The EU Education Policy in the Post-Lisbon Era

VÖLKERRECHT EUROPRECHT UND INTERNATIONALES WIRTSCHAFTSRECHT

Herausgegeben von Peter Hilpold und August Reinisch

Band 21

PL ACADEMIC RESEARCH

Caroline U. Amann

The EU Education Policy in the Post-Lisbon Era

A Comprehensive Approach

PL ACADEMIC RESEARCH

Bibliographic Information published by the Deutsche Nationalbibliothek
The Deutsche Nationalbibliothek lists this publication in the Deutsche Nationalbibliografie; detailed bibliographic data is available in the internet at http://dnb.d-nb.de.

Library of Congress Cataloging-in-Publication Data
Amann, Caroline U., 1987- author.
The EU education policy in the post-Lisbon era : a comprehensive approach / Caroline U. Amann.
pages cm. – (Völkerrecht, europarecht und internationales wirtschaftsrecht ; Band 21)
ISBN 978-3-631-66615-9
1. Educational law and legislation–European Union countries. I. Title. II. Title: European Union education policy in the post-Lisbon era.
KJE6266.A94 2015
344.24'07–dc23
2015031261

The publication of this book was kindly supported by the Vice-Rectorate for Research of Leopold-Franzens-Universität Innsbruck, the Land Tirol and the Land Vorarlberg.

ISSN 1862-457
ISBN 978-3-631-66615-9 (Print)
E-ISBN 978-3-653-05942-7 (E-Book)
DOI 10.3726/978-3-653-05942-7

Internationaler Verlag der Wissenschaften
Frankfurt am Main 2015

PL Academic Research is an Imprint of Peter Lang GmbH.

Peter Lang – Frankfurt am Main · Bern · Bruxelles · New York · Oxford · Warszawa · Wien

This publication has been peer reviewed.

www.peterlang.com

« Si c'était à refaire, je commencerais par l'education. »
Attributed to Jean Monnet

Acknowledgements

I would like to thank my supervisor Professor Peter Hilpold, who encouraged me to write this thesis. I am grateful that he allowed me to work independently while providing help and guidance whenever needed.

I am thankful to Professor Karl Weber, my second supervisor.

Further thanks go to the Vice-Rectorate for Research of Leopold-Franzens-Universität Innsbruck for granting me a thesis scholarship.

I have been fortunate to have parents who have imparted to me the value of education. The choice of topic was therefore nothing out of the ordinary. With regard to this thesis, I appreciated above all their moral support.

I especially wish to thank my sister Valerie for her invaluable advice on the English language and for proofreading the manuscript.

Finally, I wish to thank my partner Emanuel for proofreading the manuscript and for his constant support.

Caroline U. Amann
Innsbruck, October 2014

Table of Contents

List of Abbreviations

ACVT	Advisory Committee on Vocational Training
AG	Advocate General
ARGE ALP	Working Community of the Alpine Regions
BGBl.	Bundesgesetzblatt
BSR	Baltic Sea Region
BV-G	Bundes-Verfassungsgesetz
BWV	Berliner Wissenschafts-Verlag
CCC/CDCC	Council for Cultural Cooperation
CDED	Steering Committee for Education
CDESR	Steering Committee for Higher Education and Research
CEDEFOP	European Centre for the Development of Education
CERI	Centre for Educational Research and Innovation
CESS	Certificat d'Enseignement secondaire supérieur général, technique ou artistique
CETS	Council of Europe Treaty Series
cf.	confer
CF	Cohesion Fund
CFREU	Charter of Fundamental Human Rights of the European Union
CJEU	Court of Justice of the European Union
CLIL	Content and Language Integrated Learning
CLRAE	Standing Conference of Local and Regional Authorities of Europe
CoE	Council of Europe
CoR	Committee of the Regions
COTRAO	Working Community of the Western Alps
CRC	Convention on the Rights of the Child
CSRs	Country-specific Recommendations
CV	Curriculum Vitae
CYELP	Croatian Yearbook of European Law and Policy
DÖV	Die Öffentliche Verwaltung, Zeitschrift für Öffentliches Recht und Verwaltungswissenschaft

EAEC	European Atomic Energy Community
EARDF	European Agricultural and Development Fund
EC	European Community
ECHR	European Convention on Human Rights
ECJ	European Court of Justice
ECML	European Centre for Modern Languages
ECOSOC	Economic and Social Committee
ECR	European Court Reports
ECSC	European Coal and Steel Community
ECtHR	European Court of Human Rights
ECTS	European Credit Transfer System
ECVET	European Credit System for Vocational Education and Training
ed.	edition/editor
eds.	editors
EDC	Education Committee
EEA	European Economic Area
EEC	European Economic Community
EERJ	European Educational Research Journal
EESC	European Economic and Social Committee
EFTA	European Free Trade Association
eg.	exempli gratia ("for example")
EGTC	European Grouping of Territorial Cooperation
EHEA	European Higher Education Area
EHRR	European Human Rights Reports
EIF	European Investment Fund
EMFF	European Maritime and Fisheries Fund
EMU	Economic and Monetary Union
ENIC	European Network of Information Centres
EP	European Parliament
ERASMUS	European Community Action Scheme for the Mobility of University Students
ERDF	European Regional Development Fund
ESC	European Social Charter
ESF	European Social Fund
ESIF	European Structural and Investment Funds
ESS	European Employment Strategy
ET 2020	Education and Training 2020

EU	European Union
EUI	European University Institute
EuR	Zeitschrift Europarecht
Euratom	European Atomic Energy Community
EUSAIR	EU Strategy for the Adriatic-Ionian Region
EUSALP	EU Strategy for the Alpine Region
EUSBSR	EU Strategy for the Baltic Sea Region
EUSDR	EU Strategy for the Danube Region
EuZW	Europäische Zeitschrift für Wirtschaftsrecht
EYCS	Education, Youth, Culture and Sport Council
fn.	footnote
HanseLR	Hanse Law Review
HEI	Higher Education Institution
Ibid.	Ibidem ("in the same place")
ICESCR	International Covenant for Economic, Social and Cultural Rights
ICL Journal	Vienna Journal on International Constitutional Law
i.e.	id est ("that is")
IJELP	International Journal for Education Law and Policy
IVET	Initial Vocational Education and Training
JBl	Juristische Blätter
JCER	Journal of Contemporary European Research
JCMS	Journal of Common Market Studies
JORF	Journal officiel de la République Française
LLL	Lifelong Learning
NARIC	National Academic Recognition Information Centre
No./No	number
NWV	Neuer Wissenschaftlicher Verlag
nyr	not yet reported
OCTs	Overseas Countries or Territories
OECD	Organisation for Economic Co-operation and Development
OEEC	Organisation for European Economic Co-operation
OJ	Official Journal

OMC	Open Method of Coordination
OSTP	Office for Scientific and Technical Personnel
OUP	Oxford University Press
PACES	Première année commune aux études de santé
para	paragraph
PISA	Programme for International Student Assessment
QMV	Qualified Majority Voting
R&D	Research and Development
RUK	rest of UK
SAAS	Student Awards Agency for Scotland
SEA	Single European Act
SI	Statutory Instrument (UK)
SLA	Second Language Acquisition
subpara	subparagraph
TEU	Treaty on European Union
TEC	Treaty establishing the European Community
TEEC	Treaty establishing the European Economic Community
TFEU	Treaty on the Functioning of the European Union
TWGs	Thematic Working Groups
UDHR	Universal Declaration of Human Rights
UK	United Kingdom
UP	University Press
UNESCO	United Nations Educational, Scientific and Cultural Organisation
v./v	versus
VET	Vocational Education and Training
VUB	Vrije Universiteit Brussel
WEU	Western European Union

1. Introduction

> Education is indeed the linchpin needed to build the productive connection between economic and social policies, between competitiveness and social cohesion, and it is the motor force for innovation and systemic social change. Education also opens up the most effective routes to explore the richness of European diversity and to develop a sense of belonging to Europe as a vital part of the individual's sense of identity.[1]

Education is one of the policy areas in which the European Union (EU)[2] holds supporting competence[3]. This means that the Member States have attributed no legislative power to the EU. It may "carry out actions to support, coordinate or supplement" the action of the Member States, however, "[l]egally binding acts of the Union adopted on the basis of the provisions of the Treaties relating to these areas" are not to supersede Member State competence by harmonising laws on national or regional level.[4] The EU shall therefore "contribute to the development of quality education by encouraging cooperation between Member States […] while fully respecting the responsibility of the Member States for the content of teaching and the organisation of education systems and their cultural and linguistic diversity."[5] Moreover, the EU "shall implement a vocational training policy which shall support and supplement the action of the Member States, while fully respecting the responsibility of the Member States for the content and organisation of vocational training."[6]

The complexity of EU education law dates back to the early years of the European integration process. Education has always been a matter of national

1 Jones, HC, Testimony, in: Pépin, L., The History of European Cooperation in Education and Training: Europe in the Making – An Example, Office for Official Publications of the European Communities: Luxembourg, 2006, pp. 39–42, p. 39.
2 The term European Union (EU) or Union is used to refer to the construct of the European Union and its predecessors. Founded as the European Economic Community (EEC) in 1957, it changed its name to European Community (EC) in 1967 with the Merger Treaty until finally becoming the European Union (EU) in 1993. Whenever possible, the terms used will fit the respective period.
3 Previously referred to as complementary competence. For considerations on an adequate denomination cf. Final Report of the European Convention Working Group V "Complementary Competencies", CONV 375/1/02, 4 November 2002, http://european-convention.europa.eu/pdf/reg/en/02/cv00/cv00375-re01.en02.pdf.
4 Articles 2(5) and 6(e) TFEU.
5 Article 165(1) TFEU.
6 Article 166(1) TFEU.

interest. Hence, Member States were reluctant and refused to agree to a transfer of powers (i.e. "competences" in the European jargon). In fact, Community primary law lacked a legal basis for education until the Maastricht Treaty entered into force in 1993. In the 1970s and 80s, education first became relevant at the Community level. Resolutions on cooperation in the field were issued. Action programmes promoting exchange and mobility were introduced. However, what really catapulted education onto the European stage was the positive and integration-friendly approach of the European Court of Justice (ECJ). The free movement of workers, the freedom of establishment and the freedom to provide services are all in some way connected to the education sector. Hence, market-compatibility and the principle of non-discrimination on grounds of nationality quickly made the application of a policy-restricted view impossible.

The build-up process of EU education policy can best be explained with the classical neofunctionalist theory that focusses on spillover effects. Functional spillover is based on the idea that the economy is interconnected. Integration in one area builds up pressure, thereby leading to integration in others.[7] It is clear that internal market freedoms require cooperation at Member State level. In order to make mobility work, professional qualifications need to be recognised throughout the Member States. Access to education and related social advantages needs to be equally available to migrant workers or service providers and their dependants in the host Member State. The ECJ's activism and its influence on laws and regulations that are incompatible with EU law alerted the Member States. Preoccupied with sovereignty issues, they used the Maastricht Treaty to introduce a legal basis for education that explicitly forbids any harmonisation of national laws and regulations with regard to the content and organisation of education (cf. today's Article 165 TFEU). The legal basis for vocational training, which had been formally recognised as an area of Community competence with the Treaty of Rome, was brought in line with the legal basis for education equally banning harmonisation (cf. today's Article 166 TFEU).

While the Maastricht Treaty consolidated the position of the Member States, the introduction of a legal basis for education was nonetheless important for the EU as it facilitated action at the EU level. Since the ECJ had held that vocational training incorporates higher education, the legal basis for vocational training had been used to adopt the Erasmus programme. In the post-Maastricht era, action programmes were extended to pre-schools, primary and secondary schools.

---

7 Cf. Craig, P., Integration, Democracy and Legitimacy, in: P. Craig and G. de Búrca (eds.), The Evolution of EU Law, 2nd ed., OUP: Oxford, 2011, pp. 13–40, p. 14.

Moreover, the Maastricht Treaty introduced the concept of Union citizenship. For the development of EU education law, this was at least as important as the introduction of a legal basis for education. It allowed the ECJ to base its decisions on new rationales, improving the situation of the non-economically active. While the concept of Union citizenship has undoubtedly had a huge influence on education law, the non-economically active do not enjoy unconditional rights. Although there have been significant developments in the field of student maintenance aid, non-economically active students are not on par with economically active students or those retaining that status or dependants of workers or service providers who are treated as if they were economically active. Their right to access to maintenance for studies may be subject to durational residency requirements.

Due to the Union's limited competence, EU education policy may appear somewhat static. The opposite is true. Title XII of Part Three of the Treaty on the Functioning of the European Union (TFEU) provides for education, vocational training, youth and sport. While Article 165 TFEU is broadly worded and focusses on education, youth and sport, Article 166 TFEU focusses on vocational training. EU education policy has become inextricably intertwined with other policy areas including cohesion policy (also referred to as regional policy), cultural policy, economic policy, employment and social policies or research and innovation policies. The Lisbon Treaty added a horizontal provision to EU primary law. Paying tribute to the importance of inter-policy interaction, Article 9 TFEU states that "[i]n defining and implementing its policies and activities, the Union shall take into account requirements linked to the promotion of […] a high level of education". Article 14 of the Charter of Fundamental Human Rights of the European Union (CFREU) sets out a right to education. When the Lisbon Treaty entered into force in 2009, the CFREU was integrated into EU primary law, making it binding.

Because of the non-harmonisation clause in Articles 165 and 166 TFEU, the EU primarily operates with so-called "soft-law", i.e. "rules of conduct which, in principle, have no legally binding force but which nevertheless may have practical effects".[8] New modes of governance such as the open method of coordination (OMC), a policy-making instrument that translates common objectives into national policies and sets benchmarks to be reached within a certain timeframe, dominate the scene. Formally launched at the 2000 Lisbon summit, the OMC

8 Snyder, F., The Effectiveness of European Community Law: Institutions, Processes, Tools and Techniques, 56 The Modern Law Review, 1993, pp. 19–54, p. 32.

assists the Member States in the accomplishment of the goals set by Europe 2020 (hereinafter, the EU 2020 Strategy), the follow-up to the Lisbon Strategy. Emphasis on education is typical in times of economic crises. In 1973, the oil crisis, along with the resulting stock market crash, caused a depression which triggered youth unemployment all over Europe.[9] The economic crisis that hit home in 2007 severely affected the southern Eurozone countries. Hence, the EU 2020 Strategy focusses on preventing youth unemployment by tackling early school-leaving and increasing tertiary educational attainment.

The European integration process takes place at the European, national and sub-national, i.e. local and/or regional, level. Multi-level governance, "a system of continuous negotiation among nested governments at several territorial tiers – supranational, national, regional and local",[10] is rather complex when it comes to education and training because of the different systems of government of the Member States. Depending on the institutional structure, the content and the organisation of the education system is the responsibility of the national and/or the sub-national level. Education policy has been described as "almost the last [field] in which the [German] Länder retained any independence – so that any encroachment on them by Community law was regarded with some sensitivity."[11] The up-and-coming macro-regional strategies, which involve a number of Member States (separate *Länder* in the case of Germany) and third countries from the same geographical area (defined by a sea, river or mountain range) facing common challenges, focus on education and training. Cooperation does not only take place at the pan-European level. Micro-regional cooperation, i.e. cooperation at sub-national level, is at the centre of a "Europe of the Regions". Since 2007, the European Grouping of Territorial Cooperation (EGTC), which has legal personality, facilitates cross-border, transnational and interregional cooperation. It does not require the conclusion of bilateral or multilateral agreements and is an option for the sub-national level. EGTCs act within the respective powers of their members. Therefore, they are particularly interesting for regions with legislative power in the field of education and training.

---

9 Cf. Pépin, L., The History of European Cooperation in Education and Training: Europe in the Making – An Example, Office for Official Publications of the European Communities: Luxembourg, 2006, p. 77.

10 Marks, G., Structural Policy and Multilevel Governance in the EC, in: AW Cafruny and GG Rosenthal (eds.), The State of the European Community Volume 2: The Maastricht Debates and Beyond, Lynne Rienner: Boulder, 1993, pp. 391–410, p. 392.

11 Opinion of Advocate General Warner, delivered on 11 June 1974, Case C-9/74 *Casagrande v Landeshauptstadt München* [1974] ECR 773, p. 783.

In 2002, the Spanish EU Presidency referred to education as the "fourth pillar".[12] Although the pillar structure has been abandoned with the Lisbon Treaty that entered into force in 2009, this does not diminish the fact that a new era for education has been ushered in. The economy has always been at the centre of EU action. The focus on human capital, the most important factor of production and key to future growth, is but an advancement of the idea of European integration. Since the turn of the century, EU education law and policy have been undergoing changes. The concept of Union citizenship has continued to influence ECJ case law in the area. Furthermore, the relevant primary law provisions have been amended. Apart from that, the relevant action programmes have been incorporated into one single programme. Launched in 2014, Erasmus+, the action programme for education, vocational training, youth and sport for the 2014–2020 programming period, has an overall budget of almost EUR 15 billion. At no time has the EU invested as much into its student exchange scheme. Never before has it focussed on cross-border cooperation of public authorities to this extent. The best endeavours are used to create equal opportunities for everyone and encourage cross-border cooperation. Efforts are being made for increased collaboration at all levels in order to achieve the EU 2020 goals.

Because the boundaries between policies are merging, research into EU education policy requires an open-ended approach. This thesis seeks to explore the recent developments in the field. In order to explain the prevailing issues, **chapter two** delves into the underlying reasons that triggered the establishment of such policy. Analysing the founding years is without doubt essential to understand the current state of play. The development of a European dimension of education dates back to the 1950s, a time when today's intergovernmental actors started to emerge. The efforts of the Council of Europe (CoE) and the Organisation for Economic Co-operation and Development (OECD) shaped EU education policy and contributed to its establishment. The founding treaties include various references to vocational training and are essential for the examination of the ECJ's train of thought. The Maastricht Treaty amended the Treaty of Rome, significantly changing primary law. In addition to introducing a legal basis for education and Union citizenship, it also laid the foundations for EU regional policy. **Chapter three** looks at the development of the Lisbon/EU 2020 Strategy and its implications for education and training. **Chapter four** centres on

12 Cf. Nóvoa, A. and W. de Jong-Lambert, Educating Europe: An Analysis of EU Educational Policies, in: D. Phillips and H. Ertl (eds.), Implementing European Union Education and Training Policy: A Comparative Study of Issues in Four Member States, Kluwer Academic: Dordrecht, 2003, pp. 41–72, p. 41.

the Erasmus+ programme. **Chapter five** focusses on the education and training provisions in the Lisbon Treaty. It analyses the respective legal bases and the amendments and additions thereof.

Chapter six is concerned with education as a fundamental right. It analyses the sources of Article 14 CFREU and gives an overview on human rights protection in the EU. **Chapter seven** investigates the main trends in ECJ case law, where the concept of Union citizenship continues to have wide-ranging effects. In education law, the topics most prevalent are the derivative right of residence of the primary carer of a dependant who has a right to reside in the host Member State, access to study as well as the right to student maintenance aid. **Chapter eight** looks at education and training in cohesion policy and focusses on initiatives at the macro- and micro-regional level. Regarding cooperation at the macro-regional level, it investigates macro-regional strategies and their impact on education and training. The EGTC European Region Tyrol-South Tyrol-Trentino serves as an example for cooperation at the micro-regional level. Said EGTC is particularly interesting as it is made up of three regions with legislative power and covers the fields of education, vocational training, youth and sport for which the Erasmus+ programme provides funding. This thesis is therefore a most innovative one as it investigates cross-border, transnational and interregional cooperation between the Member States and their constituent units. The education systems of the Member States are rather different. Hence, the efforts to liaise with each other at the national as well as at the regional level are hugely beneficial for the further development of education and vocational training.

2. An Education Policy in the Making – A Historical Overview

> If there is a Community *law* of education, there is also a Community educational *policy*. But these two categories do not, it seems, entirely overlap. On the one hand, much of what may be called the law on education is the result of Community policies whose primary interest is not the substantive content of education but rather the functional objective of establishing a common market. On the other hand, much of what may be called common educational policy [...], does not take the form of binding Community law, but more ambiguous forms of public international law or "Community soft law".[13]

2.1 Humble Beginnings – the Initiation Phase (1948–1963)[14]

In its early days, the EU was first and foremost meant to be an economic union. Founded after a period of wartime atrocities, its prime goal for peacekeeping was to be achieved through economic ties making European countries interdependent. Education was to be left to the Council of Europe (CoE), Europe's first parliamentary and political assembly established in 1949[15], as the Member States were not keen on intrusions into what they considered part of their domaine réservé. An intergovernmental body such as the CoE was therefore deemed to be more adequate for dealing with such issues because no transfer of competences – and thus no de-nationalization – had to take place. Over the next two decades and beyond, the CoE remained the "main player" in European education cooperation.[16] Other intergovernmental actors taking part in the quest for educational

---

13 De Witte, B., Introduction, in: B. de Witte (ed.), European Community Law of Education, Nomos: Baden-Baden, pp. 9–18, pp. 9 et seq.

14 The division of key stages may vary from author to author. Also cf. Ertl, H., The European Union and Education and Training: An Overview of Policies and Initiatives, in: D. Phillips and H. Ertl (eds.), Implementing European Union Education and Training Policy: A Comparative Study of Issues in Four Member States, Kluwer Academic: Dordrecht, 2003, pp. 13–39, pp. 14 et seq.; Pépin, 2006, pp. 22 et seq. and Walkenhorst, H. The Changing Role of EU Education Policy – a Critical Assessment, Paper for the EUSA Ninth Biennial International Conference, March 31 – April 2, 2005, pp. 3 et seq.

15 The Statute of the Council of Europe was signed in 1949 and entered into force in the same year.

16 Cf. Pépin, 2006, p. 50.

improvement were the now defunct Western European Union (WEU) and the Organisation for Economic Co-operation and Development (OECD).

2.1.1 The Intergovernmental Actors[17]

The CoE mainly focussed on nuts and bolts work and, compared to the European Communities that saw education as a means of creating socio-economic benefits, it took an inclusive approach.[18] With its aim "to achieve a greater unity between its members for the purpose of safeguarding and realising the ideals and principles which are their common heritage and facilitating their economic and social progress", Article 1 of the CoE's statute provides the foundation for cooperation in the education sector. With numerous conventions, among them prominent ones such as the European Convention of Human Rights (ECHR) of 1950, which includes the right to education under Article 2 of its first Protocol (1952), the CoE counts the European Cultural Convention to its most important ones.[19] The European Cultural Convention, which lists "safeguarding and realising the ideals and principles"[20] of common heritage as its main purpose, opened for signature in 1954 and entered into force in 1955.[21] Within its preamble the treaty, which is

---

17 This sub-chapter includes information going beyond the timeframe given for the actual chapter concerned with the initiation phase. This is due to clarity and because – apart from an overview – a detailed treatment of the intergovernmental actors mentioned is not sought by the author and will not be provided in later chapters.

18 Cf. Hilpold, P., Bildung in Europa – Unter besonderer Berücksichtigung der EU-Bildungsprogramme, Nomos: Baden-Baden, 1995, p. 15.

19 Other CoE treaties regarding education include the European Convention on the Equivalence of Diplomas leading to Admission to Universities (1953) CETS No. 15, the European Convention on the Equivalence of Periods of University Study (1956) CETS No. 21, the European Convention on the Academic Recognition of University Qualifications (1959) CETS No. 32, the European Agreement on Continued Payment of Scholarships to Students Studying Abroad (1969) CETS No. 69, the European Convention on the General Equivalence of Periods of University Study (1990) CETS No. 138 and the Convention on the Recognition of Qualifications concerning Higher Education in the European Region (1997) CETS No. 165, which is more widely known as the Lisbon Recognition Convention.

20 Recital 1 of the Preamble to the European Cultural Convention (1954) CETS No. 18.

21 The total number of ratifications/accessions of the treaty is 50 (the CoE is currently made up of 47 Member States). This includes the current 28 Member States of the EU, which are all members of the CoE. Cf. http://conventions.coe.int/Treaty/Commun/ChercheSig.asp?NT=018&CM=&DF=&CL=ENG.

also open for non-members, agrees to foster the study of languages, history and civilisation among its nationals.

The European Cultural Convention laid the groundwork for European cooperation regarding education – becoming the regulatory framework for the CoE's activities in this field. In 1962, the Council for Cultural Cooperation (CCC), in French "Conseil de la Coopération Culturel", was set up to manage the Cultural Fund, which constituted a special budgetary post of the CoE allowing the signatories of the European Cultural Convention (and therefore also non-Member States of the CoE) for financial contribution and participation in the activities and programmes in its fields of education, culture, youth and sport.[22] The CCC was later replaced by the CDCC, a steering committee[23], responsible for the allocation of the resources of the Cultural Fund.[24] With the accession of almost all signatories of the convention to the CoE, the need for a separate management of the Cultural Fund was not given anymore and it has since been incorporated into the normal budget. The creation of a Rapporteur Group for Culture, Education, Youth and Sport (GR-C), has also "considerably reduced the role of the CDCC as a programme orientation and co-ordinating body".[25]

With such a framework in the background, the CoE has been able to contribute to and open up several sectors that play an important part in today's EU education policy: adult education, higher education, language learning, lifelong learning (LLL) and mobility, for example.[26] The mutual recognition of qualifications, which was first advocated by the CoE through conventions in the early

---

22 Rapporteur Group on Education, Culture, Sport and Youth, New structures for European Cultural Co-operation, GR-C(2001)38 revised 22 October 2001, https://wcd.coe.int/ViewDoc.jsp?id=232495.

23 Cf. Resolution (76) 3 of the Committee of Ministers of the Council of Europe on committee structures, terms of reference and working methods, 18 February 1976. Article 4(a) clarifies that "steering committee denotes any committee which is answerable directly to the Committee of Ministers and responsible for a substantial portion of the medium-term plan, and to which the governments of all the member states are entitled to designate persons, preferably from among national officials of the highest possible rank".

24 After this restructuring, which was undertaken in 1977, the CDCC was again transformed in 2001. It was split up into four steering committees, among them the Steering Committee for Education (CDED) and the Steering Committee for Higher Education and Research (CDESR).

25 https://wcd.coe.int/ViewDoc.jsp?id=232495.

26 Cf. Grosjean, E., Forty Years of Cultural Cooperation at the Council of Europe, 1954–94, 31 European Education, 1999, pp. 11–37.

1950s,[27] shows an approach towards mobility (which was later taken up by the EU) that was far ahead of its time. With institutions such as the European Centre for Modern Languages (ECML) that is based in Graz, Austria, the CoE still makes headway in key educational issues.

Surprisingly, even the WEU took an interest in education and the first Conference of European Rectors and Vice-Chancellors was held in Cambridge in 1955 under its aegis.[28] In the same year, the Committee on Higher Education, an intergovernmental cooperation body, was set up within the WEU.[29] Stemming from the (modified) Brussels Treaty, the preamble of which states that the economic, social and cultural ties shall be strengthened, the WEU's functions were not limited to the diplomatic and military field and included cooperation in order "to lead their peoples towards a better understanding".[30] Lastly, with funding for social and cultural dimensions – and thus education – diminished, the WEU transferred them to the CoE in 1960.[31]

The OECD, established in 1961, and its forerunner, the Organisation for European Economic Co-operation (OEEC) which was established in 1948 to coordinate the US-financed Marshall Plan, were also dealing with education issues from early on.[32] An intergovernmental organisation like the CoE, education is not explicitly included within the OECD's Convention (though Article 2(b) stipulates that the Member States shall "promote the development of their resources" and "encourage research and promote vocational training" when it comes to science and technology). But, as the former deputy director responsible for education in the OECD Directorate for Social Affairs, Manpower and Education, George Papadopoulos, pointed out:

27 Cf. fn. 19.

28 Cf. Pépin, 2006, p. 49.

29 Cf. Grosjean, 1999, p. 15.

30 Art. 3 of the Modified Brussels Treaty.

31 http://www.cvce.eu/recherche/unit-content/-/unit/en/72d9869d-ff72-493e-a0e3-bedb3e671faa/841836b7-7c9e-4fc4-b0f2-b452f31c6078.

32 The Convention of the OEEC specifies that "the Contracting Parties will make the fullest and most effective use of their available manpower" (Article 8). A Manpower Committee responsible for the promotion of the set goal was established with the creation of the OEEC. In 1958, the Office for Scientific and Technical Personnel (OSTP) was created in order to increase the number and improve the training of persons working in this sector. For more information on working papers, minutes etc. Cf. Inventory of the OEEC, Historical Archives of the European Communities, EUI, http://archives.eui.eu/en/fonds/173448?item=OEEC.

> the dominance of economic concerns within OECD has always been tempered by recognition of the social dimension of economic growth, reinforced by equal, if only gradually evolving awareness of the importance of human capital, and more generally of the "residual factor" in the process of economic growth.[33]

It is tempting to think of the OECD as a more or less economically biased organisation. The economic dimension may certainly outweigh the educational one and "[i]ntegrating education into the central objectives and mainstream activities [...] was [...] never an easy task."[34] However, even the legal framework of the OECD, the OECD convention, includes general provisions containing references pointing to the organisation's emphasis on education.

Those references figure prominently in the preamble that underlines that "economic strength and prosperity" preserve one's "individual liberty" and increase the "general well-being". This is reaffirmed by Article 1, which describes the organisation's aims as the promotion of policies that include the achievement of "the highest sustainable economic growth and employment and a rising standard of living". Economic growth and the standard of living go hand in hand, of course, both contributing to each other and being rather reciprocal. Investing in human capital – and thus in education and training that account for its "most important investments"[35] – was therefore of great importance to the OECD. Constituting a new concept in those days, "human capital" is today termed "knowledge society". A change of semantics but invariably not of its initial approach.[36]

Prompted by the so-called "Sputnik shock" of 1957, the OECD increased investment in education, leading the 1950s and 60s to see the world's first boom in education economics.[37] The OECD's approach towards its educational work can be described as policy-oriented and this is what it is particularly valued for. Called the approach's "distinctive feature", it includes the linking and relating of education "to its broader social, economic and cultural environment".[38] This

33 Papadopoulos, GS, Education 1960–1990: The OECD Perspective, OECD: Paris, 1994, p. 11.
34 Ibid. p. 12.
35 Becker, GS, Human Capital: A Theoretical and Empirical Analysis with Special Reference to Education, 3rd ed., Chicago UP: Chicago, 1993, p. 17.
36 Cf. Papadopoulos, GS, The OECD Approach to Education in Retrospect: 1960–1990, 46 European Journal of Education, 2011, pp. 85–86, p. 85.
37 Cf. Radtke, F., Die Erziehungswissenschaft der OECD – Aussichten auf die neue Performanz-Kultur, 14 Erziehungswissenschaft, 2003, pp. 109–136, pp. 110 et seq.; also cf. Papadopoulos, GS, 1994, pp. 23 et seq.
38 Papadopoulos, 1994, p. 12.

coincides with the OECD's precept that an international education policy is non-existent. The OECD "has no prescriptive role for countries, individually or collectively" but takes on a catalytic one.[39] Newly emerging policy issues with a progressive streak are identified and analysed in order to trigger "discussion and exchange within and across countries". This helps to reach general conclusions for policy development guidelines.[40]

The OECD's educational activities are conducted with the help of several different programmes. The core programmes include the Education Committee (EDC), which takes a policy-oriented approach, and the Centre for Educational Research and Innovation (CERI), which takes a research-oriented one.[41] Until today, the OECD continues to contribute to education research. With the Programme for International Student Assessment (PISA), better known as the PISA study, it allows countries to benchmark themselves against the world's education systems. Published every three years, the PISA ranking, which was first carried out in 2000, is a means to further education by getting countries to overthink their education policy.

2.1.2 The European Communities

The deeper economic integration envisaged by the European Communities, consisting of the European Coal and Steel Community (ECSC), established by the Treaty of Paris signed in 1951, as well as the European Atomic Energy Community (EAEC, Euratom) and the European Economic Community (EEC), established by the Treaty of Rome signed in 1957, did not include education as such. While it was obviously clear that the internal market (also known as the single market and formerly and back then the common market) and its principles of free movement and non-discrimination on grounds of nationality would represent challenges for the Communities' workers, tackling these by moving education to Member State level was out of the question. Education was far too sensitive a subject, the locus of policy-making being at national level.[42] Encroaching on national sovereignty was therefore not an option and the term "education" was not mentioned in any of the three founding Treaties. Nevertheless, this did not hinder the Member States to incorporate the vocational (re)training

39 Ibid. p. 13.

40 Ibid. p. 14.

41 Ibid. pp. 15 et seq.

42 Cf. Pépin, 2006, p. 22.

of employees and provide for the mutual recognition of diplomas, certificates and other evidence of formal qualifications.

Article 56 of the ECSC Treaty provides that in case of "the introduction of technical processes or new equipment" which would "lead to an exceptional reduction in labor requirements in the coal or steel industries" thereby creating difficulties for the re-employment of the released workers, non-reimbursable assistance will be granted by the High Authority if requested by governments in order to further the technical retraining for those who are led to change their employment.

Article 4 of the Euratom Treaty stipulates that the Commission shall promote and facilitate as well as complement nuclear research in the Member States "by carrying out a Community research and training programme."

According to Article 7 of said Treaty, these research and training programmes are to be determined after the Scientific and Technical Committee has been consulted. The required funding shall be included in the research and investment budget. Moreover, the Economic and Social Committee (ECOSOC, since 2002 the European Economic and Social Committee has been known under the acronym EESC), a consultative body common to the EC and the Euratom set up "in order to involve economic and social interest groups in the establishment of the common market and to provide institutional machinery for briefing the European Commission and the Council of Ministers"[43], has to be informed about the outlines of the programmes.

Article 9(1) of the Euratom Treaty concludes that within the framework of the Joint Nuclear Research Centre the Commission may set up schools for specialist training and determine further details. Article 9(2) of said Treaty calls for the establishment of an institution with university status. Such an institution has, however, never been set up.

The EEC Treaty (TEEC) contains several provisions, albeit scattered across different chapters, dealing with vocational training:

Article 41 TEEC ensures that the objectives of the common agricultural policy as set out in Article 39 TEEC may be achieved inter alia through the "effective co-ordination of efforts undertaken in the spheres of occupational training, research and the popularisation of rural economy". Projects or institutions regarding those may be financed jointly.

43 Cf. http://www.eesc.europa.eu/?i=portal.en.about-the-committee.

According to Article 50 TEEC, Member States shall encourage the exchange of young workers under a common programme. The implementation of this provision would be difficult without a common vocational training policy and therefore ought to be seen in connection with Article 128 TEEC.

Article 57 TEEC envisaged the "mutual recognition of diplomas, certificates and other evidence of formal qualifications" by means of directives. Exceptions were added for the medical, para-medical and pharmaceutical professions, where the removal of restrictions is "subject to the co-ordination of conditions for their exercise" in the Member States. Providing market access for professionals and allowing academics to continue their studies in another Member State by recognising their diplomas is a necessary prerequisite for the free movement of persons as well as the freedom of establishment and the freedom to provide services.

In regard to social policy, Article 118 TEEC leaves it to the Commission to "promote close collaboration" for "occupational and continuation training", i.e. basic and advanced vocational training, between the Member States. Para 2 stipulates that this shall be achieved by "means of studies, the issuing of opinions, and the organising of consultations both on problems arising at the national level and on those of concern to international organisations."

Article 125 TEEC determines that the European Social Fund (ESF), established to improve employment opportunities and thus raise the standard of living (cf. Article 123 TEEC), shall, if requested by a Member State, contribute 50% towards the expenses for vocational retraining. As Para 2 clarifies, this assistance is subject to certain conditions such as "the impossibility of employing the unemployed workers otherwise than in a new occupation and upon their having been, in productive employment, for a period of at least six months in the occupation for which they have been re-trained."

Article 128 TEEC, the sole provision dedicated to vocational training only, is considered the most important one:

> The Council shall, on a proposal of the Commission and after the Economic and Social Committee has been consulted, establish general principles for the implementation of a common policy of occupational training capable of contributing to the harmonious development both of national economies and of the Common Market.

Entrusting the Council with the implementation of a common vocational training policy, which is to contribute to the individual economies and the internal market, the article does not go into detail and leaves much to be inferred. Save for the establishment of the general principles thereof, nothing much is specified. The Council, acting on a Commission proposal and after the ECOSOC has been consulted,[44] is to issue the common vocational training policy. As no majority requirements are laid down, the Council decides by majority vote (Article 148(1) TEEC). It seems remarkable that the Member States would allow for such a voting procedure. After all, the education sector has always been deemed a sensitive one and, as Article 5 TEEC points out, the Member States "shall take all general or particular measures [...] for ensuring the carrying out of the obligations arising out of this Treaty" and may not jeopardise their attainment. Even though these general principles or guidelines are "not legally binding" according to Barnard, they should be adhered to due to "the duty of cooperation or fidelity" derived from said Article.[45] It therefore seems unlikely that the Member States anticipated the development the Union's education policy would once take.[46]

The scope of Article 128 TEEC was limited to vocational training. However, the Commission's proposal from 1961 on the common vocational training policy shows that a different approach was reflected upon as well. Compared to Council decision 63/266/EEC of 2 April 1963, the proposal interprets vocational training in a broader sense. According to it, vocational training shall be understood to include everyone who might be or already is employed.[47] While this expression also found its way into the Council decision[48], the Commission went further by pointing out that the common vocational training policy should shape education and training as broadly as possible.[49] Moreover, it insisted that everyone should have the opportunity to achieve whatever level of education

44 Whenever specified in the Treaty, the ECOSOC must be consulted. However, once its opinion has been received, the Council may decide not to consider it. Cf. Foster, N., EU Law: Directions, 3rd ed, OUP: Oxford, 2012, p. 65.

45 Barnard, C., Education and Vocational Training, in: D. Phillips (ed.), Aspects of Education and the European Union, Oxford Studies in Comparative Education, 5(2) (Triangle: Wallingford (OX)), 1995, pp. 13–28, p. 14. Also cf. Becker, P. and R. Primova, Die Europäische Union und die Bildungspolitik, Diskussionspapier Forschungsgruppe EU-Integration, SWP: Berlin, April 2009, p. 5.

46 Cf. Hilpold, 1995, p. 29 at fn. 86.

47 Cf. Deutscher Bundestag – 4. Wahlperiode, Drucksache IV/567, Allgemeine Grundsätze zur Durchführung einer gemeinsamen Politik der Berufsausbildung (Vorschlag der Kommission an den Rat vom 5. Oktober 1961), p. 4.

48 Cf. Council Decision 63/266/EEC of 2 April 1963 Laying Down General Principles for Implementing a Common Vocational Training Policy, English Special Edition: Series I Volume 1963–1964, pp. 25–28, p. 26.

49 Cf. Deutscher Bundestag – 4. Wahlperiode, Drucksache IV/567, Allgemeine Grundsätze zur Durchführung einer gemeinsamen Politik der Berufsausbildung (Vorschlag der Kommission an den Rat vom 5. Oktober 1961), p. 8.

and training available. Therefore, elementary education should be adjusted, enabling everyone to gain the same amount of knowledge regardless of the school's location.[50] This was taken up in the Council's decision, which concludes that special measures to promote teacher training for the less favoured regions shall be taken.[51] The Commission's view was certainly progressive and keeping in mind that "national education generally belongs to the realm of high politics in which the EU does not claim responsibility"[52], it is understandable that it was not to every Member State's taste.[53] Especially the German *Länder*, which feature a dual system for apprenticeships that consists of school-based and work-based learning, wanted the common vocational training policy to really just contain that.[54] With education a state prerogative, it was not until much later that cooperation would officially be pursued at the Community level and implemented in the treaty.

The goal of the EEC was clear, namely to lay the foundation for further economic integration. With (re)training for the workforce and the agricultural sector, financial support from the ESF and the mutual recognition of formal qualifications, the EEC Treaty already contained the seeds for further development. Facilitating and increasing mobility was (and still is) key and indeed a necessary step for the successful implementation of the internal market. It is clear, however, that education plays a fundamental role in the aforementioned fields. How can we take training and formal qualifications to an equal level without setting certain standards and harmonising education? That is simply impossible. Consequently, in terms of promoting European integration the role of education cannot be ignored and these early provisions at the Community level eventually proved to be the cornerstone of a European education policy.

50 Ibid. p. 11.

51 Cf. Council Decision 63/266/EEC, p. 27.

52 Walkenhorst, 2005, p. 2.

53 Germany and France voted against Council Decision 63/266/EEC. Cf. Becker, P. and R. Primova, 2009, p. 5 at fn. 9.

54 Cf. Bode, S., Europarechtliche Gleichbehandlungsansprüche Studierender und ihre Auswirkungen in den Mitgliedstaaten: Zur Reichweite des Diskriminierungsverbots im Hochschulbereich unter besonderer Berücksichtigung der Unionsbürgerschaft, Nomos: Baden-Baden, 2005, p. 40.

2.2 The Founding Years – the Development of a European Dimension of Education (1963–1992)

On 2 April 1963, the Council issued its decision 63/266[55] laying down ten general principles for the implementation of a common vocational training policy. Recital 5 of the preamble emphasizes that the "freedom of choice of occupation, place of training and place of work" is a fundamental right. Consequently, the freedom of choice of education must be granted. That way, the common vocational training policy is set to "bring about freedom of movement for workers" to whom it applies regardless of age and up to supervisory level (paras 4 and 7). Moreover, the Council underlines the importance of keeping skills of labour forces up-to-date with the general economic situation and with changes in production technology. This includes basic and advanced training for teachers and instructors (para 7), a basic "factor" of an effective vocational training policy (seventh principle). The first principle highlights the role of the national level. The Member States are the ones responsible for establishing and implementing programmes in accordance with the decision. The fourth principle leaves it to the Commission to propose "under the Treaty, such appropriate measures as may appear necessary" to the Council or to the Member States. However, after 1963, Community action rather took place at intergovernmental than at Community level. Hence, soft law measures in the form of "non-legally binding Resolutions" or "Conclusions of the Council and the Ministers of Education meeting within the Council" were used rather than hard law measures such as "legally binding regulations, directives or decisions."[56] This led to limited joint action in the field, leaving Member States to defer cooperation and primarily discuss vocational training at national level.[57] The fourth principle also introduces a tripartite Advisory Committee on Vocational Training (ACVT), which was set up in 1963. Chaired by the Commission, it issues "opinions on matters of vocational training, communications and other strategic documents, specific projects such as the creation of CEDEFOP [European Centre for the Development of Education] and the preparation, appraisal and promotion of Community action programmes in the field of vocational training."[58] The eighth principle calls for progressive harmonisation of training levels. Standardised descriptions

55 Cf. Council Decision 63/266/EEC, pp. 25 et seq.
56 Barnard, 1995, p. 14.
57 Cf. Ertl, 2003, p. 17.
58 Pépin, 2006, p. 57.

of the various occupations' basic qualifications enable the mutual recognition of vocational education and training and are of prime importance today.[59]

On 15 October 1968, Council Regulation 1612/68 on freedom of movement for workers within the Community (amended by Directive 2004/38 – the so-called Citizens' Rights Directive – and repealed and replaced by Regulation 492/2011), one of the basic implementing acts for migrant workers,[60] was adopted. Article 48(2) TEEC stresses that "any discrimination based on nationality between workers of the Member States, as regards employment, remuneration and other working conditions" shall be abolished. It does not, however, explicitly mention education and training. This "seemingly limited scope *rationae materiae*" did not hinder the Council to adopt provisions regarding this matter.[61] Article 7(3) of Council Regulation 1612/68 stresses that migrant workers shall not be discriminated against and "under the same conditions" which apply to national workers "have access to training in vocational schools and retraining centres". Article 12 (now Article 10 of Regulation 492/2011) provides that "[t]he children of a national of a Member State who is or has been employed in the territory of another Member State shall be admitted to that State's general educational, apprenticeship and vocational training courses under the same conditions as the nationals of that State, if such children are residing in its territory." Moreover, Member States "shall encourage all efforts to enable such children to attend these courses under the best possible conditions." Article 12 is not only interesting because it extends to the workers' direct descendants but even more so for going beyond vocational training by including an educational provision. Questioned whether the Community had exceeded the powers conferred to it by

---

59 In 2002, the Copenhagen Declaration, which initiated the Copenhagen Process on cooperation in vocational education and training, laid the foundations for the European Credit system for Vocational Education and Training (ECVET). The main goal of ECVET is to increase comparability of vocational education and training by facilitating the transfer, recognition and accumulation of assessed learning outcomes. For more information cf. Recommendation of the European Parliament and of the Council of 18 June 2009 on the Establishment of a European Credit System for Vocational Education and Training (ECVET), OJ C 155, 8.7.2009, pp. 11–18.

60 Under Article 49 TEEC "the Council, acting on a proposal of the Commission and after the Economic and Social Committee has been consulted, shall, by means of directives or regulations, lay down the measures necessary to effect progressively the free movement of workers, as defined in [Article 48 TEEC]".

61 Lenaerts, K., Education in European Community Law after "Maastricht", 31 CMLR, 1994, pp. 7–41, p. 11.

interfering in the execution of a competence lying within the Member States,[62] the ECJ held in *Casagrande* that

> [a]lthough educational and training policy is not as such included in the spheres which the Treaty has entrusted to the Community institutions, it does not follow that the exercise of powers transferred to the Community is in some way limited if it is of such a nature as to affect the measures taken in the execution of a policy such as that of education and training.[63]

In a pro-integrationist stance the Court further concluded that Article 12 "refers not only to rules relating to admission, but also to general measures intended to facilitate educational attendance."[64] Therefore, the descendant of a migrant worker can rely on educational grants "under the same conditions as nationals who are in a similar position."[65] The present judgment is not surprising in so far as "the best possible conditions" can only be created if the children of migrant workers are living in a financially sound environment to which the inclusion in the national study grant system undoubtedly contributes. Furthermore, the fifth recital of the preamble to Council Regulation 1612/68 provides that "obstacles to the mobility of workers shall be eliminated, in particular as regards the worker's right to be joined by his family and the conditions for the integration of that family into the host country". Financial worries certainly constitute such an obstacle and might well interfere with the decision to take up employment in a foreign country. Secondary Community legislation regarding the non-economically active family members of workers was therefore an important step for further European integration.

---

62 Cf. Case C-9/74 *Casagrande v Landeshauptstadt München* [1974] ECR 773, para 10: The public prosecution's office of the Bavarian Administrative Court, which had referred the case for a preliminary ruling, "stated that educational policy and educational grants were within the competence of Member States."

63 Ibid. para 12.

64 Ibid. para 9.

65 Ibid. para 7. Also cf. Case C-7/94 *Landesamt für Ausbildungsförderung Nordrhein-Westfalen v Lubor Gaal* [1995] ECR 1031, para 25 where the Court held that "Article 12 of the Regulation also encompasses financial assistance for those students who are already at an advanced stage in their education, even if they are already 21 years of age or older and are no longer dependants of their parents." This, however, only applies "to a child who has lived with his parents or either one of them in a Member State at a time when at least one of his parents resided there as a worker" (Case C-197/86 *Steven Malcolm Brown v The Secretary of State for Scotland* [1988] ECR 3205, para 30).

Apart from the implementation of Treaty articles on vocational training, which were primarily meant to enhance and facilitate worker mobility, education was not a topic in those early years. With a unified Europe in the making, a common policy on the latter was certainly not one of the objectives pursued. It was therefore left to evolve via links to the economic issues the Community held direct competence for.[66] Due to the importance attached to national sovereignty over education policy, it was not until the 1970s that aspects regarding general education eventually began to be discussed. The 1969 Hague Summit, arranged in order to relaunch European integration (which had – among other things – come to a halt after the Luxembourg Accords had established the national veto), constituted a turning point.[67] Trying to complete, widen and deepen the Communities, the Heads of State and Government pointed out in their final communiqué that it was indispensable that a "mainspring [also translated as "an exceptional source"[68]] of development, progress and culture [...] be preserved."[69] The education sector was thus acknowledged as crucial for integration.[70] Two years later, the Council itself concluded that vocational training "must not and cannot be an isolated and independent project but should be based on the achievements of a general education adapted at all its levels to the requirements of modern society." It also emphasised the need to recognise the "growing interdependence between general education and vocational [...] training". The Council opted to use its 162nd session held on 26 July 1971 to adopt general guidelines for drawing up a Community programme on vocational training because the Decision of 2 April 1963 had not been as successful as had been hoped for. It did, however, not approach general education any further.[71] General education and vocational

66 Cf. Martens, K. and KD Wolf, Boomerangs and Trojan Horses: The Unintended Consequences of Internationalising Education Policy Through the EU and the OECD, in: A. Amaral et al. (eds.), European Integration and the Governance of Higher Education and Research, Springer: Dordrecht, 2009, pp. 81–107, p. 86.

67 Foster, 2012, pp. 12 et seq.

68 Cf. Resolution of the Ministers of Education, Meeting within the Council, of 6 June 1974 on Cooperation in the Field of Education, OJ C 98, 20.8.1974, p. 2.

69 Cf. Final Communiqué of the Hague Summit, English Source: Membership of the European Communities: Implications for Ireland, Laid by the Government Before Each House of the Oireachtas, The Stationery Office: Dublin, April 1970, pp. 109–112, http://www.cvce.eu/obj/final_communique_of_the_hague_summit_2_december_1969-en-33078789-8030-49c8-b4e0-15d053834507.html.

70 Hilpold, 1995, p. 45.

71 General Guidelines for Drawing up a Community Action Programme on Vocational Training, OJ C 81, 12.8.1971, pp. 5–11 (Unofficial Translation, accessed via EUR-Lex).

training obviously were – despite the Council's propositions – just too far off, leaving the former approachable via intergovernmental means only.

The first ever meeting of Education Ministers at the EC-level did not take place until 16 November 1971.[72] Under the auspices of the Council of Europe they had, however, already met on a regular basis during the 1960s.[73] This EC-level meeting was not recognised as a Council meeting due to its configuration.[74] Resolutions (of this and the following meeting of 6 June 1974) were adopted as "Resolution of the Ministers of Education meeting within the Council",[75] thus reflecting the intergovernmental nature of the meeting.[76] It was only in 1976 that the Council began to demonstrate its commitment to the Community's activity in education. The formula "Resolution of the Council and of the Ministers of Education, meeting within the Council"[77] affirms the "mixed" nature of the adopted acts by including the Community and the intergovernmental level.[78] Those mixed resolutions require the mutual agreement of the Council (in its capacity as the Community legislator) and the representatives of the governments of the Member States (in that case the Education Ministers).[79] Still, they have to be regarded with utter care as Van Craeyenest pointed out that

72 Cf. Pépin, 2006, p. 63.

73 Cf. Corbett, A., Ideas, Institutions and Policy Entrepreneurs: Towards a New History of Higher Education in the European Community, 38 European Journal for Education, pp. 315–330, 2003, p. 320.

74 Cf. Pépin, 2006, p. 63.

75 Cf. Resolution of the Ministers for Education meeting within the Council of 16 November 1971 on Cooperation in the Field of Education, European Educational Policy Statements, 3rd ed., Office for Official Publications of the European Communities: Luxembourg, 1988, p. 11; Resolution of the Ministers of Education meeting within the Council of 6 June 1974 on Cooperation in the Field of Education, OJ C 98, 20.8.1974, p. 2.

76 Cf. Van Craeyenest, F., La nature juridique des résolutions sur la coopération en matière d'éducation, in: B. de Witte (ed.), European Community Law of Education, Nomos: Baden-Baden, 1989, pp. 127–133, p. 130.

77 Resolution of the Council and of the Ministers of Education meeting within the Council of 9 February 1976 Comprising an Action Programme in the Field of Education, OJ C 38, 19.2.1976, pp. 1–5.

78 Cf. Pépin, 2006, p. 63.

79 Cf. Van Craeyenest, 1989, p. 128.

> [s]i les Résolutions mixtes on, dans un premier temps, permis de jeter les bases d'une action ultérieure de la Communauté, il faut toutefois mettre en garde contre le danger de 'diluer' par ce biais les compétences communautaires virtuelles, ce qui serait une façon de 'contourner' les procédures législatives prévues par le traité.[80]

During the 1971 meeting the Education Ministers acknowledged that the activities provided for by the Treaty of Rome "concerning [...] the right of establishment and vocational training [...] should be supplemented by greater cooperation in the field of education as such".[81] They also decided to set up a working party that would inter alia consider a European Centre for the Development of Education. Unfortunately, this proposal by French Education Minister Olivier Guichard, which would have only meant to move with the times (cf. the OECD's CERI, created in 1967, for example), failed to get the necessary support of the Commission.[82] At the 1972 Paris Summit the Heads of State and Government concluded that it was time to add another dimension to the European Community. Top priority was assigned to regional policy, so that "structural and regional imbalances [...] which could hinder the achievement of the Economic and Monetary Union" would be corrected. This resulted in the development of the European Regional Development Fund (ERDF), a fund "backed by the Community's own resources". It joined the first of the European Structural and Investment Funds (ESIF)[83], the ESF, established by Article 123 TEEC. Furthermore, the Heads of State and Government emphasized the importance of social policy, asking for a social action programme implementing "a coordinated policy for employment and vocational training" to be drawn up.[84] Established in 1974, it stated the political will to implement a common vocational training policy, which was

---

80 Ibid. p. 131.

81 Cf. Resolution of the Ministers for Education meeting within the Council of 16 November 1971 on Cooperation in the Field of Education, European Educational Policy Statements, 3rd ed., Office for Official Publications of the European Communities: Luxembourg, 1988, p. 11.

82 Cf. Blitz, BK, From Monnet to Delors: Educational Co-operation in the European Union, 12 Contemporary European History, 2003, pp. 197–212, p. 201; Pépin, 2006, p. 64.

83 The ESIF are made up of five different funds: the European Regional Development Fund (ERDF), the European Social Fund (ESF), the European Agricultural and Development Fund (EARDF), the European Maritime and Fisheries Fund (EMFF) and the Cohesion Fund (CF). Those funds help Member States to increase and restore growth and, as of 2014, they "operate under a common framework and pursue complementary policy objectives." Cf. www.ec.europa.eu/esf.

84 Meetings of the Heads of State or Government (Summit), Paris, 19–21 October 1972, Bulletin of the European Communities, No. 10, 1972, pp. 9–26, p. 19.

to lead to an approximation of training standards as well as to the establishment of a European Vocational Training Centre. Called CEDEFOP, it was set up one year later and still serves as a vital helper for policy-makers wanting to improve vocational training systems with its expertise on skills and qualifications.

In 1973, the former Belgian Education Minister, Henri Janne, entrusted by the Commission with the formulation of the first principles of an EC-level education policy, jumped on the bandwagon and underlined the connection between regional policy and education in his report *For a Community policy on education.*[85] Citing Prof. Briggs, then the Vice-Chancellor of the University of Sussex and a former member of the Princeton Institute for Advanced Study, who pointed out the importance of "frontier interests" regarding second language acquisition (SLA) and emphasised the role of interregional cooperation, Janne already took up what seems to be getting more and more en vogue today. That education (allowing choice of SLA) should be provided through interregional cooperation of the countries concerned represents a novel aspect for the time the report was published.[86] Janne concluded that with the Education Ministers having met within the Council, education was "already a recognized responsibility in the framework of Community policy."[87] However, the report proved to be difficult to use for the Commission as it called "an operation of 'approximation' or 'harmonization' of […] policies"[88] indispensable.[89] The Commission reacted with the Communication *Education in the European Community* (COM(74) 253 final/2). Stating the importance of education policy in the Member States, it highlights the diversity of national education policies and underlines that harmonisation as well as coordination of content and structure of the latter would neither be desirable nor realistic. Drafted by the Commission's responsible departments (after the first Community enlargement in 1973, the Directorate General (DG) for Research, Science and Education was established), the communication served as a trigger for further reflection on the issue, eventually leading to the adoption of the Community's first action programme for education in 1976.[90]

In 1974, at their second meeting within the Council, the Education Ministers adopted a resolution *on cooperation in the field of education* that defined the

85 Cf. Janne, H., For a Community Policy on Education, Bulletin of the European Communities, Supplement 10/73, pp. 11 et seq.
86 Ibid. p. 32.
87 Ibid. p. 49.
88 Ibid. p. 11.
89 Cf. Pépin, 2006, p. 65.
90 Ibid.

Community's principles and priorities. They clarified that "on no account must education be regarded merely as a component of economic life". Moreover, they affirmed that educational cooperation has to "be adapted to the specific objectives and requirements of [the] field". Furthermore, it has to allow for diversity in the different Member States and thus "[h]armonization of these [education] systems or policies cannot [...] be considered an end in itself." The Education Ministers also drew up a list of "priority spheres of action" (simultaneously calling for an Education Committee, consisting of representatives of the Member States and the Commission[91], for support):

- better facilities for the education and training of nationals and the children of nationals of other Member States of the Communities and of non-member countries,
- promotion of closer relations between educational systems in Europe,
- compilation of up-to-date documentation and statistics on education,
- increased cooperation between institutions of higher education,
- improved possibilities for academic recognition of diplomas and periods of study,
- encouragement of the freedom of movement and mobility of teachers, students and research workers, in particular by the removal of administrative and social obstacles to the free movement of such persons and by the improved teaching of foreign languages,
- achievement of equal opportunity for free access to all forms of education.[92]

1976 brought about the first mixed resolution.[93] Issued by the Council and the Ministers of Education it is said to represent "the real foundation of cooperation", marking

> the start of Community work which has been progressively extended through the adoption of new texts, but which already called for improved information on education systems and their comparability, and the improvement of language teaching, as the foundation stone for better mutual understanding.[94]

91 This was unique for EC policy advisory structures at the time as it constituted "neither a Commission nor a Council body" but had dual membership. Cf. Corbett, 2003, p. 323.

92 Resolution of the Ministers of Education meeting within the Council of 6 June 1974 on Cooperation in the Field of Education, OJ C 98, 20.8.1974, p. 2.

93 Cf. Resolution of the Council and of the Ministers of Education meeting within the Council of 9 February 1976 comprising an action programme in the field of education, OJ C 38, 19.2.1976, pp. 1–5.

94 Green Paper on the European Dimension of Education, COM(93) 457 final, 29 September 1993, Annex B, para 3.

With its broad scope, the resolution *comprising an action programme in the field of education* served as a long-time atypical "legal basis" for the implementation of education cooperation activities.[95] The resolution did not confer any real powers on the Community but opted for measures such as the exchange of information and experience, cooperation in teacher training, encouraging joint study and research programmes, promoting mobility or the conduct of educational studies and research. In order to foster the mutual understanding between the Member States' educational systems, the Community was entrusted with the organisation of regular meetings for education policy officials. The organisation of study visits for national administrators of schools and higher education institutions (HEIs) was left to the Member States. In a bid to reach out to the local/regional level, local and regional administrators were also included. The introduction of a "European dimension" (already mentioned in the Janne Report[96]) – through exchanges and study visits for teachers or activities enriched with European content – was left to the Member States (a resolution *on the European dimension in education*[97] was adopted in 1988). The importance of SLA (naturally the focus is on Community languages) features prominently in the Resolution, demonstrating an interest in multilingualism, which is a necessary prerequisite for mobility and thus economically valuable. However, the significance of the education action programme does not lie in those "comparatively modest aims, but in the fact that education was legitimised as an area of policy by the Council of Ministers for the first time."[98]

The implementation of the education action programme and the further development of vocational training (i.e. the creation of CEDEFOP) did not go hand in hand (vocational training was assigned to the DG for Social Affairs). While the Education Committee ensured the development of education cooperation, the Social Affairs Committee was in charge of vocational training.[99] Education

95 Cf. Gori, G., Towards an EU Right to Education, Kluwer Law International: The Hague, 2001, p. 20.
96 Cf. Janne, 1973, pp. 26 et seq.
97 Cf. Resolution of the Council and the Ministers of Education meeting within the Council on the European dimension in education of 24 May 1988, OJ C 177, 6.7.1988, pp. 5–7.
98 Ertl, 2003, p. 19.
99 Pépin, L., The History of EU Cooperation in the Field of Education and Training: How Lifelong Learning Became a Strategic Objective, 42 European Journal of Education, 2007, pp. 121–132, p. 123.

and training were therefore going separate ways, although Janne was already very clear about the need for change in 1973 when he poignantly pointed out that

> in a society undergoing permanent change in the scientific, technical and social fields, there is no longer any good vocational training which does not comprise a sound general training at all levels, and there is no longer any good general training which is not linked with concrete practice and, in principle, with real work.[100]

In 1985, the ECJ delivered its prime landmark ruling on education with *Gravier* defining the scope of vocational training as

> any form of education which prepares for a qualification for a particular profession, trade or employment or which provides the necessary training and skills for such a profession, trade or employment is vocational training, whatever the age and the level of the training of the pupils or students, and even if the training programme includes an element of general education.[101]

With vocational training officially sporting a broad definition (i.e. inclusion of university education), the Council opted to base its decision concerning the European Community Action Scheme for the Mobility of University Students (ERASMUS) on Articles 128 and 235 TEEC, also referring to Council Decision 63/266/EEC of 2 April 1963 laying down general principles for implementing a common vocational training policy.[102] In its proposal the Commission had, however, only taken recourse to Article 128 TEEC and Council Decision 63/266/EEC.[103] Article 235 TEEC (later Article 308 TEC and predecessor of today's Article 352 TFEU[104]), a general competence norm called the "residual

---

100 Janne, 1973, p. 11.

101 Case C-293/83 *Françoise Gravier v City of Liège* [1985] ECR 593, para 30. The definition was subsequently refined in further cases: cf. Case C-309/85 *Bruno Barra v Belgian State and City of Liège* [1988] ECR 355, Case C-24/86 *Vincent Blaizot v University of Liège and Others* [1988] ECR 379, Case C-263/86 *Belgian State v René Humbel and Marie-Thérèse Humbel née Edel* [1988] ECR 5365 and Case C-308/89 *Carmina di Leo v Land Berlin* [1990] ECR 4185.

102 Cf. Council Decision 87/327/EEC of 15 June 1987 Adopting the European Community Action Scheme for the Mobility of University Students, OJ L 166, 25.6.1987, pp. 20–24.

103 Cf. Proposal for a Council Decision adopting the European Community Action Scheme for the Mobility of University Students, COM(85) 756 final, OJ C 73, 2.4.1986, pp. 4–7.

104 The wording of the article has since been changed. Article 352(3) TFEU explicitly excludes measures entailing harmonisation in areas where harmonisation has been ruled out by the Treaties. Cf. p. 97.

powers clause" (also "flexibility clause"[105]) because it allows for gap-filling if a treaty basis necessary for the attainment of Community objectives is missing,[106] was added to the Commission's proposal by unanimous vote. With Member States voicing different opinions, such as using either Article 128 TEEC or Article 235 TEEC as the sole legal basis, the request to use both articles served as a compromise basing the decision on a double legal basis.[107] As Article 235 TEEC states that

> [i]f any action by the Community appears necessary to achieve, in the functioning of the Common Market, one of the aims of the Community in cases where this Treaty has not provided for the requisite powers of action, the Council, acting by means of a unanimous vote on a proposal of the Commission and after the Assembly has been consulted, shall enact the appropriate provisions[,]

it seems a legal tour de force to use it in connection with Article 128 TEEC. Clearly, the Council sought to avoid the lax voting procedure[108] associated with Article 128 TEEC by adding an article requiring unanimity and the consultation of the European Parliament (EP).

It is not surprising that the Commission was not impressed by the addition of the aforementioned article to the initial proposal, which is why it brought a case against the Council seeking to have the ERASMUS decision annulled. The Council, fearing "creeping supranationalist tendencies",[109] was supported by several individual Member States (Germany, France, and the United Kingdom (UK)), which intervened in its support. Building on *Gravier* and subsequent rulings, the ECJ held that

> in general the studies to which the contested programme applies fall within the sphere of vocational training, and only in exceptional cases will the action planned under the programme be found to be applicable to university studies which, because of their particular character, are outside that sphere. The mere possibility of the latter cannot justify the conclusion that the contested programme goes beyond the scope of vocational

---

105 Cf. Craig, P. and G. de Búrca, EU Law: Text, Cases and Materials, 5th ed., OUP: Oxford, 2011, p. 89.

106 Cf. Conway, G., Conflicts of Competence Norms in EU Law and the Legal Reasoning of the ECJ, 11 German Law Journal, 2010, pp. 966–1005, pp. 968 et seq.

107 Cf. Lenaerts, K., ERASMUS: Legal Basis and Implementation, in: B. de Witte (ed.), European Community Law of Education, Nomos: Baden-Baden, 1989, pp. 113–125, p. 116.

108 Cf. p. 31: In conjunction with Article 148(1) TEEC, Article 128 TEEC allows for a simple majority vote.

109 Blitz, 2003, p. 204.

training and that therefore the Council was not empowered to adopt it pursuant to Article 128 of the Treaty.[110]

However, as "at least some of the initiatives planned are aimed at the spheres of both research and vocational training" and that "as the contested decision concerns not only the sphere of vocational training but also that of scientific research, the Council did not have the power to adopt it pursuant to Article 128 alone".[111] A legal basis for research was only introduced with the 1986 Single European Act (SEA) (cf. Title VI "Research and technological development"), which had not entered into force when the Council adopted the ERASMUS decision. Hence, the residual powers clause, which is restricted to situations "where no other provision of the treaty gives the Community institutions the necessary power to adopt the measure in question",[112] was necessary.

While the newly inserted Article 130g TEEC underlined the importance of cooperation of universities and research centres as well as of researcher mobility, the SEA did not grant any educational competence to the Community. This should have signalled that the Community was neither to touch education policy nor the individual aspects thereof.[113] However, in March 1987, on the eve of the 30th anniversary of the signing of the Rome Treaties, the French government proposed to its fellow Member States to push forward for a dimension of education. It issued the "Livre bleu" or blue book (named after its cover) for a Europe of education and culture calling for the teaching of modern languages, the stressing of a European dimension in education as well as exchange and mobility, among other things.[114] Because the development of a European dimension of education was lagging behind, the EP put pressure on the Council of Ministers of Education.[115] This resulted in a 1988 Council Resolution,[116] which focussed

110 Case 242/87 *Commission of the European Communities v Council of the European Communities* [1989] ECR 1425, para 27.

111 Ibid. paras 36 and 37.

112 Ibid. para 6; also cf. Case C-45/86 *Commission v Council* [1987] ECR 1493, para 13.

113 Cf. Lenaerts, 1994, p. 9.

114 Cf. Vergès, J., La voie intergovernmentale: Le "Livre Bleu" Français, in: B. de Witte (ed.), European Community Law of Education, Nomos: Baden-Baden, 1989, pp. 135–144, pp. 135 et seq.

115 Cf. Ryba, R., Educational Changes in Europe, in: D. Phillips (ed.), Aspects of Education and the European Union, Oxford Studies in Comparative Education, 5(2) (Triangle: Wallingford (OX)), 1995, pp. 63–75, p. 67.

116 Resolution of the Council and the Ministers of Education Meeting within the Council on the European Dimension in Education of 24 May 1988, OJ C 177, 6.7.1988, pp. 5–7.

on the oft-discussed European dimension of education. The Resolution stressed the contribution to the Community's development and the progress stipulated in the SEA. It picked up the earlier advances to create a European citizen concept[117] such as the Stuttgart Declaration (1983), the Conclusions of the European Council of Fontainebleau (1984) as well as the "People's Europe" report (1985) and reaffirmed their resolve for a European dimension in education.

Towards the end of the 1980s/beginning of the 1990s, several action programmes for education and training were introduced: COMETT (university-enterprise cooperation in the field of technology), ERASMUS (student mobility and transnational university cooperation projects), FORCE (continuous vocational training), LINGUA (promotion of foreign language competence), PETRA (vocational training and preparation for adult life) and TEMPUS (trans-European mobility for university studies). ERASMUS was certainly the most successful action programme and was quickly perceived as their "flagship".[118] In order to facilitate transfer of credits acquired during a study abroad period, the Commission initiated a pilot project, the European Credit Transfer System (ECTS). Intended for participants of the ERASMUS mobility scheme, participating institutions (departments) "had to agree on booking achievements in terms of study load calculated by credits", provide information on available courses in advance and agree to a course schedule (learning agreement) with the prospective students.[119] In 1989, the Commission also launched the Jean Monnet action. Despite often being overlooked in historical treatises on EU education policy, it has contributed towards a European dimension in higher education through funding EU specific teaching modules and subsidies for "Jean Monnet Chairs" focussing on European integration.[120]

---

117 Cf. Green Paper on the European Dimension of Education, Green Paper on the European Dimension of Education, COM(93) 457 final, 29 September 1993, Annex B, para 4.

118 Teichler, U., Changes of ERASMUS under the Umbrella of SOCRATES, 5 Journal of Studies in International Education, 2001, pp. 201–227, p. 202.

119 Ibid. p. 208.

120 Bache, I., The Europeanization of Higher Education: Markets, Politics or Learning?, 44 JCMS, 2006, pp. 231–248, p. 237.

2.3 The Maastricht Treaty and Beyond (1992–2000)

2.3.1 Implications for Education and Training: The Maastricht Treaty

The 1992 Maastricht Treaty – officially known as the Treaty on European Union (TEU)[121] – certainly constituted a turning point for education policy. So far, there had been reluctance to deal with education in primary law. In fact, until the entry into force of the Maastricht Treaty in 1993, the legal framework did not entail an education policy. Instead, the educational provisions served as components of treaty-based Community objectives.[122] Save for ECJ judgments that had started to churn out an education policy (also cf. Regulation 1612/68), no legal basis was available. This was a problem as "[b]etween 1957 and 1992, every proposal by the Commission was faced with assertions of sovereignty by the member states".[123] The Community had gone from remaining silent on most issue-areas dealt with at national level to experiencing a "gradual – but in retrospect – spectacular growth of policy-making at the European level".[124] This is especially true for education where secondary law began to evolve in the late 1960s and early 1970s, culminating in the Luxembourg case law, which – education-wise – acted as the engine of European integration. From the free movement of workers (Articles 48 et seq. TEEC), the freedom of establishment (Articles 52 et seq. TEEC), the freedom to provide services (Articles 59 et seq. TEEC) or vocational training (Article 128 TEEC), the provisions touching on education and free movement rights were referred to the ECJ. The application of the principle of non-discrimination on grounds of nationality resulted in interventions at national level. With primary and secondary law so diverging, it was time for change.

In order to create a valid legal basis and move beyond the system, which was basically in the hands of the courts (that is to say the ECJ), the Member States, with the exception of the UK, wished to incorporate education into primary

121 The TEU was signed in Maastricht on 7 February 1992 and entered into force on 1 November 1993.

122 Cf. Blanke, HJ, Art. 165/166 AEUV, in: E. Grabitz, M. Hilf and M. Nettesheim (eds.), Das Recht der Europäischen Union, CH Beck: München, 44. Ergänzungslieferung, May 2011, recital 1.

123 Field, J., The European Union and the Learning Society: Congested Sovereignty in an Age of Globalisation, in: F. Coffield (ed.), A National Strategy for Lifelong Learning, Newcastle University: Newcastle upon Tyne, 1997, pp. 95–111, p. 97.

124 Pollack, MA, The End of Creeping Competence? EU-Policy Making Since Maastricht, 38 JCMS, 2000, pp. 519–538, p. 521.

law.[125] Indeed, "*integration* was to be deepened, in particular, through an unprecedented extension of the powers conferred upon the European Community (or "Union")."[126] But while the Maastricht Treaty officially authorised the Union's education policy, no radical change took place.[127] Essentially, it was all about aligning primary legislation with the rest of the acquis communautaire. Not only could the Union's position officially be clarified, it was also a way of preventing the competence creep the Council and the Member States so dreaded. Although the newly inserted Article 126 TEC, dealing with education, and Article 127 TEC (reformulating and replacing Article 128 TEEC on vocational training) were placed in the 1st pillar/supranational section of the TEU, they factually limited the legal competence of the Commission. Merely supportive functions were left (though in vocational training the Union's competence went further[128]),[129] the ban on harmonisation being an absolute novelty in the development of Community law.[130] On the other hand, the EP's role was strengthened through the definition of the Union's responsibilities in the area of education. The Maastricht Treaty further introduced the co-decision procedure (Article 189b TEC), which transformed the EP into a co-legislator on an equal footing with the Council (Article 126(4) TEC). The simple majority vote that had overshadowed the application of Article 128 TEEC and prompted resorting to Article 235 TEEC because of its unanimity requirement was replaced by the cooperation procedure, i.e. qualified majority vote (QMV) and EP opinion (cf. Article 127(4) in connection with Article 189c TEC). Both Articles 126 and 127 TEC respectively, allowed the Member States to regain control over Union

---

125 Cf. Blanke, 2011, recital 59, where Blanke talks of the "prätorische Rspr. des EuGH", a legal term which is non-existent in the Anglo-American system.

126 Lenaerts, K., The Principle of Subsidiarity and the Environment in the European Union: Keeping the Balance of Federalism, 17 Fordham International Law Journal, 1993, pp. 846–895, p. 847.

127 Cf. Walkenhorst, H., Explaining Change in EU Education Policy, 15 Journal of European Public Policy, 2008, pp. 567–587, p. 571.

128 Article 127(1) TEC: The Community shall implement a vocational training policy which shall support and supplement the action of the Member States, while fully respecting the responsibility of the Member States for the content and organization of vocational training.

129 Cf. Martens and Wolf, 2009, pp. 86 et seq.

130 Cf. Hablitzel, H., Subsidiaritätsprinzip und Bildungskompetenzen im Vertrag über die Europäische Union, Pustet: Regensburg, 1994, p. 25; Hablitzel, H., Harmonisierungsverbot und Subsidiaritätsprinzip im europäischen Bildungsrecht, 55 DÖV, 2002, pp. 407–414, p. 409.

intervention in education and vocational training.[131] Still, with education intrinsically linked to other policies, a limitation of education issues to the education chapter is impossible.[132]

Inserted under Title VIII "Social Policy, Education, Vocational Training and Youth", Articles 126 and 127 TEC form chapter 3 titled "Education, Vocational Training and Youth". Based on the existing aquis, it also referred to the development of a European dimension in education (first indent of Article 126(2) TEC). Right at the beginning of the Treaty, Article 3(p) TEC determines that the Union's activities shall include "a contribution to education and training of quality". While political reasons did play a role, this extension to the Treaty was mainly made for economical reasons. Article 2 TEC that ought to be read in conjunction with Article 3 TEC, refers to the establishment of the internal market. Article 3(p) TEC is certainly the major prerequisite for the goals listed in Article 2 TEC since investment in human capital contributes to a large extent to "a harmonious and balanced development of economic activities, [...] a high degree of convergence of economic performance, a high level of employment and of social protection, the raising of the standard of living and quality of life, and economic and social cohesion" in the Member States. The notion of competitiveness through education constituted a turnaround in the integration process. Whereas previously, further development of EU education law had mainly been instigated by negative integration (cf. ECJ case law), the Maastricht Treaty and its emphasis on policy-making in the education sector was paving the way for positive integration.

With Article 126 TEC, the Union had finally overcome the lack of legal certainty. On the one hand, general education had been embedded in primary law for the first time. On the other hand, a legal framework that left no doubt about the Union's competence in the field had been put in place. Because of the perseverance of the German *Länder*, the principle of subsidiarity was established as a general rule.[133] Without it, the codification of general education would have been highly unlikely. The concept of subsidiarity as such does not constitute a novel political principle. Indeed, it also defines the relationship between the national

131 Cf. Gori, 2001, p. 77.

132 Cf. Case C-147/03 *Commission of the European Communities v Republic of Austria* [2005] ECR 5969; Case C-65/03 *Commission of the European Communities v Kingdom of Belgium* [2004] ECR 6427.

133 Cf. Scharpf, FW, The Asymmetry of European Integration or Why the EU Cannot Be a "Social Market Economy", 8 Socio-Economic Review, 2010, pp. 211–250, p. 230.

and the subnational level of the Member States.[134] Moreover, the application of the subsidiarity principle is not unprecedented in EU primary law:

> It was present in embryonic form in the ECSC Treaty (Article 5), implicit in the Treaty of Rome, and spelled out in the Single European Act in relation to the environment (Article 130r[4]).[135]

The Maastricht Treaty refers to the subsidiarity principle in recital 11 of its preamble. Article 3b(2) TEC provides a definition in the Union context. In short, in fields which do not fall into the exclusive competence of the Union, EU level action may only be taken "if and in so far as the objectives of the proposed action cannot be sufficiently achieved by the Member States and can therefore, by reason of the scale or effects of the proposed action, be better achieved by the Community". Together with para 3 that stipulates that "[a]ny action by the Community shall not go beyond what is necessary to achieve the objectives of this Treaty", a double threshold for action has been established. Para 2 presupposes a "test of comparative efficiency": are Member States able to attain an acceptable result on an intergovernmental basis (examination of available methods, e.g. administrative instructions, codes of conduct or legislation) or is there a need for EU level action? If this hurdle has been taken, the second threshold awaits the Union proposal. It has to comply with the principle of proportionality: is the intervention really justified or might it also be achieved by more lenient means?[136]

The principle of subsidiarity is firmly anchored in Articles 126 and 127 TEC. Through the institutionalisation of education, the sector became one of its prime fields of application. However, "[c]ommunity cooperation in education has applied the principle of subsidiarity since the outset, even before the term was coined — bold and active subsidiarity, for the good of its citizens."[137] Education continued to be a state prerogative. Hence, legal means for Union action remained limited (and indeed they do so until today). A few years later, federal Member States, already familiar with the concept of multi-level governance,

---

134 Depending on whether a Member State is organised as a federal, regionalised or unitary state, the extent of competence conferred upon sub-national levels varies. For sub-national competence in the education sector cf. **Chapter eight** – Regionalism in the European Union: Taking Education to a Whole New Level.

135 Communication on the principle of subsidiarity, adopted by the Commission on 27 October 1992, for transmission to the Council and Parliament, Bulletin of the European Communities, No. 10, 1992, pp. 116–126, p. 118.

136 Ibid. pp. 116 et seq.

137 1976–2006: Thirty Years of European Cooperation in Education, Press Release, 23 February 2006 (IP/06/12).

were adamant to point out in the Protocol on the implementation of subsidiarity and proportionality, attached to the Treaty of Amsterdam, that

> it is taken for granted […] that action by the European Community in accordance with the principle of subsidiarity not only concerns the Member States but also their entities to the extent that they have their own law-making powers conferred on them under national constitutional law.[138]

In the end, the subsidiarity principle "effectively relegated the Union to a secondary role"[139] and "left little [reason] for legally binding interventions on the part of the European Commission to harmonise national education systems."[140]

With the Maastricht Treaty, a demarcation of education and vocational training took place, leading to a separation of policy matters.[141] Higher education, integrated into Article 128 TEEC through judicial acquis, was reallocated to Article 126 TEC. Moreover, matters formerly not provided for at Union level such as primary and secondary schooling or LLL were incorporated. While Articles 126 and 127 TEC have a different scope of application, their structure is similar. Both highlight that it is not for the EU to undertake the responsibility for education or vocational training, but to fully respect the sovereignty of the Member States regarding "the content of teaching and the organization of education systems"/"the content and organization of vocational training" (para 1). "[C]ooperation with third countries and the competent international organisations" is to be fostered (para 3) and Union intervention is limited by proscribing "any harmonisation of the laws and regulations of the Member States" (para 4).

The amount of say of Member States was not only underpinned by the doctrine of subsidiarity, the Maastricht Treaty further introduced the Committee of the Regions (CoR) as a second advisory body (Article 198a TEC). Through the CoR the sub-national level finally got involved in the policy-making process, something the German *Länder* had been particularly keen on.[142] An additional safeguard, the assembly of regional and local representatives gives a voice to the regional and local levels. Article 126 TEC refers to the advisory body in para 4, requiring the Council to consult the CoR before adopting any measures. The CoR then states its own opinion and monitors the application of the subsidiarity

138 Declaration by Germany, Austria and Belgium on Subsidiarity, OJ C 340, 10.11.1997, p. 143.

139 Cf. Blitz, 2003, p. 212.

140 Cf. Martens and Wolf, 2009, p. 87.

141 Cf. Lenaerts, 1994, pp. 24 et seq.

142 Cf. Walkenhorst, 2005, p. 5.

principle. The CoR is divided into Commissions. Set up in 1994, it included a Commission for education and training (today the EDUC Commission for education, youth, culture and research[143]) that dealt with these consultations.[144] The wish to turn the CoR into a "subsidiarity watchdog" was expressed as early as 1995.[145] However, it was not until the Lisbon Treaty that the CoR obtained the right to initiate infringement procedures at the ECJ (Article 8, para 2 of the Lisbon Treaty Protocol No 2 on the Application of the Principles of Subsidiarity and Proportionality).[146]

Last but not least, the Maastricht Treaty introduced Union citizenship. Enshrined in Articles 8–8e TEC, it was about to have a far-reaching impact on European integration. Recital 8 of the preamble of the TEU explains the intention of the Member States as "to establish a citizenship common to nationals of their countries". It should strengthen the protection of their rights and interests (cf. third indent of Article B TEU). Article 8(1) and (2) TEC provides that "[e]very person holding the nationality of a Member State shall be a citizen of the Union" and that "[c]itizens of the Union shall enjoy the rights conferred by this Treaty". Apart from this overall provision, Article 8a TEC stipulates that "[e]very citizen of the Union shall have the right to move and reside freely within the territory of the Member States, subject to […] limitations and conditions". The concept of Union citizenship was not something completely new. Indeed, embryonic forms thereof had already been present in the TEEC. The free movement of workers, the freedom of establishment and the freedom to provide services as well as the principle of non-discrimination on grounds of nationality had already been established in 1957.[147] Although the pre-Maastricht idea had been that of an economically active

143 Cf. http://cor.europa.eu/en/activities/commissions/educ/Pages/role.aspx#.

144 Cf. Committee of the Regions, Key Dates in the History of the Committee of the Regions: 1994–2009, Publications Office of the European Union: Luxembourg, 2009, p. 6.

145 Ibid. p. 9.

146 Cf. Lisbon Treaty Turns Committee of the Regions into Subsidiarity Watchdog, Press Release, 4 December 2009 (COR/09/113).

147 Cf. Jacobs, FG, Citizenship of the European Union – A Legal Analysis, 13 European Law Journal, 2007, pp. 591–610, pp. 592–593. Also cf. O'Leary, S., Free Movement of Persons and Services, in: P. Craig and G. de Búrca (eds.), The Evolution of EU Law, 2nd ed., OUP: Oxford, 2011, pp. 499–545, p. 506; Shaw, J., Citizenship: Contrasting Dynamics at the Interface of Integration and Constitutionalism, in: P. Craig and G. de Búrca (eds.), The Evolution of EU Law, 2nd ed., OUP: Oxford, 2011, pp. 575–609, p. 584: "incipient form" of Union citizenship through "proto-citizenship" ECJ case law from the 1970s onwards.

citizen, the ECJ had used teleological interpretation pushing the limits of what was feasible and possible.[148] This is best illustrated by the *Gravier* ruling, in which the ECJ interpreted the provisions of the TEEC in a very broad manner.[149]

The Amsterdam Treaty (signed in 1997, entered into force in 1999) inserted a ninth recital into the TEC preamble underlining the Union's determination "to promote the development of the highest possible level of knowledge for their peoples through a wide access to education and through its continuous updating". An emphasis of such extent clearly added to the political weight of the up-and-coming policy area. The Amsterdam Treaty further led to a renumbering of Article 3(p) TEC to Article 3(q) TEC as well as of Articles 126 and 127 TEC to Articles 149 and 150 TEC (this included a change of Title VIII to Title XI). Additionally, the decision-making procedure provided for by Article 150(4) TEC was changed. The co-decision procedure described in Article 251 TEC (ex Article 189b), which had previously only been prescribed in Article 149 TEC (formerly the cooperation procedure referred to in Article 252 (ex Article 189c) had applied regarding Article 150 TEC), gave the EP a stronger say in vocational training. Moreover, para 4 of Article 150 TEC was changed, so that the Council – as in Article 149 TEC – had to consult the CoR before adopting any measures on vocational training. The Treaty of Nice (signed in 2001, entered into force in 2003) did not bring about any changes for the education sector. It was only with the Lisbon Treaty (signed in 2007, entered into force in 2009) that further innovations were provided.

2.3.2 Marching towards Lisbon: an Interim Period

The time between 1993 and 1999 is alluded to as an interim period for education with other issues dominating the scene.[150] The integrationist dynamic that had been part of the emerging policy was capped, leaving it primarily confined to the newly established legal framework.[151] The activities at the EU level were thus limited to publishing Commission Green and White Papers as well as expanding the existing action programmes. Green Papers are adopted by the Commission

148 Cf. Shaw, 2011, p. 588.

149 Cf. Case C-293/83 *Gravier*.

150 Cf. Walkenhorst, 2005, p. 8; Walkenhorst, 2008, p. 571.

151 Cf. Walkenhorst, 2005, p. 7.

to stimulate discussion on topics,[152] while White Papers contain "proposals for Community action in a specific area" and may be triggered by Green Papers.[153]

Based on the 1988 Resolution *on the European dimension in education*, the Commission adopted the 1993 Green Paper *on the European Dimension of Education* (COM(93) 457 final). In the same year the White Paper *Growth, Competitiveness, Employment: The Challenges and Ways Forward into the 21st Century* (COM(93) 700 final) was issued, referring especially to the importance of basing "[a]ll measures on the concept of developing, generalizing and systematizing lifelong learning and continuing training."[154] With its emphasis on the "essential pillar of European construction" in the form of economic growth and social cohesion,[155] it served as a stimulus for the Lisbon Strategy agreed upon in 2000.[156] The 1993 White Paper further proposed a "European Year of Education" to create Union-wide awareness.[157] Ultimately turned into the 1996 European Year of LLL, it was the starting point for active LLL promotion and increasing LLL awareness on all levels.[158] In 1995, the Commission adopted the White Paper *on Education and Training – Teaching and Learning – Towards the Learning Society* (COM(95) 590 final), the first ever policy document breaking with the division between education and training,[159] it marked the Union's emergence as a key player of LLL promotion.[160]

LLL, however, soon became a key objective of the European Employment Strategy (ESS), which was launched at the European Council's 1997 special Luxembourg Employment Summit.[161] This led to an "inter-sectoral rivalry" between the EU's education and employment policies, with education, and LLL in

152 http://europa.eu/legislation_summaries/glossary/green_paper_en.htm.
153 http://europa.eu/legislation_summaries/glossary/white_paper_en.htm.
154 Bulletin of the European Communities, Supplement 6/93, p. 120.
155 Ibid. p. 15.
156 Cf. Corbett, 2003, p. 326.
157 Bulletin of the European Communities, Supplement 6/93, p. 122.
158 Cf. Dehmel, A., Making a European Area of Lifelong Learning a Reality? Some Critical Reflections on the European Union's Lifelong Learning Policies, 42 Comparative Education, 2006, pp. 49–62, p. 53.
159 Cf. Pépin, 2006, p. 28.
160 Cf. Hake, BJ, Lifelong Learning Policies in the European Union: Developments and Issues, 29 Compare: A Journal of Comparative and International Education, 1999, pp. 53–69, p. 55.
161 Pépin, 2007, p. 127.

particular, becoming a "tool of employment policy".[162] LLL was further alluded to in the preamble to the 1997 Treaty of Amsterdam, underlining the importance of the continuous updating of education.[163] However, because LLL was part of the Union's employment strategy, decisions that concerned "core educational issues" were made by the Member States' Employment Ministers and prepared by DG Employment. Moreover, the LLL definition of the DG Employment differed from the broadly framed LLL definition of the DG Education, which included all levels of formal learning as well as non-formal learning. The Education Ministers of the Member States were therefore eager to reclaim LLL.[164] The EES was also remarkable because it was the first example of the OMC, which would later be associated with the Lisbon Strategy and its successor, the EU 2020 Strategy. Instead of rules, the EES employs guidelines and indicators to keep track of progress with regard to the latter.[165]

The mid 90s also saw the rationalisation and streamlining of the Union's action programmes. With the 1995–1999 programming period, the six existing action programmes were fused into two: SOCRATES[166] for education and LEONARDO for vocational training. However, the first rationalisation of the action programmes was not successful in developing closer links between education and vocational training. This changed with the 2000–2006 programming period, which introduced the possibility to develop joint actions in order to support the implementation of LLL and a knowledge-based Europe.[167]

The limitations set by the Treaty of Maastricht had made greater integration in the education area impossible. With Member States unable to pursue targets on supranational Union level without fearing competence conferral, the Education Ministers had to look elsewhere – go "forum shopping" so to say – in order to

162 Cf. Gornitzka, A., Bologna in Context: A Horizontal Perspective on the Dynamics of Governance Sites for a Europe of Knowledge, 45 European Journal of Education, 2010, pp. 535–548, p. 541; Corbett, A., Education and the Lisbon Strategy, in: P. Copeland and D. Papadimitriou (eds.), The EU's Lisbon Strategy: Evaluating Success, Understanding Failure, Palgrave: Basingstoke, 2012, pp. 149–167, p. 154.

163 Cf. p. 52.

164 Gornitzka, A., The Open Method of Coordination as Practice – A Watershed in European Education Policy?, ARENA Working Paper No. 16, December 2006, pp. 14–15; Gornitzka, 2010, pp. 541–542.

165 Cf. Trubek, DM and LG Trubek, Hard and Soft Law in Europe, 11 European Law Journal, 2005, pp. 343–364, pp. 348–349.

166 SOCRATES introduced the COMENIUS actions for school, making the promotion of cooperation at school level (e.g. school partnerships) reality.

167 Cf. Pépin, 2007, p. 126.

find a venue allowing for political initiatives without loss of sovereignty. Extra-EU measures, more precisely the Bologna Process launched in 1999, proved to be significant for the harmonisation of the European higher education systems. An intergovernmental initiative at European level, it stretches beyond the confines of the EU. With "considerable national systemic diversity[,] both in terms of structure and content",[168] the Bologna process is a means to increase compatibility between higher education systems in Europe. Due to Europe being a region in which "each country's system of higher education has been developed independently of each other over the centuries, the prospect of convergence seems complex, the job laborious and the outcome(s) likely to be diverse, compound and multifaceted."[169] While this is undoubtedly true, educational cooperation is indispensable in a Europe of knowledge as set out in the 1998 Sorbonne Declaration.

The main objective of the Bologna Process, which is regularly reviewed by the Ministers for Higher Education in the Ministerial Communiqués and Declarations, is the implementation of a European Higher Education Area (EHEA). It includes inter alia the introduction of the three-cycle degree system (bachelor/master/doctorate), the use of credits (ECTS), the promotion of mobility of students and teachers and cooperation in quality assurance. With the foundations of the EHEA in place, the Bologna Process currently counts 47 participating countries.[170] The EU Commission joined the Bologna Process as a full member in 2001. It goes without saying that the Bologna Process has since influenced the Union's agenda for higher education.[171]

168 Gornitzka, 2006, p. 6.
169 Cf. Papatsiba, V., Making Higher Education More European through Student Mobility? Revisiting EU Initiatives in the Context of the Bologna Process, 42 Comparative Education, 2006, pp. 93–111, p. 93.
170 Cf. European Commission, The European Higher Education Area in 2012: Bologna Process Implementation Report, Education, Audiovisual and Culture Executive Agency: Brussels, 2012, p. 15.
171 Cf. Tauch, C., EU Higher Education Issues and Priorities for 2010–2020, 1 Journal of the European Higher Education Area, 2011, pp. 65–90, p. 66.

3. The Lisbon Strategy: High Flying Ambitions for Education and Training

> Europe's wealth lies in the knowledge and ability of its people; that is the key to growth, employment and social cohesion.[172]

In March 2000, the Lisbon European Council set itself a lofty goal: making the EU "the most competitive and dynamic knowledge-based economy in the world capable of sustainable economic growth with more and better jobs and greater social cohesion."[173] Referred to as the "second turning point" for EU education policy,[174] the Lisbon Strategy, also known as Lisbon Agenda or Lisbon Process, put focus on education and training and introduced the open method of coordination (OMC). The OMC, the "engine" of the Lisbon Strategy,[175] had in fact, despite being hailed a new governance tool, already been employed for the co-ordination of policies before. Developed with the above-mentioned EES, it had also been used within the Economic and Monetary Union (EMU). It was only with the Lisbon Summit, however, that it was placed within a "broader strategy", combining competitiveness and social cohesion.[176] A policy-making instrument, it does neither lead to binding legislative measures nor does it require Member States to change their national law.[177] It is a form of soft law, a "means of spreading best practice and achieving greater convergence towards the main EU goals [...] designed to help Member States to progressively develop their own policies". Creating a kind of template, the European Council described the OMC's elements as

172 Berlin Declaration, German Presidency of the Council of the European Union, 2007, http://en.wikisource.org/wiki/Berlin_Declaration.

173 Lisbon European Council 23 and 24 March 2000, Presidency Conclusions, para 5.

174 Cf. Nóvoa and De Jong-Lambert, 2003, p. 55.

175 Cf. Pépin, L., Education in the Lisbon Strategy: Assessment and Prospects, 46 European Journal of Education, 2011, pp. 25–35, p. 25.

176 Smismans, S., How to Be Fundamental with Soft Procedures? The Open Method of Coordination and Fundamental Social Rights, in: G. de Búrca and B. de Witte (eds.), Social Rights in Europe, OUP: Oxford, 2005, pp. 217–238, p. 217.

177 European Parliament, Committee on Legal Affairs, Rapporteur: MM Ortega, Working Document on Institutional and Legal Implications of the Use of "Soft Law" Instruments, 14.2.2007, PE 384.581v02-00 (DT\653346EN.doc).

- fixing guidelines for the Union combined with specific timetables for achieving the goals which they set in the short, medium and long terms;
- establishing, where appropriate, quantitative and qualitative indicators and benchmarks against the best in the world and tailored to the needs of different Member States and sectors as a means of comparing best practice;
- translating these European guidelines into national and regional policies by setting specific targets and adopting measures, taking into account national and regional differences;
- periodic monitoring, evaluation and peer review organised as mutual learning processes.[178]

The OMC has turned into the policy-making instrument of choice for overall policy orientation. However, there is no such thing as a single OMC: it is time-variant and dependent on the specific policy.[179] Because it is mainly used to share experiences and promote best practice, it is ideal for policy areas that exclude harmonisation.[180] The use of the OMC has significantly changed the attitude towards coordination in education so that "in the early 2000s the question was [...] no longer whether it was a good idea to coordinate Member States' education policy, but how this could be made possible."[181] However, it is likely that the Bologna Process as well as the EES's involvement in LLL had an impact on the Member States, making them more willing to agree to cooperation in education at the EU level.[182]

The OMC in education and training is very similar to the template set out in the Lisbon Strategy. Common objectives and benchmarks (and a time schedule) are defined by the Member States. Best practices are identified with the help of clusters (expert groups) and peer learning activities. The implementation is constantly reviewed: with the help of the respective data, monitoring is carried

---

178 Lisbon European Council 23 and 24 March 2000, Presidency Conclusions, para 37.

179 Cf. Lange, B. and N. Alexiadou, New Forms of European Union Governance in the Education Sector? A Preliminary Analysis of the Open Method of Coordination, 6 EERJ, 2007, pp. 321–335, p. 322; Halász, G., European Coordination of National Education Policies from the Perspective of the New Member Countries, in: R. Standaert (ed.), Becoming the Best: Educational Ambitions for Europe, CIDREE: Enschede, 2003, pp. 89–118, p. 90.

180 Bernard, N., A "New Governance" Approach to Economic, Social and Cultural Rights in the EU, in: T. Hervey and J. Kenner (eds.), Economic and Social Rights under the EU Charter of Fundamental Rights, Hart Publishing: Oxford, 2003, pp. 247–268, pp. 263–264.

181 Gornitzka, 2006, p. 13.

182 Ibid. p. 15.

out. Clusters involve public and private actors in the form of representatives of the Member States, Commission experts and social partners. The Council and the Commission serve as the main actors in the OMC in education and training. The Council has "the first word, deciding on the objectives, indicators and benchmarks and the last word, adopting the reports and Council conclusions." The Commission, on the other hand, is – at least most of the times – "the initiator, driver, and main agenda setter" (also cf. below for the European semester). With regard to the participation of regional governments, federally organised Member States tend to involve their regions much more than unitary states. The inclusion of the social partners and the civil society is also largely down to the individual Member State.[183]

The Lisbon Strategy was devised as an overall strategy for a ten-year period (2000–2010) to promote growth and jobs. Envisaging a transformation to a knowledge-based society, it formulated strategic goals "for building knowledge infrastructures, enhancing innovation and economic reform, and modernising social welfare and education systems."[184] It is the forerunner of today's EU 2020 Strategy. The Lisbon Strategy was "translated into specific sectoral strategies, including one for the education sector",[185] the Education and Training 2010 Work Programme (ET 2010). However, the Lisbon Strategy was not successful. This was already visible in the 2004 mid-term review.[186] In 2005, the Lisbon Strategy was revised, however, by the time it was coming to an end, it was clear that it had failed.[187] In fact, only one of the benchmarks set out in ET 2010, the increase of the number of graduates in mathematics, science and technology [MST] by 15%, was achieved.[188] The other benchmarks were revised and integrated into

183 Warleigh-Lack, A. and R. Drachenberg, Policy Making in the European Union, in: M. Cini and N. Perez-Solorzano Borragan (eds.), European Union Politics, 4th ed., 2013, OUP: Oxford, pp. 199–212, p. 209.

184 Lisbon European Council 23 and 24 March 2000, Presidency Conclusions, para 2.

185 Halász, G., European Union: The Strive for Smart, Sustainable and Inclusive Growth, in: Y. Wang (ed.), Education Policy Trends in G20 Members, Springer: Heidelberg, 2013, pp. 267–286, p. 268.

186 Report from the High Level Group chaired by Wim Kok, Facing the Challenge: The Lisbon Strategy for Growth and Employment, Office for Official Publications of the European Communities: Luxembourg, 2004.

187 Sweden admits Lisbon Agenda "failure", EurActiv, 3 June 2009, http://www.euractiv.com/priorities/sweden-admits-lisbon-agenda-fail-news-221962.

188 Cf. Tauch, 2011, p. 68.

the Strategic Framework for European Cooperation in Education and Training (ET 2020), the follow-up to ET 2010, which was adopted in 2009.[189]

ET 2020 was adopted before the EU 2020 Strategy, with two of its benchmarks becoming one of the headline targets of the EU 2020 Strategy. This goes to show that the education sector is not just implementing the overall strategy, but in fact aspires to lead the way.[190] EU 2020, the EU's ten-year growth strategy for "smart, sustainable and inclusive growth", was adopted by the European Council in 2010. It includes five inter-related headline targets in the areas of employment, research and development (R&D), climate change and energy, education, and the fight against poverty and social exclusion to be reached by 2020. Each Member State is encouraged to adopt specific measures implementing those headline targets at national level. Concerning education, the headline target has twin goals, namely to "improv[e] education levels, in particular by aiming to reduce school drop-out rates to less than 10% and by increasing the share of 30–34 years old having completed tertiary or equivalent education to at least 40%". The unique position of education policy is emphasised by the European Council, which stresses that the Member States retain the sole competence "to define and implement quantitative targets in the field of education."[191]

Education is key to reach other headline targets such as that by 2020 75% of the 20–64 year-olds be employed, that 3% of the EU's GDP are invested in R&D (this presupposes that there are enough researchers available) or reducing the number of people at risk of poverty and social exclusion by at least 20 million. Therefore, Member States need to invest in knowledge, skills and competences. This includes all sectors of education and training: from early childhood education and care to higher education or vocational education and training, including LLL.[192] In order to organise policy coordination, the EU has introduced the so-called European Semester. Towards the end of the year, the Commission adopts its Annual Growth Survey, outlining the priorities for the year to come. In March, the European Council debates the Annual Growth Survey and decides

---

189 Council Conclusions of 12 May 2009 on a Strategic Framework for European Co-operation in Education and Training (ET 2020), OJ C 119, 28.5.2009, pp. 2–10.

190 Halász, 2013, p. 269.

191 European Council Conclusions, Brussels, 17 June 2010.

192 European Commission, DG EAC, Education and Training within Europe, DGVT Meeting in Ireland, 21–22 May 2013, Agenda Item II, Document 1, https://www.education.ie/en/Press-Events/Conferences/Ireland-s-Presidency-of-the-EU/Conference-21-22-May-2013/Education-and-Training-within-Europe-2020-Strategy.pdf.

on the directions to be taken. In April, Member States submit their National Reform Programmes. Then the Commission adopts Country-specific Recommendations (CSRs). After the European Council has approved the CSRs, the Council adopts them formally at the end of June/early July.[193]

The four strategic objectives of ET 2020 include:

(1) Making lifelong learning and mobility a reality;
(2) Improving the quality and efficiency of education and training;
(3) Promoting equity, social cohesion and active citizenship;
(4) Enhancing creativity and innovation, including entrepreneurship, at all levels of education and training.[194]

In 2012, the Strategic Framework ET 2020 was revised, bringing it in line with the EU 2020 Strategy (and the European semester specifically). Furthermore, the Council and Commission set out priorities for education and training in 2012–2014 (ET 2020 second cycle).[195] The four ET 2020 strategic objectives are supported by benchmarks which constitute "reference levels of European average performance".[196] Initially five benchmarks (two of them being taken up as an EU 2020 headline target), the benchmarks have since been increased to seven, with one proposed benchmark for foreign language skills. The current benchmarks read

- at least 95% of children between 4 years old and the age for starting compulsory primary education should participate in early childhood education;
- the share of low-achieving 15-years olds in reading, mathematics and science should be less than 15%;
- the share of early leavers from education and training[197] should be less than 10%;
- the share of 30–34 year olds with tertiary educational attainment should be at least 40%;

---

193 Cf. http://ec.europa.eu/europe2020/making-it-happen/index_en.htm.

194 Council Conclusions of 12 May 2009 on a Strategic Framework for European Cooperation in Education and Training (ET 2020), OJ C 119, 28.5.2009, pp. 2–10, pp. 3–4.

195 2012 Joint Report of the Council and the Commission on the implementation of the Strategic Framework for European Cooperation in Education and Training (ET 2020): Education and Training in a Smart, Sustainable and Inclusive Europe, OJ C 70, 8.3.2012, pp. 9–18.

196 Council Conclusions of 12 May 2009 on a Strategic Framework for European Cooperation in Education and Training (ET 2020), OJ C 119, 28.5.2009, pp. 2–10, p. 7.

197 The term "early leaver from education and training" refers to "a person aged 18 to 24 who has finished no more than a lower secondary education and is not involved in further education or training". Cf. http://epp.eurostat.ec.europa.eu/statistics_explained/index.php/Glossary:Early_leaver_from_education_and_training.

- an average of at least 15% of adults should participate in lifelong learning;
- at least 20% of higher education graduates and 6% of 18–34 year-olds with an initial VET qualification should have had a period of study or training abroad;
- the share of employed graduates (20–34 year-olds) having left education and training no more than three years before the reference year should be at least 82%.[198]

Since 2007, Europe has been suffering from an economic crisis. In the meantime, it has also had impacts on the education landscape. Between 2008 and 2011, sixteen Member States have decreased their expenditure for education, with six of them further cutting the budget for education in 2012. Furthermore, from 2008 to 2011 the employment rate of recent graduates with at least upper secondary education has decreased from 82% to 75.7%. Moreover, there is evidence of a skills mismatch: 21% of the tertiary education graduates are employed in jobs that require lower qualifications.[199] Between 2009 and 2012, adult participation in LLL has decreased from 9.2% to 9%.[200] It is far below the ET 2020 benchmark, which stands at 15%. With regard to the share of "low-achievers" in basic skills, the numbers available are from PISA 2009.[201] Benchmark data on international student mobility (extra-EU) and initial vocational education and training (IVET) across the EU are fragmented. So far, very little is known about the respective mobility flows. This is why the Commission (Eurostat) and the Member States have agreed on a regulation foreseeing "the obligatory transmission of tertiary education mobility data". Moreover, Eurostat is currently undertaking work on IVET benchmark data (sample survey), with results expected at the end of 2015.[202] Progress has been made, however, in achieving the ET 2020 benchmark of 95% in early childhood education and care, with participation increasing from 91.7% in 2009 to 93.2% in 2011.[203] The persisting economic crisis does not make the attainment of the ET 2020 targets any easier and as it stands, some Member States are a very long way from achieving the ET 2020 benchmarks.

The EU 2020 education and training headline target is broadly achievable. From 2005 to 2012, the school dropout rate has been gradually reduced from 15.7% to 12.7%. In 2009, it still stood at 14.2%. In the meantime, half of the

---

198 European Commission, Education and Training Monitor 2012, Publications Office of the European Union: Luxembourg, 2012, p. 8.

199 Cf. European Commission, Education and Training Monitor 2013, Publications Office of the European Union: Luxembourg, 2013, p. 6.

200 Ibid. p. 12.

201 Ibid. p. 8.

202 Ibid. pp. 48–49 and p. 55.

203 Ibid. p. 12.

Member States have already reached their targets or are about to reach them. There is evidence of structural improvements, however, part of the reduction may be due to the tight labour market.[204] The share of 30–34 years old having completed tertiary or equivalent education has increased from 27.9% in 2005 to 35.7% in 2012. In 2009, the tertiary education attainment rate stood at 32.1%. In 2012, the share of the population aged 30–34 having completed tertiary or equivalent education reached 35.7%. Current attainment rates vary, with some Member States being far from the EU headline target. Moreover, national targets vary from 26–27% in Italy to 60% in Ireland. Meeting national targets would lead to a tertiary education attainment rate of 38%. However, trends suggest that the increase is structural and that the 40% headline target is likely to be met.[205]

				Current	Target
Headline target	1	Early leavers from education and training	The share of the population aged 18-24 fulfilling the following two conditions: (1) the highest level of education or training attained equals International Standard Classification of Education (ISCED) level 0, 1, 2 or 3c short; (2) respondents declared not having received any education or training in the four weeks preceding the survey. Data comes from the EU Labour Force Survey.	12.7% (2012)	Below 10% (2020)
	2	Tertiary education attainment	The share of the population aged 30-34 years who have successfully completed university or university-like (tertiary-level) education that equals International Standard Classification of Education (ISCED) level 5 or 6. Data comes from the EU Labour Force Survey.	35.7% (2012)	At least 40% (2020)
Other targets	1	Early childhood education and care	The share of the population aged 4 to the age when the compulsory education starts who are participating in early education. Data comes from the UOE data collection.	93.2% (2011)	95% (2020)
	2	Achievement in reading, maths and science	The share of 15-year-olds failing to reach Level 2 in reading, mathematics and science as measured by the OECD's Programme for International Student Assessment (PISA).	Reading: 19.6% (2009) Maths: 22.2% (2009) Science: 17.7% (2009)	15% (2020)
	3	Employment rate of recent graduates	The share of employed people aged 20-34 having successfully completed upper secondary or tertiary education 1 to 3 years before the reference year of the survey and who are no longer in education or training. Data comes from the EU Labour Force Survey.	75.7% (2012)	82% (2020)
	4	Adult participation in lifelong learning	The share of the population aged 25-64 who stated that they received formal or non-formal education or training in the four weeks preceding the survey. Data comes from the EU Labour Force Survey.	9.0% (2012)	15% (2020)

Source: European Commission, Education and Training Monitor 2013, p. 8.

204 Communication from the Commission to the European Parliament, the Council, the European Economic and Social Committee and the Committee of the Regions, Taking Stock of the Europe 2020 Strategy for Smart, Sustainable and Inclusive Growth, Brussels, 19.3.2014, COM(2014) 130 final/2, p. 13.

205 Ibid. and http://ec.europa.eu/europe2020/pdf/themes/28_tertiary_education.pdf.

			EU average		HIGHEST performer	LOWEST performer
			2009	2012	2012	2012
Europe 2020 headline targets						
Early leavers from education and training *Europe 2020 headline target: less than 10%*			14.2%	12.7%	4.2%	24.9%
Tertiary education attainment *Europe 2020 headline target: at least 40%*			32.1%	35.7%	51.1%	21.7%
ET 2020 benchmarks						
Early childhood education and care *ET 2020 target: 95%*			91.7%	93.2%[11]	100%[11]	70.6%[11]
Low achievers in basic skills *ET 2020 target: 15%*		Reading	19.6%	:	8.1%[09]	41.0%[09]
		Maths	22.2%	:	7.8%[09]	47.1%[09]
		Science	17.7%	:	6.0%[09]	41.4%[09]
Learning mobility	IVET	Leonardo da Vinci outbound	0.6%	0.7%[11]	7.1%[11]	0.1%[11]
	Higher education	Erasmus inbound	:	1.1%[11]	8.4%[11]	0.0%[11]
		Inbound degree mobile students	:	7.0%[11]	40.6%[11]	0.5%[11]
Employment rate of recent graduates *ET 2020 target: 82%*			78.3%	75.7%	91.9%	42.9%
Adult participation in lifelong learning *ET 2020 target: 15%*			9.2%	9.0%	31.6%	1.4%

Source: European Commission, Education and Training Monitor 2013, p. 12.

4. The Erasmus+ Programme

> Erasmus of Rotterdam was an early beneficiary of funding to study abroad. The then bishop of Cambray, Henry of Bergen (for whom Erasmus had started to work as secretary), gave him both leave and a stipend in 1495 to go and study at the University of Paris. Erasmus never looked back; and, in a career that spanned Paris, Leuven, Cambridge and Basel, he became arguably the outstanding scholar of his generation: the 'Prince of the Humanists'. It is tolerably safe to say that he put the funding for his university studies abroad to excellent use – and, indeed, the current exchange programmes between EU universities bear his name.[206]

On 21 December 2013, the Erasmus+ Regulation, which applies from 1 January 2014, entered into force.[207] The Erasmus+ programme puts an end to the fragmentation of cooperation programmes in education, training and youth. Moreover, it provides support for sports activities. The Erasmus+ programme, which runs from 2014–2020, incorporates the LLL Programme (pre-school, primary and secondary school education (Comenius), higher education (Erasmus), vocational training (Leonardo da Vinci), adult learning (Grundtvig) and teaching and research in European integration (Jean Monnet)), the Youth in Action programme, the five international cooperation programmes (Erasmus Mundus, Tempus, Alfa, Edulink and the programme for cooperation with industrialised countries) and sport. As recital 10 of the preamble to the Erasmus+ Regulation sets out, the single programme which includes "formal, non-formal and informal learning […] should create synergies and foster cross-sectoral cooperation across the various […] sectors." During its implementation "where appropriate, the role of local and regional authorities should be duly taken into account."

The general objectives of the Erasmus+ programme include contributing towards the achievement of "the objectives of the Europe 2020 strategy, including the headline education target" and "the objectives of the strategic framework for European cooperation in education and training ('ET 2020'), including the corresponding benchmarks" (Article 4(a) and (b) of the Erasmus+ Regulation).

---

206 Opinion of Advocate General Sharpston, delivered on 16 February 2012, Case C-542/09 *European Commission v Kingdom of the Netherlands*, nyr, para 1.

207 Cf. Article 38 of Regulation (EU) No 1288/2013 of the European Parliament and of the Council of 11 December 2013 establishing 'Erasmus+': the Union programme for education, training, youth and sport and repealing Decisions No 1719/2006/EC, No 1720/2006/EC and No 1298/2008/EC Text with EEA relevance, OJ L 347, 20.12.2013, pp. 50–73.

The focus lies on learning mobility, cooperation between education and training and the world of work, LLL, multilingualism and intercultural awareness, teaching and research in European integration and transnational and international cooperation (cf. Article 5(1)(a)-(f) of the Erasmus+ Regulation). The international – extra-EU – dimension plays a major role. Currently there are five non-EU programme countries: the EEA EFTA States (Iceland, Liechtenstein and Norway) and the candidate countries Turkey and the former Yugoslav Republic of Macedonia.[208] Moreover, numerous partner countries may take part in certain actions (cf. Article 24(3) of the Erasmus+ Regulation).[209]

The Erasmus+ programme is based on three key actions: "learning mobility of individuals", "cooperation for innovation and the exchange of good practices" and "support for policy reform" (cf. Articles 6(1), 12 of the Erasmus+ Regulation). These involve actions in the fields of education, training and youth. Besides the three key actions, the Erasmus+ programme includes the Jean Monnet activities and actions in the field of sport (cf. Articles 10, 16 and 17 of the Erasmus+ Regulation).

Key action 1, "learning mobility of individuals", makes up the lion's share of the new programme. There are mobility activities for students in higher education (short,[210] first, second and third cycle) as well as for students (or apprentices) in vocational education and training. HEI students may study at partner HEIs or undertake traineeships. Apprentices and students in vocational education and training can gain experience abroad. Moreover, the Erasmus+ programme has introduced a student loan guarantee for students studying abroad for a full degree at Master's level, i.e. not just for part of the second cycle (cf. Articles 7(1)(a) and 20 of the Erasmus+ Regulation). 3.5% of the financial envelope is set aside for the student loan guarantee facility (cf. Article 18(2)(c) of the Erasmus+ Regulation). The student loan guarantee is available to students resident in any of the 28 Member States or the extra-EU programme countries who pursue their graduate degree at a HEI in a programme country "which is neither their country of residence nor the country in which they obtained their qualification granting access to the Master's programme" (cf. Article 20(1) of the Erasmus+ Regulation).

---

208 Cf. pp. 104 et seq.

209 Cf. pp. 108 et seq.

210 "[T]he missing link between secondary and higher education", the short cycle can be described as a intermediate qualification. Some or all credits earned during a short cycle degree may be used towards a first cycle degree. Cf. Kirsch, M. and Y. Beernaert, Short Cycle Higher Education in Europe: Level 5: The Missing Link, EURASHE: Brussels, 2011, p. 10.

The student loan guarantee is managed by the European Investment Fund (EIF), which concludes "agreements with financial inter-mediaries, such as banks, national and/or regional student lending institutions or other financial institutions" (cf. Article 20(3) of the Erasmus+ Regulation). Staff mobility is possible in "form of teaching or assistanceships or participation in professional development activities abroad" (cf. Article 7(1)(b) of the Erasmus+ Regulation). Young people may take part in "non-formal and informal learning activities" (e.g. youth exchanges or volunteering). Moreover, training and networking activities for youth workers are supported (cf. Article 13(1)(a) and (b) of the Erasmus+ Regulation).[211]

Key action 2, "cooperation for innovation and the exchange of good practices", involves strategic partnerships between institutions and/or organisations,[212] partnerships between education and training institutions and the world of work (knowledge and sector skills alliances)[213] as well as IT support platforms, which inter alia allow for virtual mobility, peer learning and exchange of good practices (cf. Articles 8(1) and 14(1) of the Erasmus+ Regulation).

Key action 3, "support for policy reform", is key to achieve the education and training headline target of the Europe 2020 Strategy and to reach the benchmarks set by ET 2020. This is why the Erasmus+ programme supports "country-specific and thematic analysis, including through cooperation with academic networks" and "peer learning and peer reviews through the [OMC]".[214] Moreover, it supports the implementation of the transparency and recognition tools of the Union in the programme countries. These include, among others, the EQF, the ECTS and the counterpart for vocational education and training, ECVET, the Europass and the Youthpass. The Europass consists of up to five documents: the Curriculum Vitae (CV) and the Language Passport are freely accessible and may be completed online, while the Europass Mobility records (e.g. student exchange, work experience abroad), the Certificate Supplement (vocational education and training) and the Diploma Supplement (higher education) may be issued by education and training authorities.[215] The Youthpass is a certificate for youth actions supported under the Erasmus+ programme. It describes non-formal and informal learning and is issued to the participating young people and

211 For the international dimension of learning mobility of individuals cf. pp. 109 et seq.

212 Cf. pp. 79–80, p. 110 and pp. 240 et seq.

213 Cf. pp. 87–88 and p. 110.

214 European Commission, Erasmus+ Programme Guide: Valid as of 1 January 2014, Version 3, 9.4.2014, p. 15.

215 https://europass.cedefop.europa.eu.

youth workers.[216] Furthermore, support for policy reform includes policy dialogue with European stakeholders in the fields of education, training and youth as well as various networks such as NARIC (cf. Articles 9(1) and 15(1) of the Erasmus+ Regulation).[217]

The Jean Monnet activities aim to disseminate knowledge about European integration. Among other things, the Erasmus+ programme supports the "Jean Monnet Chairs", HEIs that pursue "an aim of European interest" such as the European University Institute (EUI) in Florence or the College of Europe in Bruges and Natolin and promotes exchanges and policy debate between academics and Union policy-makers (Article 10 of the Erasmus+ Regulation).[218]

The actions in the field of sport include transnational activities in the form of collaborative partnerships[219], "not-for-profit European sport events", "strengthening the evidence base for policy-making" and "dialogue with relevant European stakeholders" (Article 17 of the Erasmus+ Regulation).

With the 2014–2020 programming period, the budget for education and training has been beefed up. The financial envelope for the Erasmus+ programme amounts to nearly EUR 15 billion (cf. Article 18(1) of the Erasmus+ Regulation). The bulk of it, 77.5%, is allocated to education and training, whereby 43% thereof (33.3% of the total budget) are set aside for higher education, 22% (17% of the total budget) for vocational education and training, 15% (11.6% of the total budget) for school education and 5% (3.9% of the total budget) for adult learning. The rest is allocated to youth (10%), the Student Loan Guarantee Facility (3.5%), Jean Monnet (1.9%), sport (1.8%), operating grants to national agencies (3.4%) and administrative expenditure (1.9%). At least 63% of the allocations for education, training and youth are earmarked for the learning mobility of individuals, whereas at least 28% are designated for cooperation for innovation and the exchange of good practices and 4.2% for support for policy reform. The margin of flexibility may not exceed 5% of each of the allocations (cf. Article 18(2) and (3) of the Erasmus+ Regulation).

216 https://www.youthpass.eu.

217 For the international dimension of policy reform cf. pp. 108 et seq.

218 For the international dimension of Jean Monnet activities cf. pp. 108 et seq.

219 Cf. p. 110 and pp. 242 et seq.

5. Education and Training in the Lisbon Treaty

The 2007 Lisbon Treaty, also known as the Reform Treaty, entered into force in 2009. It amended the TEU and the TEC, renaming the latter Treaty on the Functioning of the European Union (TFEU). This was a necessary step, for the EU replaced and succeeded the EC (Article 1 para 3 TEU), ending confusion through "one single legal entity and structure".[220] The primary source of EU law, the TEU and the TFEU now share "the same legal value" (Article 1 para 3 TEU and Article 1(2) TFEU). Article 6(1) first subpara TEU stipulates that the Charter of Fundamental Human Rights of the European Union (CFREU) "shall have the same legal value as the Treaties." On equal standing with the Treaties, the CFREU is now part of primary law. This is of particular importance for all things education-related as the CFREU includes a fundamental right to education (cf. Article 14 CFREU).

The Lisbon Treaty has brought about substantial change making EU law less prone to competence creep. For the first time ever, a definition of the powers attributed to the EU is incorporated into the founding Treaties. The Lisbon Treaty distinguishes between three types of competence: exclusive, shared and supporting (cf. Article 2 TFEU). Article 5 TEU (ex Article 5 [ex Article 3b] TEC) draws on its predecessor, explicitly stating that competences are conferred by the Member States and that "[c]ompetences not conferred upon the Union in the Treaties remain with the Member States" (Article 5(2) TEU). Article 5(3) TEU adds a new dimension to subsidiarity control by involving national parliaments to ensure compliance, thus "continu[ing] the process of creating an ever closer union among the peoples of Europe, in which decisions are taken as closely as possible to the citizen" (recital 13 of the preamble of the TEU). Article 2 TFEU is concerned with the adoption and transposition of legislative and implementing measures. Depending on the competence type, the roles assigned to the Union and the Member States vary. Para 5 states that

> [i]n certain areas and under the conditions laid down in the Treaties, the Union shall have competence to carry out actions to support, coordinate or supplement the actions of the Member States, without thereby superseding their competence in these areas.
>
> Legally binding acts of the Union adopted on the basis of the provisions of the Treaties relating to these areas shall not entail harmonisation of Member States' laws or regulations.

---

220 European Parliament Resolution of 20 February 2008 on the Treaty of Lisbon (2007/2286(INI)), OJ C 184 E, 6.8.2009, pp. 25–30, p. 28.

Article 6 TFEU, which is by no means finite,[221] sets out the areas in which the EU has supporting competence. Education, vocational training, youth and sport are one of them (cf. Article 6(e) TFEU). With the activities of the Union confined to supporting, coordinating and complementing action, it is clear that "it has no legislative power in these fields and may not interfere in the exercise of these competences reserved for Member States."[222] As can be inferred from Article 2(5) TFEU, the EU may "pass legally binding acts on the basis of the provisions specific to these areas",[223] provided that they do not lead to harmonisation at Member State level.

Interestingly, the TFEU does not expressly mention the OMC. It does, however, introduce OMC characteristics in Treaty articles referring to "coordination, the establishment of guidelines and indicators, the organization of exchange of best practice, and the preparation of the necessary elements for periodic monitoring and evaluation" (cf. Articles 149, 153, 156, 168, 173 and 181 TFEU). Unfortunately, the signatories of the Lisbon Treaty failed to include such a reference in the TFEU provisions for education and training. The reasons for this are unclear as the OMC in this area was launched in 2002[224] and therefore already in place when the Treaty of Lisbon was signed by the plenipotentiaries of the Member States. There is no reason to suggest that this was a deliberate omission. Still, enshrining the OMC in education and training in primary law through an explicit provision would have been a possibility to dispel any doubts whatsoever.[225]

Right at the beginning, the Lisbon Treaty draws attention to the value attached to education. Recital 2 of the amended preamble of the TEU makes sure to point out the impact of Europe's humanist roots, reading that the Union

> DRAW[S] INSPIRATION from the cultural, religious and humanist inheritance of Europe, from which have developed the universal values of the inviolable and inalienable rights of the human person, freedom, democracy, equality and the rule of law[.]

The fourth subpara of Article 3(3) TEU emphasizes that the Union "shall respect its rich cultural and linguistic diversity, and shall ensure that Europe's cultural

---

221 Cf. Craig and De Búrca, 2011, p. 86.

222 Cf. Division of competences within the European Union, http://europa.eu/legislation_summaries/institutional_affairs/treaties/lisbon_treaty/ai0020_en.htm.

223 Cf. Craig and De Búrca, 2011, p. 87.

224 Cf. Detailed work programme on the follow-up of the objectives of education and training systems in Europe, OJ C 142, 14.6.2002, pp. 1–22.

225 Cf. Garben, S., EU Higher Education Law: The Bologna Process and Harmonization by Stealth, Kluwer: Alphen aan den Rijn, 2011, p. 89.

heritage is safeguarded and enhanced", whereas recital 9 of the preamble of the TFEU specifically mentions the Union's determination "to promote the development of the highest possible level of knowledge for their peoples through a wide access to education and through its continuous updating".

Introduced by the Lisbon Treaty, Article 9 TFEU further accentuates the importance of education and training. The so-called horizontal social clause ensures the general application (i.e. mainstreaming) of education and training throughout the Union's policy-making. Echoing more than a few of the goals set by Article 3(3) TEU, the latter provision and the other social clauses (i.e. Articles 8, 10, 11 and 12 TFEU) give the impression of constituting the missing link between the TEU and the TFEU: "[t]hey thus serve to establish consistency between the activity of the EU and its fundamental missions."[226] Viewed "as an expression of the desire to mainstream social policies in all areas of policy",[227] Article 9 TFEU affirms the ongoing quest for greater social cohesion. It is now up to the European institutional actors as well as the Member States to evaluate their policies and actions in accordance with this provision. Consequently, legal acts not abiding to said Article will come under scrutiny and the ECJ would technically be able to declare them null and void. Together with the CFREU the horizontal social clause may therefore well contribute to a "reorientation of EU legislation and jurisprudence towards social aims."[228] Although Article 9 TFEU does not differentiate between actions, the general understanding tends to be that the provision's main aim is to act as a filter regarding adverse effects on the Union's social acquis through legislative measures.[229]

In order to achieve the Europe 2020 Strategy headline targets, integrated policy-making is a prerequisite. Taking education and training into account when exercising other Union competences – and therefore adhering to the horizontal social clause – is key. Whereas Article 9 TFEU applies to hard and

226 Vielle, P., How the Horizontal Social Clause Can be Made to Work: The Lessons of Gender Mainstreaming, in: N. Bruun, K. Lörcher and I. Schömann (eds.), The Lisbon Treaty and Social Europe, Hart Publishing: Oxford, 2012, pp. 105–121, p. 114 et seq.

227 Bruun, N., Lörcher, K. and I. Schömann, Introduction, in: N. Bruun, K. Lörcher and I. Schömann (eds.), The Lisbon Treaty and Social Europe, Hart Publishing: Oxford, 2012, p. 4.

228 Vielle, 2012, p. 105.

229 Cf. Schoukens, P., From Soft Monitoring to Enforceable Action: A Quest for New Legal Approaches in the EU Fight Against Social Exclusion, Policy Paper by Euroforum KU Leuven, April 2013, p. 22, https://www.kuleuven.be/euroforum/viewpic.php?LAN=E&TABLE=DOCS&ID=858.

soft law, it is the OMC that springs to mind. Indeed, it is the "familiarity" with soft law "that provides a key to the particular shapes and meanings underlying its formulation." Against the background of the OMC, Article 9 TFEU "will be understood as an unequivocal reference to a determination to redress the balance in favour of socially directed purposes."[230]

Title XII of Part Three of the TFEU provides the foundations for education, vocational training, youth and sport. From a structural perspective this is an upgrade. Compared to the previous Treaty versions (i.e. ex Title XI, chapter 3), education and training now has its very own title. Like the Treaty of Amsterdam, the Lisbon Treaty renumbered the two relevant articles. Article 165 TFEU (ex Article 149 TEC) covers the education domain, whereas Article 166 TFEU (ex Article 150 TEC) is concerned with vocational training. They include a finite list of the Union's power to act in the respective areas.[231] However, Title XII is not exhaustive. There are further primary law provisions dealing with education and training aspects such as Articles 41(a), 53, 145, 156, 167(2), 174, 175, 179, 180(d) or 207(4)(b) TFEU. The main purpose or the centre of gravity of the measure serves as a demarcation criterion between the various provisions.[232] Moreover, ECJ jurisprudence hinges on internal market competences such as the free movement rights, the principle of non-discrimination on grounds of nationality and Union citizenship. Significant changes to earlier Treaty versions include the introduction of an EU sport policy (cf. the second subpara of Article 165(1) TFEU and the seventh indent

230 Vielle, 2012, p. 115.

231 Cf. Frenz, W., Bildung, Jugend, Sport, in: W. Frenz, Handbuch Europarecht, Band 6: Institutionen und Politiken, Springer: Berlin, 2011, pp. 1139–1163, recital 4012; Niedobitek, M., Artikel 165 AEUV, in: R. Streinz (ed.), EUV/AEUV: Vertrag über die Europäische Union und Vertrag über die Arbeitsweise der Europäischen Union, 2nd ed., CH Beck: München, 2012, recital 50; Niedobitek, M., Artikel 166 AEUV, in: R. Streinz (ed.), EUV/AEUV: Vertrag über die Europäische Union und Vertrag über die Arbeitsweise der Europäischen Union, 2nd ed., CH Beck: München, 2012, recital 9; Ruffert, M., Artikel 165 AEUV, in: C. Calliess and M. Ruffert, EUV/AEUV, 4th ed., CH Beck: München, 2011, recital 13; Ruffert, M., Artikel 166 AEUV, in: C. Calliess and M. Ruffert, EUV/AEUV, 4th ed., CH Beck: München, 2011, recital 4. Contrary cf. EP-Resolution on Education and Training in the Run-up to 1993, OJ C 150, 15.6.1992, pp. 366–370, p. 368: "[the] fields of action referred to in [ex] Articles 126 and 127 [TEC] are not exhaustive but are rather in the nature of examples".

232 Cf. Kotzur, M., Die Bildungskompetenzen der Europäischen Union nach Art. 165, 166 AEUV, in: K. Odendahl (ed.), Europäische (Bildungs-)Union?, BWV: Berlin/NWV: Wien, 2011, pp. 107–130, p. 118.

of Article 165(2) TFEU), an extension of the Union's youth policy (cf. the fifth indent of Article 165(2) TFEU) and the insertion of a new ultimate phrase into Article 166(4) TFEU allowing the Council to adopt recommendations (i.e. the introduction of a non-binding soft law instrument into Article 166 TFEU). Furthermore, a reference to the ordinary legislative procedure, i.e. co-decision and QMV, was introduced into Articles 165(4) and 166(4) TFEU. Article 294 TFEU on the ordinary legislative procedure draws on ex Article 251 TEC. However, together with the newly inserted Article 289 TFEU, it finally defines the legal instruments used in connection with Articles 165(4) and 166(4) TFEU.[233] It should also be noted that changes to the QMV rules are due to enter into force in November 2014. The "old" QMV rule will apply until 31 October 2014 and possibly until 31 March 2017, when it will be replaced by the double majority of Member States and citizens (cf. Article 16(4) TEU, Article 238(2) TFEU and Article 3 of Protocol (No 36) on transitional provisions).

The structure of Articles 165 and 166 TFEU has not changed since their introduction as Articles 126 and 127 TEC. Para 1 points out the Union's supporting and supplementing competence. Para 2 subsequently lists the Union's power to act regarding the substantive area. Para 3 is concerned with the cooperation with third countries and the competent international organisations. Para 4 defines the Union's means of action and inserts a prohibition on harmonisation.

5.1 Article 165 TFEU – Scope and Objectives

Article 165 TFEU provides the scope of the Union's policy in education, youth and sport. As already pointed out, the attributed competence is quite limited. The EU is confined to the "development of quality education" by encouraging Member State cooperation and *if necessary* (i.e. application of the principles of subsidiarity and proportionality) it may support and supplement action. The development of quality education, which has become the leitmotif of EU education policy, ties in with recital 9 of the preamble of the TFEU that refers to the promotion of the "development of the highest possible level of knowledge". The first subpara of Article 165(1) TFEU contains a non-affection clause. According to it, the Union must respect the competence of the Member States in terms of "the content of teaching and the organisation of education systems and their cultural and linguistic diversity." However, it "shall contribute to the development of quality education by encouraging cooperation between Member States

233 Cf. pp. 89 et seq.

and, if necessary, by supporting and supplementing their action". Through the non-affection clause the national sovereignty in cultural and educational matters ("Kultur- und Bildungshoheit") is particularly emphasised.[234] At the same time, it implies that the regional autonomy in the area shall not be undermined.[235] This can also be inferred from Article 4(2) TEU that stipulates that the Union is to respect the Member States' "national identities, inherent in their fundamental structures, political and constitutional, inclusive of regional and local self-government." An innovation of the Lisbon Treaty, primary law now includes an express definition of the system of multi-level governance that comprises four levels: the EU, Member States, regions and municipalities.[236] The non-affection clause of Article 165(1) TFEU further links to the Union's support of multilingualism, a cross-cutting policy area that is especially important for the maintenance of the Union's diversity.

Except for the fifth indent on youth policy and the seventh and ultimate indent that applies to the newly introduced sport policy, Article 165(2) TFEU defines the scope of EU education policy. First and foremost, it points out that the Union is to develop the European dimension in education. This includes in particular "the teaching and dissemination of the languages of the Member States" (first indent). The European education dimension, a constant fixture since the emergence of EU education policy,[237] seems to be the key objective and encompass the other education-related indents (note, however, that the structure and wording of Article 165(2) TFEU suggests otherwise).[238] This also goes for vocational training, especially as the European dimension is not mentioned in Article 166(2) TFEU.[239] The implementation of the objective contained within the first indent remains with the Member States.[240] The second indent of Article 165(2) TFEU establishes that Union action shall be aimed at "encouraging

234 Cf. Vedder, C., Artikel 165 AEUV, in: C. Vedder and W. Heintschel von Heinegg (eds.), Europäisches Unionsrecht, Nomos: Baden-Baden, 2012, pp. 699–703, recital 4.

235 Also cf. EP-Resolution on Education and Training in the Run-up to 1993, OJ C 150, 15.6.1992, pp. 366–370, pp. 367 et seq.

236 Cf. Blanke, HJ, Article 4, in: HJ Blanke and S. Mangiameli (eds.), The Treaty on European Union (TEU): A Commentary, Springer: Heidelberg, 2013, pp. 185–253, recital 62.

237 Cf. p. 39 (Janne).

238 Also cf. Blanke, 2011, recital 76: "leitbildartig"; Ruffert, Artikel 165 AEUV, 2011, recital 14.

239 Cf. Niedobitek, Artikel 165 AEUV, 2012, recitals 38 and 52.

240 Cf. Bode, 2005, p. 94.

mobility of students and teachers, by encouraging inter alia, the academic recognition of diplomas and periods of study". Indents one and two are of framework nature. They include an exemplary list of measures on how to satisfactorily attain the objectives contained. While they leave sufficient leeway for implementation, they do not diminish the finite character of Article 165(2) TFEU.[241]

The objectives set forth in indents one and two are without doubt the ones EU education policy mainly focusses on. While the European dimension constitutes a wide spectrum (e.g. furthering awareness of the European idea through various forms of educational activities),[242] the TFEU singles out the promotion of SLA. Language acquisition goes hand in hand with the development of crosscultural competence.[243] Therefore, fostering multilingualism increases career opportunities and facilitates mobility, enabling students and teachers to take advantage of the existing action programmes. Suffice it to say that the educational activities of the Union particularly aim at a substantial boost of mobility.[244]

It must be observed, however, that the academic recognition of diplomas and periods of study mentioned in the second indent must not be confused with the mutual recognition of diplomas, certificates and other evidence of formal qualifications provided for by Article 53 TFEU. Whereas the latter is seeking to complete free movement law by easing the transition from one Member State to another for the self-employed, the academic recognition envisaged by the second indent of Article 165(2) TFEU is predominantly meant to increase student mobility. While this too is part and parcel of free movement law, it covers the period prior to seeking access to the labour market. This double function of diploma recognition, i.e. for academic and professional purposes, makes a two-pronged definition necessary.[245] Therefore, the TFEU contains two different legal bases for diploma recognition.

The academic recognition of diplomas and periods of study (i.e. ECTS credits) obtained in a Member State other than the one in which the diploma holder or student would like to pursue or continue their undergraduate, graduate and/or

---

241 Also cf. Niedobitek, Artikel 165 AEUV, 2012, recital 51.

242 Cf. Blanke, 2011, recital 76.

243 Cf. Amann, CU, Bilingual Education: A Token for Crosscultural Pragmatics?, Diploma Thesis, University of Innsbruck, 2011.

244 Cf. Margedant, U., Bildungspolitik, in: J. Bergmann (ed.), Handlexikon der Europäischen Union, 4th ed., Nomos: Baden-Baden, 2012, pp. 148–152, p. 148.

245 Cf. Zilioli, C., The Recognition of Diplomas and Its Impact on Educational Policies, in: B. de Witte (ed.), European Community Law of Education, Nomos: Baden-Baden, 1989, pp. 51–70, p. 52.

postgraduate studies, is a prerequisite for future education. Professionally, recognition becomes relevant later on. However, Article 53 TFEU may have indirect effects on students, such as dissuading them from studying in Member States other than their own or the one in which they plan to ultimately settle because insufficient recognition or lack thereof may result in penalties regarding career or pay terms.[246]

The legal bases regarding the matter (cf. the second indent of Article 165(2) TFEU, Article 53 TFEU) attribute different levels of competence to the EU, leading to double standards. Academically and professionally, the recognition clauses feature varying legal designs. Due to the term "diploma" including "both the degree conferred by institutions of higher education confirming the completion of a course of at least three years' duration […] and the license to practise",[247] different recognition provisions have been enshrined in EU primary law. According to Article 53(1) TFEU,

> the European Parliament and the Council shall, acting in accordance with the ordinary legislative procedure, issue directives for the mutual recognition of diplomas, certificates and other evidence of formal qualifications, and for the coordination of the provisions laid down by law, regulation or administrative action in Member States concerning the taking-up and pursuit of activities as self-employed persons.

It seems odd that the EU should have full competence to issue directives for the mutual recognition of professional qualifications of Member State nationals belonging to the liberal professions wishing to pursue a regulated profession in a Member State other than the Member States in which they obtained them,[248] whereas academic recognition basically lies in the hands of the Member States. The limited scope of the Union is further diminished by the non-harmonisation clause of Article 165(4) TFEU. Any changes to national law are therefore prohibited, though the Member States must not infringe rights derived from the freedom of movement or the principle of non-discrimination on grounds of nationality. Due to professional recognition being "more closely connected to the labour market, and hence an EU affair",[249] the Union's involvement in recognition is of diverging nature. Professions of most sensitive nature are regulated

246 Also cf. Bode, 2005, pp. 129 et seq.
247 Cf. Zilioli, 1989, p. 52.
248 Cf. Article 2 of Directive 2005/36/EC of the European Parliament and of the Council of 7 September 2005 on the recognition of professional qualifications, OJ L 255, 30.9.2005, pp. 22–142.
249 Garben, 2011, p. 187.

through directives issued under Article 53 TFEU (i.e. in the fields of architecture, law, medicine or pharmacy), whereas others which are not do not even fall within the latter's scope, being subject to the sovereignty of the Member States. In addition to this, the freedom of establishment and the freedom to provide services are not conditional on the issuance of directives. Individuals may invoke rights derived from Articles 49 and 57 TFEU even if a harmonising directive has not (yet) been issued because these provisions are directly effective.[250] Anyone who is able to avail of professional recognition under Article 53 TFEU therefore clearly has an advantage. According to academics, the Union would be able to implement regulatory measures in order to facilitate academic recognition regarding the commencement or continuation of higher education by taking recourse to the TFEU's principle of non-discrimination on grounds of nationality (cf. Article 18 TFEU).[251] So far, however, academic recognition has been confined to the boundaries of Article 165 TFEU.

The second indent of Article 165(2) TFEU expressly includes academic recognition. It does not, however, refer to Article 53 TFEU in any way or lay claim that academic recognition may only be dealt with by Title XII. There is also no factual evidence that Article 53 TFEU does not include academic recognition. A diploma may not only give the holder access to vocational training (e.g. to the Bar Professional Training Course for those wishing to secure pupillage in England or Wales in order to become barristers), it can also constitute a necessary prerequisite to start working in a regulated profession (e.g. teaching). Starting off one's career can be subject to prior academic recognition. Therefore, overlap between the two provisions of the TFEU is possible.[252] The boundaries between Articles 53 and 165 TFEU are certainly blurred, leaving a fine line to tread between academic and professional recognition. While some are of the opinion that Article 53 TFEU "extends the recognition of qualifications beyond the professional and into the 'purely' academic",[253] statements like this must certainly conjure up fear in those believing that a collision between the pro-harmonisation Article 53 TFEU and Articles 165 and 166 TFEU that have put a ban on it, is best to be avoided. After all, some even dread that support measures might go beyond the second indent of Article 165(2) TFEU as regards

250 Cf. Miles, G. et al., Foundations for the LPC 2013–2014, OUP: Oxford, 2013, p. 253.
251 Cf. Niedobitek, Artikel 165 AEUV, 2012, recital 53.
252 Cf. Ruffert, Artikel 165 AEUV, 2011, recital 15.
253 Davies in Garben, 2011, pp. 187 et seq.

university autonomy.[254] However, harmonising the field of education through the back door is certainly not possible within the Union's ambit (as far as the Lisbon Treaty is concerned, the Member States are still very much the masters of education policy) and further not within its aims. A standardisation of teaching methods and programmes on offer is not what the EU wants to establish. Its "purpose of [...] action is rather to give European students the possibility of looking for the best education anywhere in the [Union] and of taking advantage of the peculiarities of any given educational system."[255] The ECJ has yet to explore the issue further. A clear statement on the demarcation between Articles 53 and 165 TFEU would be most useful.

Information regarding academic recognition is available via the National Academic Recognition Information Centre (NARIC) network of the EU. The national agencies, i.e. the constituent national units, share advice and provide expert opinion regarding questions of academic recognition at national level. Advisory services are not only available to individuals but also to institutions involved in education or future employers.[256] The NARIC network is supported by the European Commission "through the exchange of information and experience between countries, the identification of good practices, the comparative analysis of systems and policies in this field, and the discussion and analysis of matters of common educational policy interest."[257] It cooperates closely with the European Network of Information Centres (ENIC), a joint initiative of the CoE and UNESCO, established to implement the Lisbon Recognition Convention. The Lisbon Recognition Convention, officially the Convention on the Recognition of Qualifications concerning Higher Education in the European Region, is an international convention of the CoE together with UNESCO. Although the NARIC and ENIC networks are separate legal entities, they act as one and as "[t]he ENIC [n]etwork has a somewhat wider composition [...] all NARICs are also ENICs".[258]

In 2008, the EP and the Council issued a recommendation regarding a European Qualifications Framework (EQF). It is essentially "a common reference framework", which acts as "a translation device between different qualifications

---

254 Cf. Blanke, 2011, recital 79; Hablitzel, 1994, p. 24; Hablitzel, 2002, p. 414; Mächtle, CI, Bildungsspezifische Implikationen des allgemeinen Diskriminierungsverbots und der Freizügigkeit, Peter Lang: Frankfurt am Main, 2010, p. 95.

255 Zilioli, 1989, p. 69.

256 Cf. http://ecctis.co.uk/naric.

257 European Commission, Erasmus+ Programme Guide, 2014, p. 21.

258 Bergan, S., The Recognition of Qualifications: Legal Basis and Practical Implementation, 2 Journal of the EHEA, 2012, pp. 73–92, p. 79.

systems and their levels, whether for general and higher education or for vocational education and training."[259] It is based on eight European reference levels, which refer to both academic and professional qualifications. They describe theoretical and/or factual knowledge, cognitive and practical skills and competence "in terms of responsibility and autonomy".[260] Levels 5 (short cycle), 6 (first cycle), 7 (second cycle) and 8 (third cycle) refer to the qualifications available at a higher education level. In accordance with the recommendation, Member States were encouraged to "relate their national qualifications systems to the European Qualifications Framework by 2010" and to adopt the necessary measures to ensure that from 2012 onwards qualification certificates issued in a Member State include a reference to the EQF level.[261]

The third indent of Article 165(2) TFEU concerns the promotion of cooperation between educational establishments, thereby pooling expertise and adding to its level. The cooperation aims at all stages within the framework of general education (i.e. pre-primary, primary, secondary and tertiary level). Cooperation between public and private educational establishments is possible.[262] Sharing experience and knowledge is emphasised by the Erasmus+ Regulation. Various recitals and articles refer to cooperation at transnational level. Article 5(1)(b) of the Erasmus+ Regulation emphasizes the importance of enhanced cooperation at transnational level in order to achieve the programme's specific objective "to foster quality improvements, innovation excellence and internationalisation". Recital 17 of the preamble of the Erasmus+ Regulation indicates the need to strengthen the extent as well as the intensity of European cooperation between schools, referring to the Agenda for European Cooperation on Schools for the 21st century[263]. In OMC manner, Article 8(1)(a) of said Regulation stipulates that cooperation for innovation and the exchange of good practices shall support strategic partnerships between institutions and/or organisations involved in education and training "aimed at developing and implementing joint initiatives

259 Recital 12 of the preamble to the Recommendation of the European Parliament and of the Council of 23 April 2008 on the establishment of the European Qualifications Framework for lifelong learning, OJ C 111, 6.5.2008, pp. 1–7.
260 Ibid. Annex II.
261 Ibid. Points 2 and 3.
262 Cf. Blanke, 2011, recital 81.
263 Communication from the Commission to the European Parliament, the Council, the European Economic and Social Committee and the Committee of the Regions of 3 July 2008 – Improving Competences for the 21st Century: An Agenda for European Cooperation on Schools, COM(2008) 425 final.

and promoting peer learning and exchanges of experience." Such partnerships are always transnational and involve a group of institutions and/or organisations in different programme countries, which carry out joint European activities in the field. Institutions and/or organisations from partner countries may take part under certain conditions.[264] At school level these may include class exchanges or individual long-term mobility while consisting of more extensive programmes in higher education (cf. Article 2(18) TFEU).

The fourth indent of Article 165(2) TFEU focusses on "developing exchanges of information and experience on issues common to the education systems of the Member States", thus adding to said Article's third indent. The objectives of the third and fourth indents are certainly intertwined and measures based on them will often be in line with each other. Article 8(1)(a) of the Erasmus+ Regulation is an example of how transnational cooperation and the exchange of information and experience go hand in hand.

The sixth indent of Article 165(2) TFEU is concerned with the encouragement of distance education. More and more HEIs are starting to embrace virtual mobility and offer distance learning courses. However, one must distinguish between virtual mobility, i.e. "activities supported by information and communications technology [ICT], including e-learning, organised at institutional level, that realise or facilitate transnational and/or international, collaborative experiences in a context of teaching and/or learning",[265] and learning mobility, i.e. "moving physically to a country other than the country of residence".[266] As recital 31 of the Erasmus+ Regulation sets out, virtual mobility may complement learning mobility, however, it should not replace it.[267] Distance learning can be useful for LLL, because it enables those that live and/or work in less favoured regions to take advantage of the abundance of courses on offer at European HEIs.[268] However, while distance education adds to transnational and/or international experience, it cannot be compared to a study abroad experience.

The fifth indent of Article 165(2) TFEU is concerned with youth policy. The Union's objective includes "encouraging the development of youth exchanges and of exchanges of socio-educational instructors". Through the Lisbon Treaty the aim of Union action has been expanded to "encouraging the participation of

---

264 Cf. pp. 109–110.

265 Article 2(10) of the Erasmus+ Regulation.

266 Article 2(7) of the Erasmus+ Regulation.

267 Cf. Recital 31 of the preamble of the Erasmus+ Regulation.

268 Cf. Commission Working Document Consultation on the Future "EU 2020" Strategy, Brussels, 24.11.2009, COM(2009) 647 final, p. 6.

young people in democratic life in Europe". This links to Article 10(3) TEU that affirms every citizen's "right to participate in the democratic life of the Union" and thus "expresses the intention to promote popular participation in the Union's democratic life".[269] With the scant consideration of citizens' opinions ever so often criticized, the fifth indent of Article 165(2) TFEU is a step towards a "grassroots democracy"[270]. Active involvement in the drafting and implementation of future legal acts (e.g. the citizens' initiative (cf. Article 11(4) TEU)) is important. Thus, creating greater awareness among young people is a means to counter democratic deficit. Youth policy is, however, not limited to the fifth indent. Owing to the age of the main addressees, education policy and youth policy go hand in hand. Hence, youth policy forms an integral part of the Union's education policy.[271] Based on the Commission's White Paper on Youth[272], thematic priorities in the framework of European cooperation in the youth field include participation, information, voluntary activities among young people and the greater understanding and knowledge of youth.[273] The youth dimension is also to be taken into account regarding other policies.[274] These horizontal aspects are not taken up by the TFEU, however, youth policy is so immersed in education policy that a separate mention would probably not have made much difference.

Pursuant to Article 165(1) second subpara TFEU, the Union "contribute[s] to the promotion of European sporting issues, while taking account of the specific nature of sport, its structures based on voluntary activity and its social and educational function." However, Article 165 TFEU will only ever have (at least in the current Treaty version) "a limited impact on the EU's legal powers over sport". This is due to the absence of horizontality. Contrary to other provisions such as Article 147(2) TFEU on employment, Article 165 TFEU does not stipulate that its objectives need to be taken into account when defining and implementing the Union's policies and activities. With respect to education and training, Article 9

269 Ramirez, P., Article 10, in: HJ Blanke and S. Mangiameli (eds.), The Treaty on European Union (TEU): A Commentary, Springer: Heidelberg, 2013, pp. 417–447, recital 30.

270 Ibid. recital 31.

271 Cf. Frenz, Bildung, Jugend, Sport, 2011, recital 4003; Vedder, Artikel 165 AEUV, 2012, recital 6.

272 European Commission White Paper – A New Impetus for European Youth, COM(2001) 681 final, 21.11.2001.

273 Cf. Resolution of the Council and of the representatives of the Governments of the Member States, meeting within the Council of 27 June 2002 regarding the framework of European cooperation in the youth field, OJ C 168, 13.7.2002, pp. 2–5, p. 3.

274 Ibid. p. 4.

TFEU ensures that the promotion of a high level is maintained throughout the Union's fields. The horizontal social clause does not include sport, however. That is not to say that sporting issues will not be considered regarding EU actions but they do not have to.[275] In case the educational aspects do not take effect, sport may still be subject to other fields of EU law. Therefore, further horizontal clauses such as Articles 8 (gender equality) or 10 (combating discrimination) TFEU may well come into play.[276]

According to Article 2(1)(a) of the European Sports Charter of the CoE[277], sport concerns "all forms of physical activity which, through casual or organised participation, aim at expressing or improving physical fitness and mental well-being, forming social relationships or obtaining results in competition at all levels." With regard to EU law, the social significance of sport (i.e. its role in bringing people together and forging identity) was emphasised by Declaration 29 annexed to the Treaty of Amsterdam. Urging the Union bodies to take notice of sports associations when important questions are at stake, it also called for special consideration of amateur sport. The 2000 Nice European Council Meeting adopted a Declaration on "the specific characteristics of sport and its social function in Europe, of which account should be taken in implementing common policies".[278] It noted the educational function inherent in sport and expressed hopes that "the cohesion and ties of solidarity binding the practice of sports at every level, fair competition and both the moral and material interests and the physical integrity of those involved in the practice of sport, especially minors, may be preserved."[279]

Associated with competition law and the fundamental freedoms of the internal market, the ECJ had already been having a potentially far-reaching impact on sport. Similar to education, the lack of an express competence regulating Union influence led to concern. This was especially so in regard to the "specificity of

---

275 Cf. Parrish, R. et al., The Lisbon Treaty and EU Sports Policy: Study, European Parliament: Brussels, 2010, p. 10, http://www.europarl.europa.eu/meetdocs/2009_2014/documents/cult/dv/esstudyeusportspolicy/esstudyeusportspolicyen.pdf.

276 Cf. Niedobitek, Artikel 165 AEUV, 2012, recital 47.

277 Recommendation No. R (92) 13 Rev of the Committee of Ministers to Member States on the Revised European Sports Charter, adopted by the Committee of Ministers on 24 September 1992 at the 480th meeting of the Ministers' Deputies and revised at their 752nd meeting on 16 May 2001.

278 Annex IV to the Presidency Conclusions of the Nice European Council Meeting, 7, 8 and 9 December 2000.

279 Ibid. point 2.

sport".[280] This expression refers to its specific nature – its characteristics – and can generally be approached via two prisms: the "specificity of sporting activities and of sporting rules" and the "specificity of the sport structure".[281] The sporting context of Article 165 TFEU does, however, not interfere with the commercial aspects.[282] Those remain to be dealt with by the relevant competition law and internal market provisions.

The seventh indent of Article 165(2) TFEU draws heavily on the declarations of Amsterdam and Nice. Providing that the Union's aim shall be on

> developing the European dimension in sport, by promoting fairness and openness in sporting competitions and cooperation between bodies responsible for sports, and by protecting the physical and moral integrity of sportsmen and sportswomen, especially the youngest sportsmen and sportswomen[,]

it is a codification of the latters' philosophy and phraseology.[283] The seventh indent of Article 165(2) TFEU includes "all the characteristics that make sport special, such as for instance the interdependence between competing adversaries or the pyramid structure of open competitions."[284] In 2008, the European Council called for a combined sports training and education for young people.[285] The Commission has underlined the importance of the matter by issuing guidelines on dual careers, inviting the EU to initiate supplementary action in the area.[286] This has been further emphasised through Article 16(1)(b) of the new Erasmus+ Regulation, which stipulates that the Union shall promote and support the dual careers of athletes meaning a "combination of high-level sports training with general education or work" (cf. Article 2(23) of said Regulation). This measure is especially important with regard to achieving the Europe 2020 headline education target as it prevents early school leaving and leads to more

280 Cf. Parrish et al., 2010, p. 15.
281 White Paper on Sport, COM(2007) 391 final, p. 13.
282 Cf. Ruffert, Artikel 166 AEUV, 2011, recital 16.
283 Cf. Siekmann, R., Introduction to International and European Sports Law: Capita Selecta, T.M.C. Asser Press: The Hague, 2012, p, 80.
284 Cf. Communication from the Commission to the European Parliament, the Council, the European Economic and Social Committee and the Committee of the Regions: Developing the European Dimension in Sport, COM(2011) 12 final, 18.1.2011, p. 11.
285 Annex V to the Presidency Conclusions of the Brussels European Council Meeting, 11 and 12 December 2008.
286 Cf. European Commission, EU Guidelines on Dual Careers of Athletes, Publications Office of the European Union: Luxembourg, 2013, p. 1.

graduates in higher education, which will ultimately result in higher employability.

It might be debatable whether Article 165 TFEU also refers to amateur sports activities. However, the Commission has already affirmed that it does.[287] According to Article 16(1) of the Erasmus+ Regulation, the programme for the years 2014–2020 shall in particular focus on grassroots sport, i.e. "organised sport practised at local level by amateur sportspeople, and sport for all."[288] Article 16(1)(c) of said Regulation therefore establishes that the Union's specific objectives in sport include inter alia the "promotion of voluntary activities [...], together with social inclusion, equal opportunities and awareness of the importance of health-enhancing physical activity through increased participation in, and equal access to, sport for all."

Throughout the seventh indent of Article 165(2) TFEU the educational function is paramount. This is in particular demonstrated through the last phrase that focusses on the youngest, thereby leading to an overlap with youth policy. Before the Lisbon Treaty came into force, sports-related funding programmes were already linked to education policy (among other Union competences) in order to avoid being accused of acting ultra vires.[289] Consequently, the insertion into Article 165 TFEU was not completely unexpected. All in all, the Treaty of Lisbon put an end to a fragmentary as well as inorganic arrangement by recognising sport as falling within the EU's jurisdiction.[290]

5.2 Article 166 TFEU – Scope and Objectives

Article 166 TFEU provides for the Union's competence regarding vocational training. It applies to all forms of vocational training, i.e. initial and continuing vocational training as well as retraining (cf. Article 166(2) TFEU). Vocational training is therefore closely connected with the Union's employment and social policies (cf. Articles 145 and 151 TFEU et seq.). According to the third indent of

---

287 Cf. Communication from the Commission to the European Parliament, the Council, the European Economic and Social Committee and the Committee of the Regions: Developing the European Dimension in Sport, COM(2011) 12 final, 18.1.2011, p. 11.

288 Article 2(24) of the Erasmus+ Regulation.

289 Cf. Parrish et al., 2010, p. 11.

290 Cf. Nino, M., The Protection and Promotion of Sport in the European Union Following the Treaty of Lisbon and the Bernard Ruling, in: G. Ziccardi Capaldo (ed.), 1 The Global Community Yearbook of International Law and Jurisprudence 2010, OUP: New York, 2012, pp. 179–194, p. 183.

Article 156, para 1 TFEU, the Commission, in order to achieve the objectives of the EU's social policy (cf. Article 151 TFEU), shall encourage Member State co-operation and facilitate coordination of action in particular as regards basic and advanced vocational training. Article 166(2) TFEU is closely intertwined with Article 162 TFEU, even repeating the tasks of the ESF. Compared to Article 128 TEEC, an explicit reference to the internal market was avoided. Following the Maastricht Treaty, the EU is more than a purely economic community. However, against the background of the growth, competitiveness and employment goals enshrined in Article 166(2) TFEU, the Union's attitude clearly has not changed and is all the more so oriented towards a functioning economy. All in all, the Union's efforts in vocational training can be narrowed down to the following:

(1) to prevent and reduce unemployment,
(2) to provide for innovation in order to remain competitive at international level.[291]

Article 166(1) TFEU does not explicitly refer to the Union's leitmotif of contributing to the "development of quality education" (Article 165(1) TFEU). However, considering that Article 166(1) TFEU stipulates that "[t]he Union shall implement a vocational training policy which shall support and supplement the action of the Member States", the scope of action goes well beyond. Whereas Article 166 TFEU has its limitations (it is a supporting competence after all), it is not as restricted as Article 165 TFEU. Although both Articles 165 and 166 TFEU draw on ex Article 128 TEEC, it is Article 166 TFEU that acts as a replacement of Article 128 TEEC, taking over the existing acquis' legacy.[292] However, following the substantive changes due to the reformulation of the vocational training provision, Article 166 TFEU is much more restricted and "drafted to prevent any extension of [...] competence."[293] Conferring supporting competence on the Union, the Member States consolidated their status as the "masters of the Treaty".

Unlike Article 165(1) TFEU, Article 166(1) TFEU does not include a criterion of necessity. However, as the principles of subsidiarity and proportionality are enshrined in the Treaty, the Union has to comply with them anyway. Any reference to necessity is thus no more than a simple reminder. Article 166(1) TFEU includes a non-affection clause acknowledging that the Member States remain responsible for determining the content and the organisation of vocational training.

291 Cf. Bode, 2005, p. 96.
292 Cf. Gori, 2001, pp. 92 et seq. For the common vocational training policy cf. pp. 30 et seq.
293 Gori, 2001, p. 94.

It is unfortunate that the Lisbon Treaty did not provide for an express reference to LLL, for the common vocational training policy has long turned into a LLL strategy.[294] The underlying concept of Article 166(2) TFEU may well be described as to "contribute to the development of quality lifelong learning, and to promote high performance, innovation and a European dimension in systems and practices in the field",[295] a phrase used to circumscribe the 2007–2013 action programme in the field of LLL (Comenius, Erasmus, Leonardo da Vinci, Grundtvig and Jean Monnet).

Para 2 of Article 166 TFEU describes the Union's five objectives in the field of vocational training. Interestingly, the third, the fourth and the fifth objective draw on objectives listed in Article 165(2) TFEU (cf. the third, fourth and fifth indent of Article 166(2) TFEU), adapting them to vocational training.[296] This concerns the objectives regarding mobility, cooperation "between educational or training establishments and firms" and "exchanges of information and experience" between the Member States. The first and the second objective listed in Article 166(2) TFEU, on the other hand, focus on the facilitation of vocational (re)integration.

The first indent of Article 166(2) TFEU stipulates that the Union shall aim to "facilitate adaptation to industrial changes, in particular through vocational training and retraining". Repeating part of the wording of Article 162 TFEU on the ESF, it embodies the key objective for vocational training.[297] Measures pursuant to the first indent of Article 166(2) TFEU may thus be financed through the ESF.[298] However, this requires domestic public funding matching the ESF funds. The ESF is committed to improving employment opportunities. This is why, according to some, its denomination is a bit of a misnomer because the tasks entrusted to it are very much work-related.[299]

---

294 Cf. Cort, P., The EC Discourse on Vocational Training: How a 'Common Vocational Training Policy' Turned into a Lifelong Learning Strategy, 2 Vocations and Learning, 2009, pp. 87–107.

295 Article 1(3)(a) of Decision No 1720/2006/EC of the European Parliament and of the Council of 15 November 2006 Establishing an Action Programme in the Field of Lifelong Learning, OJ L 327, 24.11.2006, pp. 45–68.

296 Also cf. Niedobitek, Artikel 166 AEUV, 2012, recital 10.

297 Cf. Blanke, 2011, recital 90.

298 Also cf. Hilpold, 1995, p. 123.

299 Cf. Budischowsky, J., Art. 162 AEUV, in: Mayer, H., Kommentar zu EUV und AEUV unter Berücksichtigung der österreichischen Judikatur und Literatur, Manz: Wien, 2010, pp. 3–7, recital 3: "Arbeitsmarktstrukturfonds".

According to the second indent of Article 166(2) TFEU, the Union is to "improve initial and continuing vocational training in order to facilitate vocational integration and reintegration into the labour market" (also cf. Article 153(2)(b) TFEU). The second objective goes hand in hand with the third one, focussing on the facilitation of access to vocational training as well as encouraging mobility of both instructors and trainees and in particular young people. The third indent of Article 166(2) TFEU is partly congruent with Article 162 TFEU, which describes the aim of the ESF as to "render the employment of workers easier and to increase their geographical and occupational mobility within the Union". Mobility of workers may, likewise to the first objective, be financed by the ESF. Both objectives are part of the EU 2020 Strategy. "Youth on the move", a package of policy initiatives, inter alia covers the facilitation of entry of young people to the labour market, whereas mobility in vocational training is emphasised under the Flagship Initiative: "An Agenda for new skills and jobs".[300]

The fourth objective centres on the prevention of youth unemployment by increasing employability through improving skills. Pursuant to the fourth indent of Article 166(2) TFEU, the Union aims to "stimulate cooperation on training between educational or training establishments and firms". This has been incorporated into the fourth strategic objective of ET 2020, which focusses inter alia on the enhancement of entrepreneurship by emphasising the importance of partnerships between education and training providers and businesses. In recital 14 of the preamble of the Erasmus+ Regulation, the Union legislature indicates that cooperation with the world of work should receive particular attention at transnational level. Article 8(1)(b) of the Erasmus+ Regulation provides for such cooperation in the form of knowledge and sector skills alliances. Knowledge alliances may be established, in particular, between HEIs and enterprises.[301] They aim "at promoting creativity, innovation, work-based learning and entrepreneurship by offering relevant learning opportunities, including developing new curricula and pedagogical approaches" (cf. first indent of Article 8(1)(b) of the Erasmus+ Regulation). Sector skills alliances may be established between education and training providers and sectors in which European Sector Skills Councils have been set up (the textile, clothing and leather as well as the commerce sector (i.e. retail and wholesale)) and "those with skills imbalances to which current Commission policies respond" (advanced manufacturing, information and

300 Cf. Communication from the Commission, Europe 2020: A Strategy for Smart, Sustainable and Inclusive Growth, COM(2010) 2020 final, 3.3.2010.

301 Cf. European Commission, Erasmus+ Programme Guide, 2014, p. 110.

communication technologies, environmental technologies and the cultural and creative sectors).[302] They aim "at promoting employability, contributing to the creation of new sector-specific or cross-sectoral curricula, developing innovative methods of vocational teaching and training and putting the Union transparency and recognition tools into practice" (cf. second indent of Article 8(1)(b) of the Erasmus+ Regulation). Such partnerships are particularly valuable for Member States where education and vocational training do not overlap, i.e. that do not feature a dual system.[303]

The fifth objective is concerned with issues common to the training systems of the Member States and the only one to openly encourage Member State cooperation.[304] It stipulates that the Union's action shall aim at "develop[ing] exchanges of information and experience on issues common to the training systems of the Member States."

5.3 The Legal Instruments of Articles 165 and 166 TFEU

Para 4 of Articles 165 and 166 TFEU is concerned with the legal means, i.e. (incentive) measures and recommendations, available to the Union. For the external dimension of education policy and the Union's means of action cf. the next chapter on para 3.

The first indent of Article 165(4) TFEU provides that

> the European Parliament and the Council, acting in accordance with the ordinary legislative procedure, after consulting the Economic and Social Committee and the Committee of the Regions, shall adopt incentive measures, excluding any harmonisation of the laws and regulations of the Member States[.]

With the Treaty of Lisbon QMV became the default voting method.[305] That is to say that the Council shall act by QMV unless the Treaties provide otherwise (cf. Article 16(3) TEU). The co-decision procedure was renamed ordinary legislative procedure (cf. Article 294 TFEU (ex Article 251 TEC)).[306] This has led to a restructuring of Article 165(4) TFEU, changing the former provision so as to adapt it to the new circumstances. The second indent of Article 165(4) TFEU reads "[t]he Council, on a proposal from the Commission, shall adopt

---

302 Ibid. p. 119.

303 Also cf. Ruffert, Artikel 166, 2011, recital 6.

304 Also cf. Bode, 2005, p. 96; Ruffert, Artikel 166, 2011, recital 5.

305 Cf. House of Lords, European Union Committee, The Treaty of Lisbon: An Impact Assessment, Volume I: Report, The Stationery Office Limited: London, 2008, p. 49.

306 Cf. Foster, 2012, p. 88.

recommendations." The second indent of ex Article 149(4) TEC had included the phrase "acting by a qualified majority". With QMV becoming the default voting method, this reference was no longer necessary.

Whereas Article 165(4) is structured with the help of indents, Article 166(4) TFEU features a continuous paragraph stating that

> [t]he European Parliament and the Council, acting in accordance with the ordinary legislative procedure and after consulting the Economic and Social Committee and the Committee of the Regions, shall adopt measures to contribute to the achievement of the objectives referred to in this article, excluding any harmonisation of the laws and regulations of the Member States, and the Council, on a proposal from the Commission, shall adopt recommendations.

The main difference to Article 165(4) TFEU concerns the wording of the legal act. Contrary to Article 165(4) TFEU that provides for the adoption of incentive measures, Article 166(4) TFEU provides for the adoption of measures. It was only with the entry into force of the Lisbon Treaty that the provision for Council recommendations was added to Article 166(4) TFEU. Previously, the Article on vocational training had provided for the adoption of measures only.

5.3.1 Incentive Measures

Article 165(4) TFEU empowers the Union to take incentive measures to "contribute to the achievement of the objectives referred to". EU primary law does not contain a definition of the term "incentive measures", although Article 165 TFEU is not the only provision by a long stretch (cf. Articles 19(2), 79(4), 149, 167(5), 168(5) TFEU). Those provisions feature "[t]he same combination of soft law [i.e. recommendations] and legal incentive measures falling short of harmonization".[307] Incentive measures have been described as a legal act of sui generis nature.[308] However, since the entry into force of the Lisbon Treaty, the first indent of Article 165(4) TFEU includes a reference to the ordinary legislative procedure (cf. Article 294 TFEU), which is closely linked to Article 288 TFEU. According to the newly inserted Article 289(1) TFEU, the ordinary legislative procedure consists of the joint adoption of a regulation, directive or decision (for definitions cf. Article 288 TFEU) by the EP and the Council. Article 296, para 3 TFEU stipulates that the EP and the Council shall "refrain from adopting acts not provided for by the relevant legislative procedure". In substance, Article 288 TFEU is the same as ex Article 249 TEC. However, there

307 Also cf. Craig and De Búrca, 2011, p. 86.
308 Cf. Blanke, 2011, recital 100.

is a subtle yet significant difference. Pursuant to Article 249, para 4 TEC, decisions were only binding upon those to whom they were addressed. The new Article 288, para 4 TFEU states that "[a] decision shall be binding in its entirety." Unless it refers to specific addressees, it is therefore generally binding. Before the Lisbon Treaty came into force, decisions without addressees were adopted in "an unspecified form of binding legislation". Contrary to the "decision" provided for in ex Article 251 TEC, it was "a *sui generis* act with a general scope of application".[309] With the changes to Article 288 TFEU and the introduction of Article 289 TFEU, the classification of incentive measures as legal acts of sui generis nature is no longer viable.

Owing to this lack of definition, the scope of Union power regarding incentive measures has to be deduced from the relevant TFEU provisions. Pursuant to Article 2(5) TFEU, legally binding acts adopted in areas where the Union holds supporting competence, shall not entail harmonisation of the laws or regulations of the Member States. Due to the limited extent of competence, i.e. to contribute by encouraging cooperation between Member States and to support and supplement their actions if necessary, incentive measures may be described as being "aimed at providing a framework [in which] such [cooperation] may take place and to offer financial support for its implementation."[310] In order for them to become legally effective, incentive measures are usually implemented in the form of decisions.[311] This is not to say that the first indent of Article 165(4) TFEU does not allow for other legally binding forms provided for in Article 288 TFEU (cf. the Erasmus+ Regulation, for example).[312] Therefore, even if incentive measures do not per se supersede the competence of the Member States, they will constrain it "to the degree entailed by the EU legal act."[313] Thus, incentive measures may impose an obligation of cooperation on the Member States.[314] The Lisbon Treaty, although not providing for a definition of "incentive measures", has brought clarity regarding their binding nature. The newly inserted Article 289 TFEU defines the ordinary legislative procedure (i.e. jointly adopted regulations, directives and decisions) and stipulates that "[l]egal acts adopted by legislative

309 Cf. Lenaerts, 1994, p. 31 at fn. 75.

310 Cf. Gori, 2001, p. 90.

311 Cf. Blanke, 2011, recital 100.

312 Also cf. Frenz, W., Europäische Bildungspolitik, 64 DÖV, 2011, pp. 249–259, p. 256; Niedobitek, Art. 165 AEUV, 2012, recital 59.

313 Cf. Craig and De Búrca, 2011, p. 87.

314 Cf. Lenaerts, 1994, p. 31.

procedure shall constitute legislative acts". In the past, the binding nature of incentive measures had been disputed, leading AG Léger to state that

> when the legislature intends to limit powers so that only actions of a non-binding nature can be taken, this is clearly expressed, as in Articles 126, 128 and 129 of the Treaty [now Articles 165, 167 and 168 TFEU], where the measures intended to contribute to the attainment of objectives connected with education, culture and public health are classified as 'incentive measures'.[315]

With a non-harmonisation clause in place, non-binding acts would be incompatible. With regard to form, incentive measures are therefore clearly binding.[316] Pursuant to Article 297(2) TFEU, however, regulations, directives and decisions (i.e. all acts of secondary legislation) may also be of non-binding nature. However, these "are taken to be the delegated administrative or executive acts" of Union bodies, easily distinguishable by not being published in the L Series of the Official Journal (OJ) which contains the binding acts.[317]

5.3.2 Measures

As with "incentive measures", the Treaties do not provide for a definition of "measures". It is understood that measures go beyond incentive measures. However, the "difference is one of wording rather than substance."[318] According to Article 166(1) TFEU, the Union is to implement a vocational training policy, supporting and supplementing "the action of the Member States". With regard to content, Article 166 TFEU therefore goes further than Article 165 TFEU (the focus of which is to encourage Member State cooperation, e.g. through financial incentives). Due to Article 166(4) TFEU expressly prohibiting any harmonisation of the Member States' laws and regulations, the measures adopted by the Union may effectively not go beyond incentive measures.[319] Moreover, the demarcation between measures and incentive measures has become less important. Before the Lisbon Treaty entered into force, the binding nature of incentive measures was disputed.[320] Whereas it was generally accepted that measures could be implemented in the form of the binding legal acts specified

---

315 Opinion of Advocate General Léger, delivered on 10 December 1996, Case C-233/94 *Germany v European Parliament and Council* [1997] ECR 2405, para 57.
316 Cf. Niedobitek, Artikel 165 AEUV, 2012, recital 58.
317 Cf. Foster, 2012, pp. 103 et seq.
318 Cf. Gori, 2001, p. 95.
319 Cf. Frenz, Europäische Bildungspolitik, 2011, p. 256.
320 Also cf. Ruffert, Artikel 165 AEUV, 2011, recital 23.

in Article 288 TFEU (also cf. ex Article 249 TEC/ex Article 189 TEEC), some concluded that incentive measures were to be adopted in an unspecified form not provided for by Article 288 TFEU.[321] While action programmes were indeed adopted in the form of Council decisions (not to be confused with decisions within the meaning of Article 288 TFEU) allowing "Member States to evade the automatic legal effects associated with the legislative instruments provided for in [Article 288 TFEU]",[322] this does not reflect the current legal position. The reference to the ordinary legislative procedure leaves no doubt as to the nature of incentive measures.

5.3.3 The Non-Harmonisation Clause

While it is clear that the application of Article 114 TFEU concerning the approximation of laws is ruled out regarding the education policy domain,[323] the scope of the non-harmonisation clause contained in Articles 165(4) and 166(4) TFEU has been disputed. According to Hablitzel, the proscription of harmonisation is absolute, i.e. it constitutes a comprehensive ban.[324] He states that the ECJ's judgment on advertising and sponsorship of tobacco products[325] (cf. Article 168(5) TFEU on the prohibition of harmonisation in the area of public health) gives rise to optimism that the Court will accept and value the non-harmonisation clause of Articles 165 and 166 TFEU should they ever be put to test.[326] However, in the tobacco advertising case the ECJ had argued that public health policy was the centre of gravity of the directive concerned. While the protection of Member States' power regarding education policy is certainly true for Articles 165 and 166 TFEU and the EP and Council have neither been empowered to harmonise the youth and sport policy covered by the latter, the TFEU includes other potentially relevant policy domains. The education title proper, i.e. Title XII of the TFEU, deals with aspects of education but does not limit other policy domains.[327] ECJ jurisprudence "suggests that harmonising measures can be taken despite this type of prohibition so long as the harmonising measures are nominally based on

321 Cf. Hilpold, 1995, pp. 122 et seq.
322 Cf. Lenaerts, 1994, p. 31 at fn. 75.
323 Cf. Craig and De Búrca, 2011, p. 87.
324 Also cf. Ruffert, Artikel 165 AEUV, 2011, recital 22.
325 Cf. Case C-376/98 *Germany v European Parliament and Council* [2000] ECR 8419.
326 Cf. Hablitzel, 2002, pp. 409 et seq.
327 Cf. Frenz, Bildung, Jugend, Sport, 2011, recital 4032.

another Treaty competence."[328] In practice, convergence in the field may thus be achieved through the use of legal bases other than Articles 165 and 166 TFEU.

According to settled case law of the ECJ, "the choice of a legal basis for a measure must be based on objective factors which are amenable to judicial review. Those factors include, in particular, the aim and content of the measure".[329] In order to adopt a legal act, the centre of gravity, i.e. the primary purpose, must be determined. On condition that the primary purpose is not education, the legal act can be based on other Treaty articles. It is prohibited to do so "in order to circumvent the express exclusion of harmonisation".[330] Two or more legal bases may be used if two or more objectives are pursued. However, legal bases can only be cumulated in case they provide for the same decision-making procedure (regarding the education provisions that would be QMV).[331] This was effectively a problem before the entry into force of the Amsterdam Treaty.[332] Due to ex Articles 126 and 127 TEC including different decision-making procedures (i.e. co-decision procedure v. cooperation procedure), preference (according to the case law set by the ECJ) had to be given to ex Article 126 TEC as it contained "[t]he more democratic decision-making procedure".[333]

If a prospective legal act also touches upon issues education-related besides its main objective(s), the non-harmonisation clause of Articles 165(4) and 166(4) TFEU will not prevent the adoption of harmonising measures.[334] The limitation expressed in Article 165(4) TFEU is not in conflict with other Treaty provisions and "affects, in its own terms, only the 'incentive measures' for which it provides."[335] Consequently, the same must of course apply to Article 166(4) TFEU. However, this is not a carte blanche for harmonisation. Recourse to Article 114 TFEU[336] (in policy domains other than education, i.e. if the main objective is not

---

328 Cf. Parrish et al., 2010, p. 13.

329 Cf. Case C-155/91 *Commission v Council* [1993] ECR 939, para 7.

330 Case C-376/98 *Germany v European Parliament and Council*, para 79.

331 Cf. Case C-300/89 *Commission v Council* [1991] ECR 2867.

332 Also cf. pp. 111 et seq. on the demarcation between Articles 165 and 166 TFEU.

333 Lenaerts, 1994, p. 30.

334 Also cf. Budischowsky, J., Art. 165, 166 AEUV, in: Mayer, H., Kommentar zu EUV und AEUV unter Berücksichtigung der österreichischen Judikatur und Literatur, Manz: Wien, 2010, pp. 10–31, recital 59.

335 Opinion of Advocate General Fennelly, delivered on 15 June 2000, Case C-376/98 *Germany v European Parliament and Council* [2000] ECR 8419, para 71.

336 Also cf. Article 115 TFEU which provides for the approximation of laws that "directly affect the establishment or functioning of the internal market" by unanimity in the Council.

education-related) "is not justified where the measure to be adopted has only the incidental effect of harmonizing market conditions within the [Union]".[337] In other words: "the EU may intervene to cure diversity between national laws only where that diversity is shown to be harmful to the achievement of the EU's internal market."[338] It should be pointed out that Article 114 TFEU does not apply to provisions relating to the free movement of persons or the rights and interests of employed persons (cf. para 2 thereof). Thus, the areas prone to overlap with education issues are deemed too sensitive for QMV. This is where Article 115 TFEU, which acts as the residual legal basis for areas excluded from Article 114 TFEU, comes in.[339] Providing for the approximation of laws that "directly affect the establishment or functioning of the internal market" by means of directives, it requires unanimity in the Council following consultations of the EP and the EESC.

The non-harmonisation clause does not, however, interdict the indirect approximation of laws. It is necessary to distinguish between two scenarios: on the one hand, there is voluntary convergence at intergovernmental level on the basis of international law (i.e. the Bologna process), on the other hand, the EU provides for indirect harmonising effect through financial incentives (e.g. the funding made available through the ESF/ERDF). The first scenario is clear-cut: education primarily falls under the competence of the Member States. The second scenario is an intra-EU one. Pursuant to Article 174, para 1 TFEU, economic, social and territorial cohesion shall be strengthened. In view of that, Article 175, para 1 TFEU provides that cohesion be taken into account and contributed to when formulating and implementing the policies and actions of the Union. Without prejudice to Article 166 TFEU, Article 153(1)(h) TFEU ensures "the integration of persons excluded from the labour market" through the adoption of minimum requirements by means of directives (Article 153(2)(b) TFEU). Therefore, providing match-funding for the implementation of cohesion policy, may well have implications for the education domain.[340]

---

337 Case C-155/91 *Commission v Council*, para 19.

338 Weatherill, S., The Limits of Legislative Harmonization Ten Years After *Tobacco Advertising*: How the Court's Case Law has Become a "Drafting Guide", 12 German Law Journal, 2011, pp. 827–864, p. 830.

339 Cf. Barnard, C., Competence Review: The Internal Market, pp. 23 et seq., https://www.gov.uk/government/uploads/system/uploads/attachment_data/file/226863/bis-13-1064-competence-review-internal-market.pdf.

340 Cf. Blanke, 2011, recital 112; also cf. Bode, 2005, pp. 99 et seq. and Mächtle, 2010, p. 80.

5.3.4 The Adoption of (Incentive) Measures and the Enhanced Role of the CoR

Whenever an (incentive) measure is to be adopted, the Commission submits a proposal to the EP and the Council (Article 294(2) TFEU). After that, the ordinary legislative procedure is set in motion. If after two readings the EP and the Council still do not concur, a Conciliation Committee composed of members of the EP and the Council is set up. If an agreement cannot be reached within six weeks, the proposal is rejected. Otherwise, the joint text is sent to the EP and the Council for a third reading. If they fail to adopt the joint text within six weeks, the proposal is finally rejected (cf. Article 294(10)-(13) TFEU). In addition, the EESC and the CoR have to be consulted (Articles 304, para 1 and 307, para 1 TFEU). They will then adopt an opinion, which is not binding and therefore not legally enforceable (cf. Article 288, para 5 TFEU). Since the entry into force of the Lisbon Treaty, however, the CoR may bring actions before the ECJ in two instances:

(1) for the purpose of protecting its own prerogatives before the ECJ (Article 263, para 3 TFEU),
(2) "on grounds of infringement of the principle of subsidiarity by a legislative act" for the adoption of which the TFEU provides that the CoR be consulted (Article 8 of the Lisbon Treaty Protocol No 2 on the Application of the Principles of Subsidiarity and Proportionality).[341]

5.3.5 Recommendations

According to the second indent of Article 165(4) TFEU, the Council may adopt recommendations following a Commission proposal. Since 2009, Article 166(4) TFEU allows for the adoption of Council recommendations. Virtually, this had been the distinguishing mark between Articles 165(4) and 166(4) TFEU. Contrary to the (incentive) measures that are adopted jointly by the EP and the Council, the adoption of measures is not subject to the ordinary legislative procedure. In line with Article 16(3) TEU the Council acts by QMV when adopting recommendations under the second indent of Article 165(4) TFEU and/or Article 166(4) TFEU. According to Article 288, para 5 TFEU, recommendations, like opinions, "have no binding force." Hence, they constitute a form of soft law. The scope of recommendations in Union law thus concurs with the term's literal

341 Also cf. p. 51.

meaning.[342] However, to state that recommendations have no legal effect at all would not be correct. As has been clarified in the *Grimaldi* ruling, Article 267(b), para 1 TFEU "confers on the Court jurisdiction to give a preliminary ruling on the validity and interpretation of all acts of the institutions of the [Union] without exception."[343] Recommendations thus have to be taken into consideration by the national courts "in order to decide disputes submitted to them, in particular where they cast light on the interpretation of national measures adopted in order to implement them or where they are designed to supplement binding Community provisions."[344] The specific mention of recommendations adopted by a simplified decision-making procedure in connection with Articles 165 and 166 TFEU stresses the importance of soft law in education policy.[345] However, in its Resolution *on institutional and legal implications of the use of 'soft law' instruments* the EP recalled that "soft law cannot be a substitute for legal acts and instruments, which are available to ensure the continuity of the legislative process, especially in the field of culture and education".[346]

5.3.6 Excursus on Article 352 TFEU

According to Article 352(1) TFEU which draws on ex Article 308 TEC/ex Article 235 TEEC, the general competence norm may only be used as a residual legal basis to attain "objectives set out in the Treaties" if the Treaties themselves do not provide for "the necessary powers". Whereas ex Article 308 TEC had referred to "action [...] necessary to attain, in the course of the operation of the common market", Article 352 TFEU is framed more broadly referring only to the "policies defined in the Treaties". Ex Article 235 TEEC was used to introduce the Erasmus programme.[347] However, times (and Treaties) have changed and education has officially been inserted into the Treaties and provided with its own Treaty provision. Nevertheless, ex Article 308 TEC has since been used in connection with education. For example, Tempus IV (programming period

---

342 Cf. Senden, L., Soft Law in European Union Community Law, Hart Publishing: Oxford, 2004, p. 159.

343 Cf. Case C-322/88 *Grimaldi v Fonds des maladies professionelles* [1989] ECR 4407, para 8.

344 Ibid. para 18.

345 Cf. Niedobitek, Artikel 165 AEUV, 2012, recital 61.

346 European Parliament Resolution of 4 September 2007 on institutional and legal implications of the use of 'soft law' instruments (2007/2028(INI)), OJ C 187E, 24.7.2008, pp. 75–79, point 1.

347 Cf. pp. 42 et seq.

2007–2013), which promoted institutional cooperation with partner countries of Eastern Europe, Central Asia, the Western Balkans and the Mediterranean region, focussing on the reform and modernisation of higher education systems, still referred to it. However, it was not formally adopted. Instead the Commission opted to extend Tempus III[348] which had been based on Article 235 TEC (Maastricht consolidated version), financing it through the European external assistance policy instruments.[349] Given that Tempus IV involved reforming and modernising higher education systems, recourse to the flexibility clause was a prerequisite as this goes beyond the scope of Articles 165 and 166 TFEU.[350] Actions in the field of education may therefore be based on Article 352 TFEU. However, this presupposes that they cannot be based on Articles 165 and 166 TFEU.

According to the newly inserted para 3 of Article 352 TFEU, "[m]easures based on this Article shall not entail harmonisation of Member States' laws or regulations in cases where the Treaties exclude such harmonisation." If harmonisation is an issue, recourse to Article 352 TFEU may therefore not be taken in the field of education. Nevertheless, Article 352 TFEU can also be used in connection with other Treaty objectives. Thus, Blanke argues that the flexibility clause could indirectly lead to harmonisation in education.[351] This would presuppose that the legal act cannot be based on Articles 165 and 166 TFEU and that education is not its main objective. However, it is debatable whether this would be in line with Article 352(3) TFEU. The introduction of para 3 of Article 352 TFEU has further led some to object to the use of the flexibility clause in the field of education in any case.[352] Nevertheless, it is unlikely that the use of Article 352 TFEU in connection with other Treaty objectives would lead to harmonisation in the education field. Whenever Article 352 TFEU is used, the EP is not just

348 Cf. Council Decision 1999/311/EC of 29 April 1999 adopting the third phase of the trans-European cooperation scheme for higher education (Tempus III) (2000–2006), OJ L 120, 8.5.1999, pp. 30–36.

349 Cf. Commission Decision 2008/785/EC of 9 October 2008 amending Commission Decision 2005/56/EC setting up the Education, Audiovisual and Culture Executive Agency for the management of Community action in the fields of education, audiovisual and culture in application of Council Regulation (EC) No 58/2003, OJ L 269, 10.10.2008, pp. 11–13. Also cf. Niedobitek, Artikel 165 AEUV, 2012, recital 78.

350 Cf. Gori, 2001, p. 188.

351 Cf. Blanke, 2011, recital 114.

352 Cf. Chalmers, D., Davies, G. and G. Monti, European Union Law: Cases and Materials, 2nd ed., Cambridge UP: Cambridge, 2010, p. 216.

consulted (as was the case before the Lisbon Treaty), but must consent (cf. Article 352(1) TFEU). Furthermore, the national parliaments of the Member States must be notified of the proposal (Article 352(2) TFEU). The changes introduced by the Lisbon Treaty will make it harder to adopt a legal act on the basis of Article 352 TFEU. Moreover, the German Constitutional Court has decided that the use of the flexibility clause

> constitutionally requires ratification by the German *Bundestag* and the *Bundesrat* on the basis of Article 23.1 second and third sentence of the Basic Law. The German representative in the Council may not express formal approval on behalf of the Federal Republic of Germany of a corresponding lawmaking proposal of the Commission as long as these constitutionally required preconditions are not met.[353]

Amid concerns regarding Article 352 TFEU, precautionary measures have also been taken in the UK. Pursuant to Section 8, Subsection 1 of the European Union Act 2011, a Minister may not vote in favour of a proposal based on Article 352 TFEU unless one of several conditions such as the draft proposal being approved by Act of Parliament (Subsection 3 of said Section) is met. With the unanimity requirement in the Council a prerequisite, it is highly unlikely that a proposal trying to circumvent Articles 165 and 166 TFEU and/or to encroach upon Member State sovereignty in the education field via other Treaty objectives would ever be adopted.

5.4 The External Dimension of Articles 165 and 166 TFEU

According to Articles 165(3) and 166(3) TFEU, the Union and its Member States shall foster cooperation with both third countries and the competent international organisations in the fields of education and training. Article 165(3) TFEU, which compared to the pre-Lisbon Treaty versions now includes the external dimension of sport, stipulates that this shall in particular entail cooperation with the CoE, the intergovernmental actor that has been amassing expertise in the area since the early days of European integration.[354] The CoE is not referred to in Article 166(3) TFEU. Argumentum a contrario one could thus conclude that the Union and the CoE mainly collaborate in general education matters.[355] With regard to scope, the external actions of the Union are confined to the boundaries

353 Lisbon Judgment, BVerfG, 2 BvE 2/08 vom 30.6.2009, para 328 (available in English under http://www.bverfg.de/entscheidungen/es20090630_2bve000208en.html).

354 Cf. pp. 23 et seq.

355 Cf. Hilpold, 1995, p. 123.

set by Articles 165(2) and 166(2) TFEU.[356] The Union's treaty-making power in education and training is generally seen as restricted to the fostering of cooperation.[357] Whenever the Union enters into an agreement, it cannot go beyond the powers conferred upon it by the Member States (Article 5(2) TFEU). In that respect the external dimension of Articles 165 and 166 TFEU does not differ from the internal one. Although Member States may continue to pursue an external relations policy of their own in education and training (this is also reflected in the wording of Articles 165(3) and 166(3) TFEU),[358] they shall refrain from taking measures that would compromise the Union's objectives (cf. third sentence of Article 4(3) TEU). Mirroring the internal dimension, cohesion is thus guaranteed regarding the external dimension. In accordance with the principle of sincere cooperation (first sentence of Article 4(3) TEU), the Union shall assist the Member States when carrying out tasks flowing from the Treaties. The same applies vice versa.[359] This allows for a coherent education and training strategy of the EU regardless of which dimension (i.e. internal or external) applies.

Title V of the TFEU deals with the conclusion of international agreements. The newly inserted Article 216 TFEU stipulates that the Union can conclude bilateral and multilateral agreements with third countries as well as international organisations (para 1). According to para 1, the circumstances under which the Union may conclude such agreements are given

> where the Treaties so provide or where the conclusion of an agreement is necessary in order to achieve, within the framework of the Union's policies, one of the objectives referred to in the Treaties, or is provided for in a legally binding Union act or is likely to affect common rules or alter their scope.

Such agreements are binding upon the Union's institutions and the Member States (para 2). As a provision Article 216 TFEU is of utmost importance for the external dimension of the Union's education policy. Whereas Articles 165(3) and 166(3) TFEU allow the Union to further international cooperation by means attributed to it in Articles 165(4) and 166(4) TFEU (i.e. incentive measures and measures), they do not empower it to pursue the objectives of Articles 165(2) and 166(2) TFEU in the conduct of external relations. Before the entry into force of the Lisbon Treaty, the Union had to make do with implied external competence.

356 Cf. Frenz, Bildung, Jugend, Sport, 2011, recital 4045; Ruffert, Artikel 165 AEUV, 2011, recital 30.
357 Cf. Budischowsky, Art. 165, 166 AEUV, 2010, recital 56.
358 Cf. Margedant, 2012, p. 149; Niedobitek, Artikel 165 AEUV, 2012, recital 48.
359 Also cf. Hilpold, 1995, p. 121.

The ECJ has held that the Union's "competence to enter into international commitments may arise not only from express conferment by the Treaty but also by implication from provisions of the Treaty."[360] In Opinion 1/76 the Court explained that it had

> concluded inter alia that whenever [Union] law has created for the institutions of the [Union] powers within its internal system for the purpose of attaining a specific objective, the [Union] has authority to enter into the international commitments necessary for the attainment of that objective even in the absence of an express provision in that connexion.[361]

Thus, the external competence of the Union was seen as the necessary corollary of the internal one.[362] Through Article 216 TFEU, the absence of an explicit reference to external competence has been done away with. Within the framework of said Article the Union has been provided with explicit treaty-making power. Making the previous practice of having recourse to case law obsolete, it allows the Union to act accordingly in regard to Articles 165(3) and 166(3) TFEU.[363] Streinz argues that because the Union lacks exclusive competence in the field of education, mixity is a necessary prerequisite for international agreements.[364] Naturally, a common position of the Union and its Member States may be necessary as regards relations with third countries or international organisations.[365] However, while international agreements concluded by the Union pursuant to Title XII may often be concluded as mixed agreements with the Union and its Member States as Contracting Parties, a procedure of this kind is not necessarily a prerequisite. The Union may act on its own as long as it sticks to its mission to support and supplement the action of the Member States. The bottom line

360 Case C-476/98 *Commission v Germany* [2002] ECR 9855, para 82.

361 Opinion 1/76 [1977] ECR 741, para 3.

362 Cf. Ott, A. and R. Wessel, The EU's External Relations Regime: Multilevel Complexity in an Expanding Union, in: S. Blockmans and A. Lazowski (eds.), The European Union and Its Neighbours: A Legal Appraisal of the EU's Policies of Stabilisation, Partnership and Integration, T.M.C. Asser Press: The Hague, 2006, pp. 19–60, p. 24.

363 Also cf. Niedobitek, Artikel 165 AEUV, 2012, recital 49.

364 Cf. Streinz, T., Fraternal Twins: The European Union and the Council of Europe, in: H. de Waele and JJ Kuipers (eds.), The European Union's Emerging International Identity: Views from the Global Arena, Brill: Leiden, 2013, pp. 101–129, p. 105.

365 Cf. Niedobitek, Artikel 165, 2012, recital 49.

is that the Union must not undermine the scope of the respective Articles.[366] The former bilateral cooperation programmes between the EU and Canada (EU-Canada Programme) or the US (EU-US Atlantis Programme) are examples of international agreements concluded sine mixity.[367]

Moreover, the common commercial policy, which "shall be conducted in the context of the principles and objectives of the Union's external action" (Article 207(1) TFEU), comprises the field of trade in education services (cf. Article 207(4)(b) TFEU). Article 3(1)(e) TFEU provides that the Union has exclusive competence regarding the common commercial policy. Considering that the Union holds supportive competence for internal actions in the education sector, such a provision may set the alarm bells ringing. However, the power of the Union with regard to education services is limited. With the backing of public service unions in the education services sector, a number of Member States pushed for special provisions.[368] These provisions have been embedded in Article 207 TFEU. The Council is to act unanimously with regard to the negotiation and conclusion of agreements "where these agreements risk seriously disturbing the national organisation of such services and prejudicing the responsibility of Member States to deliver them" (Article 207(4)(b) TFEU). Besides the unanimity clause in Article 207(4)(b) TFEU, a non-harmonisation clause has been added stipulating that "[t]he exercise of the competences [...]

366 Cf. Vedder, Artikel 165 AEUV, 2012, recital 9; Odendahl, K., Bildung, Kultur, Forschung und technologische Entwicklung, in: M. Niedobitek (ed.), Europarecht – Politiken der Union, De Gruyter: Berlin, 2014, pp. 1005–1064, recital 19.

367 Cf. Council Decision 2006/910/EC of 4 December 2006 concerning the conclusion of the Agreement between the European Community and the United States of America renewing the cooperation programme in higher education and vocational education and training: Agreement between the European Community and the United States of America renewing a programme of cooperation in higher education and vocational education and training, OJ L 346, 9.12.2006, p. 33–40; Council Decision 2006/964/EC of 18 December 2006 on the conclusion of the Agreement between the European Community and the Government of Canada establishing a framework for cooperation in higher education, training and youth: Agreement between the European Community and the Government of Canada establishing a framework for cooperation in higher education, training and youth, OJ L 397, 30.12.2006, pp. 14–21.

368 Cf. Leal-Arcas, R., The European Union's New Common Commercial Policy after the Treaty of Lisbon, in: M. Trybus and L. Rubini (eds.), The Treaty of Lisbon and the Future of European Law and Policy, Edward Elgar: Cheltenham, 2012, pp. 262–284, p. 266; Woolcock, S. The Treaty of Lisbon and the European Union as an Actor in International Trade, ECIPE Working Paper No. 1, 2010, p. 9.

shall not affect the delimitation of competences between the Union and the Member States, and shall not lead to harmonisation of legislative or regulatory provisions of the Member States in so far as the Treaties exclude such harmonisation." The second subpara of Article 133(6) TEC provided that agreements relating to educational services "shall fall within the shared competence of the Community and its Member States. Consequently [...] the negotiation of such agreements shall require the common accord of the Member States." Hence, the predecessor of Article 207 TFEU explicitly foresaw mixity for agreements on education services. Article 207(6) TFEU limits the explicit competence of the Union. However, the protection of national sovereignty through Article 133(6) TEC was considerably more extensive. After all, Article 207(6) TFEU only limits the exercise of the Union's competence if agreements would lead to harmonisation in the education sector.[369] Thus, provided that harmonisation is not an issue, agreements may be concluded sine mixity.

The growing importance of moving cooperation in education and training to an international level is highlighted by the Commission's efforts. Advocating an active role in the cooperation with non-EU countries, it lists its five main objectives as

- To advance the EU as a centre of excellence in education and training;
- To support partner countries outside the EU in their modernisation efforts;
- To promote common values and closer understanding between different peoples and cultures;
- To support Member States and HEIs in the EU and beyond in their internationalisation efforts;
- To improve the quality of services and human resources in the EU and beyond through mutual learning, comparison and exchange of good practice.[370]

The main focus of the Union's external dimension lies on higher education, as most areas of common interest are in this field and contacts have already been established.[371] Recently, the Union expanded its objectives from four to five. The new (fourth) indent vouching support for Member States and HEIs did not feature in earlier listings of objectives. In 2013, the Commission launched a Communication regarding European higher education in the world, aiming to contribute to the EU 2020 Strategy through helping Member States and HEIs

369 Weiß, W., Artikel 207 AEUV, in: E. Grabitz, M. Hilf, and M. Nettesheim (eds.), Das Recht der Europäischen Union, CH Beck: München, 49. Ergänzungslieferung, 2012, recital 70.

370 http://ec.europa.eu/education/policy/international-cooperation/index_en.htm.

371 Cf. Tauch, 2011, p. 76.

"develop strategic partnerships that will allow Europe to tackle global challenges more effectively."[372] According to the Commission, a comprehensive internationalisation strategy should include

> the development of international curricula, strategic partnerships, finding new ways of delivering content, and ensuring complementarity with broader national policies for external cooperation, international development, migration, trade, employment, regional development, research and innovation.[373]

In order to stay competitive on the international level, European HEIs need to promote student and staff mobility ("two-way mobility" scheme, recognition of competences and qualifications), ensure that curricula are innovative, endeavour academic excellence in teaching and research, conclude cooperation agreements and enter into strategic partnerships (joint and double degrees, partnerships with other institutions and/or organisations) and discuss common challenges with partners from third countries or regions (policy dialogue). Moreover, HEIs shall take into account labour market demands (target skills shortages), make use of the "knowledge triangle" between business, higher education and research (European Industrial Doctorates) and serve the growing need for digital learning, enabling non-mobile students to profit from "internationalisation at home" ("off-campus" learners).[374]

The Commission clearly states its intention to move beyond intra-EU cooperation and make global cooperation reality. However, it acknowledges that there is no one-size-fits-all approach and that it is ultimately for the Member States to

> tailor their national strategies to reinforce their strengths, their international presence, and attract talent, taking into account identified national and intercultural skills shortages and bearing in mind the knowledge and research needs of their developing partner countries.[375]

All in all, the options for individuals, institutions and/or organisations (even the private sector and civil society) from third countries are manifold. Depending on the relations between the EU and the country in question, various cooperation options may be put to use.

372 Communication from the Commission to the European Parliament, the Council, the European Economic and Social Committee and the Committee of the Regions: European higher education in the world, COM(2013) 499 final, Brussels, 11.7.2013, p 2.

373 Ibid. p. 3.

374 Ibid. pp. 3 et seq.

375 Ibid. p. 4.

5.4.1 The EEA EFTA States

Since the adoption of the Agreement on the European Economic Area (EEA)[376], which entered into force on 1 January 1994, the European Free Trade Association (EFTA) States Iceland, Liechtenstein and Norway have been able to participate in the Union's various education-related activities. Due to a December 1992 referendum rejecting EEA membership, Switzerland did not ratify the EEA Agreement. This only leaves bilateral agreements. Switzerland is thus confined to a form of cooperation used since the end of the 1980s.

Cooperation in education and training was first established by means of bilateral agreements between the Community and the EFTA States. Opening up the Community's education and training programmes, the EFTA States were enabled to participate in the two largest ones: COMETT II and ERASMUS.[377] In the course of negotiations for the EEA, further cooperation in education and training ensued.[378] Since 1 January 1995, the EEA EFTA States participate in all education and training programmes then in force or adopted (cf. Article 4(2) Protocol 31 to the EEA Agreement).

According to Article 1(1) EEA Agreement, the aim of the agreement as such is generally economic, promoting "a continuous and balanced strengthening of trade and economic relations". Pursuant to Article 1(2)(f) EEA Agreement, closer cooperation in other (i.e. non-economic) fields such as education shall contribute to this achievement. The fourth indent of Article 78 EEA Agreement, inserted under Part VI dealing with cooperation outside the four freedoms, stipulates that the Contracting Parties shall focus on strengthening and broadening cooperation in the framework of the Union's activities in the fields of education, training and youth. The provisions of Part VI differ from the rest of the Agreement as they do not create rights or obligations for individuals but are concerned with the Contracting Parties. The beneficiaries or target groups, however, are research institutions, students or workers, for example.[379] Article 84 EEA Agreement refers to Protocol 31 that sets out provisions governing cooperation in specific fields outside the four freedoms. In addition to Protocol 31 and its Article 4 on education, training, youth and sport (the original heading of

376 Agreement on the European Economic Area, OJ L 1, 3.1.1994, pp. 3–522; and EFTA States' official gazettes.

377 Cf. Norberg, S. et al., The European Economic Area: EEA Law: A Commentary on the EEA Agreement, Fritzes (Kluwer): Stockholm, 1993, p. 658.

378 Cf. Blanke, 2011, recital 124.

379 Norberg et al., 1993, p. 640.

Article 4 "Education, training and youth" was replaced so as to include sport),[380] the EEA Agreement contains Protocol 29 on vocational training.

According to the second sentence of Article 4(2) of Protocol 31, the planning and development of Union programmes in this field is "subject to the procedures referred to in Part VI, in particular Article 79(3)" EEA Agreement. Thus, the EEA EFTA States are included in the preparatory stage (cf. Article 100 EEA Agreement) and the drafting of new legislation (cf. Article 99 EEA Agreement). Pursuant to Article 99(1) EEA Agreement, the Commission seeks advice on the elaboration of proposals from EEA EFTA State experts in the same manner as from EU Member State experts. Until the Council makes a decision, the Contracting Parties are in "a continuous information and consultation process" (Article 99(3) EEA Agreement). The EEA EFTA States contribute financially to the programmes and actions referred to in paras 1–2(n) of Protocol 31 whereby they cover their own costs and make an appropriate contribution to the Union's overhead costs (cf. Article 4(3) of Protocol 31 in accordance with Article 82(1)(a) of the Agreement).

Article 98 EEA Agreement provides that the EEA Joint Committee can amend Protocol 31 through decisions. With new Union legislation becoming available on a regular basis, Protocol 31 has to be updated frequently.[381] The programmes and actions adopted will then become valid retroactively. Recital 35 of the preamble to the Erasmus+ Regulation and Article 24(1)(c) of the Erasmus+ Regulation refer to the EEA EFTA States. The Commission adopted a proposal for a Council decision on the position to be adopted, on behalf of the European Union, in the EEA Joint Committee concerning an amendment to Protocol 31 to extend the cooperation of the Contracting Parties to the EEA Agreement to include the Erasmus+ Regulation.[382] The EEA Joint Committee has meanwhile adopted the decision amending Protocol 31 in order to allow for extended cooperation to take place with effect from 1 January 2014.[383]

380 Article 1(2) of the Decision of the EEA Joint Committee amending Protocol 31 to the EEA Agreement, on cooperation in specific fields outside the four freedoms No 140/2012 of 13 July 2012, OJ L 309, 8.11.2012, pp. 23–24.

381 Cf. Article 4(2)(a) et seq. of Protocol 31.

382 Proposal for a Council Decision on the position to be adopted, on behalf of the European Union, in the EEA Joint Committee concerning an amendment to Protocol 31 to the EEA Agreement, on cooperation in specific fields outside the four freedoms, 11.3.2014, COM(2014) 142 final.

383 Decision No 110/2014 (OJ L [to be published] and EEA Supplement No [to be published]), e.i.f. 17.5.2014.

Protocol 29 to the EEA Agreement on vocational training provides that

> [i]n order to promote the movement of young people within the EEA, the Contracting Parties agree to strengthen their cooperation in the field of vocational training and to endeavour to improve conditions for students wishing to study in an EEA State other than their own. In this context they agree that the provisions of the Agreement concerning the right of residence for students do not alter the possibilities of individual Contracting Parties, existing before the entry into force of the Agreement, as to the tuition fees charged to foreign students.

Its wording evokes the notion of a pre-Maastricht provision. Unlike Protocol 31 it has never been updated. Scouring literature there is no indication as to why it remains unchanged. The work on the EEA Agreement was concluded in 1992 (if not for Switzerland's refusal to ratify, it would have entered into force on 1 January 1993).[384] Since then, Article 128 TEEC has been rendered out of date. Article 166 TFEU now covers vocational education and training, whereas Article 165 TFEU covers general education including higher education. Apart from the ECJ that keeps on reiterating the pre-Maastricht version, higher education is generally taken to be covered by Article 165 TFEU. However, Article 98 EEA Agreement states that the EEA Joint Committee may amend the Annexes to the EEA Agreement as well as Protocols 1 to 7, 9 to 11, 19 to 27, 30 to 32, 37, 39, 41 and 47. The EEA Agreement does not contain specific provisions as to the amendment of the other protocols. An amendment of Protocol 29 would be subject to negotiations between the Contracting Parties.[385] The only way to amend Protocol 29 would therefore be to amend the EEA Agreement itself. This would require ratification through the Contracting Parties. Such amendments have so far, however, only been done in connection with enlargements of the EU (and therefore the EEA). Whenever this was the case, the EEA EFTA States opted to not discuss the EEA Agreement in general and "limited the changes to a revision of Protocol 38 on the EEA financial mechanism as well as matters that are directly related to the enlargement of the EU/EEA."[386] Unofficial talks with EU Member States regarding Protocol 29 have been conducted at various

---

384 Cf. Norberg et al., 1993, p. 68.

385 Cf. Written evidence from Erna Hjaltested, Senior Legal Officer, EEA Co-ordination Division, EFTA, 14 January 2013, in: House of Commons, Foreign Affairs Committee, The Future of the European Union: UK Government Policy, First Report of Session 2013–14, Vol. II, p. 185.

386 Written evidence from Tore Grønningsæter, Senior Information and Communication Officer, EFTA, 26 March 2014 (file with author).

times. However, the feedback received was clear in that at least some EU Member States would most probably turn down a proposal for an amendment.[387]

5.4.2 The Particular Case of Switzerland

Switzerland, the only non-EEA member of the EFTA States, has so far been able to participate in the Union's programmes subject to bilateral agreements. From the academic year 2011/12 to the academic year 2013/14, Switzerland had been able to participate in the Erasmus programme as an associated country. Article 24(1)(d) of the Erasmus+ Regulation stipulates that the Swiss Confederation may participate in the Erasmus+ programme as a non-EU programme country subject to a bilateral agreement (also cf. recital 36 of the preamble of the Erasmus+ Regulation). However, due to a February 2014 popular initiative against mass immigration (Eidgenössische Volksinitiative "Gegen Masseneinwanderung") in which the Swiss voted to reintroduce quotas for EU citizens, the ongoing negotiations regarding the Swiss participation in the Erasmus+ programme have been suspended. As a result of the initiative approved, the Swiss Federal Council has not been able to sign the Protocol extending the EU-Swiss agreement on the free movement of persons to Croatia, the EU's newest Member State. According to the Commission, the outcome of the referendum "call[s] into question the principle of free movement of persons between the EU and Switzerland." Given that the Union "has always made clear that there is a close link between Swiss participation in Erasmus+ and the Protocol, as the programme is closely linked to the free movement of persons (exchange of researchers and students)", the Swiss participation in Erasmus+ for the Erasmus+ 2014 call for proposals has been reduced to that of a partner country.[388]

5.4.3 Turkey and the Former Yugoslav Republic of Macedonia

According to Article 24(1)(b) of the Erasmus+ Regulation, candidate countries may participate in the Erasmus+ programme as non-EU programme countries. Except for Iceland, which participates as an EEA EFTA State, Turkey and the former Yugoslav Republic of Macedonia are the only EU candidates that take part on an equal footing with the Member States. The participation as a non-EU programme country is subject to an agreement between the Commission and

387 Ibid.
388 Cf. Information Note on the Participation of Switzerland in Erasmus+, http://ec.europa.eu/programmes/erasmus-plus/news/2014/20140209_en.htm.

the competent authorities of the candidate countries.[389] After an exchange of letters on 26 May 2014, the Commission received the former Yugoslav Republic of Macedonia's written notification, which provides for the entry into force of the Erasmus+ agreement on 4 June 2014.[390] On 19 May 2014, Turkey signed the Erasmus+ agreement. Ratified by the Turkish Council of Ministers, it was published in the Official Gazette of 17 June (reference No 2014/6458) and entered into force on 18 June 2014.[391]

5.4.4 Erasmus+: Cooperation for Partner Countries

The five international cooperation programmes Erasmus Mundus, Tempus, Alfa, Edulink and the programme for cooperation with industrialised countries have all been incorporated into the Erasmus+ programme. These programmes came to an end on 31 December 2013. However, the ongoing projects (in the case of Erasmus Mundus this includes the selection of students for scholarships) will continue until the end of the respective grant period. As of 1 January 2014, calls for proposals are issued under the Erasmus+ programme.[392]

As set out in recital 8 of the preamble to the Erasmus+ Regulation, the Erasmus+ programme

> should include a strong international dimension, particularly as regards higher education, in order not only to enhance the quality of European higher education in pursuit of the broader ET 2020 objectives and the attractiveness of the Union as a study destination, but also to promote understanding between people and to contribute to the sustainable development of higher education in partner countries, as well as their broader socio-economic development, inter alia by stimulating "brain circulation" through mobility actions with partner-country nationals.

Partner countries neighbouring the EU consist of the Eastern Partnership countries (Armenia, Azerbaijan, Belarus, Georgia, Moldova, Ukraine), the Southern Mediterranean countries (Algeria, Egypt, Israel, Jordan, Lebanon, Libya, Morocco, Palestine, Syria, Tunisia), the Western Balkans (Albania, Bosnia and Herzegovina, Kosovo, Montenegro, Serbia) and the Russian Federation. Moreover, any country

---

389 European Commission, Erasmus+ Programme Guide, 2014, p. 10.

390 The former Yugoslav Republic of Macedonia joins Erasmus+, http://ec.europa.eu/programmes/erasmus-plus/news/2014/20140610-erasmus_en.htm.

391 Turkey latest country to join Erasmus+, http://ec.europa.eu/programmes/erasmus-plus/news/2014/20140620_en.htm.

392 Cf. http://eacea.ec.europa.eu.

of the world may take part in some of the programme actions.[393] Furthermore, Switzerland, which, subject to the conclusion of a bilateral agreement, was supposed to be a non-EU programme country, currently participates as a partner country.

According to Article 1(4) of the Erasmus+ Regulation, "[t]he Programme shall include an international dimension aimed at supporting the Union's external action, including its development objectives, through cooperation between the Union and partner countries." The general objectives of the Erasmus+ programme include "the sustainable development of partner countries in the field of higher education" and "the promotion of European values in accordance with Article 2 of the Treaty on European Union" (Article 4(c) and (f) of the Erasmus+ Regulation). Pursuant to Article 5(1)(d) of the Erasmus+ Regulation, the Erasmus+ programme aims

> to enhance the international dimension of education and training, in particular through cooperation between Union and partner-country institutions in the field of VET and in higher education, by increasing the attractiveness of European higher education institutions and supporting the Union's external action, including its development objectives, through the promotion of mobility and cooperation between the Union and partner-country higher education institutions and targeted capacity-building in partner countries[.]

The participation of partner countries is subject to limitations. However, they may participate in all of the three key actions.[394] In the higher education field, the following actions are open to partner countries:

- **International credit mobility of individuals and Joint Master Degrees** (under Key Action 1) promoting the mobility of learners and staff from and to Partner Countries;
- **Capacity Building** projects in higher education (under Key Action 2) promoting cooperation and partnerships that have an impact on the modernisation and internationalisation of higher education institutions and systems in Partner Countries, with a special focus on Partner Countries neighbouring the EU;
- Support to **policy dialogue** (under Key Action 3) through the network of Higher Education Reform Experts in Partner Countries neighbouring the EU, the international alumni association, policy dialogue with partner countries and international attractiveness and promotion events;

393 Cf. European Commission, Erasmus+ Programme Guide, 2014, p. 24.
394 Cf. p. 66.

- **Jean Monnet** activities with the aim of stimulating teaching, research and reflection in the field of European Union studies worldwide.[395]

In the youth field, the following actions are open to partner countries:

- **Mobility for young people and youth workers** (under Key Action 1) promoting Youth Exchanges, European Voluntary Service and mobility of youth workers in cooperation with Partner Countries neighbouring the EU;
- **Capacity Building** projects in the youth field (under Key Action 2) promoting cooperation and mobility activities that have a positive impact on the qualitative development of youth work, youth policies and youth systems as well as on the recognition of non-formal education in Partner Countries, notably in African, Caribbean and Pacific (ACP), Asian and Latin American countries;
- Involvement of young people and youth organisations from Partner Countries neighbouring the EU in the youth **Structured Dialogue** (under Key Action 3) through their participation in international meetings, conferences and events that promote dialogue between young people and decision-makers.[396]

Moreover, institutions and/or organisations from partner countries may also participate in strategic (education, training and youth) or collaborative partnerships (sport),[397] knowledge and sector skills alliances ("partnerships between the world of work and education and training institutions", cf. Article 8(1)(b) of the Erasmus+ Regulation). This cooperation is, however, reduced to institutions and/or organisations that bring "an added value to the project."[398]

5.4.5 Excursus on the Transatlantic Cooperation Programmes

The EU-Canada Programme and the EU-US Atlantis Programme were both cooperation programmes in the field of education and vocational training. The EU-Canada Programme consisted of the Transatlantic Exchange Partnership (TEP) and the Transatlantic Degree Partnership (TDP), funding joint study and training programmes. The focus was on the development of curricula (including double/joint degrees), student exchanges with provision for credit recognition, faculty exchanges and international internships. The EU-US Atlantis Programme supported the cooperation of HEIs regarding the improvement of educational

395 European Commission, Erasmus+ Programme Guide, 2014, p. 12.

396 Ibid.

397 Also cf. pp. 240 et seq.

398 European Commission, Erasmus+ Programme Guide, 2014, p. 12.

services, the comparison and modernisation of curricula and the development of joint study programmes with full recognition of credits and qualifications.[399]

Due to Canadian and US budget cuts, both bilateral cooperation programmes have been put on hold. In order for the EU to financially contribute to projects, Canada and the US need to provide matching funding. The EU-US Atlantis Call for Proposals EACEA/36/10 published on 5 January 2011[400] and later amended by a corrigendum published on 7 April 2011[401] (cf. formal cancellation notice in the OJ)[402], and the EU-Canada Call for Proposals EACEA/37/10 published on 30 November 2010,[403] were both cancelled in 2011. With these cancellations having taken place, all calls for proposals were cancelled until 2013. Both the EU-Canada Cooperation Programme and the EU-US Atlantis Programme were last renewed for the programming period of 2007–2013. It remains to be seen what the future holds. Technically, the renewal of the transatlantic cooperation programmes would be possible if comparable funding is provided. The Erasmus+ Regulation has led to an end of the fragmentation of the international programmes (cf. recitals 2 and 8 of the preamble of the Erasmus+ Regulation). Higher education cooperation with Canada and/or the US would thus run via Erasmus+.

5.5 The Demarcation between Articles 165 and 166 TFEU

Right after the implementation of the Maastricht Treaty, discussion ensued about the demarcation between education and vocational training. There was never any doubt about general education being covered by Article 165 TFEU alone. It was the fact that the existing acquis had covered higher education (at least partially) by Article 128 TEEC that led to confusion. Article 128 TEEC was basically split up (i.e. higher education was explicitly added to Article 165 TFEU) "to refine the distinction between vocational training and education",[404] leading to the term "vocational training" losing its original broader meaning. With Article 165 TFEU

399 http://eacea.ec.europa.eu/bilateral_cooperation/eu_canada/index_en.php and http://eacea.ec.europa.eu/bilateral_cooperation/eu_us/index_en.php.

400 Cf. OJ C 2, 5.1.2011, pp. 2–4.

401 Cf. OJ C 108, 7.4.2011, p. 26.

402 Cf. Cancellation of the EU-US Atlantis Call for Proposals EACEA/36/10, OJ C 142, 13.5.2011, p. 29.

403 Cf. OJ C 323, 30.11.2010, pp. 20–22.

404 Cf. Stalford, H., Transferability of Qualifications and EU Migrant Children, in: J. Shaw (ed.), Social Law and Policy in an Evolving European Union, Hart Publishing: Oxford, 2000, pp. 243–258, p. 251.

(or back then ex Article 126 TEC) in place, the Union was finally able to pursue an education policy without having to take a detour via vocational training.[405] With the "need to dissemble" lost, Union action can be based on a firmer legal footing.[406] This is a substantive improvement as it allows legislation in the field to provide the necessary clarity of standards. Since the Maastricht Treaty, two schools of thought have evolved: One arguing that there is a lex generalis/lex specialis relationship between Articles 165 and 166 TFEU with Article 166 TFEU constituting a lex specialis with respect to Article 165 TFEU,[407] the other one believing that the introduction of a separate provision on education reinforces the boundaries between education and vocational training.[408]

The heading "Education, Vocational Training, Youth and Sport" of Title XII of Part Three of the TFEU might suggest that there are several provisions dealing with each of the fields addressed. This is, however, not the case. Whereas youth is part of Articles 165 and 166 TFEU (cf. the fifth indent of Article 165(2) TFEU as well as the third indent of Article 166(2) TFEU, where it receives special mentioning), sport is covered by the ultimate indent of Article 165(2) TFEU. Article 165 TFEU refers to general education including higher education, while Article 166 TFEU is concerned with initial and continuing vocational training and retraining. Compared to Article 166 TFEU, the wording of Article 165 TFEU is more general. Article 165(1) TFEU features the Union's commitment to contribute to "quality education". Applying to "all forms of education, irrespective of their relevance from the point of view of access to the labour market or to an occupation", it has become a leitmotif for education and vocational training.[409] The development of a European dimension, the key objective of Article 165 TFEU, applies to education and vocational training alike.[410] Article 165 TFEU is thus far

---

405 Cf. Lenaerts, 1994, p. 26.

406 Cf. Field, J., European Dimensions: Education, Training and the European Union, Higher Education Policy Series 39, Jessica Kingsley: London, 1998, p. 62; Gori, 2001, p. 97.

407 Cf. Hilpold, 1995, p. 122; Mächtle, 2010, p. 70; Lenaerts, 1994, pp. 26 et seq.; Niedobitek, Artikel 166 AEUV, 2012, recital 5; Vedder, C., Artikel 166 AEUV, in: C. Vedder and W. Heintschel von Heinegg (eds.), Europäisches Unionsrecht, Nomos: Baden-Baden, 2012, pp. 703–705, recital 1.

408 Cf. Field, 1998, p. 62.

409 Cf. Lenaerts, 1994, p. 27.

410 Also cf. the Commission's Action Plan for skills and mobility, Communication from the Commission to the Council, the European Parliament, the Economic and Social Committee and the Committee of the Regions, COM(2002) 72 final, 13.2.2002, p. 8.

more extensive than its counterpart, foreshadowing a lex generalis/lex specialis relationship.

The task to precisely define the boundaries between education and vocational training is a challenging one. It is also more of a gedankenexperiment found in German literature, stemming from the distinction between education and training in the German-speaking countries. Of course, the semantics of a legal term is bound to differ within the Member States. It is not unusual for denotation to vary, depending on whether it is used within Union law or national law.[411] Non-German speakers may want to compare the German Treaty version of the TFEU with the English or the French one. In German the terms used by Title XII are "allgemeine und berufliche Bildung", whereas it is "education and vocational training" in English and "éducation et formation professionelle" in French. This subtle difference may well account for confusion as Article 165 TFEU in contrast to Title XII does not use the term "allgemeine Bildung" but "Bildung" only. Furthermore, Austria and Germany feature a "dual system" of vocational training, meaning that an apprentice receives work-based training in a company while at the same time attending part-time vocational school. While general education and higher education are covered by Article 165 TFEU, dual vocational training programmes fall under Article 166 TFEU.[412] Consequently, Article 166 TFEU also comprises dual study programmes (i.e. a combination of work-based training and study at HEIs).

Until the entry into force of the Amsterdam Treaty in 1999, different decision-making procedures applied for the respective articles.[413] Furthermore, the CoR did not have to be consulted regarding vocational training measures. With the worlds of education and work converging and the same decision-making procedure (i.e. QMV) applying in both Articles 165 and 166 TFEU, the demarcation discussion has become less significant.[414] In practice, large-scale proposals are based on Articles 165 and 166 TFEU.[415] Ex Article 149 TEC was seldom used as the sole legal basis and so far no measures based on Article 165 TFEU alone have been adopted.[416] A joint legal basis combining Articles 165(4) and 166(4) TFEU

411 Also cf. Niedobitek, Artikel 165 AEUV, 2012, recital 37.

412 Cf. Hilpold, 1995, p. 122.

413 Cf. p. 52.

414 Also cf. Hablitzel, 2002, p. 409; Rechberger-Bechter, C., Europäische Gemeinschaft in der Bildungspolitik: Zuständigkeiten und Handlungsmöglichkeiten, Nomos: Wien, 2008, p. 73.

415 Cf. Rechberger-Bechter, 2008, p. 71.

416 Cf. Niedobitek, Artikel 165 AEUV, 2012, recital 63.

has been chosen for the Erasmus+ Regulation.[417] Moreover, the ECJ has yet to come up with a definition of education and vocational training for the post-*Gravier* era. It is questionable whether this is ever going to happen, however. Recital 10 of the preamble of the Erasmus+ Regulation stresses that the programme "should create synergies and foster cross-sectoral cooperation across the various [...] sectors", making a demarcation between Articles 165 and 166 TFEU practically redundant. Since the entry into force of the Lisbon Treaty, both Articles feature a reference to the ordinary legislative procedure. Thus, (incentive) measures according to Articles 165(4) and 166(4) TFEU may only be adopted using the binding legal instruments listed in Article 288 TFEU. Further alignment was achieved by adding Council recommendations to the field of vocational training.

Due to the broad scope of Article 165 TFEU and the specific one of Article 166 TFEU, it stands to reason that the maxim of lex specialis derogat legi generali applies. The assumption that the introduction of separate provisions severs the relationship between education and training is not convincing, particularly as Articles 165 and 166 TFEU share almost the same structure and similar objectives. So far, the ECJ has not adapted its jurisdiction and still reiterates its pre-Maastricht views. The TFEU does not define vocational education, however, the second indent of Article 165(2) TFEU speaks volumes. It is unfortunate that the discrepancy between ECJ jurisprudence and the current Treaty version has not yet been resolved. As indicated earlier, it is unlikely that the ECJ will ever raise the issue. On the other hand, defining higher education as vocational training does not have any consequences for students that have a case pending because they are facing discrimination related to their studies. Quite the contrary, this can be an advantage for those who are currently or were employed at the time.

417 Cf. Erasmus+ Regulation.

6. A Right to Education – The Fundamental Rights based Approach/The Legal Perspective

> Education has the potential to unlock the door to equality and participation[;] it constitutes the basis necessary for empowerment of each individual, and for the promotion of all human rights.[418]

6.1 Fundamental Rights Protection in the EU

It was not until the Maastricht Treaty that fundamental rights were formally recognised in EU primary law (cf. ex Article F(2) TEU). Although the TEEC did not include any reference to fundamental rights and it took some time for the "first distinct contours" of an EU constitutional framework for fundamental rights protection to emerge,[419] the ECJ has always been vocal about its commitment to protect fundamental rights stating that

> [i]n fact, respect for fundamental rights forms an integral part of the general principles of law protected by the ECJ. The protection of such rights, whilst inspired by the constitutional traditions common to Member States, must be ensured within the framework of the structure and objectives of the Community.[420]

In 1977, the EP, the Council and the Commission issued a joint declaration declaring their commitment "to the protection of fundamental rights, as derived in particular from the constitutions of the Member States and the European Convention for the Protection of Human Rights and Fundamental Freedoms."[421] Although the declaration was no more than an affirmation of little practical effect, it was nonetheless of symbolic significance, for the institutions indicated their willingness to respect fundamental rights when exercising their powers.[422]

---

418 http://www.ua.ac.be/main.aspx?c=.ELA&n=63187.

419 Cf. De Búrca, G., The Evolution of EU Human Rights Law, in: P. Craig and G. de Búrca (eds.), The Evolution of EU Law, 2nd ed., OUP: Oxford, 2011, pp. 465–497, p. 480.

420 Case C-11/70 *Internationale Handelsgesellschaft mbH v Einfuhr und Vorratsstelle für Getreide und Futtermittel* [1970] ECR 1125, para 4.

421 Cf. Joint Declaration by the European Parliament, the Council and the Commission, OJ C 103, 27.4.1977, p. 1.

422 Cf. De Búrca, 2011, p. 479.

Fundamental rights were first mentioned in primary law in recital three of the preamble to the 1987 SEA expressing the Community's determination

> to promote democracy on the basis of the fundamental rights recognized in the constitutions and laws of the Member States, in the Convention for the Protection of Human Rights and Fundamental Freedoms and the European Social Charter, notably freedom, equality and social justice[.]

1989 saw the adoption of the Community Charter of Fundamental Social Rights for Workers by all the Member States except the UK (also cf. Article 151 TFEU). Nonetheless, the entrenchment of human rights and fundamental freedoms as guaranteed by the European Convention for the Protection of Human Rights and Fundamental Freedoms (ECHR) in the TEU was a revolutionary milestone for EU fundamental rights protection. While the subsequently adopted Amsterdam Treaty represented a "decisive step on the way to an ever clearer recognition of the principle of fundamental rights protection",[423] it did not introduce a bill of rights but stuck to the system of references.

In 1999, the Cologne European Council took the view that the fundamental rights relevant at the EU level should be consolidated to make them more visible.[424] What followed was the solemn declaration of the CFREU at the Nice European Council. On behalf of their institutions, the presidents of the Commission, the Council and the EP adopted and promulgated the CFREU on 7 December 2000. However, the CFREU was not incorporated into the Nice Treaty. Published in the C series of the OJ, it was not of binding effect and remained a political declaration.[425] While it took some time until the ECJ first referred to the CFREU,[426] the European judiciary in the form of the AGs and the General Court led the way.[427] The EP and the Commission emphasised their compliance

423 Cf. European Commission, Affirming Fundamental Rights in the European Union: Time to Act, Report of the Expert Group on Fundamental Rights, Office for Official Publications of the European Communities: Luxembourg, 1999, pp. 9 et seq.

424 Cf. Cologne European Council, Presidency Conclusions, 3 and 4 June 1999, Document 150/99 REV 1, para 44 and Annex IV European Council Decision on the Drawing up of a Charter of Fundamental Rights of the European Union.

425 Cf. Charter of Fundamental Rights of the European Union, OJ C 364, 18 December 2000, pp. 1–22.

426 Cf. Case C-540/03 *European Parliament v Council* [2006] ECR 5769, para 38.

427 Cf. Anderson, D. and C. Murphy, The Charter of Fundamental Rights: History and Prospects in Post-Lisbon Europe, EUI LAW Working Papers, 2011, p. 2.

with the rights and principles contained in the CFREU.[428] With the entry into force of the Lisbon Treaty, the CFREU has finally been accorded legally binding status. The incorporation of the Charter of Fundamental Rights, albeit only with the help of a cross reference (cf. subpara 1 of Article 6(1) TEU) and in a slightly revised version,[429] put an end to the "praetorian jurisprudence" of the ECJ.[430] Whereas the protection of fundamental rights has always been one of the basic tenets of EU law, the CFREU – now codified and of binding effect – takes them to a whole new level.

6.2 Fundamental Rights Protection in EU Primary Law Post-Lisbon

The TEU includes several references to the protection of fundamental rights. These are found in the preamble and under Title I on common provisions, whereby Article 6 TEU constitutes the main provision in this regard. In the preamble to the TEU the Member States confirm their "respect for human rights and fundamental freedoms" (fourth recital) and their "attachment to fundamental social rights" (fifth recital). Article 2 TEU emphasises that "the Union is founded on the values of [...] respect for human rights, including the rights of persons belonging to minorities", values that are common to the Member States. Respect and commitment to promote such values is therefore conditio sine qua non for the accession to the EU (cf. Article 49, para 1 TEU). It is the Union's aim to promote its values (cf. Article 3(1) TEU) and to "combat social exclusion and discrimination, and [...] promote social justice and protection, equality between women and men, solidarity between generations and protection of the rights of the child" (Article 3(3) TEU). Article 7 TEU acts as a "monitoring mechanism" for fundamental rights violations (cf. para 1, "clear risk of a serious breach") by the Member States.[431] Article 6 TEU makes up "the core of human rights protection and

428 Cf. Towara, C. Das Rechts auf Bildung gemaß Art. 14 der Charta der Grundrechte der EU, in: Odendahl, K. (ed.), Europäische (Bildungs-)Union?, 2011, NWV: Wien/ BWV: Berlin, pp. 75–106, pp. 77 et seq.

429 Cf. Charter of Fundamental Rights of the European Union, OJ C 303, 14 December 2007, pp. 1–16.

430 Cf. Kollonay-Lehoczky, C., Lörcher, K. and I. Schömann, The Lisbon Treaty and the Charter of Fundamental Rights of the European Union, in: N. Bruun, K. Lörcher, and I. Schömann (eds.), The Lisbon Treaty and Social Europe, Hart Publishing: Oxford, 2012, pp. 61–105, pp. 62 et seq.

431 Cf. De Búrca, 2011, p. 484.

its multilevel system" within the framework of the Treaties.[432] Sporting the same numbering since the Amsterdam Treaty (Article 6 TEU, Article F(2) TEU in the Maastricht Version), it has been substantively amended following its introduction into primary law.

Article 6(3) TEU reads that the "[f]undamental rights, as guaranteed by the European Convention for the Protection of Human Rights and Fundamental Freedoms and as they result from the constitutional traditions common to the Member States, shall constitute general principles of the Union's law." It is essentially identical with ex Article F(2) TEU (Maastricht Version) and ex Article 6(2) TEU. The Lisbon Treaty provides for the Union's accession to the ECHR (Article 6(2) TEU). Article 2 of Protocol (No 8) relating to Article 6(2) of the Treaty on European Union on the Accession of the Union to the European Convention on the Protection of Human Rights and Fundamental Freedoms stipulates that accession to the ECHR shall affect neither the Union's competences or its institutions powers' nor the situation of its Member States in relation to the ECHR (e.g. reservations entered).

The accession of the EU to the ECHR has been discussed for well over 40 years. The Court of Justice of the European Union (CJEU)[433] regularly refers to the ECHR and the European Court of Human Rights (ECtHR). However, the fundamental rights enshrined in the ECHR are not legally binding on the CJEU or the other Union institutions. On the other hand, they do apply to the Member States, all of which are parties to the ECHR, "even when the latter are applying or implementing EU law."[434] Upon accession of the EU to the ECHR, legal acts of the Union will thus not only be measured by Union law itself but be subject to the jurisdiction of the ECtHR. Some have therefore suspected that it was "the institutional implication which would submit the Court of Justice, like its constitutional brethren in the Member States, to scrutiny by the Strasbourg Court" that has delayed the Union's accession to the ECHR for such a long time.[435]

432 Kollonay-Lehoczky, Lörcher, and Schömann, 2012, p. 70.

433 The CJEU includes the ECJ, the General Court and specialised courts (Article 19(1) TEU).

434 Cf. Accession by the European Union to the European Convention on Human Rights: Answers to Frequently Asked Questions, 30 April 2013, http://www.coe.int/t/dghl/standardsetting/hrpolicy/accession/Accession_documents/EU_accession-QA_updated_2013_E.pdf.

435 Cf. Weiler, J. and S. Fries, A Human Rights Policy for the European Community and Union: The Question of Competences, in: P. Alston, M. Bustelo and J. Heenan (eds.), The EU and Human Rights, OUP: Oxford, 1999, pp. 147–165, p. 150.

Notwithstanding that the Member States of the Union are parties to the ECHR, the accession of the EU has proven difficult. Both the EU and the CoE had to establish conditions allowing for such a move. In 1996, the ECJ ruled in Opinion 2/94 that the accession (of the Community) to the ECHR would lead to

> a substantial change in the present Community system for the protection of human rights in that it would entail the entry of the Community into a distinct international institutional system as well as integration of all the provisions of the Convention into the Community legal order.[436]

At the time there was "[n]o Treaty provision confer[ring] on the Community institutions any general power to enact rules on human rights or to conclude international conventions in this field."[437] The ECJ thus held that due to its "constitutional significance" an accession would go beyond the scope of the flexibility clause (cf. ex Article 235 TEC (Maastricht Version); now, after amendment, Article 352 TFEU). Therefore, the only way to accede to the ECHR was "by way of Treaty amendment."[438]

Under the Lisbon Treaty, the EU has been vested with legal personality (cf. Article 47 TEU). Article 6(2), first sentence of the TEU empowers the Union to accede to the ECHR. However, as the wording "[t]he Union shall accede to" suggests, the accession is also mandatory. Consequently, the Union – in order to comply with said Article – has to take the necessary steps allowing for the accession to the ECHR. According to Article 218(6)(a)(ii) TFEU, the Council may only "adopt the decision concluding the agreement" to accede to the ECHR after the EP has given its consent. The Council further has to act unanimously and the decision can only enter into force after the Member States have approved it "in accordance with their respective constitutional requirements" (Article 218(8) subpara 2 TFEU). Therefore, the Member States are equally bound by the obligation of Article 6(2), first sentence of the TEU. Member States that fail to fulfil this obligation under the Treaties could therefore be facing infringement proceedings (cf. Articles 258 et seq.). Also, Member States or institutions of the EU could bring actions against EU institutions failing to act in accordance with said Article (cf. Article 265 TFEU).[439]

---

436 Opinion 2/94 *Accession by the Community to the European Convention for the Protection of Human Rights and Fundamental Freedoms* [1996] ECR 1763, para 34.

437 Ibid. para 27.

438 Ibid. para 35.

439 Cf. Obwexer, W., Der Beitritt der EU zur EMRK: Rechtsgrundlagen, Rechtsfragen und Rechsfolgen, EuR, 2012, pp. 115–148, pp. 116 et seq.

Preparatory measures also needed to be taken on the side of the CoE. Protocol No. 14 to the ECHR had been open for signature since 13 May 2004 and entered into force on 1 June 2010. Article 17 of the Protocol amends Article 59 of the ECHR. A new para 2 has been inserted, stipulating that the EU may accede to the ECHR. However, at the time of drafting, it was not possible to enter into negotiations let alone conclude an agreement with the EU in this regard due to its lack of competence. The fact that no reference to a possible accession treaty could be made in Protocol No. 14 necessitated a second ratification procedure.[440] Whereas it was not clear whether this would take the form of a new amending protocol or an accession treaty when the Explanatory Report was compiled, the latter will now be the case. Prior to the Council adopting the decision authorising the signature to the accession agreement after having obtained the EP's consent, the ECJ will be asked for its opinion on the draft agreement's compatibility with the Treaties (cf. Article 218(11) TFEU). As Article 1(1) of the draft Accession Agreement provides, the EU will accede to the ECHR as well as to its Protocols No. 1 and 6.[441] Owing to the necessary signature and ratification by all of the 47 States Parties, it will take several years for the accession to complete.[442]

The most important change regarding the TEU's fundamental rights provisions can be found in Article 6(1) subpara 1 TEU. According to said Article, "[t]he Union recognises the rights, freedoms and principles set out in the Charter of Fundamental Rights" and gives legal effect (i.e. "the same legal value as the Treaties") to it. Although the first-ever codified bill of rights of the EU is not an integral part of the Treaties, it is binding on all of the Member States except the UK and Poland which chose an opt-out.[443] Fundamental rights as listed in the CFREU are not just considered general principles of EU law. Following the

---

440 Cf. Explanatory Report to Protocol No. 14 to the Convention for the Protection of Human Rights and Fundamental Freedoms, amending the control system of the Convention (2004) CETS No. 194, paras 101 et seq.

441 Cf. Fifth Negotiation Meeting Between the CDDH AD HOC Negotiation Group and the European Commission on the Accession of the European Union to the European Convention on Human Rights, Final Report to the CDDH, 47+1(2013)008rev2, Strasbourg, 10 June 2013, http://www.coe.int/t/dghl/standardsetting/hrpolicy/accession/Meeting_reports/47_1(2013)008rev2_EN.pdf.

442 Cf. Accession by the European Union to the European Convention on Human Rights: Answers to Frequently Asked Questions, 30 April 2013, http://www.coe.int/t/dghl/standardsetting/hrpolicy/accession/Accession_documents/EU_accession-QA_updated_2013_E.pdf.

443 Cf. Protocol No. 30 to the Lisbon Treaty on the Application of the Charter of Fundamental Rights of the European Union to Poland and to the United Kingdom.

adoption of the Lisbon Treaty, they are part of EU primary law. This goes to show that the Union attaches greater importance to fundamental rights protection than ever before. Union policy used to be "beset by a paradox" in this regard. Whereas the EU was "a staunch defender of human rights" in its internal and external dimension, it lacked "a coherent policy at either level".[444] The virtually non-existent human rights policy in the not too distant past is history. Fundamental rights now feature in the Union's "constitutional self-understanding" as well as its "international self-representation."[445]

According to Article 6(1) subpara 2 TEU, "[t]he provisions of the Charter shall not extend in any way the competences of the Union as defined in the Treaties." The Charter itself confirms this with an even more in-depth provision stating that it "does not extend the field of application of Union law beyond the powers of the Union or establish any new power or task for the Union, or modify powers and tasks as defined in the Treaties" (Article 51(2) CFREU). The principle of conferral (cf. Article 5(2) TEU) is also addressed by the second sentence of Article 51(1) CFREU, which states that when applying the Charter "the limits of the powers of the Union as conferred on it in the Treaties" must be respected. The first sentence of Article 51(1) CFREU stipulates that the Union shall act "with due regard for the principle of subsidiarity" (cf. Article 5(3) TEU). The principle of subsidiarity is further referred to in recital 5 of the preamble to the CFREU. The principle of proportionality (cf. Article 5(4) TEU) is referred to in Article 52(1) CFREU which ensures that "[a]ny limitation on the exercise of the rights and freedoms recognised by this Charter must be provided for by law and respect the essence of those rights and freedoms." Limitations may only be made if necessary and if they "genuinely meet objectives of general interest recognised by the Union or the need to protect the rights and freedoms of others." Hence, the application of the Charter as well as the interpretation of the rights and principles set out therein require compliance with the principle of conferred powers as well as the principles of subsidiarity and proportionality.

Pursuant to the first sentence of Article 51(1) CFREU, the Charter applies to the Union's institutions, bodies, offices and agencies, i.e. "all the authorities set up by the Treaties or by secondary legislation".[446] Concerning the Member

444 Cf. Alston, P. and J. Weiler, An 'Ever Closer Union' in Need of a Human Rights Policy: The European Union and Human Rights, in: P. Alston, M. Bustelo and J. Heenan (eds.), The EU and Human Rights, OUP: Oxford, 1999, pp. 3–66, p. 6.

445 Cf. De Búrca, 2011, pp. 465 and 495.

446 Cf. Explanations relating to the Charter of Fundamental Rights, OJ C 303, 14 December 2007, pp. 17–35, p. 32.

States, the Charter only applies "when they are implementing Union law." Unfortunately, the explanations relating to the CFREU, although drawn up in order to provide guidance for the CJEU and the courts of the Member States (cf. Article 52(7) CFREU), do not go into too much detail. While they do explain the rationale behind the provision, i.e. that it follows from the case law of the ECJ "that the requirement to respect fundamental rights defined in the context of the Union is only binding on the Member States when they act in the scope of Union law", the explanations do not explore the issue any further. Lenaerts distinguishes between two types of Union law implementation: firstly, "EU obligations that require a member state to take action" (e.g. transposing a directive into national law) and secondly, "EU obligations that must be complied with when a member state derogates from EU law" (e.g. the derogation from the fundamental freedoms of the internal market, cf. the ERT case[447], for example).[448] However, according to the ECJ, "implementing Union law" may also involve the adoption of "national measures which aim to apply a normative scheme put in place by the EU legislator".[449] While it is clear that the Charter only applies to Member States when there is a connection to Union law, it is ultimately up to the ECJ to provide for an interpretation until further notice.[450] With regard to the term "Member States", the explanations relating to the CFREU do, however, clarify that it is to be interpreted broadly, i.e. that it includes "the central authorities as well as [...] regional or local bodies, and [...] public organisations".[451] The first sentence of Article 51(1) CFREU refers to public parties only. Consequently, "unlike general principles of EU law [...] the provisions of the Charter do not apply in a private dispute."[452] This is also confirmed by AG Trstenjak who stated that owing to the latter provision, "the Charter does not create justiciable rights as between private individuals."[453] The fact remains that the creation of the CFREU was "an exercise

---

447 Cf. Case C-260/89 *ERT v DEP* [1991] ECR 2925.

448 Lenaerts, K., Exploring the Limits of the EU Charter of Fundamental Rights, 8 ECLR, 2012, pp. 375–403, p. 378.

449 Ibid. p. 379.

450 Cf. Lenaerts, K., Die EU-Grundrechtecharta: Anwendbarkeit und Auslegung, EuR, 2012, pp. 3–17, p. 4.

451 Explanations relating to the Charter of Fundamental Rights, p. 32.

452 Lenaerts, K., Exploring the Limits of the EU Charter of Fundamental Rights, 2012, p. 377 at fn. 11.

453 Opinion of Advocate General Trstenjak, delivered on 22 September 2011, Case C-411/10 *N. S. v Secretary of State for the Home Department* [2011] ECR 13905, para 173.

in consciousness-raising", drawing the attention of citizens to the Union's commitment to the protection of rights.[454]

6.3 A Fundamental Right to Education: The Legal Implications of Article 14 CFREU

Except for the UK which does not have a codified constitution (instead cf. the Human Rights Act 1998, which incorporated Article 2 of the First Protocol to the ECHR into UK law, as well as the Education and Skills Act 2008 and the Education Act 2011), all of the Union's Member States have provided for a right to education in constitutional law.[455] The right to education comprises various aspects:

> [i]t has been variously classified as an economic right, a social right and a cultural right. It is all of these. It is also, in many ways, a civil right and a political right, since it is central to the full and effective realization of those rights as well. In this respect, the right to education epitomizes the indivisibility and interdependence of all human rights.[456]

---

454 Wallace, C. and J. Shaw, Education, Multiculturalism and the Charter of Fundamental Rights of the European Union, in: T. Hervey and J. Kenner (eds.), Economic and Social Rights under the EU Charter of Fundamental Rights – A Legal Perspective, Hart Publishing: Oxford, 2003, pp. 223–246, p. 234.

455 Austria (Articles 17, 17a and 18 of the Austrian Basic Law (Staatsgrundgesetz)), Belgium (Article 24 of the Constitution), Bulgaria (Articles 23 and 53 of the Constitution), Croatia (Articles 63, 64, 66, 67, 68 and 69 of the Constitution), Cyprus (Article 20 of the Constitution), Czech Republic (Articles 16, 26 and 33 of the Charter of Fundamental Rights and Freedoms), Denmark (Section 76 of the Constitution (Danmarks Riges Grundlov)), Estonia (Article 37 of the Constitution), Finland (Section 16 of the Constitution), France (Section 13 of the Preamble to the Constitution), Germany (Articles 6 and 7 of the German Basic Law (Grundgesetz)), Greece (Article 16 of the Constitution), Hungary (Article XI of the Fundamental Law), Ireland (Article 42 of the Constitution (Bunreacht na hÉireann)), Italy (Articles 30, 33 and 34 of the Constitution), Latvia (Article 112 of the Constitution), Lithuania (Articles 40, 41 and 42 of the Constitution), Luxembourg (Article 23 of the Constitution), Malta (Articles 2, 10, 11, 12 and 17 of the Constitution), the Netherlands (Article 23 of the Constitution), Poland (Article 70 of the Constitution), Portugal (Articles 43, 73, 74, 75, 76 and 77 of the Constitution), Romania (Article 32 of the Constitution), Slovakia (Article 42 of the Constitution), Slovenia (Articles 54, 57 and 58 of the Constitution), Spain (Article 27 of the Constitution), Sweden (Section 2 of Chapter 1 and Section 18 of Chapter 2 of the Instrument of Government (Regeringsformen)).

456 Committee on Economic, Social and Cultural Rights, General Comment 11 on the plans of action for primary education (Twentieth session, 1999), UN Doc. E/C.12/1999/4 (1999), para 2.

An "empowerment right", the right to education is key – indispensable so to say – for the realisation of other fundamental rights.[457] It is enshrined in many international and regional human rights instruments such as Article 26 of the Universal Declaration of Human Rights (UDHR), Article 13 of the International Covenant for Economic, Social and Cultural Rights (ICESCR), Articles 28 and 29 of the Convention on the Rights of the Child (CRC) which are international as well as in Article 2 of the First Protocol to the ECHR, Article 17 of the revised European Social Charter (ESC) (also cf. Articles 9 and 10 thereof on the right to vocational guidance and training as well as Articles 9 and 10 of the 1961 ESC which is still in place for ten Contracting Parties which have not yet ratified the revised version)[458] or Article 14 of the CFREU which are regional.

The definition of the term "education" varies and "may be construed in a wide or narrow sense."[459] Article 1(a) of the UNESCO *Recommendation concerning Education for International Understanding, Co-operation and Peace and Education relating to Human Rights and Fundamental Freedoms* refers to education as "the entire process of social life by means of which individuals and social groups learn to develop consciously within, and for the benefit of, the national and international communities, the whole of their personal capacities, attitudes, aptitudes and knowledge." However, international human rights instruments (or in the case of the EU regional ones) usually refer to education in a narrow sense, i.e. formal institutional instruction at the national or regional level.[460] In General Comment No. 13 on the right to education (also cf. Art. 13 of the ICESCR), the Committee on Economic, Social and Cultural rights adopted four features, i.e. the 4 A's: Availability, Accessibility, Acceptability and Adaptability, which the

457 Cf. Committee on Economic, Social and Cultural Rights, General Comment 13 on the right to education (Twenty-first session, 1999), UN Doc. E/C.12/1999/10 (1999), para 1.

458 The 1996 revised ESC came into force in 1999. It is now gradually replacing the initial 1961 treaty and has so far been ratified by 33 Member States of the CoE: Albania, Andorra, Armenia, Austria, Azerbaijan, Belgium, Bosnia and Herzegovina, Bulgaria, Cyprus, Estonia, Finland, France, Georgia, Hungary, Ireland, Italy, Latvia, Lithuania, Malta, Moldova, Montenegro, the Netherlands, Norway, Portugal, Romania, Russia, Serbia, Slovakia, Slovenia, Sweden, "the former Yugoslav Republic of Macedonia", Turkey and Ukraine. The 1961 ESC is still in place for Croatia, the Czech Republic, Denmark, Germany, Greece, Iceland, Luxembourg, Poland, Spain and the UK.

459 Hodgson, D., International Protection of the Right to Education, Max Planck Encyclopedia of Public International Law, Max Planck Institute for Comparative Public Law and International Law: Heidelberg and OUP, 2013, recital 1.

460 Ibid.

right to (receive an) education exhibits. Initially developed by former UN Special Rapporteur on the Right to Education, Katarina Tomaševski,[461] it means that a sufficient number of educational institutions and programmes need to be available and accessible to all (i.e. no discrimination or insurmountable economic hurdles). The content of teaching (i.e. curricula and teaching methods) has to be acceptable and adaptable to changing societies and students' needs in diverse settings.[462]

6.3.1 Article 14 CFREU and (Inter)related EU Law – A Pot Pourri of Provisions

Following the entry into force of the Lisbon Treaty, the right to education as set out in Article 14 CFREU has become an integral part of EU law. A "hybrid provision", Article 14 CFREU draws on existing provisions such as the constitutions of the Member States as well as other human rights instruments.[463] However, when applying the CFREU the Union must comply with the principle of conferred powers (cf. Article 5(2) TFEU) and may not extend or modify the Union's competences as specified in the TFEU (cf. Article 51(2) CFREU). According to Articles 165 and 166 TFEU, the Union holds supporting competence in matters relating to education and vocational training. The Union has no say in the content of teaching and the organisation of education systems as well as the organisation of vocational training. Furthermore, harmonisation of national education laws and regulations is explicitly excluded. It is of no surprise that the Union's education provisions (to which Article 14 CFREU adds) have been described as "a slightly odd little *pot pourri*."[464] Moreover, the Charter contains other provisions related to education such as Article 10(1) CFREU (freedom of thought, conscience and religion), Article 13 CFREU (freedom of the arts and sciences), Article 15 CFREU (freedom to choose an occupation and right to engage in work), Article 16 CFREU (freedom to conduct a business), Article 21 CFREU

461 Cf. Tomaševski, K., Human Rights Obligations: Making Education Available, Accessible, Acceptable and Adaptable, Right to Education Primers No. 3, Novum Grafiska: Gothenburg, 2001.

462 Cf. Committee on Economic, Social and Cultural Rights, General Comment 13 on the right to education (Twenty-first session, 1999), UN Doc. E/C.12/1999/10 (1999), para 6.

463 Cf. Mentick, D. and F. Goudappel, The Education Provision in the Charter of Fundamental Rights of the European Union: A Bleak Perspective, 4 European Journal for Education Law and Policy, 2000, pp. 145–148, p. 145.

464 Cf. Wallace and Shaw, 2003, p. 223.

(non-discrimination), Article 22 CFREU (cultural, religious and linguistic diversity), Article 32 CFREU (prohibition of child labour and protection of young people at work), Article 34(2) CFREU (social security and social assistance) or Article 45 CFREU (freedom of movement and of residence).

Article 14 CFREU includes different aspects of the right to education. Para 1 stipulates that "[e]veryone has the right to education and to have access to vocational and continuing training." Besides the explicit recognition of the right to education for all, the provision extends to access to initial and continuing vocational training. Thus, para 1 creates a link to Articles 165 and 166 TFEU as well as Articles 7(3) and 10 of Regulation 492/2011 on freedom of movement for workers within the Union. In this context, it is also noteworthy to point out the connection to Articles 7(1)(c), 11(2), 12(3), 16(3) and 24(2) of Directive 2004/38 on the right of citizens of the Union and their family members to move and reside freely within the territory of the Member States. Para 2 lays down the principle of free compulsory education. Unlike paras 1 and 3, it does not link to other provisions of EU law. Para 3 provides for "[t]he freedom to found educational establishments with due respect for democratic principles" as well as "the right of parents to ensure the education and teaching of their children in conformity with their religious, philosophical and pedagogical convictions". This provision connects to Article 10(1) CFREU on the right to freedom of thought, conscience and religion which includes freedom "to manifest religion or belief [...] in teaching".

6.3.2 Rights, Freedoms or Principles?

The CFREU contains rights, freedoms and principles (cf. Article 6(1) TEU or the ultimate recital of the preamble to the CFREU). As can be seen from Article 14 CFREU, provisions may involve several of these categories. "Freedoms" are set out as a separate category. Nevertheless, "in practice they fall under either "rights" or "principles"."[465] Title II of the CFREU comprises a list of "freedoms". However, like Article 14 CFREU on the right to education, most of the articles listed under Title II are headed rights or refer to the respective freedoms as rights. Others such as Article 13 CFREU on the freedom of the arts and sciences are not referred to as rights in the text of the Charter. Although the explanations relating to the CFREU refer to Article 13 CFREU as a right, it is unclear whether this provision involves a right or a principle.[466] The explanations relating to the

465 House of Lords, European Union Committee, The Treaty of Lisbon: An Impact Assessment, Vol. I: Report, recital 5.16.

466 Cf. Kaczorowska, A., European Union Law, Routledge: Abingdon, 2013, p. 227.

CFREU acknowledge that articles may contain elements of rights and principles.[467] Unfortunately, the CFREU and its explanations do not always clearly differentiate and may be opaque. With obscurity on where to draw the line, it will be up to the ECJ to work out the distinction in this respect.[468]

Pursuant to Article 51(1) CFREU, rights shall be respected while principles shall be observed and the application thereof promoted. Article 52(5) CFREU stipulates that Charter provisions containing principles may be implemented through legislative and executive acts of the Union as well as through acts of the Member States "implementing Union law". According to it, principles "shall be judicially cognisable only in the interpretation of such acts and in the ruling on their legality." Therefore, they do not "give rise to direct claims for positive action by the Union's institutions or Member States authorities." Consistent with ECJ case law, the approach towards "principles" can also be found in the constitutional systems of the Member States.[469] All in all, it is probably best to describe rights as "something which an individual perhaps potentially can rely on and may be justiciable", whereas principles are "guidance to the legislator, not capable of justiciability".[470] Thus, rights are directly enforceable in the courts. Principles, on the other hand, are justiciable only if they have been implemented as laid down in Article 52(5) CFREU.

6.3.3 The Sources of Article 14 CFREU

Article 14 CFREU on the right to education is based on, in particular, the common constitutional traditions of the Member States as well as Article 2 of the First Protocol to the ECHR.[471]

All of the Member States of the Union have enshrined a right to education in their constitutions in one way or the other, the sole exception being the UK which has a constitutional system different from continental Europe, Ireland or Malta. The UK has a partly written constitution which is not codified and large parts thereof are parliamentary statute law. In the UK Parliament may pass statutes (acts) which cannot be overruled by the courts. However, Parliament has

---

467 Cf. Explanations relating to the Charter of Fundamental Rights, p. 35.
468 Cf. House of Lords, European Union Committee, The Treaty of Lisbon: An Impact Assessment, Vol. I: Report, recital 5.22.
469 Explanations relating to the Charter of Fundamental Rights, p. 35.
470 House of Lords, European Union Committee, The Treaty of Lisbon: An Impact Assessment, Vol. II: Evidence, The Stationery Office Limited: London, 2008, Q289 on p. E60.
471 Cf. Explanations relating to the Charter of Fundamental Rights, p. 22.

also passed laws which limit its own sovereignty such as the Human Rights Act 1998 that incorporated the ECHR and – most importantly – Article 2 of its First Protocol on the right to education into UK law.[472] The Human Rights Act 1998 provides "a degree of constitutional protection" as judges may issue a "declaration of incompatibility" if they consider domestic primary legislation to be incompatible with the ECHR.[473] An accumulation of education acts passed in Parliament is concerned with the right to education and its various manifestations (cf. the Education and Skills Act 2008 or the Education Act 2011).

The other 27 Member States have provided for a right to education in different forms. Whereas it is considered a freedom right for the most part, it has also been constructed as an equality right (e.g. recital 13 to the preamble to the French Constitution of 27 October 1946: "La Nation garantit l'égal accès [...] à l'instruction [et] à la formation professionnelle".).[474] Hence, the right to education may be formulated as a civil and political "first generation" right (liberté) or as an economic, social and cultural "second generation" right (égalité). While civil and political rights are directly enforceable, economic, social and cultural rights are not enforceable until implemented.[475] Apart from different classifications, the constitutional provisions vary in length. The constitutions of some Member States contain quite elaborate provisions (e.g. Article 16 of the Greek constitution), whereas others are short and basic. According to Article 6(2) of the German Basic Law (Grundgesetz), it is the parents' duty to provide for their children's care and upbringing. The performance of such duty is controlled by the German State.

Not all of the constitutions of the Member States cover every aspect of Article 14 CFREU. Free compulsory education as laid down in Article 14(2) CFREU is provided for in Article 24(3) of the Belgian constitution, for example. Other Member States guarantee free primary education (cf. Section 76 of the Danish Constitution (Danmarks Riges Grundlov), Article 42(4) of the Constitution of Ireland (Bunreacht na hÉireann) or Article 23, first sentence, of the Constitution of Luxembourg), whereas Article 16(4) of the Greek Constitution provides that education at State educational institutions is free for Greeks at all levels.

---

472 Cf. http://www.parliament.uk/about/how/sovereignty.

473 Harris, N., Equal Rights in Education in the UK (England), 4 IJELP, 2008, pp. 4–15.

474 Cf. Bernsdorff, N., Charta Artikel 14 Recht auf Bildung, in: Meyer, J. (ed.), Charta der Grundrechte der Europäischen Union, 3rd ed., 2010, recital 2.

475 Cf. Weston, BH, Human Rights, Encyclopædia Britannica Online, last updated 20.3.2014, http://www.britannica.com/EBchecked/topic/275840/human-rights; Gori, 2001, p. 316.

The parental right to ensure that education and teaching are in conformity with their religious convictions is expressed in Article 7(2) of the German Basic Law (Grundgesetz) which stipulates "die Erziehungsberechtigten haben das Recht, über die Teilnahme des Kindes am Religionsunterricht zu bestimmen." Article 42(1) of the Constitution of Ireland (Bunreacht na hÉireann) guarantees "the inalienable right […] of parents to provide […] for the religious and moral […] education of their children." Article 24(1) of the Belgian constitution is very similar to Article 14(3) CFREU as it guarantees inter alia « le respect des conceptions philosophiques, idéologiques ou religieuses des parents ».

The interpretation rule laid down in Article 52(4) CFREU provides that "[i]n so far as this Charter recognises fundamental rights as they result from the constitutional traditions common to the Member States, those rights shall be interpreted in harmony with those traditions." Hence, when consulting the constitutional provisions of the Member States, it is not about finding the "lowest common denominator". Instead, "the Charter rights concerned should be interpreted in a way offering a high standard of protection which is adequate for the law of the Union and in harmony with the common constitutional traditions."[476]

Article 2 of the First Protocol to the ECHR provides that

> no person shall be denied the right to education. In the exercise of any functions which it assumes in relation to education and to teaching, the State shall respect the right of parents to ensure such education and teaching in conformity with their own religious and philosophical convictions.

According to Article 52(3) CFREU, rights contained in the Charter that correspond to rights guaranteed by the ECHR shall have the same meaning and scope as those laid down in the ECHR. The same goes for the protocols to the ECHR. The ECHR only constitutes a minimum standard. Therefore, the Charter provisions may well go beyond the scope of the provisions contained in the ECHR and its protocols by providing for more extensive protection. This is the case with Article 14 CFREU. Whereas Article 14 CFREU uses a positive formulation (i.e. "[e]veryone has"), Article 2 of the First Protocol to the ECHR "is the only regional or international human rights provision to adopt a negative […] formulation of the right to education in the sense that the High contracting parties must not take steps to interfere with the right to education" (i.e. "no person shall be denied").[477] Owing to its negative formulation, the ECtHR held that said provision does not require the Contracting Parties to the ECHR to "establish at

476 Explanations relating to the Charter of Fundamental Rights, p. 34.

477 Cf. Hodgson, 2013, recital 13.

their own expense, or to subsidise, education of any particular type or at any particular level". Instead it constitutes "a right of access to educational institutions existing at a given time". However, the ECtHR explained that all Member States of the CoE possess "a general and official educational system" and that it was therefore not necessary to require the Contracting Parties to the ECHR to set up such a system.[478] Nevertheless, Article 2 of the Protocol to the ECHR is understood to contain an obligation incumbent on each Contracting Party to ensure that "a minimum of educational establishments" is available as the right to education would be rendered meaningless otherwise.[479]

Unlike the ECHR, which applies to everyone under the jurisdiction of a Contracting State (i.e. nationals and non-nationals), the CFREU only comes into play in cross-border situations. Generally, only Union citizens may rely on the CFREU. However, under certain circumstances third-country nationals can also rely on Article 14 CFREU (cf. Directive 2004/38). Whereas the personal scope of the ECHR can be described as "static" in so far as that Article 2 of the first Protocol to the ECHR may only be invoked by those already under its jurisdiction, the CFREU allows for transnational mobility.[480] In fact, Article 14 CFREU presupposes a transnational dimension. According to literature, Union citizens may not base any claims against their home State on Article 14 CFREU.[481] However, there may well be a cross-border element in place if Union citizens have exercised their right to freedom of movement (cf. *Prinz and Seeberger*[482] and *Elrick*[483]). Future requests for preliminary rulings before the ECJ may therefore well include actions brought by nationals of the Member States concerned and based on Article 14 CFREU.

---

478 Cf. Case "Relating to Certain Aspects of the Laws on the Use of Languages in Education in Belgium" v Belgium (Merits) [1968] 1 EHRR 252.

479 Wagner, V., Article 14 – Right to Education, in: EU Network of Independent Experts on Fundamental Rights, Commentary of the Charter of Fundamental Rights of the European Union, 2006, pp. 141–148, p. 142.

480 Also cf. Gori, G., Article 14, in: S. Peers, T. Hervey and J. Kenner, The EU Charter of Fundamental Rights: A Commentary, Hart Publishing: Oxford, 2014, pp. 401–422, recitals 30 et seq.

481 Cf. Wagner, 2006, p. 144.

482 Joined Cases C-523/11 and C-585/11 *Laurence Prinz v Region Hannover and Philipp Seeberger v Studentenwerk Heidelberg*, Judgment of the Court of Justice (Third Chamber) of 18 July 2013, nyr.

483 Case C-275/12 *Samantha Elrick v Bezirksregierung Köln*, Judgment of the Court of Justice (Third Chamber) of 24 October 2013, nyr.

Article 14 CFREU further draws on the Social Charters of the Union and the CoE (cf. recital 5 of the preamble to the CFREU as well as recital 5 of the preamble to the TEU confirming the attachment to fundamental social rights). Point 15 of the Community Charter of the Fundamental Social Rights of Workers stipulates that "[e]very worker of the [EU] must be able to have access to vocational training and to receive such training throughout his working life." Articles 9 and 10 of the (revised) ESC ensure the right to vocational guidance and training (also cf. Articles 9 and 10 of the 1961 ESC). According to Article 9 of the (revised) ESC, the Contracting Parties

> undertake to provide or promote [...] a service which will assist all persons [...] to solve problems related to occupational choice and progress, with due regard to the individual's characteristics and their relation to occupational opportunity: this assistance should be available free of charge, both to young persons, including schoolchildren, and to adults.

Article 10(1) of the (revised) ESC provides that the Contracting Parties undertake "to provide or promote [...] vocational training of all persons [...] and to grant facilities for access to higher technical and university education, based solely on individual aptitude." Article 10(5) of the revised ESC (Article 10(4) of the 1961 ESC) adds that the Contracting Parties should take measures such as to: (a) reduce or abolish fees or charges, (b) grant financial assistance if necessary, (c) allow for supplementary training requested by the employer during normal working hours and (d) ensure supervision of young workers in order to provide for training efficiency and protection. There is no length of residence requirement for students and trainees "residing in any capacity, or having authority to reside in reason of their ties with persons lawfully residing, on the territory of the Party concerned before starting training." This is not the case for students and trainees who do not possess such ties and "entered the territory with the sole purpose of attending training."[484] According to Article 20(b) of the revised ESC, the Contracting Parties are to recognise the right to equal opportunities and equal

484 Cf. Council of Europe, European Committee of Social Rights: Conclusions 2012, France, p. 19 (not yet published in the Volumes of Conclusions, text may be subject to editorial revision), http://www.coe.int/t/dghl/monitoring/socialcharter/conclusions/State/France2012_en.pdf. The Committee has repeatedly (cf. European Social Charter (revised), European Committee of Social Rights, Conclusions 2008 – Volume 1 (Albania, Andorra, Armenia, Azerbaijan, Belgium, Bulgaria, Cyprus, Estonia, Finland, France, Georgia, Ireland, Italy), Council of Europe Publishing: Strasbourg, 2008, p. 325) found France not to be in conformity with the ESC owing to indirect discrimination regarding "access to scholarships granted on the basis of social criteria for higher education."

treatment in matters of employment and occupation without discrimination on the grounds of sex regarding vocational guidance, training and retraining (the 1961 ESC does not provide for such protection; Article 20(b) of the revised ESC corresponds to Article 1(1) of the 1988 Additional Protocol to the ESC).

The 1961 ESC does not contain a general right to education. However, Article 17(1)(a) of the revised ESC on the right of children and young persons to social, legal and economic protection imposes an obligation on Contracting Parties "to ensure that children and young persons [...] have [...] the education and the training they need, in particular by providing for the establishment or maintenance of institutions and services sufficient and adequate for this purpose". Pursuant to Article 17(2) of the revised ESC, the Contracting Parties are to provide free primary and secondary education as well as encourage regular school attendance. While this applies to public education, children and young persons do not have a right to access private educational establishments for free.[485] The appendix to Article 17 explains that the provision's scope includes "all persons below the age of 18 years, unless under the law applicable to the child majority is attained earlier, without prejudice to the other specific provisions provided by the Charter". Therefore, the Contracting Parties are not obliged to provide compulsory education until the age of 18 years but rather must provide it in accordance with national law.

In fact, the reason that compulsory education is not mentioned in Article 17(2) of the revised ESC is that the duration of compulsory education varies from State to State.[486] Nevertheless, the European Committee of Social Rights, which decides on the conformity of national law and practice with the provisions of the ESC, thinks it best to provide for "a reasonable period" of compulsory education and coordinate it with the minimum age for admission to employment. According to the Secretariat of the ESC, the Charter's education and training provisions guarantee "an accessible and effective primary and secondary education and vocational training system, as well [as] equal access to higher education."[487] Moreover, as regards protection of persons with disabilities, the ESC in its revised version specifically obliges Contracting Parties to take

485 Cf. Explanatory Report to the revised European Social Charter (1996) CETS 163, para 73.

486 Ibid. para 74.

487 Council of Europe, The Right to Education under the European Social Charter: Information Document prepared by the Secretariat of the ESC, 17 November 2006, https://www.coe.int/t/dghl/monitoring/socialcharter/Theme%20factsheets/FactsheetEducation_en.pdf.

measures in order to provide for "guidance, education and vocational training in the framework of general schemes wherever possible or, where this is not possible, through specialised bodies, public or private" (cf. Article 15(1) of the revised ESC).

Besides the common constitutional traditions of the Member States, the Community Charter of the Fundamental Social Rights of Workers and the human rights instruments of the CoE, Article 14 CFREU further draws on the rights deriving from the international obligations common to the Member States (e.g. Article 26 of the UDHR, Article 13 of the ICESCR or Articles 28 and 29 of the CRC) as well as ECJ and ECtHR case law (cf. recital 5 of the preamble to the CFREU).

The UDHR, the ICESCR and the CRC are all UN Treaties. Article 13 of the ICESCR contains the most wide-ranging provision on the right to education.[488] Article 13(1) ICESCR determines the objective of education to be "the full development of the human personality and the sense of its dignity, and [the strengthening of] the respect for human rights and fundamental freedoms." However, international human rights instruments tend to have broader provisions than regional ones.[489] Pursuant to Article 26(1) UDHR, Article 13(2)(a) ICESCR and Article 28(1)(a) CRC, primary education shall be free and compulsory. Article 26(1) UDHR, Article 13(2)(b) and (c) ICESCR and Article 28(1)(b) and (c) CRC stipulate that secondary education (in all its forms, i.e. including vocational training) and higher education shall be equally accessible, whereby access to higher education is determined on the basis of capacity. According to Article 13(2)(b) and (c) ICESCR, free education shall be progressively introduced at all levels. Article 26(1) UDHR reads "[e]ducation shall be free, at least in the elementary and fundamental stages", implying that free education beyond primary education would be desirable. Article 28(1)(b) CRC goes further by putting an obligation on the States Parties to introduce free education at secondary level.

According to Article 13(3) ICESCR, the States Parties are obliged to respect the parents' liberty to "ensure the religious and moral education of their children in conformity with their own convictions." Article 26(3) UDHR similarly provides that "[p]arents have a prior right to choose the kind of education that

488 Cf. Hüfner, K., The Human Rights Approach to Education in International Organisations, 46 European Journal of Education, 2011, pp. 117–126, p. 126.

489 Cf. Wallace and Shaw, 2003, p. 235.

shall be given to their children." Article 13(4) ICESCR and Article 29(2) CRC stipulate that

> [n]o part of [Article 13 ICESCR or Articles 28 and 29 CRC] shall be construed so as to interfere with the liberty of individuals and bodies to establish and direct educational institutions, subject always to the observance of the principles set forth in paragraph 1 [...] and to the requirement that the education given in such institutions shall conform to such minimum standards as may be laid down by the State.

The second sentence of Article 18(1) CRC further provides that "[p]arents [...] have the primary responsibility for the upbringing and development of the child." The third sentence of Article 18(1) CRC stresses that "[t]he best interests of the child will be their basic concern." Thus, States Parties are obliged to "respect the rights and duties of the parents [...] to provide direction to the child" (Article 14(2) CRC).

Article 2 of the first Protocol to the ECHR partly corresponds to Article 14 CFREU. In accordance with Article 52(3) CFREU, the corresponding parts have the same meaning and scope as Article 2 of the first Protocol to the ECHR. Limitations to Article 14 CFREU "must comply with the same standards as are fixed by the detailed limitation arrangements laid down in the ECHR" and "the level of protection afforded by the Charter may never be lower than that guaranteed by the ECHR." Moreover, the meaning and scope of Article 2 of the first Protocol to the ECHR are not only determined by its wording but by the relevant ECtHR and ECJ case law.[490]

To a large extent, the development of education policy traces back to ECJ case law. From the early 1980s onwards, the ECJ has had to bring the free movement of workers in line with the principle of non-discrimination on grounds of nationality. Since the Maastricht Treaty, non-economically active Union citizens have benefitted from free movement rights. Students who move to another Member State to pursue their education are able to invoke Articles 18 and 21 TFEU. If they have lived in the host Member State for a sufficient number of years, they may even claim maintenance grants and loans.[491] Third-country nationals are able to base their right of residence on the Union citizenship of their children who are in education. Owing to constant development, the case law of the ECJ is a living source of law. Consequently, the same goes for ECtHR case

490 Cf. Explanations relating to the Charter of Fundamental Rights, p. 33.

491 Cf. Case C-209/03 *The Queen, on the application of Dany Bidar v London Borough of Ealing and Secretary of State for Education and Skills* [2005] ECR 2119.

law. It is therefore save to say that case law is one of the most important sources as regards Article 14 CFREU.

6.3.4 Article 14(1) CFREU: The Right to Education and to Access to Vocational and Continuing Training

Pursuant to Article 14(1) CFREU, the right to education comprises positive obligations incumbent on the Member States. Although the explanations relating to the CFREU conclude that Article 14(1) CFREU corresponds to Article 2 of the first Protocol to the ECHR as regards to meaning,[492] this is much too sweeping a statement. The wording of Article 14(1) CFREU suggests that Member States are obliged "to not only refrain from interfering with the [right to] education, but to facilitate it through positive action."[493] Article 14(2) CFREU also points towards such an interpretation, stipulating that the right to education "includes the possibility to receive free compulsory education." "[P]hrased as a mere subset" of Article 14(1) CFREU,[494] Article 14(2) CFREU adds to the latter's substance. Thus, one could reason that Article 14(1) CFREU presupposes that Member States provide for educational establishments. However, the responsibility of the Member States as regards content and organisation of education and vocational training is firmly rooted in para 1 of Articles 165 and 166 TFEU. The Union cannot adopt legally binding acts if they entail the harmonisation of the laws and regulations of the Member States in the area of education and vocational training (cf. para 4 of Articles 165 and 166 TFEU). Member States may therefore not be obliged to introduce changes to their education systems (e.g. to establish free compulsory education).

While the interpretation borne out by the wording of Article 14(1) CFREU clearly differs from Article 2 of the first Protocol to the ECHR, the meaning of the provisions is not so different after all. Both Article 14(1) CFREU and Article 2 of the first Protocol to the ECHR constitute a right of access to existing educational establishments.[495] Article 2 of the first Protocol to the ECHR requires a minimum of educational establishments to be available.[496] Hence, the same applies to Article 14(1) CFREU. The right to education presupposes that a

492 Cf. Explanations relating to the Charter of Fundamental Rights, p. 34.

493 Also cf. Wagner, 2006, p. 145.

494 Cf. Winkler, R., The Right to Education according to Article 14 of the Charter of Fundamental Rights, 1 IJELP, 2005, pp. 60–65, p. 64.

495 Cf. pp. 127 et seq.

496 Cf. pp. 129–130.

functioning education system is in place. The Member States of the Union must therefore not fall short of providing for a minimum of educational establishments.[497] Thus, the addition (i.e. the possibility of free compulsory education as stipulated by Article 14(2) CFREU) and the extension (i.e. widening the scope of Article 14(1) CFREU to vocational and continuing training), do in principle not lead to a derogation from the meaning of the right to education as provided for in Article 2 of the first Protocol to the ECHR. Consequently, the right to education according to Article 14(1) CFREU constitutes a primarily negative obligation,[498] guaranteeing equal access to existing educational establishments.

Compared to Article 2 of the first Protocol to the ECHR, the scope of Article 14(1) CFREU has been extended to cover access to vocational and continuing training.[499] Becoming the most competitive and dynamic knowledge-based economy lies at the heart of the EU 2020 Strategy. LLL is a part of EU education policy. A right of access to vocational and continuing training, which after all inspired a line of education-related jurisprudence of the Court, is thus more than justifiable. As has been pointed out before, the CFREU draws on Point 15 of the Community Charter of the Fundamental Social Rights of Workers as well as on Article 10 of the (revised) ESC. Contrary to Article 14(1) CFREU, however, the provisions on vocational training of the Social Charters specifically provide for retraining. Article 14(1) CFREU puts emphasis on the access to vocational and continuing training. Hence, it constitutes a right that is essentially weaker than the right to education.[500] Member States are not obliged to provide for vocational education to the same extent as for general education. After all, Article 14(1) CFREU constitutes nothing more than a "basic right of access to such training". The provision has thus been criticized as having the potentially fatal effect of excluding persons with little previous education or training as well as persons with disabilities.[501]

The right to education as enshrined in the CFREU applies to primary, secondary as well as tertiary education, thereby including access to initial and continuing vocational training. Although Article 14(1) CFREU does not specifically refer to higher education, it expressly comprises access to higher education by

497 Cf. Bernsdorff, 2010, recital 13; Frenz, W., Kommunikationsgrundrechte, in: W. Frenz, Handbuch Europarecht, Band 4: Europäische Grundrechte, Springer: Berlin, 2009, pp. 531–730, recital 2407.

498 Cf. Winkler, 2005, p. 62.

499 Also cf. Explanations relating to the Charter of Fundamental Rights, p. 34.

500 Cf. Frenz, 2009, recital 2424.

501 Cf. Wallace and Shaw, 2003, p. 236.

referring to vocational training. Article 10(1) of the (revised) ESC refers to access to higher education but restricts it to the individual aptitude of persons. Whereas the duration of compulsory education varies from Member State to Member State,[502] upper secondary education is not compulsory in most. Therefore, the right to upper secondary education is generally limited to a right to access as Member States are not required to provide for educational establishments outside of compulsory education. Education at upper secondary schools and HEIs may be subject to enrolment or tuition fees. Moreover, the number of available places can be limited. In accordance with EU law, the introduction of measures to limit the number of applicants in upper secondary and tertiary education (e.g. the *numerus clausus* in Germany) is legitimate as long as places are allocated in accordance with the right to equal treatment.[503]

6.3.5 Article 14(2) CFREU: The Principle of Free Compulsory Education

Article 14(2) CFREU introduces "the possibility to receive free compulsory education." A further expression of the right to education, it goes beyond the wording of Article 2 of the First Protocol to the ECHR. However, the explanations relating to the Charter provide that free compulsory education constitutes a principle.[504] According to Article 52(5) CFREU, principles "may be implemented" but there is no general obligation demanding their implementation.[505] After all, the Union has supporting competence in education and may only support, coordinate or supplement the actions of the Member States. The organisation of education systems is entirely up to the Member States. The competence of the Union is also referred to in the explanations stating that "[i]n so far as the Charter applies to the Union, this means that in its training policies the Union must respect free compulsory education, but this does not, of course, create new powers."[506] Therefore, the principle of free compulsory education "guides Union action, but does not require the Union to take action."[507] Free compulsory education is thus not justiciable except if the Member States have made provision for it in legislation.

502 Cf. pp. 138–139.
503 Also cf. Gori, 2014, recital 23.
504 Cf. Explanations relating to the Charter of Fundamental Rights, p. 22.
505 Also cf. Winkler, 2005, p. 64.
506 Explanations relating to the Charter of Fundamental Rights, p. 22.
507 Winkler, 2005, p. 64.

Some Member States provide for free compulsory education in their constitutions.[508] Union citizens can thus rely on the principles of free movement and non-discrimination on grounds of nationality in order to receive free compulsory education in another Member State. However, while the ECJ may hand down a ruling prohibiting discrimination on grounds of nationality to the effect that Union citizens moving to another Member State must be admitted to educational establishments on the same conditions as the nationals of that Member State, it cannot force a Member State to offer compulsory education for free.[509] It has been argued that it is possible that the ECJ "will interpret the freedom of movement of workers [...] in such a way as to impose an obligation on Member States to have free, elementary education facilities in place".[510] However, from a legal point of view this suggestion is questionable. According to Article 6(1) subpara 2 TEU and Article 51(2) CFREU, the provisions of the Charter do not extend the powers of the Union. Moreover, as outlined above, the explanations relating to the Charter reiterate that the principle of free compulsory education does not create new powers. According to Article 6(1) subpara 3 TEU and recital 5 of the preamble to the CFREU, the Charter is to be interpreted with "due regard to the explanations". Such a ruling would take the method of competence creep to the extreme. It would disregard the national responsibility for the content of teaching and the organisation of education systems, which is enshrined in Article 165(1) subpara 1 TFEU, and lead to the harmonisation of the national education laws and regulations.

Each Member State may implement the principle of free compulsory education into national law. However, this does not preclude private institutions from charging tuition fees. Each child may attend an educational establishment which is free of charge. Nevertheless, it is entirely up to the parents whether they want to avail of such an offer and send their child to a publicly funded school. Private institutions can implement tuition fees as they see fit. Provided that measures for financial compensation are in place, Article 14(2) CFREU does not prohibit tuition fees for State funded establishments offering "certain specific forms of education".[511] The explanations do not elaborate on this matter. This may include music lessons or other extracurricular activities like school trips. The concern of Article 14(2) CFREU is to ensure that every child is able to receive compulsory education free of charge. However, the Member States have set different

508 Cf. p. 128.

509 Also cf. Wagner, 2006, pp. 146 et seq.

510 Ibid. p. 147.

511 Explanations relating to the Charter of Fundamental Rights, p. 22.

starting and ending ages for compulsory education. The duration of full-time compulsory education varies from eight years in Croatia to thirteen years in the Netherlands.[512] Thus, the principle of free compulsory education – if implemented – does not lead to Union-wide national legislation providing for free education of the same age group.

It remains to be questioned whether free compulsory education at State schools puts children of less well-off parents at a disadvantage. Equal opportunity may well be at risk if privately educated children receive better tuition. Moreover, social cohesion could be undermined. Often, private schools have an international orientation or use progressive teaching methods. Those who can afford it might therefore choose such an institution in order to make it easier for their child to embark upon a professional career. However, the CFREU does not provide for State support for children who attend privately owned and operated schools.[513] This should not deter Member States from creating educational equality. Every State spends part of its tax money to fund public education and everyone pays into the system regardless of whether they send their children to public or private schools. Allowing for free school choice, i.e. without tuition fees or an affordable top-up, would be a step towards a fairer school system. It would further lead to more competitiveness. If the money follows the student, public schools need to offer education which is at least as good as the education offered at private ones in order to be able to attract students.

Sweden, for example, uses an education voucher system. Introduced in the early 1990s, both public and "independent" schools are financed through the State. Although independent schools ("fristående skolor" in Swedish) are publicly funded, they are independently owned and operated. Essentially private schools, they may not top-up their budget with the help of tuition fees. Once approved by the Swedish National Agency for Education, they are fully financed through the local government receiving vouchers according to the number of students they attract. Consequently, the municipality budget will decline if the municipality's public schools are not sought after.[514] Swedish independent schools may "deviate from the national curriculum, but they must be open to all

512 Cf. European Commission, Eurydice – Facts and Figures: Compulsory Education in Europe 2013/14: http://eacea.ec.europa.eu/education/eurydice/documents/facts_and_figures/compulsory_education_EN.pdf.

513 Also cf. Frenz, 2009, recital 2438.

514 Cf. Böhlmark, A. and M. Lindahl, Independent Schools and Long-run Educational Outcomes – Evidence from Sweden's Large Scale Voucher Reform, CESifo Working Paper No. 3866, 2012, pp. 2 et seq.

students [and] are not allowed to select students by ability, socio-economic characteristics or ethnicity."[515] In case of oversubscription, selection may take place on the basis of proximity to the school, a waiting list and the prior enrolment of siblings. Except for three private schools (Gränna, Lundsberg and Sigtuna), which are not participating in the education voucher system, Sweden's schools are freely accessible.[516]

In 1992, Sweden's Minister of Education Per Unckel stated that "[e]ducation is so important that you can't just leave it to one producer. Because we know from monopoly systems that they do not fulfil all wishes."[517] The advantage of being able to attend independent schools regardless of wealth or place of residence – although the latter may act as an elimination criterion if schools are oversubscribed – has expanded the right to education. Education voucher systems have been criticized for contributing to segregation due to "a smaller share of students [interacting] with ethnically and socioeconomically diverse peers".[518] However, there is no indication that the Swedish education voucher system has undermined social cohesion. Shafiq and Myers attribute this to the design of the Swedish education voucher system and, in particular, to anti-discrimination regulations that were endorsed by the Swedish teachers' unions. They suggest that this probably had a minimising effect concerning "segregation by ability, ethnicity, and socioeconomic status", with the resulting student diversity likely to have "contributed to favorable civic attitudes".[519]

6.3.6 Article 14(3) CFREU: The Freedom to Found Educational Establishments and the Right of Parents to Ensure the Education and Teaching of Their Children in Conformity with Their Religious, Philosophical and Pedagogical Convictions

According to the explanations relating to the CFREU, Article 14(3) CFREU corresponds to the second sentence of Article 2 of the first Protocol to the ECHR as regards the rights of parents.[520] Article 2 of the first Protocol to the

515 Ibid. p. 7.

516 Ibid. pp. 7–8.

517 Cf. Shafiq, M. and J. Myers, Educational Vouchers and Social Cohesion: A Statistical Analysis of Student Civic Attitudes in Sweden, 1999–2009, American Journal of Education, forthcoming, p. 1, http://www.ncspe.org/publications_files/OP218.pdf.

518 Ibid p. 2.

519 Ibid. p. 22.

520 Cf. Explanations relating to the Charter of Fundamental Rights, p. 34.

ECHR ensures the right of parents that their children may receive an education in conformity with their religious and philosophical convictions. An "adjunct" of the fundamental right to education, it makes up for the discharge of the parents' natural duty which manifests itself in the responsibility for the upbringing of their children.[521] The CFREU broadens the scope of the right of parents by adding pedagogical convictions. However, it remains to be seen whether there actually is a difference between philosophical and pedagogical convictions. Pedagogical approaches (e.g. Montessori or Waldorf) are built on both a philosophy and the corresponding pedagogical methods. Pursuant to the explanations relating to the Charter, the right of parents must be interpreted in conjunction with Article 24 CFREU on the rights of the child.[522] According to Article 24(1) CFREU, "[c]hildren shall have the right to such protection and care as is necessary for their wellbeing." Article 24(2) CFREU stipulates that the primary consideration must be "the child's best interests".

The right of parents as enshrined in Article 14(3) CFREU, however, cannot be interpreted in such a way that Member States must provide for education in accordance with their religious, philosophical and pedagogical convictions. The said provision stipulates that such right shall be respected "in accordance with the national laws governing [its] exercise". Therefore, it is by no means "an absolute right for individuals to be educated wherever and however they want."[523] The ECtHR has held that the right of parents "to ensure [...] education and teaching in conformity with their own religious and philosophical convictions" does not prevent Contracting States "from imparting through teaching or education information or knowledge of a directly or indirectly religious or philosophical kind." Parents may not "object to the integration of such teaching or education in the school curriculum, for otherwise all institutionalised teaching would run the risk of proving impracticable." However, the Contracting States "must take care that information or knowledge included in the curriculum is conveyed in an objective, critical and pluralistic manner."[524] Whereas education and teaching may not be conducted in an indoctrinating manner, it is up to the parents whether they can and would like to shell out for an education which conforms to their religious, philosophical and pedagogical convictions.

521 Cf. Kjeldsen, Busk Madsen and Pedersen v Denmark [1976] 1 EHRR 711, para 52.

522 Cf. Explanations relating to the Charter of Fundamental Rights, p. 22.

523 House of Lords, European Union Committee, The Treaty of Lisbon: An Impact Assessment, Vol. I: Report, recital 5.51.

524 Kjeldsen, Busk Madsen and Pedersen v Denmark [1976] 1 EHRR 711, para 53.

Besides the right of parents laid out above, Article 14(3) CFREU guarantees the freedom to found educational establishments. It is certainly not by chance that the latter right and freedom are both to be found in Article 14(3) CFREU. Due to Member States not having to provide for an education which conforms to the parents' religious, philosophical and pedagogical convictions, parents who would like their child to go on to a faith-based school or take advantage of progressive education will have to send them to private educational establishments. According to Article 14(3) CFREU, anyone may found private educational establishments provided that they do so "with due respect for democratic principles" and "in accordance with the national laws governing the exercise of such freedom". The freedom to found private educational establishments constitutes an aspect of the freedom to conduct a business (cf. Article 16 CFREU).[525] However, compared to this lex generalis the freedom to found educational establishments is limited by the respect for democratic principles. The TFEU has enshrined the freedom to found educational establishments through two of the fundamental freedoms of the internal market, the freedom of establishment (cf. Article 49 TFEU) and the freedom to provide services (cf. Article 56 TFEU). According to Article 57 TFEU, only services "normally provided for remuneration" are services "within the meaning of the Treaties". In *Humbel and Edel* the ECJ held that this "characteristic is [...] absent in the case of courses provided under the national education system".[526] In the event that the State demands a "certain contribution to the operating expenses of the system" through enrolment or tuition fees, this does not affect the nature of the class or course.[527] Since private educational establishments mostly provide for fee-paying students (there may be scholarships available for the particularly gifted), they fall under the freedom to provide services.

6.3.7 Limitations to and Derogations from Article 14 CFREU

AG Colomer once pointed out that "[i]n education, several aspects combine to make up its essential core, such as teaching plans or the organisation of the system, which the national legislatures are responsible for defining, specifying and limiting, the institutions merely assuming roles providing guidance and

525 Cf. Explanations relating to the Charter of Fundamental Rights, p. 22.

526 Cf. C-263/86 *Belgian State v René Humbel and Marie-Thérèse Edel* [1988] ECR 5365, para 18.

527 Ibid. para 19.

incentive."[528] The question is, therefore, how far may national law deviate from Article 14 CFREU? According to Article 52(2) CFREU, "[r]ights recognised by this Charter for which provision is made in the Treaties shall be exercised under the conditions and within the limits defined by those Treaties." Articles 165 and 166 TFEU do not confer a right to education on individuals. Nevertheless, the right to education is a right provided for under the Treaties. Through the evolution of EU law, the right to education has been linked to the right to freedom of movement of Union citizens.[529] Thus, Article 14 CFREU falls under Article 52(2) CFREU.

Article 14 CFREU embodies the ECJ's case law on non-discriminatory access to education and vocational and continuing training and the right to freedom of movement. The ECJ has made it clear that every Union citizen is entitled to participation in education. In accordance with Union citizenship, the EU nationals "have the right to move and reside freely within the territory of the Member States subject to the limitations and conditions laid down in the Treaties and by the measures adopted to give them effect" (Article 21(1) TFEU). Article 18 TFEU prohibits discrimination on grounds of nationality. However, discrimination can be classified as direct or indirect. Direct discrimination occurs "where one person is treated less favourably than another is, has been or would be treated in a comparable situation on grounds of racial or ethnic origin" (Article 2(2)(a) of Directive 2000/43[530], hereinafter the "Race Equality Directive"). It is strictly forbidden and cannot be justifiable. Indirect discrimination occurs "where an apparently neutral provision, criterion or practice would put persons of a racial or ethnic origin at a particular disadvantage compared with other persons". However, indirect discrimination may be allowed if that "criterion or practice is objectively justified by a legitimate aim and the means of achieving that aim are appropriate and necessary" (Article 2(2)(b) of the Race Equality Directive).

Article 45(3) TFEU allows for limitations to the freedom of movement of workers "on grounds of public policy, public security or public health". This also applies to the freedom of establishment and the freedom to provide services (cf. Articles 52(1) and 62 TFEU). In addition, secondary law reiterates the limitations

528 Opinion of Advocate General Ruiz-Jarabo Colomer, delivered on 20 March 2007, Joined Cases C-11/06 and C-12/06 *Rhiannon Morgan v Bezirksregierung Köln and Iris Bucher v Landrat des Kreises Düren* [2007] ECR 9161, para 91.

529 Cf. Gori, 2014, recital 39.

530 Council Directive 2000/43/EC of 29 June 2000 implementing the principle of equal treatment between persons irrespective of racial or ethnic origin, OJ L 180, 19.7.2000, pp. 22–26.

laid down in primary law. The Citizens' Rights Directive stipulates that "Member States may restrict the freedom of movement and residence of Union citizens and their family members, irrespective of nationality, on grounds of public policy, public security or public health." Moreover, it adds that "[t]hese grounds shall not be invoked to serve economic ends" (Article 27(1) of the Citizens' Rights Directive). Of those express derogations, the one on grounds of public health has been rarely used.[531] However, it is this derogation, which has been accepted by the ECJ in education-related cases. The ECJ allows Member States to protect themselves against a large influx of students if the public health (system) is at risk. Austria and Belgium, the Member States most at risk of "free riders" who do not pay into their tax systems and therefore do not contribute towards the cost of their education because they reside elsewhere, have introduced quota systems. However, these only apply to applicants for medical and paramedical courses. The onus is on the Member States to show that the quota system is both appropriate and necessary. Austria and Belgium have until December 2016 to prove that the measures are in accordance with Union law.[532] Otherwise, the right to freedom of movement will apply without limitation.

Article 7(1)(c) of the Citizens' Rights Directive confers a right of residence for more than three months upon Union citizens if they

- are enrolled at a private or public establishment, accredited or financed by the host Member State on the basis of its legislation or administrative practice, for the principal purpose of following a course of study, including vocational training; and
- have comprehensive sickness insurance cover in the host Member State and assure the relevant national authority, by means of a declaration or by such equivalent means as they may choose, that they have sufficient resources for themselves and their family members not to become a burden on the social assistance system of the host Member State during their period of residence[.]

If Union citizens have been lawfully resident in the host Member State for a continuous period of five years, they acquire the right of permanent residence (cf. Article 16(1) of the Citizens' Rights Directive). In accordance with Union law, lawful residence is given if Union citizens fulfil the criteria listed in Article 7 of the Citizens' Rights Directive. Union citizens have a right to equal treatment in the host Member State. However, if they do not (yet) qualify for permanent residence, the host Member State neither has to grant them student grants nor

531 Cf. Shaw, J., Hunt, J. and C. Wallace, Economic and Social Law of the European Union, Palgrave Macmillan: Basingstoke, 2007, p. 296.

532 Cf. Austria and Belgium given more time to justify quotas, Press Release, 18 December 2012 (IP/12/1388).

student loans (cf. Article 24(2) of the Citizens' Rights Directive). This derogation does not apply to those who fall under Regulation 492/2011. If students are employed (this includes the service providers) or retain worker status or if they are the dependent children of a migrant worker, they qualify for student maintenance aid even if they have not been lawfully resident in the host Member State for a continuous period of five years (cf. Articles 7(2) and 10 of Regulation 492/2011). Article 7(3)(d) of the Citizens' Rights Directive stipulates that Union citizens, unless they are involuntarily unemployed, only retain the status of a worker if the vocational training is related to their previous employment. Hence, their right to student maintenance aid depends on their chosen course.

7. Main Trends in ECJ Case Law

Over two decades ago, the ECJ was criticized for being "an excessively activist judiciary".[533] However, owing to the framework nature of the TEEC, there was bound to be judicial activism. In fact, the Court was (and still is) supposed to find solutions for legal questions left open by Community/EU law.[534] Naturally, functional spillover is on the agenda. In order to meet the requirements of the internal market, the ECJ may take decisions which are not benefitting the Member State(s) concerned. In the education sector, this is the case with regard to access to study, student maintenance in form of student grants and loans or the right of residence for third-country nationals who act as the primary carer for Union citizens still in education. However, Member States that perceive a ruling as going too far are limited in terms of action. They may seek amendment of the Treaties. This in turn requires unanimity in the European Council as well as ratification by all the Member States (cf. Article 48 TEU). As De Waele poignantly puts it: "one lone dissenting voice is enough to uphold the unwanted judgment and the eventual undesired consequences thereof."[535]

While the ECJ has been referred to as "the main culprit" behind competence creep,[536] its contribution to shaping the EU of today must also be acknowledged. Indeed, the current EU education policy may well be described as the product of extensive Court rulings. The changes made to the TEEC by the Maastricht Treaty were at least partially caused by the judges in Luxembourg. Whereas the Commission considered a sound legal basis for education and vocational training important in order to further economic progress, the Member States wanted to prevent future interference with one of their core competences.[537] By the time the European Council met in Maastricht in December 1991, it was apparent that the ECJ was becoming overambitious. Since 1974, the ECJ had dealt with cases concerning education. It all started out with *Casagrande*, the son of a (deceased)

533 De Waele, H., The Role of the European Court of Justice in the Integration Process: A Contemporary and Normative Assessment, 6 HanseLR, 2010, pp. 3–26, p. 3.

534 Ibid. p. 9.

535 Ibid. p. 15.

536 Corrias, L., The Passivity of Law: Competence and Constitution in the European Court of Justice, Springer: Heidelberg, 2011, p. 13.

537 Also cf. Käsper, K., Free Movement of Students in the EU, in: T. Kerikmäe (ed.), Protecting Human Rights in the EU: Controversies and Challenges of the Charter of Fundamental Rights, Springer: Heidelberg, 2014, pp. 145–159, p. 151.

migrant worker.[538] With the Court's landmark *Gravier* ruling, it was clear that the impact on national law was potentially huge. Interpreting vocational training "extremely wide, wider than the phrase's meaning in everyday speech [...] and in technical use by education policy makers",[539] the ECJ drew a connection between tertiary education and vocational training. Admitting that the TEEC does not include both educational organisation and policy, the Court ruled that "access to and participation in courses of instruction and apprenticeship, in particular vocational training, are not unconnected with Community Law."[540] It is not surprising that the Member States sought to secure their powers through the codification of education upon realising how the Community's competence could be expanded with the help of case law.

Although the Maastricht Treaty was a quantum leap forward for the EU's education policy, it also had the agreeable side effect of consolidating the sovereignty of the Member States in the area. Until today, Article 165(1) TFEU guarantees that the responsibility of the Member States as regards the content of teaching and the organisation of education systems is respected at the EU level. The same goes for the content and organisation of vocational training (cf. Article 166(1) TFEU). The introduction of a legal basis for education was a turning point. However, the recognition of Union citizenship status represented a shift of equal importance. For an economically driven Community characterised by functionalist tendencies, the concept of Union citizenship must have seemed unusual.[541] Whereas the ECJ had to take recourse to the economically active (workers, the self-employed and service providers) in the pre-Maastricht era, Union citizenship was now "destined to be the fundamental status" of EU nationals.[542] At the beginning, it was not clear whether non-economically active Union citizens fell within the scope ratione personae of the provisions of the Treaty on Union citizenship,

---

538 Cf. p. 35.

539 Flynn, J., Gravier: Suite du Feuilleton, in: B. de Witte (ed.), European Community Law of Education, Nomos: Baden-Baden, 1989, pp. 95–112, p. 99.

540 Case C-293/83 *Gravier*, para 19.

541 Cf. Hilpold, P., Unionsbürgerschaft und Bildungsrechte oder: Der EuGH-Richter als "Künstler", in: GH Roth and P. Hilpold (eds.), Der EuGH und die Souveränität der Mitgliedsstaaten: eine kritische Analyse richterlicher Rechtssschöpfung auf ausgewählten Rechtsgebieten, Linde/Stämpfi/Boorberg: Wien/Bern/Stuttgart, 2008, pp. 11–53, p. 13.

542 Case C-184/99 *Rudy Grzelczyk v Centre public d'aide sociale d'Ottignies-Louvain-la-Neuve* [2001] ECR 6193, para 31.

which is a prerequisite for invoking the right to equal treatment.[543] In 1998, five years after the Maastricht Treaty entered into force, the ECJ ascertained that this was the case for "a national of a Member State lawfully residing in the territory of another Member State".[544] Thus, the concept of Union citizenship is proof that a legal norm, which was primarily assumed to be a postulate for legal reasoning, can transform EU law in a never before seen manner.[545] The explicit mentioning of "the right to move and reside freely within the territory of the Member States" in Article 21(1) TFEU adds to the free movement rights. Previously dependent on economic factors, this aspect is now of little relevance for Union citizens.[546]

The invocation of the right to free movement of persons is no longer restricted to economically active Union citizens and their dependants. Students no longer need to prove that they fall under the free movement of workers as enshrined in Article 45 TFEU (although undoubtedly a number of students will do so or accrue worker status during their studies), the freedom of establishment (cf. Article 49 TFEU) or the freedom to provide services (cf. Article 56 TFEU). Instead, they may simply rely on Article 18 TFEU which states that "[w]ithin the scope of application of the Treaties [...] any discrimination on grounds of nationality shall be prohibited." The principle of non-discrimination on grounds of nationality is the centrepiece of the Treaties. In *Grzelczyk* the Court held that "Article 6 [now Article 18 TFEU] must be read in conjunction with the provisions of the Treaty concerning citizenship of the Union in order to determine its sphere of application."[547] Hence, there is a correlation between the concept of Union citizenship and the principle of non-discrimination on grounds of nationality, i.e. the right to equal treatment. This link has become even more evident since the Lisbon Treaty integrated both concepts into Part Two of the TFEU headed "Non-discrimination and Citizenship of the Union". It is therefore not surprising that the right to equal treatment and the right to free movement have been referred to as the "twin principles".[548]

543 Cf. Guild, E., Peers, S. and J. Tomkin, The EU Citizenship Directive: A Commentary, OUP: Oxford, 2014, p. 224.

544 Case C-85/96 *María Martínez Sala v Freistaat Bayern* [1998] ECR 2691, para 61.

545 Cf. Hilpold, P., Unterhaltsstipendien für Unionsbürger – Die Rechtssache "Förster" und die Grenzen mitgliedstaatlicher Solidarität, EuZW, 2009, pp. 40–43, p. 41.

546 Cf. Hilpold, P., Unionsbürgerschaft und Sprachenrechte in der EU, 122 JBl, 2000, pp. 93–101, p. 97.

547 Case C-184/99 *Grzelczyk*, para 30.

548 O'Leary, 2011, p. 499.

A natural extension of the principle of non-discrimination on grounds of nationality, Union citizenship status represents a metamorphosis from a market-driven community to a community that is primarily oriented towards, safeguards and fosters individual rights.[549] As AG Mazák put it, "the concept of Union citizenship [...] marks a process of emancipation of Community rights from their economic paradigm."[550] Whereas the principle of non-discrimination on grounds of nationality is essentially formulated as a negative obligation, the concept of Union citizenship comprises a positive, rather than negative obligation.[551] Like the right to equal treatment, the rights deriving from Union citizenship are residual.[552] Therefore, the ECJ examines any other possible rights such as the right to free movement of workers before elaborating on the status of Union citizenship. Essentially, the right to free movement and residence for Union citizens is weaker than other rights under the Treaties. Economic ties are still useful. With regard to education, those covered by Regulation 492/2011 are able to invoke the most extensive rights. Students who are or have been employed in the host Member State (provided that they retain worker status) or who are still dependent on their parents that are or have been employed in the host Member State, are entitled to equal treatment with regard to maintenance aid via Regulation 492/2011. However, there is no doubt that the concept of Union citizenship has revolutionised EU law.

A new era has dawned for Union citizens and for students in particular. Since the ratification of the Maastricht Treaty, the line of ECJ jurisprudence linked to education has evolved. The free movement rights have seen an extension to the non-economically active, making them eligible for social benefits. In the past, the Court differentiated between Union citizens who had already been in an employment relationship in the Member State concerned (provided that there was "a link between the previous occupational activity and the studies in question"[553]) and those who had not. The right to equal treatment only applied with regard

549 Cf. Hilpold, P. Nichtdiskriminierung und Unionsbürgerschaft, in: M. Niedobitek (ed.), Europarecht – Politiken der Union, Walter de Gruyter: Berlin, 2014, pp. 1–96, recital 93.

550 Opinion of Advocate General Mazák, delivered on 10 July 2008, Case C-158/07 *Jacqueline Förster v Hoofddirectie van de Informatie Beheer Groep* [2008] ECR 8507, para 54.

551 Cf. Hilpold, 2014, recital 7.

552 Cf. Edward, D. and R. Lane, Edward and Lane on European Union Law, Edward Elgar: Cheltenham, 2013, recital 11.98.

553 Case C-39/86 *Sylvie Lair v Universität Hannover* [1998] ECR 3161, para 39.

to “assistance […] intended to cover registration and other fees, in particular tuition fees, charged for access to education that by virtue of the judgment in Gravier it falls, as relating to conditions of access to vocational training, within the scope of the EEC Treaty”.[554] Only those covered by Regulation 1612/68 were entitled to maintenance grants which constitute a social advantage in accordance with Article 7(2) of said Regulation.[555] However, the Court was obviously aware that future developments were to be expected when it held that

> at the present stage of development of Community law the first paragraph of Article 7 of the EEC Treaty [now Article 18 TFEU] applies to assistance for maintenance and training given by a Member State to its nationals for the purposes of university studies only in so far as such assistance is intended to cover registration and other fees, in particular tuition fees, charged for access to education.[556]

This line of jurisprudence changed after Maastricht with Union citizens being given access to maintenance aid in form of student grants and loans, if they had acquired a right of permanent residence. This was a move both “unsurprising and inevitable.”[557]

These new developments in EU law have subsequently been integrated into the Citizens’ Rights Directive, which repealed and replaced several sectoral directives, among them the Services Directive 73/148, the Persons of Independent Means Directive 90/364 and the Students Directive 93/96, and into Regulation 492/2011, which repealed and replaced Regulation 1612/68 on freedom of movement for workers within the Union. Consequently, the Citizens’ Rights Directive and Regulation 492/2011 are the most consulted legal instruments besides the Treaties and the CFREU. However, the ECJ has not yet started to use Regulation 492/2011, which entered into force in 2011, but instead keeps on using Regulation 1612/68, which was repealed with effect from 25 April 2011. This concerns even those cases that were referred for a preliminary ruling in 2012, long after Regulation 492/2011 entered into force. The reason being, obviously, that the old Regulation was still in force when the relevant incidents occurred. Therefore, the cases discussed in detail will include references to Regulation 1612/68, although it has already been repealed. However, Article 7 of Regulation 1612/68

554 Ibid. para 14.
555 Ibid. para 24.
556 Ibid. para 16.
557 Van der Mei, AP, Union Citizenship and the ‘De-Nationalisation’ of the Territorial Welfare State: Comments on Case C-456/02 *Trojani* and Case C-209/03 *Bidar*, 7 European Journal of Migration and Law, 2005, pp. 203–211, p. 207.

on employment and equality of treatment has neither been changed nor renumbered (cf. Article 7 of Regulation 492/2011). Article 12 of Regulation 1612/68 on workers' families was renumbered to Article 10 of Regulation 492/2011 but its wording has not changed.

EU education policy is rich in cross-cutting issues. Therefore, the ECJ's work is usually complex and guidance is drawn from past judgments. The following sub-chapters deal with the most recent developments in the field. Nowadays, most cases fall into the category of the so-called "cross-over cases" that "deal with both a consideration of a specific aspect such as whether the person is a worker, or work seeker or entitled student, but [...] wrapped in the context of citizenship."[558] The judgments are usually based on the free movement of workers and their dependants or the free movement of the non-economically active and the principle of non-discrimination on grounds of nationality. Occasionally, the freedom of establishment or the freedom to provide services comes in. Most obstacles to the freedom of movement have been removed. The first sub-chapter starts out with education and the derivative right of residence. It focusses on Union citizenship and the primary carer's right of residence. A child may have a right of residence by means of Union citizenship or, if it is a third-country national, it may derive a right of residence because it is the child of a Union citizen migrant worker. However, as soon as the child has acquired a right of residence, the primary carer of the child (Union citizens and third-country nationals alike) may derive a right of residence from the child's right of residence. The second sub-chapter deals with access to study. A much-discussed topic that divides the Member States, current legal issues will be debated. At the moment, higher education is not equally accessible to all Union citizens. In Austria, Belgium and Scotland, admission to HEIs is restricted. Whereas Austria and Belgium rely on indirect discrimination in order to keep applicants from neighbouring countries at bay, Scotland directly discriminates against students from England, Wales and Northern Ireland. The third sub-chapter analyses the entitlement of mobile students to maintenance aid in form of student grants and loans towards the home and the host Member States.

7.1 Education and the Derivative Right of Residence

There are different ways of becoming an addressee of EU law: either as a primary addressee (i.e. as a Union citizen) or as a derivative addressee (i.e. as someone

558 Foster, 2012, pp. 316 et seq.

who enjoys a relationship with a Union citizen). Derivative addressees enjoy as the term suggests "derived" rights. This does not mean that those rights are conferred "less directly" by EU law but rather that the interest of "conferring rights upon them derives from the relationship which these individuals enjoy with another person, whose benefit is the main interest of [EU] law."[559] A derivative addressee must not necessarily be a third-country national. Union citizens may find themselves to be primary addressees but they may just as well find themselves to be derivative addressees, depending on whether they themselves are exercising one of the fundamental freedoms. Of course, with Union citizenship evolving into a fifth fundamental freedom,[560] Union citizens do not necessarily have to avail of derivative rights. However, depending on the personal situation, this may be their only choice.

With regard to education, third-country nationals (or Union citizens) may derive a right to reside if they act as a Union citizen's primary carer. However, as Barrett points out, a derivative right of residence requires more than just a dependant with Union citizen status. In order to come within the scope of EU law, one must be the primary carer of a primary addressee of EU law "by virtue of (a) his or her nationality and (b) some activity or status other than merely that of being a [...] EU citizen."[561] In short, there needs to be a cross-border element. Hence, if Union citizen U resides with his third-country national relative R in his Member State of Origin O, the rules of EU law do not apply. If, however, U moves from O to host Member State H, EU law applies by virtue of the cross-border element and R will, if certain conditions apply, enjoy a derivative right of residence. However, although the "purely internal rule", i.e. situations lacking a cross-border element because none of the free movement provisions are exercised, had been one of the "cardinal features" of EU law,[562] there has been change with regard to national measures that result in a Union national being deprived of the "genuine enjoyment of the substance of the rights attaching to the status of European Union citizen."[563] The situations in which EU law applies regardless

559 Barrett, G., Family Matters: European Community Law and Third-Country Family Members, 40 CMLR, 2003, pp. 369–421, pp. 370 et seq.

560 Editorial, Editorial Comments: Two-speed European Citizenship? Can the Lisbon Treaty Help Close the Gap?, 45 CMLR, 2008, pp. 1–11, pp. 1 and 3.

561 Barrett, 2003, p. 377.

562 Tryfonidou, A., Redefining the Outer Boundaries of EU Law: The Zambrano, McCarthy and Dereci Trilogy, 18 European Public Law, 2012, pp. 493–526, p. 506.

563 Case C-34/09 *Gerardo Ruiz Zambrano v Office national de l'emploi (ONEm)* [2011] ECR 1177, para 45.

of a cross-border element are, however, very limited. If Union citizen U lives in Member State N, of which he is a national, and his third-country national relative R, who acts as his primary carer and on whom U is emotionally and financially dependent, is not granted a right of residence (and a right to work), this would deprive U of the genuine enjoyment of his Union citizenship status as U would presumably have to leave N in order to be with R.

7.1.1 *Chen and Zhu*: Birthright Citizenship and EU Law

A case that was particularly striking in that it showcased the "potentially transformative power of EU citizenship"[564] goes back to Section 6(1) and 6(3) of the Irish Nationality and Citizenship Act 1956 (No. 26 of 1956) as amended by the Irish Nationality and Citizenship Act 2001 (No. 15 of 2001), which applies retroactively as from 2 December 1999. According to it, "[e]very person born in the island of Ireland is entitled to be an Irish citizen" if this person "is not entitled to citizenship of any other country." While this provision was amended again shortly afterwards by the Irish Nationality and Citizenship Act 2004 (No. 38 of 2004)[565] because it happened to conjure up a political crisis caused by the perception that "illegal immigration and asylum-seeking by non-Europeans of child-bearing age have resulted in the attribution of Irish nationality to unacceptably

564 Barnard, C., Of Students and Babies, 64 Cambridge Law Journal, 2005, pp. 560–563, p. 561.

565 Also cf. Article 2 of the Constitution of Ireland (Bunreacht na hÉireann): "It is the entitlement and birthright of every person born in the island of Ireland, which includes its islands and seas, to be part of the Irish Nation. That is also the entitlement of all persons otherwise qualified in accordance with law to be citizens of Ireland." Since the referendum on Irish citizenship (i.e. yes or no to ius soli) on 11 June 2004 and the subsequent amendment of the Constitution of Ireland with the twenty-seventh amendment to the Constitution of Ireland on 24 June 2004, the right to Irish citizenship has changed. Article 9(2)(1) of the Constitution of Ireland, which was inserted by said referendum, provides that "[n]otwithstanding any other provision of this Constitution, a person born in the island of Ireland, which includes its islands and seas, who does not have, at the time of the birth of that person, at least one parent who is an Irish citizen or entitled to be an Irish citizen is not entitled to Irish citizenship or nationality, unless provided for by law." Hence, it partly reverses changes made to the Constitution of Ireland on 2 December 1999 as a result of the British-Irish Agreement of 1998, the "Good Friday Agreement". Also cf. Ward, P., Family Law in Ireland, Kluwer Law International: Alphen aan den Rijn, 2010, p. 46.

large numbers of inappropriate beneficiary babies",[566] it was enough to trigger short-time birth tourism.

Mrs Chen and her husband Mr Zhu, both Chinese nationals, wanted to circumvent the country's one-child policy as Mrs Chen had already given birth to a child in China. Six months before giving birth, Mrs Chen entered the UK. Shortly afterwards, she travelled to Belfast, Northern Ireland, where she eventually gave birth to baby Catherine Zhu. Following the birth, Mrs Chen and Catherine, issued with an Irish passport, settled in Cardiff, Wales.[567] As the Court noted, Mrs Chen is the primary carer of her daughter, who is emotionally and financially dependent on her mother. Mrs Chen provides for both private medical and child-care services for her daughter in the UK by virtue of her employment, so that both she and her daughter do not rely upon UK public funds. By having been born in Northern Ireland and acquiring Irish citizenship, Catherine had lost the right to Chinese citizenship and, consequently, was only allowed to enter Chinese territory with a 30-day visa.[568]

The Irish and UK Governments claimed that Catherine could not invoke the right to free movement and residence because she had simply never moved from one Member State to another.[569] However, the Court held that

> [t]he situation of a national of a Member State who was born in the host Member State and has not made use of the right to freedom of movement cannot, for that reason alone, be assimilated to a purely internal situation, thereby depriving that national of the benefit in the host Member State of the provisions of Community law on freedom of movement and of residence[.][570]

The Court first examined Catherine's right to free movement by virtue of being a recipient of services as she was receiving privately paid child-care services in the UK. However, it held that Directive 73/148[571] (repealed and replaced by

---

566 Grossman, A., Birthright Citizenship as Nationality of Convenience, Proceedings, Council of Europe, Compendium of Texts on the 3rd European Conference on "The Nationality and the Child", Strasbourg: 11–12 October 2004, published 17 April 2008, pp. 109–121, pp. 113–114, http://uniset.ca/naty/CJ-S-NAT_2008_2_en.pdf.

567 Cf. Case C-200/02 *Kunqian Catherine Zhu and Man Lavette Chen v Secretary of State for the Home Department* [2004] ECR 9925, para 8.

568 Ibid. para 13.

569 Ibid. para 18.

570 Ibid. para 19.

571 Council Directive 73/148/EEC of 21 May 1973 on the abolition of restrictions on movement and residence within the Community for nationals of Member States with regard to establishment and the provision of services, OJ L 172, pp. 14–16.

Directive 2004/38) does not cover a Union citizen who established primary residence in another Member State in order to receive services for an indefinite period of time.[572] It has been said that the order in which the Court approached the questions put before it, i.e. examining the freedom to provide services before taking recourse to "the right of the citizen directly" by virtue of Article 21(1) TFEU, is significant in that it shows that it does not consider Union citizenship "as a first status" as of yet. However, with the economic agent benefitting "from more rights than the simple citizen, who will be expected to take care of him or herself and thus have sufficient means of subsistence",[573] such an approach is not surprising.

The Court accepted that as a Union citizen, Catherine fell under the "Playboy"[574] Directive 90/364[575] (repealed and replaced by Directive 2004/38) on persons of independent means, and pursuant to it and her Union citizenship status, had a right to long-term residence. It dismissed the claim of the Irish and UK Governments that Catherine needed to possess sufficient resources herself and must not rely on her mother as unfounded. According to Article 1(1) of Directive 90/364, a Member State national must only "have" sufficient resources. Requiring a specific origin of the resources is not necessary in order to attain the objective pursued (i.e. no unreasonable burden on the finances of the host Member State), which "would constitute a disproportionate interference with the exercise of the fundamental right of freedom of movement and of residence".[576] The Court also rejected the UK Government's contention that neither Catherine nor Mrs Chen could rely on EU law due to Mrs Chen's deliberate move to Northern Ireland in order to allow her child to acquire Irish nationality. Consistent with international law, the Court held that every Member State, with due regard to EU law, is competent to determine the conditions for nationality acquisition and loss on its own.[577] Had the Court decided otherwise, it would have deconstructed European citizenship as we know it – based on multiple demoi – and based it on

---

572 Cf. Case C-200/02 *Chen*, paras 21 and 22.

573 Carlier, JY, Case C-200/02, *Man Lavette Chen and Kunqian Catherine Zhu v Secretary of State for the Home Department*, Judgment of the Court of Justice (Full Court) of 19 October 2004, 42 CMLR, 2005, pp. 1121–1131, p. 1124.

574 Ibid. p. 1123; Edward, D. and R. Lane, Edward and Lane on European Union Law, Edward Elgar: Cheltenham, 2013, recital 11.104.

575 Council Directive 90/364/EEC of 28 June 1990 on the right of residence, OJ L 180, 13.7.1990, pp. 26–27.

576 Case C-200/02 *Chen*, paras 26 and 29–33.

577 Ibid. para 37.

a unique demos. In other words, there would have been a competence transfer from the Member States to the EU which could have had "the long term consequence [...] of replacing the nationality law regimes of the Member States."[578] The Court therefore ruled that Mrs Chen, though a third-country national, had a right to reside in the host Member State as the primary carer of her child.[579]

7.1.2 *Ibrahim* and *Teixeira*: the Primary Carer's Right of Residence or the Parasitic Right of the Parasitic Right

Ibrahim[580] and *Teixeira*[581] both concern the right of residence for parents of children of migrant workers who are not able to provide sufficient resources to support themselves. Mrs Ibrahim and Mrs Teixeira entered the UK as spouses of migrant workers but subsequently separated or divorced. Whereas Mrs Ibrahim was a third-country national who had never been in employment, Mrs Texeira was a Union citizen who had previously worked in the UK. Moreover, Mrs Ibrahim's children were aged between one and nine, whereas Mrs Texeira's daughter was 18. Both cases originated from the UK (the questions for preliminary rulings were referred by the Court of Appeal for England and Wales) and were practically dealt with in parallel, with the respective judgments issued the same day.

The Court had already ruled in an earlier judgment that the primary carer of the child of a former migrant worker who was in education in the host Member State could derive a right of residence from Article 12 of Regulation 1612/68. In *Baumbast* a third-country national was granted a right of residence in the UK to tend to her children after her husband, a German national and former migrant worker, had left the UK due to employment reasons. As the Court held

> [t]he right conferred by Article 12 of Regulation No 1612/68 on the child of a migrant worker to pursue, under the best possible conditions, his education in the host Member State necessarily implies that that child has the right to be accompanied by the person who is his primary carer and, accordingly, that that person is able to reside with him in that Member State during his studies. To refuse to grant permission to remain to a

578 Kunoy, B., A Union of National Citizens: The Origins of the Court's Lack of Avant-Gardisme in the Chen Case, 43 CMLR, pp. 179–190, p. 188.

579 Cf. Case C-200/02 *Chen*, para 48.

580 Case C-310/08 *London Borough of Harrow v Nimco Hassan Ibrahim and Secretary of State for the Home Department* [2010] ECR 1065.

581 Case C-480/08 *Maria Teixeira v London Borough of Lambeth and Secretary of State for the Home Department* [2010] ECR 1107.

parent who is the primary carer of the child exercising his right to pursue his studies in the host Member State infringes that right.[582]

The Court's ruling thus resulted in the creation of a primary carer right which is "parasitic upon the child's right of residence, which in turn is parasitic upon the original worker's right of residence."[583]

Ibrahim and *Teixeira* were different from *Baumbast*, however. Both Mrs Ibrahim and Mrs Teixeira did not have sufficient resources, thereby relying on benefits in the UK. Indeed, it was their application for social assistance that had ultimately given rise to the question of their right of residence. The national court was particularly sceptical regarding Mrs Ibrahim's case.[584] Her husband had only resided in the UK as a migrant worker for a short period of time. A positive decision by the ECJ was therefore expected to open up the floodgates for derivative rights of children of migrant workers who had only recently begun their education in the host Member State and were dependent upon a not self-sufficient primary carer.

Mrs Ibrahim, a Somali citizen, was married to Mr Yusuf, a Danish citizen. Her husband moved to and worked in the UK from October 2002 to May 2003. Thereafter, he claimed incapacity benefit and eventually left the UK in 2004 after his benefits were stopped. Mrs Ibrahim had moved to the UK in February 2003 with her three oldest children, the fourth and youngest child being born there. All her children held Danish citizenship. Mrs Ibrahim separated from her husband after he had left the UK. She never worked and was entirely dependent on benefits. Her application for housing assistance in January 2007 for her and her children was rejected on the grounds that neither she nor her husband, who had returned to the UK in December 2006, qualified as resident in the UK under EU law.[585]

Mrs Teixeira, a Portuguese citizen, came to the UK in 1989 together with her husband, a fellow Portuguese. In 1991, their daughter Patricia was born in the UK. However, the couple subsequently divorced. Mrs Teixeira, who had been in employment from 1989 to 1991, worked intermittent periods after the birth

582 C-413/99 *Baumbast and R v Secretary of State for the Home Department* [2002] ECR 7091, para 73.

583 O'Brien, C., Case C-310/08 *London Borough of Harrow v. Nimco Hassan Ibrahim and Secretary of State for the Home Department*, Judgment of the Court (Grand Chamber) of 23 February 2010, nyr., Case C-480/08 *Maria Teixeira v. London Borough of Lambeth and Secretary of State for the Home Department*, Judgment of the Court (Grand Chamber) of 23 February 2010, nyr., 48 CMLR, 2011, pp. 203–225, p. 204.

584 Ibid. pp. 205–206.

585 Cf. Case C-310/08 *Ibrahim*, paras 15–21.

of her daughter, with her last employment being in 2005. When her daughter, who had previously stayed with her father, went to live with her in March 2007, Mrs Teixeira unsuccessfully applied for housing assistance.[586]

The UK Government contested that the applicants in the main proceedings could rely on Article 12 of Regulation 1612/68. It argued that since its entry into force, Directive 2004/38 "constitutes the sole basis for the conditions governing the exercise of the right of residence in the Member States of citizens of the Union and the members of their families". Consequently, it noted that a right of residence could not be derived from Article 12 of Regulation 1612/68. However, the Court held that there was nothing to suggest that the Union legislature had any intentions of reducing the scope of Article 12 of Regulation 1612/68 to "a mere right of access to education." After all, the Citizens' Rights Directive did not repeal Article 12 of Regulation 1612/68.[587]

The Court argued that if Article 12 of Regulation 1612/68 had been limited in the way suggested, i.e. not providing a right of residence for the children of migrant workers, leaving it in force would have been pointless as a right to education may also be derived from Article 24(1) of Directive 2004/38. Furthermore, it stated that Directive 2004/38 aims "to simplify and strengthen the right of free movement and residence of all Union citizens". Citing the travaux préparatoires to Directive 2004/38 which specifically mention that said Directive was in line with the *Baumbast* ruling, the Court held that "the children of a national of a Member State who works or has worked in the host Member State and the parent who is their primary carer can claim a right of residence in the latter State on the sole basis of Article 12 of Regulation No 1612/68, without being required to satisfy the conditions laid down in Directive 2004/38."[588]

After having determined that the legal situation had not changed since *Baumbast*, the Court still had to rule whether such a right of residence was conditional on having sufficient resources and comprehensive sickness insurance in that State. The Court stated that the wording of Article 12 of Regulation 1612/68 does not entail any conditions regarding self-sufficiency or comprehensive sickness insurance cover in that State. Referring to *Baumbast*, the Court reiterated that Article 12 of said Regulation "cannot be interpreted restrictively and must not,

586 Cf. Case C-480/08 *Teixeira*, paras 20–24.
587 Case C-310/08 *Ibrahim*, paras 44–50; Case C-480/08 *Teixeira*, paras 55–60; also cf. Amended proposal for a Directive of the European Parliament and of the Council on the right of citizens of the Union and their family members to move and reside freely within the territory of the Member States, COM(2003) 199 final, p. 7.
588 Case C-310/08 *Ibrahim*, para 50.

under any circumstances, be rendered ineffective". Refusing the parent who is the primary carer to remain in the host Member State would deprive the children of "the best possible conditions" and therefore of a right granted to them by the Union legislature. Moreover, it concluded that such a requirement could neither be derived from the case law of the Court. Referring to Article 12(3) of Directive 2004/38 (although not applicable in the main proceedings), which stipulates that "[t]he Union citizen's departure from the host Member State or his/her death shall not entail loss of the right of residence of his/her children or of the parent who has actual custody of the children, irrespective of nationality, if the children reside in the host Member State and are enrolled at an educational establishment, for the purpose of studying there, until the completion of their studies", the Court ruled that children of a Union citizen who is or has been employed in the host Member State and the parent acting as a primary carer may claim a right of residence solely on the basis of Article 12 of Regulation 1612/68. This right is not in any way conditional on the dependant and the primary carer having sufficient resources or comprehensive sickness insurance cover in the host Member State.[589]

Furthermore, the Court clarified that Article 12 of Regulation 1612/68 does not presuppose that the child of a former migrant worker must have begun its education in the host Member State while the migrant worker was still employed. Even if the child started its education when none of its parents retained a migrant worker status anymore, it could rely on Article 12 of that regulation. The only thing that matters is that the child became installed in the host Member State at a time when one of its parents exercised a right of residence as a migrant worker.[590] A parent and primary carer of a child of a migrant worker derives a right of residence from Article 12 of Regulation 1612/68 until that child reaches the age of majority. However, due to the fact that the right of access to education (and therefore the right to residence) of the child of a migrant worker continues until the child has completed its education, the parent and primary carer of the child may derive a right of residence beyond the age of majority if his or her presence and care are still required in order that the child may pursue and complete its education.[591]

---

589 Cf. Case C-310/08 *Ibrahim*, paras 51–59; Case C-480/08 *Teixeira*, paras 65–70.

590 Case C-480/08 *Teixeira*, paras 72–74.

591 Ibid. para 86.

7.1.3 *Ruiz Zambrano*: The Derivative Right of Residence in Internal Situations or "Civis Europeus Sum"

Mr Ruiz Zambrano, a Colombian national, applied for asylum in Belgium in 1999. While his application was rejected and he was ordered to leave Belgium, the order included a non-refoulement clause stipulating that he would not be sent back to his country of origin. Despite a further application for residence rejected, Mr Ruiz Zambrano stayed in Belgium with his family. He signed a contract of employment of indefinite duration, although he did not have a work permit.[592] While in Belgium, his wife gave birth to two children. Pursuant to the then applicable version of Article 10(1) of the Belgian Nationality Code,[593] Belgian nationality went to any child born in Belgium that, if it was not for Belgian nationality, would be left stateless.[594] According to Colombian Law, children of Colombian parents born outside Colombia do not receive Colombian citizenship unless the parents take steps in order to have them recognised. Thus, Mr Ruiz Zambrano's children (born in 2003 and 2005) were given Belgian citizenship.[595]

Mr Ruiz Zambrano had tried to legalise his residence in Belgium at various points in time and twice lodged applications for unemployment benefits, which were rejected due to his failure to obtain a work permit beforehand. He then challenged the decisions regarding the refusal of his unemployment benefits before the Tribunal du travail de Bruxelles (Brussels Employment Tribunal). Mr Ruiz Zambrano argued that he had a right of residence by virtue of the EC Treaty or, in the alternative with reference to *Chen*[596], at the very least a derivative right of residence by virtue of being the ascendant of a minor child holding

592 Cf. Case C-34/09 *Ruiz Zambrano*, paras 14 et seq.

593 *Moniteur belge*, 12 July 1984, p. 10095.

594 Article 10 of the Belgian Nationality Code has been revised in the meantime (Law of 27 December 2006). Pursuant to the new version of Article 10, acquiring Belgian nationality by birth is impossible unless administrative action by the child's legal representatives with the diplomatic or consular authorities of the country of origin of its parents or the country of origin of one parent in order to obtain a different nationality for the child proves fruitless ("[…] si l'enfant peut obtenir une autre nationalité moyennant l'accomplissement par son ou ses représentants légaux d'une démarche administrative auprès des autorités diplomatiques ou consulaires du pays de ses auteurs ou de l'un de ceux-ci.").

595 Cf. Case C-34/09 *Ruiz Zambrano*, paras 19 and 22.

596 Case C-200/02 *Chen*.

Union citizenship and that he was, therefore, exempt from any obligation of obtaining a work permit.[597]

In its referral to the ECJ, the Tribunal du travail de Bruxelles essentially asked whether the European citizenship provisions in the TFEU are to be interpreted as meaning that a third-country national, upon whom his minor children holding European citizenship are dependent, has a right of residence in the Member State of which they are nationals and in which they reside, and whether he is further exempt from any obligation of obtaining a work permit. The Governments submitting observations were of the opinion that this was not possible, as Mr Ruiz Zambrano's children had never exercised their right to free movement and residence. The ECJ, however, while noting that the Citizens' Rights Directive did not apply (cf. Article 3(1): "all Union citizens who move to or reside in a Member State other than that of which they are a national, and to their family members"), took a different stance. It highlighted the "fundamental status" of Union citizenship and held that in the circumstances given, "Article 20 TFEU precludes national measures which have the effect of depriving citizens of the Union of the genuine enjoyment of the substance of the rights conferred by virtue of their status as citizens of the Union". Moreover, "[a] refusal to grant a right of residence to a third-country national with dependent minor children in the Member State where those children are nationals and reside, and also a refusal to grant such a person a work permit, has such an effect" and would presumably "result in the children, citizens of the Union, having to leave the territory of the Union".[598]

The brevity of the judgment's operative part has given rise to speculation that there had been "much disagreement among the judges about the legal issues."[599] This would not at all be surprising, given the importance of the decision. However, the Court was quick to narrow the application of EU law in internal situations. Shortly after the ruling, the Court issued its decisions in *McCarthy*[600] and

---

597 Case C-34/09 *Ruiz Zambrano*, para 34.

598 Ibid. paras 36–39 and paras 41–44.

599 Guild, E., The Court of Justice of the European Union and Citizens of the Union: A Revolution Underway? The Zambrano Judgment of 8 March 2011, http://eudo-citizenship.eu/search-results/453-the-court-of-justice-of-the-european-union-and-citizens-of-the-union-a-revolution-underway-the-zambrano-judgment-of-8-march-2011.

600 Case C-434/09 *Shirley McCarthy v Secretary of State for the Home Department* [2011] ECR 3375.

Dereci[601], in which it basically took a step backwards. In the Court's view, the *Ruiz Zambrano* principle may only be used in situations "that are akin to those of that case, thus making it rather hard for a situation to be brought within the scope of Article 20 TFEU through that route."[602] As the Court clarified in *Dereci*, "the genuine enjoyment of the substance of the rights conferred by virtue of European Union citizen status refers to situations in which the Union citizen has, in fact, to leave not only the territory of the Member State of which he is a national but also the territory of the Union as a whole."[603] Thus, it seems that as groundbreaking as the decision in *Ruiz Zambrano* may be, the Court is really only willing to apply the *Ruiz Zambrano* principle if the Union citizen is a minor (presumably also a dependant who has reached the age of majority and is still in education) who is emotionally and financially dependent on his or her third-country national parent and primary carer. If there would be a case of *Chen* reloaded so to say, the Citizens' Rights Directive would be applicable as it applies "to all Union citizens who move to or reside in a Member State other than that of which they are a national, and to their family members" (Article 3 of the Citizens' Rights Directive).[604]

7.2 Access to Study

Different Member States have different conditions for access to HEIs. Especially restrictive selection procedures have been put in place regarding courses for the medical professions. Candidates are usually selected on the basis of the grade average of their upper secondary diploma corresponding to university entrance level and/or admissions and aptitude tests. Non-academic criteria may include prior work experience or shadowing of doctors. Furthermore, Germany has introduced the so-called "Wartesemester", a waiting period for applicants. Applicants with a German Abitur or equivalent who have not achieved the minimum grades (*numerus clausus*) may wait to be accepted for their chosen course. During the waiting period, they are not allowed to enrol in any other course of study at a German university. In the meantime, alternatives are studying abroad

601 Case C-256/11 *Murat Dereci and Others v Bundesministerium für Inneres* [2011] ECR 11315.

602 Tryfonidou, 2012, p. 514.

603 Case C-256/11 *Dereci*, para 66.

604 Also cf. Lenaerts, K., 'Civis Europaeus Sum': From the Cross-border Link to the Status of Citizen of the Union, 3 Online Journal on free movement of workers within the European Union, 2011, pp. 6–18, p. 17 at fn. 94.

or training to be a nurse or a dental technician. However, depending on one's grades, waiting for a place for medical school may be time consuming. In 2011, the Verwaltungsgericht Gelsenkirchen (a German administrative court) ruled that applicants with "Wartesemester" of six years, which corresponds to the time it takes to complete a medical degree in Germany, had to be admitted to medical school as there was no realistic chance for admission otherwise. However, the Oberverwaltungsgericht Nordrhein-Westfalen (the higher administrative court) suspended the obligation to implement the decisions by the Verwaltungsgericht Gelsenkirchen and eventually amended them.[605] Thus, waiting for a place without knowing how long admission will ultimately take is not a very attractive option. The system France put in place is similarly unattractive to the one in Germany. Although all students with a French baccalauréat or equivalent are admitted, the grade average of the first year – PACES (première année commune aux études de santé) – which is a jointly taught course for everyone wanting to study medicine, dentistry, pharmacy or midwifery determines whether a student is allowed to proceed to the second year (PCEM2). Students may take the PACES twice, which means they can re-enrol once.[606]

With such hurdles in place, it is not surprising that prospective students are willing to go abroad to study to be able to pursue the profession of their choice. This in turn influences the higher education systems of other Member States. Not designed to meet demands for that many students, the cross-border mobility that comes with the freedom of movement is beginning to take its toll. Austria and Belgium are particularly affected as Germany and France are among the countries with the most restrictive admission requirements. Furthermore, these two countries are also the most populous Member States. As they share the same official language and therefore the medium (or language) of instruction with Austria and the French Community of Belgium, prospective students flock to their neighbouring countries in order to kick off their medical career. Higher education offered in their mother tongue (i.e. German or French) as well as no or very low tuition fees have attracted the students who did not qualify for

605 Cf. Verwaltungsgericht Gelsenkirchen, Beschlüsse vom 28.9.2011, Aktenzeichen 6 L 941/11; 6 L 929/11; 6 L 940/11 und 6 L 942/11; Oberverwaltungsgericht Nordrhein-Westfalen, Beschlüsse vom 6.10.2011, Aktenzeichen 13 B 1214/11, 13 B 1215/11, 13 B 1216/11, 13 B 1217/11 and 13 B 1218/11; Oberverwaltungsgericht Nordrhein-Westfalen, Beschlüsse vom 8.11.2011, Aktenzeichen 13 B 1209/11, 13 B 1210/11, 13 B 1211/11, 13 B 1212/11, 13 B 1213/11 and 13 B 1224/11.

606 Cf. Articles 1, 2 and 12 of Arrêté du 28 octobre 2009 relatif à la première année commune aux études de santé, JORF, No. 266, 17.11.2009, p. 19838.

admission in their home States. Much to the dismay of the Member States that provided for their education, they usually return to their country of origin upon earning their degrees. Austria and Belgium therefore generally serve as net importers of students. With 11.36% of the total number of students being foreign students in Austria and the total number of foreign students amounting to 6.98% in Belgium, Austria and Belgium receive a lot more foreign students than most of the other Member States of the Union. Furthermore, the balance of mobility, i.e. "the number of outgoing students minus the number of incoming students, divided by the total number of students (Erasmus students excluded)", amounts to −8.02% in Austria and −4.62% in Belgium (calculations based on numbers from 2008).[607] Hence, Austria and Belgium shoulder a considerably large portion of education costs for foreign students.

According to the OECD, Germany is the biggest net exporter of students with 132,000 students studying abroad with 98% thereof studying in OECD countries, followed by France with 80,000 students studying abroad with 97% thereof studying in OECD countries.[608] However, this leaves the question of who should bear the costs of higher education of those mobile students. Generally, this is down to four parties: the graduate, the host country, the country of origin and the country that ultimately benefits from the skills the graduate obtained in the host country.[609] However, except for England (which charges high tuition fees), the Member States of the EU apply the host country principle, i.e. higher education is financed by the host country that "imports post secondary students and some months or years later exports an enriched human capital".[610] It has thus been remarked that Germany and France free ride on their neighbouring countries.[611] The country of origin principle, which is used in Switzerland where the 26 cantons reimburse each other for students' imbalances,[612] has not yet been

607 Gérard, M., Who Is to Pay for Mobile Students?, in: A. Curaj et al. (eds.), European Higher Education at the Crossroads: Between the Bologna Process and National Reforms, Springer: Dordrecht, 2012, pp. 727–748, p. 728.

608 Cf. OECD, How Is International Student Mobility Shaping Up?, Education Indicators in Focus, No. 14, OECD Publishing, 2013, p. 2.

609 Cf. Gérard, M. and S. Uebelmesser, Globalization and Access to Higher Education – Policy Implications, CESifo DICE Report 2013/2, pp. 3–10, p. 4.

610 Gérard, M., Financing Bologna Students' Mobility, Taxation Paper No 26, Office for Official Publications of the European Communities: Luxembourg, 2010, p. 7.

611 Cf. Gérard and Uebelmesser, 2013, p. 4.

612 Cf. Gérard, M., Financing Bologna, the Internationally Mobile Students in European Higher Education, CESifo Working Paper No 2391, 2008, pp. 30 et seq.

taken on in the EU. This means that education of mobile students is funded inter alia by the tax revenues generated by the workers of the host country. However, this financing model is based on the assumption that those students will one day pay taxes in the respective host country, therefore financing the education of the next generation. In the long term, the status quo is therefore not an option. In order to render tax-based regimes sustainable, transfer agreements will be inevitable.[613]

7.2.1 The Case of Austria

Austria used to have an open admission policy, allowing everyone who had passed the Austrian Matura (the Austrian upper secondary diploma) to enrol at university. However, in order to keep prospective students from Germany at bay, Austria made provisions in Section 7 of its General Law of Higher Education (Allgemeines Hochschul-Studiengesetz, the "AHStG")[614]. According to it, foreigners who had not obtained an Austrian Matura were eligible for admission only if they could prove admissibility in their country of origin (note the different admission requirements for Austrian nationals and foreigners regarding upper secondary diplomas from abroad). However, with Austria's accession to the EU on 1 January 1995 it was clear that national legislation could no longer be directly discriminating on grounds of nationality (cf. Article 18 TFEU). This is why the General Law of Higher Education was amended so that applicants who had not obtained an Austrian Matura but an upper secondary diploma in a State other than Austria had to prove that they fulfilled the conditions for access in that same State regardless of their nationality (this was termed "specific university admissibility").[615]

Consequently, Austrian nationals who had completed their secondary education abroad also had to prove that they were eligible for admission in the State that had issued their upper secondary diploma (e.g. minimum grades to be included in the *numerus clausus* or passing an entrance examination). The Law on University Studies (Universitäts-Studiengesetz, the "UniStG"), which repealed

613 Cf. Gérard and Uebelmesser, 2013, p. 6.

614 Bundesgesetz vom 15. Juli 1966 über die Studien an den wissenschaftlichen Hochschulen (Allgemeines Hochschul-Studiengesetz – AHStG), BGBl. Nr. 177/1966.

615 Kasparovsky, H., The Impact of EU Law on Austrian Higher Education Curricula, 4 ICL Journal, 2010, pp. 582–589, p. 586.

and replaced the General Law of Higher Education[616], also provided for such a regulation. Section 36(1) of the Universitäts-Studiengesetz stipulated that

> [i]n addition to possession of a general university entrance qualification, students must demonstrate that they meet the specific entrance requirements for the relevant course of study, including entitlement to immediate admission, applicable in the State which issued the general qualification.

The decision whether applicants were eligible was thus handed over to the country in which they had obtained their upper secondary diploma. It was evident that it was to the detriment of those who had not obtained their upper secondary diplomas in Austria as everyone in possession of an Austrian Matura was immediately admitted to their course of choice at any Austrian university. Although Austrians having completed their upper secondary education abroad had to provide evidence that they were eligible for their chosen course of study in the country where their upper secondary diplomas had been issued, it is clear that the provision targeted non-nationals in particular. Exemptions from Section 36(1) of the UniStG were possible as Section 36(4) of the UniStG established that

> [t]he Federal Minister may by regulation designate groups of persons whose university entrance qualification is to be regarded, by reason of their close personal ties with Austria or their activity on behalf of the Republic of Austria, as issued in Austria for the purposes of establishing possession of the specific university entrance requirements.

This, however, only applied (and in fact it still does!) to the holders of upper secondary diplomas from South Tyrol issued by upper secondary schools using German or Ladin as the medium of instruction. Due to historic reasons (i.e. South Tyrol belonged to Austria until 1918), this exemption had been enshrined in Section 3 of the Verordnung des Bundesministers für Wissenschaft und Verkehr über die Festlegung von Personengruppen bei der Zulassung zu ordentlichen Studien (the "Personengruppenverordnung")[617], a regulation on groups of persons eligible for university studies. This regulation has just been repealed and replaced by the Verordnung des Bundesministers für Wissenschaft und Forschung über die Festlegung von Personengruppen bei der Zulassung zu ordentlichen Studien (the "Personengruppenverordnung 2014" – PersGV

616 Bundesgesetz über die Studien an den Universitäten (Universitäts-Studiengesetz – UniStG), BGBl. I Nr. 48/1997.

617 Verordnung des Bundesministers für Wissenschaft und Verkehr über die Festlegung von Personengruppen bei der Zulassung zu ordentlichen Studien (Personengruppenverordnung), BGBl. II Nr. 211/1997.

2014).[618] Like Section 3 of the Personengruppenverordnung, Section 3(2) of the Personengruppenverordnung 2014 establishes that upper secondary diplomas issued by upper secondary schools using German or Ladin as the medium of instruction, which do not allow for immediate admission to Italian universities (e.g. for medicine, dentistry or veterinary medicine, which require entrance examinations), are regarded as having been issued in Austria.

In 1999, the Commission sent Austria a letter of formal notice claiming that Section 36 of the UniStG infringed Articles 12, 149 and 150 TEC (now Articles 18, 165 and 166 TFEU).[619] Not satisfied with the replies submitted by Austria, the Commission sent Austria a reasoned opinion in 2002, calling on Austria "to ensure that holders of secondary education diplomas awarded in other Member States can gain access to Austrian higher or university education under the same conditions as holders of secondary education diplomas awarded in Austria."[620] Due to this request not being carried out, the Commission ultimately instigated legal proceedings against Austria.[621] Austria opined that Section 36 of the UniStG governed the academic recognition of upper secondary diplomas – a prerequisite for admission to Austrian universities – and therefore did not fall within the scope of the Treaty.[622] The ECJ, referring to *Gravier*[623] and *Commission v Belgium*[624], reiterated that "the conditions of access to vocational training fall within the scope of the Treaty". Pursuant to Article 18 TFEU, discrimination on grounds of nationality within the scope of the Treaty is prohibited. Since, according to settled case law, higher education and university education are regarded as vocational training and Section 36 of the UniStG concerns the access to higher education or university education in Austria, the question at issue falls within the scope of the Treaty.[625]

618 Verordnung des Bundesministers für Wissenschaft und Forschung über die Festlegung von Personengruppen bei der Zulassung zu ordentlichen Studien (Personengruppenverordnung 2014 – PersGV 2014), BGBl. II Nr. 340/2013.

619 Cf. Case C-147/03 *Commission v Austria*, para 7.

620 Ibid. para 10.

621 Ibid. para 11.

622 Ibid. para 30.

623 Cf. Case C-293/83 *Gravier*, para 25.

624 Cf. Case C-65/03 *Commission of the European Communities v Kingdom of Belgium* [2004] ECR 6427, para 25.

625 Cf. Case C-147/03 *Commission v Austria*, paras 31–35; also cf. Case C-24/86 *Blaizot*, paras 15–20, and Case 42/87 *Commission of the European Communities v Kingdom of Belgium* [1988] ECR 5445, paras 7 and 8.

The judges in Luxembourg argued that

> Paragraph [sic[626]] 36 of the UniStG introduces not only differential treatment to the detriment of students who have obtained their secondary education diplomas in a Member State other than the Republic of Austria, but also between those same students according to the Member States in which they obtained their secondary education diploma.[627]

Hence, they found that this provision hindered the right to free movement, penalising a person for wanting to profit of the opportunities provided under Union law. Referring to *D'Hoop*[628], they took account of the second indent of Article 149(2) TEC (now the second indent of Article 165(2) TFEU), which expressly provides that Union action is to be aimed at "encouraging mobility of students and teachers, by encouraging inter alia, the academic recognition of diplomas and periods of study".[629] Thus, the argument presented by Austria that admission to its universities was "subject to proof of general aptitude and of specific aptitude for university studies and no condition other than academic recognition of the qualification giving access to university studies is required",[630] was doomed from the start.

The ECJ maintained that Union citizenship was the fundamental status of the nationals of the Member States, reiterating its previous line of jurisprudence established in *Grzelczyk*.[631] It held that although Section 36 of the UniStG applies to all students regardless of nationality, "it is liable to have a greater effect on nationals of other Member States than on Austrian nationals, and therefore the difference in treatment introduced by that provision results in indirect

626 The section sign "§" (signum sectionis in Latin) indicates "a subdivision of a document or a subdivision of an article in a document, statutory title, or code." Section is "commonly (and unfortunately)" used interchangeably with paragraph. Garner, BA, Garner's Dictionary of Legal Usage, http://www.oxforddictionaries.com. Hence, the correct denomination of "§" is section. While the section sign is indeed called "Paragraph" in German (the German expression for paragraph is "Absatz"), using "paragraph" in English accounts for confusion as a section like an article may consist of several paragraphs. Unfortunately, it seems that the ECJ has taken to use "paragraph" in the English language version of rulings in which the language of the case (i.e. the "official language") is German.

627 Case C-147/03 *Commission v Austria*, para 43.

628 Cf. Case C-224/98 *Marie-Nathalie D'Hoop v Office national de l'emploi* [2002] ECR 6191, para 32.

629 Case C-147/03 *Commission v Austria*, para 44.

630 Ibid. para 40.

631 Ibid. para 45. Also cf. Case C-184/99 *Grzelczyk*, para 31.

discrimination."[632] Referring to *Bickel and Franz*[633] and *D'Hoop*[634], the Court stated that such differential treatment "could be justified only if it were based on objective considerations independent of the nationality of the persons concerned and were proportionate to the legitimate aim of the national provisions".[635] Taking up the idea of non-discriminatory measures, which AG Jacobs had expressed in his opinion,[636] the ECJ suggested that the excessive demand for study places could be dealt with through the introduction of entrance examinations or the requirement of minimum grades.[637]

The Austrian Government submitted three justifications. Firstly, it claimed that differential treatment was necessary in order to safeguard the homogeneity of the Austrian higher or university education system because an influx of persons with upper secondary diplomas from other Member States would lead to financial as well as structural and staffing problems. Secondly, it alleged that it was necessary to prevent the abuse of Community law by those who "improperly evad[ed] the application of their national legislation as regards training for a trade or profession". Thirdly, it concluded that Section 36 of the UniStG complied with the 1953 European Convention on the Equivalence of Diplomas leading to Admission to Universities and the 1997 Convention on the Recognition of Qualifications concerning Higher Education in the European Region (the Lisbon Recognition Convention).[638]

However, the ECJ did not accept any of the justifications submitted. It held that, as to the homogeneity argument, the very same risks alleged were present in other Member States such as Belgium and that Austria had failed to provide "an analysis of the appropriateness and proportionality of the restrictive measure adopted [...] and specific evidence substantiating its arguments".[639] With regard to the prevention of abuse of Community law, the ECJ referred to the second indent of Article 149(2) TEC (now Article 165(2) TFEU) and to the third indent

632 Case C-147/03 *Commission v Austria*, para 47.

633 Cf. Case C-274/96 *Criminal proceedings against Horst Otto Bickel and Ulrich Franz* [1998] ECR 7637, para 27.

634 Cf. Case C-224/98 *D'Hoop*, para 36.

635 Case C-147/03 *Commission v Austria*, para 48.

636 Cf. Opinion of Advocate General Jacobs, delivered on 20 January 2005, Case C-147/03 *Commission of the European Communities v Republic of Austria* [2005] ECR 5969, para 52.

637 Cf. Case C-147/03 *Commission v Austria*, para 61.

638 Ibid. paras 49–59.

639 Ibid. paras 62–66.

of Article 150(2) TEC (now Article 166(2) TFEU), which aim to encourage mobility of students and trainees. It observed that

> the possibility for a student from the European Union, who has obtained his secondary education diploma in a Member State other than Austria, to gain access to Austrian higher or university education under the same conditions as holders of diplomas awarded in Austria constitutes the very essence of the principle of freedom of movement for students guaranteed by the Treaty, and cannot therefore of itself constitute an abuse of that right.[640]

The last argument that alluded to conventions of the CoE was a transparently feeble one. In the event of a prior conflicting right rooted in international law, a discrimination infringing EU law is clearly untenable.[641] This position was also supported by the ECJ. Referring to *Commission* v *Luxembourg*[642], the ECJ explained that any rights and obligations arising from such agreements concluded before accession may, if not compatible with Union law, not be exercised with regard to other Member States. Consequently, the ECJ stated that "Austria may not invoke by way of justification either the 1953 Convention or *a fortiori* the 1997 Convention, which was concluded after [Austria had] acceded to the Union."[643]

Hence, the ECJ concluded that Austria had failed to fulfil its obligations under Articles 12, 149 and 150 TEC (now Articles 18, 165 and 166 TFEU) because it had not taken

> the necessary measures to ensure that holders of secondary education diplomas awarded in other Member States can gain access to higher and university education organised by it under the same conditions as holders of secondary education diplomas awarded in Austria[.][644]

Following the ECJ's decision and the subsequent repeal of the admission scheme in 2005, Austria was literally invaded by German students. This was especially so in regard to the medical degree programmes offered at the medical universities of Graz, Innsbruck and Vienna.[645] The former admission scheme had acted like

---

640 Ibid. paras 69–70.

641 Cf. Hilpold, P., Hochschulzugang und Unionsbürgerschaft: Das Urteil EuGH vom 7.7.2005 in der Rechtssache C-147/03, Kommission gegen Österreich, EuZW, 2005, pp. 647–652, p. 649.

642 Case C-473/93 *Commission of the European Communities v Grand Duchy of Luxemburg* [1996] ECR 3207, para 40.

643 Case C-147/03 *Commission v Austria*, para 74.

644 Ibid. para 75.

645 With the beginning of the fall semester 2014, the Johannes Kepler Universität Linz will also offer a course in medicine which will be the first one offered as a bachelor/

a "firewall", protecting Austrian universities from "numerus clausus refugees" from Germany.[646] In order to take control of the situation, Austria decided to re-establish access restrictions. Since the academic year 2006/07, anyone wanting to enrol in medicine or dentistry at a public Austrian university needs to take an entrance examination. The allocation of study places is determined by the results obtained, as well as by an additional quota system. According to Section 124b(5) of the Universities Act 2002 (Universitätsgesetz, the "UG")[647], 75% of the study places in medicine and dentistry are reserved for applicants with an Austrian Matura (this includes the respective upper secondary diplomas issued in South Tyrol as well as upper secondary diplomas issued in Liechtenstein and Luxembourg which are regarded as having been issued in Austria[648]). The number of study places for applicants who obtained their upper secondary diplomas elsewhere is capped at 25%, whereby 20% of the study places are reserved for those with upper secondary diplomas issued in other EU Member States and 5% for those with upper secondary diplomas issued in third countries.

By establishing supplementary provisions concerning the admission to degree programmes where the *numerus clausus* applies in Germany, Austria once again introduced indirect discrimination on grounds of nationality, which is prohibited by Article 18 TFEU. According to the current legal situation, holders of upper secondary diplomas issued in other EU Member States cannot gain access to medicine or dentistry programmes at Austrian public universities under the same conditions as holders of an Austrian Matura. Section 124b(5) of the UG stipulates that both the right to education and the access to higher education for those with Austrian upper secondary diplomas have been substantially curtailed due to an increased influx of persons who obtained their upper secondary diplomas abroad. Hence, the quota system serves to safeguard the homogeneity

master programme. The Paracelsus Medizinische Privatuniversität in Salzburg is a private medical university with its own admission criteria. It charges high tuition fees which currently amount to EUR 13,500 per year.

646 Funk, BC, Verfassungsrechtliche Dimensionen des österreichischen Hochschulrechts, in: W. Berka, C. Brünner and W. Hauser (eds.), Handbuch des österreichischen Hochschulrechts (2nd ed.), NWV: Wien, 2012, pp. 31–50, p. 49.

647 Bundesgesetz über die Organisation der Universitäten und ihre Studien (Universitätsgesetz 2002 – UG), BGBl. I Nr. 120/2002, consolidated version.

648 Cf. Österreich – Liechtenstein: Abkommen über Gleichwertigkeiten im Bereich der Reifezeugnisse und des Hochschulwesens, BGBl. III Nr. 176/1997; Kulturabkommen zwischen der Republik Österreich und dem Großherzogtum Luxemburg, BGBl. Nr. 372/1972, in der Fassung des Zusatzprotokolls, BGBl. Nr. 588/1986.

in the respective degree programmes, which is also supposed to help maintain the quality of the Austrian public health system. Having amended the UG 2002 twice, first in July 2005 to abide the ECJ's ruling and again in June 2006 in order to introduce a quota system, the Commission considered that Austria had still not complied with the respective ruling.

In January 2007, the Commission sent a letter of formal notice based on Article 228 TEC (now Article 260 TFEU) opining that Austria had not applied the ECJ ruling.[649] However, ten months later it decided to suspend the infringement proceedings for five years. Formally, the Commission explained "that there [was] prima facie evidence that without these restrictive measures, a problem could arise in the future for the Austrian health system, as a result of a potential shortage of health professionals practising in Austria." Thus, it allowed the Austrian authorities time to gather "more complete and detailed data to justify that the measures imposed are necessary and proportionate."[650] The Commission did not mend its ways for no reason. Austria was driving a hard bargain regarding the negotiations surrounding the Lisbon Treaty, calling for a special Treaty protocol in order to be able "to set a cap on the number of foreign students they would take in."[651] Hence, off the record, the Commission had suspended the infringement proceedings so as not to defer the conclusions of the negotiations. In December 2012, the Commission announced that it would prolong the 2007 freeze on the infringement proceedings for another four years until December 2016. This, it noted, was "conditional on [...] gathering definitive evidence on why these courses should be an exception to EU Treaty rules on free movement of citizens, which normally guarantee EU nationals with relevant entry qualifications full access to higher education in any Member State."[652]

7.2.2 The Case of Belgium

Over the years, the French Community of Belgium has seen an influx of foreign students. Since the 1970s, the country has tried to tackle the situation by

---

649 Cf. Free movement of students: the Commission sends letters of formal notice to Austria and Belgium, Press Release, 24 January 2007 (IP/07/06).

650 Cf. Access to higher education: the Commission suspends its infringement cases against Austria and Belgium, Press Release, 28 November 2007 (IP/07/1788).

651 Garben, S., Case C-73/08, *Nicolas Bressol and Others, Céline Chaverot and Others v. Gouvernement de la Communauté française*, Judgment of the Court (Grand Chamber) of 13 April 2010, nyr, 47 CMLR, 2010, pp. 1493–1510, p. 1497.

652 Austria and Belgium given more time to justify quotas, Press Release, 18 December 2012 (IP/12/1388).

introducing various laws concerned with the access to higher education. In the academic year 1976/77, an enrolment fee, the so-called Minerval, was introduced for pupils and students who attended state educational institutions or institutions supported by the state although their parents did not reside in Belgium.[653] The Minerval has been likened to the "out-of-state tuition" charged by public colleges/universities in the US. The rationale being that income tax is neither levied from the foreign students nor from their parents.[654] However, the Minerval was found to constitute discrimination on grounds of nationality. In 1985, the ECJ ruled in its landmark case *Gravier* that the imposition of a registration fee for the access to vocational training on non-nationals was contrary to Article 7 TEEC (now Article 18 TFEU).[655]

However, the story did not end there. Like Austria, Belgium had taken measures to restrict the access to university courses for foreigners. According to Belgian law, the recognition of foreign diplomas and certificates of study was "under no circumstances [to] have the effect […] of giving the recipient access to studies to which he does not have access in the country in which the diploma or certificate was awarded".[656] Hence, anyone who had not obtained a Belgian Certificat d'Enseignement secondaire supérieur général, technique ou artistique (CESS) was at a disadvantage. The Government of the French Community had, however, provided for an exemption for holders of upper secondary diplomas issued in Luxembourg (this provision was repealed on 3 April 2003).[657] The Commission opined that the Belgian rule infringed Articles 12, 149 and 150 TEC (now Articles 18, 165 and 166 TFEU). Moreover, it underlined "that the discrimination complained of against holders of diplomas awarded in another Member State was coupled with discrimination between nationals of other

653 Cf. Case C-293/83 *Gravier*, para 3.

654 Cf. Van der Mei, AP, Free Movement of Students and the Protection of National Educational Interests: Reflections on Bressol and Chaverot, 13 European Journal of Migration and Law, 2011, pp. 123–134, p. 125.

655 Cf. Case C-293/83 *Gravier*, para 26.

656 Cf. Article 1(b) of the Arrêté royal déterminant les conditions et la procédure d'octroi de l'équivalence des diplômes et certificats d'études étrangers, 20 July 1971, published in Moniteur belge, 5 Ausgust 1971, p. 9254.

657 Cf. Article 2 of the Arrêté du Gouvernement de la Communauté française établissant l'équivalence entre certains titres étrangers de fin d'études secondaires et le certificat homologué d'enseignement secondaire supérieur, 17 May 1999, published in Moniteur belge, 25 September 1999, p. 36182.

Member States according to the Member State in which they were awarded their secondary education diploma."[658]

On 23 October 2001, after launching an infringement procedure against Belgium, the Commission requested that Belgium take the necessary measures to comply with Union law.[659] Although the Government of the French Community assured the Commission that it would comply with its request, the relevant provision was not amended until 3 April 2003, when an exemption for qualifications awarded in Member States of the EU was added.[660] On 14 February 2003, the Commission thus brought an action before the ECJ alleging that Belgium had failed to fulfil its obligations under the Treaty by not complying with Articles 12, 149 and 150 TEC (now Articles 18, 165 and 166 TFEU). *Commission v. Austria*[661] is virtually identical to *Commission v. Belgium*[662]. However, unlike Austria, Belgium did not put forward any grounds for justification. The judges therefore ruled that

> by failing to take the measures necessary to ensure that holders of secondary education diplomas awarded in other Member States can gain access to higher education organised by the French Community under the same conditions as holders of the CESS, the Kingdom of Belgium has failed to fulfil its obligations under Article 12 EC, read in conjunction with Articles 149 EC and 150 EC [now Articles 18, 165 and 166 TFEU].[663]

While the case was pending, as well as in the aftermath of the judgment, the French Community was faced with a huge influx of students who had obtained their upper secondary diploma abroad. In its efforts to address the situation, the French Community organised entrance examinations in veterinary medicine from 2003 to 2005. Out of 795 applicants for veterinary medicine in the 2005 entrance examination, 192 had obtained their upper secondary diploma in the French Community. Out of the 250 successful applicants in said year, 216 had obtained their upper secondary diploma abroad. Hence, only 34 applicants with an upper secondary diploma obtained in the French Community were allowed to start veterinary medicine.[664] This was problematic in so far as almost a third

658 Case C-65/03 *Commission v Belgium*, para 19.
659 Ibid. para 9.
660 Ibid. paras 6 and 10.
661 Cf. Case C-147/03 *Commission v Austria*.
662 Cf. Case C-65/03 *Commission v. Belgium*.
663 Ibid. para 31.
664 Cf. Opinion of Advocate General Sharpston, delivered on 25 June 2009, Case C-73/08 *Nicolas Bressol and Others and Céline Chaverot and Others v Gouvernement de la Communauté française* [2010] ECR 2735, para 115.

of the veterinarians who established themselves in France every year had received their education in Belgium's French Community.[665] Furthermore, French applicants were at an advantage since in France students interested in pursuing a career as a veterinarian are required to do a two-year preparatory course before a competitive entrance examination for admission to basic training. This, in addition to the fact that there were so many French applicants, was taken as an argument that Belgian applicants were at a disadvantage.[666] Thus, it was not long until the French Community started to put measures in place in order to provide enough places for its residents.

On 16 June 2006, the Parliament of the French Community adopted the Décret régulant le nombre d'étudiants dans certains cursus de premier cycle de l'enseignement supérieur.[667] This decree regulates the number of students for certain undergraduate degree programmes. Those include the bachelor's degree programmes at university level in physiotherapy and rehabilitation as well as veterinary medicine. Further bachelor's degree programmes at university level were added to the decree after the case had been brought to court. Since the academic year 2009/10, the bachelor's degree programme psychology and education: speech and language therapy falls within the scope of the decree. Since the academic year 2012/13, this is also the case for the bachelor's degree programmes in medicine and dentistry.[668] Furthermore, the decree concerns the following bachelor's degree programmes at university colleges (haute écoles), which are non-university HEIs preparing for specific professions: midwifery, occupational therapy, speech therapy, podiatry-chiropody, physiotherapy and audiology. It also applies to the programme for educators specialised in psycho-educational counselling.[669] However, except for physiotherapy, the Belgian Constitutional Court has annulled Article 8 of the decree, meaning that the restrictions affecting the six other degree programmes at university colleges listed above have subsequently been lifted.[670]

It is not surprising that the French community saw the need to act following the judgment in *Commission v Belgium*[671]: in the academic year 2005/06, between

665 Ibid. para 24.

666 Cf. Garben, 2010, p. 1499.

667 Cf. Décret régulant le nombre d'étudiants dans certains cursus de premier cycle de l'enseignement supérieur, 16.6.2006, published in Moniteur Belge 6.7.2006, p. 34055.

668 Ibid. Article 3.

669 Ibid. Article 7.

670 Cf. Arrêt de la Cour constitutionnelle No. 89/2011 du 31 mai 2011, numéros du rôle: 4034 et 4093.

671 Cf. Case C-65/03 *Commission v Belgium*.

78% and 86% of the students enrolled in university degree programmes covered by the decree had obtained their upper secondary diplomas in another Member State.[672] From the academic year 2006/07 onwards, universities and university colleges have only been allowed to admit a limited number of non-resident students within the meaning of the decree. Whereas resident students have unrestricted access to the relevant degree programmes covered by Articles 3 and 7 of the decree, the threshold for non-resident students usually amounts to 30% of the total number of places. Exceptions are possible should the number of students who have obtained their upper secondary diploma in a country other than the one in which they are studying ever go beyond 10% on average in the HEIs of the EU.[673]

According to Article 1 of the decree, everyone with principal residence in Belgium at the time of registration in a HEI qualifies as a resident student if they have

(1) the right to remain in Belgium permanently,
(2) have had their principal residence in Belgium for at least six months (this was changed to 15 months on 15 May 2007) prior to their registration in a HEI while carrying on a remunerated or unremunerated professional activity or benefitting from a replacement income granted by a Belgian public service,
(3) have permission to remain in Belgium for an unlimited period of time according to the relevant Belgian legislation,
(4) have permission to remain in Belgium because they have been granted refugee status according to the relevant Belgian legislation or have submitted a request for this to happen,
(5) have the right to reside in Belgium because they benefit from temporary protection according to the relevant Belgian legislation,
(6) have a father, mother, legal guardian or spouse who fulfils one of the conditions above (in this case the change brought about on 15 May 2007 regarding the period of six months is not relevant),
(7) have had their principal residence in Belgium for at least three years at the time of registration in a HEI or
(8) have been granted a scholarship within the framework of development cooperation for the academic year and the studies for which the request for registration was submitted.

672 Cf. Opinion of Advocate General Sharpston delivered on 25 June 2009 in Case C-73/08 *Bressol and Chaverot*, para 20.

673 Cf. Articles 4 and 8 of the Décret régulant le nombre d'étudiants dans certains cursus de premier cycle de l'enseignement supérieur, 16.6.2006, published in Moniteur Belge 6.7.2006, p. 34055.

Pursuant to Articles 5 and 9 of the decree, those who do not qualify as residents within the meaning of Article 1 of the decree may apply for registration in a course listed in Articles 3 or 7 of the decree at the earliest three working days before 2 September preceding the relevant academic year. If the number of non-resident applicants who lodged an application for registration in one of the courses covered by the decree at the latest on the last working day before 2 September preceding the academic year exceeds the threshold fixed, places will be allocated by drawing lots (Articles 5 and 9 of the decree). Hence, non-residents have exactly three working days on which they can apply for a place and the allocation of places is entirely up to fate if the limited number of places is not sufficient for all the applicants. It is hardly surprising that the selection process was eyed with suspicion by the ECJ that obviously found it peculiar that non-resident applicants were not admitted on the basis of aptitude.[674]

It did not come as a surprise that the Commission considered the adoption of said decree another infringement of EU law and decided to open a new procedure against Belgium in January 2007. The Commission argued that the Belgian system, or more precisely the French Community system, was discriminatory and that Belgium had "failed to justify the introduction of this system."[675] Nevertheless, ten months later, at the same time as the Commission announced the suspension of the infringement proceedings against Austria, it also did so regarding Belgium. The Commission stated that data provided by Belgium allowed "the assumption of a risk that, without an appropriate safeguard measure, the French Community would be unable to maintain sufficient levels of territorial coverage and of quality in its public health system."[676] Nevertheless, the suspension resulting from the Austro-EU deal could not protect Belgium from students going to court and in fact they had already done so before the moratorium was announced.[677] In mid-2006, Nicolas Bressol and others had brought an action before the Belgian Constitutional Court seeking annulment of the decree. At the end of the year, Céline Chaverot and others brought another action.

674 Cf. Case C-73/08 *Nicolas Bressol and Others and Céline Chaverot and Others v Gouvernement de la Communauté française* [2010] ECR 2735, para 81.

675 Cf. Free movement of students: the Commission sends letters of formal notice to Austria and Belgium, Press Release, 24 January 2007 (IP/07/06).

676 Cf. Access to higher education: the Commission suspends its infringement cases against Austria and Belgium, Press Release, 28 November 2007 (IP/07/1788).

677 Also cf. Van der Mei, Free Movement of Students and the Protection of National Educational Interests, 2011, p. 127.

The applicants in the main proceedings sought to challenge the constitutionality of the decree and have it annulled. Considering the ECJ's legal interpretation in *Commission v Austria*[678] and *Commission v Belgium*[679], it must have seemed a clear-cut case when it was brought before the Belgian Constitutional Court. However, when the Belgian Constitutional Court halted proceedings pending a preliminary ruling from the ECJ in February 2008, the Commission had already enacted its moratorium. Some of the applicants in the main proceedings were students who did not qualify as residents in accordance with Article 1 of the decree and had applied for one of the (back then) nine courses mentioned in Articles 3 and 7 of the decree for the coming academic year.[680] The other applicants in the main proceedings were lecturers at the universities and university colleges of the French Community who felt that the "decree directly and immediately place[d] their jobs in jeopardy, as it w[ould], ultimately, lead to a reduction in the number of students enrolled in their higher education institutions."[681] Interestingly, the number of lecturers exceeded the number of students by far. The applicants in the main proceedings were composed of nearly 50 lecturers but only 15 students from France.[682]

Contrary to previous ECJ cases in the field, the Belgian Government for once submitted justifications to the Court.[683] It put forward that such differential treatment was necessary due to excessive burdens on the financing of higher education resulting from the influx of non-resident students. Nevertheless, the ECJ countered that this was not an essential reason as the explanations of the French Community in regard to the adoption of the decree indicated otherwise. According to them, a so-called "closed envelope" system "in which the overall allocation does not vary depending on the total number of students" is used to finance higher education.[684] However, as has been cleverly remarked, such a statement is a dangerous one to make considering that a "closed envelope" system does not bear any relationship to the number of students. Hence, an increase of students, especially one which is so excessive, would lead to a deterioration of the quality

678 Cf. Case C-147/03 *Commission v Austria*.

679 Cf. Case C-65/03 *Commission v Belgium*.

680 Cf. Case C-73/08 *Bressol and Chaverot*, para 21.

681 Ibid. para 23.

682 Cf. Garben, 2010, p. 1498.

683 Also cf. Hoogenboom, A., Mobility of Students and the Financial Sustainability of Higher Education Systems in the EU: A Union of Harmony or Irreconcilable Differences?, 9 CYEL, 2013, pp. 15–59, p. 23 at fn. 42.

684 Case C-73/08 *Bressol and Chaverot*, paras 49 and 50.

of education as HEIs would not see more funding.[685] This ties in neatly with the Belgian Government's next argument in the justification of the measures taken.

The Belgian Government claimed that deterioration of the quality of higher education due to overcrowding was a substantial factor for its actions. It maintained that in order to safeguard the system's homogeneity and be able to provide vital practical training for the medical and paramedical professions, the capacities could not be exploited any further. A decline in quality would put the public health system in jeopardy and, moreover, the education of such a huge number of students from abroad would eventually lead to a shortage of medical and paramedical personnel in the French Community. With non-resident students returning home after graduation, the health system of the French Community would eventually be undermined.[686] The ECJ maintained that the only valid and acceptable reason on which to base a claim was public health. It acknowledged that indirect discrimination may be justified if it serves to keep up the quality of the public health system. However, labelling the discrimination an indirect one is highly questionable. Indeed, AG Sharpston found the differential treatment in the case to be directly discriminating.[687] Whereas the first condition, i.e. principal residence in Belgium at the time of registration, is undoubtedly indirectly discriminating, the second condition, i.e. satisfying one of eight criteria exhaustively listed in Article 1 of the decree one of them being the right to permanent residence, most certainly is not.

The judges stressed that any measures derogating from the principles of EU law must comply with the principles of proportionality and necessity with regard to the means taken and objective pursued. Hence, any justifications by a Member State must include an analysis thereof. The Court underlined that in this particular case it was not enough to focus on non-resident students. Moreover, the fact that resident students might pursue their career elsewhere after graduation needs to be taken into account. Furthermore, graduates who did not receive their education in the French Community might establish themselves there.[688] Along the same lines, it also held that it could not be ruled out a priori that reducing the number of students, in particular with regard to preventing the quality of

---

685 Cf. Garben, 2010, p. 1501 at fn. 31.

686 Cf. Case C-73/08 *Bressol and Chaverot*, paras 52, 56 and 59.

687 Cf. Opinion of Advocate General Sharpston, Case C-73/08 *Bressol and Chaverot*, para 67.

688 Cf. Case C-73/08 *Bressol and Chaverot*, paras 62, 63, 71 and 73.

education from deteriorating, might not conjure up a shortage of medical and paramedical personnel in the area concerned.[689]

It is unfortunate that the ECJ did not take up the suggestion of AG Sharpston who had wished for a clarification of what constituted direct and what constituted indirect discrimination. The decree in question stipulates that everyone who has the right to remain in Belgium permanently is admitted to the degree programmes in question (cf. Article 1(1) of the decree). According to AG Sharpston, this right is "necessarily linked to a characteristic indissociable from nationality". That non-Belgian Union citizens may obtain such a right through the Citizens' Rights Directive does not change anything. Pursuant to Article 16(1) of said Directive, Union citizens must have legally resided in the respective Member State "for a continuous period of five years". Obviously, most non-resident applicants will neither qualify under the Citizens' Rights Directive nor under any other of the exhaustively listed criteria in Article 1(2) et seq. of the decree. AG Sharpston additionally relies on the "but for" test: "but for" the fact that students have Belgian nationality, they would not automatically have satisfied the right of permanent residence and therefore one of the criteria listed in the decree. She further points out that the Belgian Council of State had expressed doubts in its opinion on the draft of the decree, commenting that French applicants were directly targeted by the decree. It had also remarked that the legal provision in question in *Commission v Austria*[690] had treated Austrian citizens the same as everybody else, focussing on where the upper secondary diploma had been obtained.[691]

In December 2012, again simultaneously with Austria, the Commission suspended the infringement proceedings against Belgium for another four years, not without remarking that as restrictions had now also been put in place for medicine and dentistry (cf. Article 3 of the decree), these were also being examined by the Commission on the basis of the same principles.[692]

7.2.3 Austria and Belgium: Conclusion

It is a pity that the ECJ avoided the question of financing. Whereas it is true that financially a student increase has no consequences for Belgian HEIs due to the

---

689 Ibid. para 68.

690 Cf. Case C-147/03 *Commission v Austria*.

691 Cf. Opinion of Advocate General Sharpston, Case C-73/08 *Bressol and Chaverot*, paras 67–72.

692 Cf. Austria and Belgium given more time to justify quotas, Press Release, 18 December 2012 (IP/12/1388).

"closed envelope" system, this does not hold true for all the higher education systems of EU Member States. In the Netherlands, for example, HEIs receive financing on the basis of student numbers. Thus, an increase in students at Dutch HEIs also has financial consequences.[693] The Nordic countries Denmark, Finland, Norway and Sweden have adopted an agreement among themselves, which allows for compensation for those Nordic countries that have more incoming students than outgoing ones. Effective from 1 January 2013 (a previous agreement had been signed as early as 1996), Denmark, which has seen an excessive increase in students from Nordic countries since the academic year 2001/02, will receive yearly compensations. In 2014, compensation amounts to DKK 30,000 per student, which equals about EUR 4,023. Although Denmark, like all other EU Member States, is obliged to admit students from other EU/EEA countries, the former Danish Minister of Education, Morten Østergaard, remarked that Denmark welcomed students from its neighbouring countries but would not finance Norwegian and Swedish medical education. However, the Nordic countries were obviously more understanding than Germany and France, discussing the question of financing in the Nordic Council and as the former Norwegian Minister of Education, Kristin Halvorsen, observed, "the Danes ha[d] a good point".[694]

Alas, the discussion of financing higher education for students from other Member States centres on the medical and paramedical programmes. Particularly costly, these programmes are often limited by a *numerus clausus* or entrance examinations. Consequently, those who do not get a place in their country of origin, opt to go abroad in order to pursue their chosen course of study. For smaller Member States taking in an excessive influx of students comes at a cost, they are burdened with mounting expenditure for education and the need to reform their own HEIs. As the ECJ has clearly stated, Member States are

> free to opt for an education system based on free access – without restriction on the number of students who may register – or for a system based on controlled access in which the students are selected. However, where they opt for one of those systems or for a combination of them, the rules of the chosen system must comply with European Union law and, in particular, the principle of non-discrimination on grounds of nationality.[695]

---

693 Cf. Van der Mei, Free Movement of Students and the Protection of National Educational Interests, 2011, p. 131.

694 Myklebust, JP, New Nordic agreement on compensation for students, University World News, Issue No. 246, 31 October 2012, http://www.universityworldnews.com/article.php?story=20121031163939447.

695 Case C-73/08 *Bressol and Chaverot*, para 29.

Thus, while the organisation of education systems is up to the Member States (cf. Articles 165(1) and 166(1) TFEU), they need to comply with the right to move and reside freely within the territory of the Member States.[696] Whereas many – and especially the smaller Member States – used to prefer free access to their HEIs, this might no longer be possible, at least not regarding the most sought-after courses. The current situation may be summed up as follows: smaller Member States "are caught between a rock (political/budgetary realities) and a hard place (the Court's case law)."[697] Indeed, the advantages of the internal market may come at a high price for smaller Member States, whereas those that cause the increased student mobility benefit from the EU rules by having their nationals educated abroad before they return to put their newly acquired skills to use. Of course, this may not always be the case. Graduates may stay in the country or emigrate to settle in another country which is not their country of origin after all. However, Member States whose nationals excessively profit from higher education systems of other Member States would do well to emulate the example set by the Nordic countries, even though they are not required to do so under Union law.

While the influx of "*numerus clausus* refugees" affects medical and paramedical degree programmes in particular, it is also noticeable in others. In Austria, for example, this is the case regarding business administration, pharmacy and psychology. This prompted the former Rector of the University of Innsbruck and later Austrian Federal Minister for Science and Research, Karlheinz Töchterle, to wonder whether one could ask the Austrian tax payer to provide university infrastructure for students from large parts of Central Europe who had started to flood Austria because it provided places to study without charging tuition fees.[698] In fact, Austria has already tightened its once open admission scheme, having introduced admission regulations for popular degree programmes (cf. Section 14(h) of the UG 2002). In architecture and town planning (2,020 study places), biology and biochemistry (3,700 study places), computer science (2,500 study places), business administration, economics and management (10,630 study places) and pharmacy (1,370 study places) admission is restricted. The number of places is distributed among the universities. If the number of applicants exceeds the number of study places, there is an entrance examination. If a university receives fewer

696 Ibid. para 28.

697 Hoogenboom, 2013, p. 56.

698 Cf. Frank, M. and T. Schultz, Dr. Austria, Süddeutsche Zeitung, 17 May 2010, http://www.sueddeutsche.de/karriere/deutsche-studenten-in-oesterreich-dr-austria-1.45835-2.

applications than it has study places available, applicants that registered for the same programme at another university may also be admitted until the fixed number of study places is reached. Pursuant to Section 124(b) of the UG 2002 on the supplementary provisions relating to admission to degree programmes subject to the German *numerus clausus*, there are entrance examinations for psychology and veterinary medicine.

Contrary to the entrance examination in medicine and dentistry, Austria has not introduced quotas for any other degree programmes. Regarding the quota system in medicine and dentistry, the onus is on Austria to show that restrictions are justified. The same goes for Belgium and its quota system, which affects slightly more degree programmes. It is now up to Austria and Belgium to provide data and projections as to the actual inflow and outflow of students and graduates. As the Commission put it

> [a]t the end of 2016, there should be sufficient data covering several cohorts of graduates and enough information on future trends affecting the number of qualified professionals in the areas concerned to make an informed decision on whether the strict conditions for the public health exception have been met. If they have not, the normal freedom of movement rules will apply.[699]

7.2.4 The Special Case of Scotland

In Scotland admission to studies is subject to the payment of tuition fees. However, these are paid by the Scottish Government subject to eligibility (i.e. students studying full time for their first degree). Students ordinarily resident in Scotland and non-UK EU students ordinarily resident in the EEA have a Home/EU fee status (the standard tuition fee amounts to £1,820 per year) and may apply to the Student Awards Agency for Scotland, short SAAS, to have their tuition fees paid to the university. Rest of UK (RUK) students, i.e. students ordinarily resident in England, Wales or Northern Ireland, have a RUK fee status, which is significantly higher than the Home/EU fee status (up to £9,000 per year) and not payable by the SAAS.[700] A classic example of reverse discrimination, Scotland has taken advantage of the fact that differential treatment of one's own nationals is not prohibited under EU law. Reverse discrimination "occurs at the decentralized level

699 Austria and Belgium given more time to justify quotas, Press Release, 18 December 2012 (IP/12/1388).

700 For further clarification cf. The Education (Fees) (Scotland) Regulations 2011.

of provinces, municipalities and the like."[701] Whereas discrimination of Union citizens on grounds of nationality is prohibited within the scope of the Treaties (cf. Article 18 TFEU), the right to equal treatment may only be invoked if a cross-border dimension is involved. Reverse discrimination is therefore a phenomenon which "occurs as a result of a simultaneous application of EU law and national law."[702]

The high fees for RUK students were triggered by the Westminster Government's decision to increase tuition fees for undergraduate students to up to £9,000 per year. As the Scottish Government pointed out, the funding policy driven by Scotland is different from the English one, with the Westminster Government pursuing "an increasingly market-driven approach" to higher education. Scotland, on the other hand, sees free education for the able as a core part of its educational tradition and system. Fearing an influx of students due to tuition fees in England having been raised to up to £9,000 per year from the academic year 2012/13, the Scottish Government decided to raise tuition fees for RUK students. So far, this has not led to a decrease of RUK students studying in Scotland, with an increase of acceptances of 4% for the academic year 2012/13.[703]

Due to Scotland's referendum on independence on 18 September 2014, tuition fees for RUK students have become a highly debated topic. The Scottish Government proposed that following independence it would "maintain the *status quo* by continuing our current policy of charging fees to students from the rest of the UK".[704] However, it is prohibited under EU law to discriminate against students on grounds of nationality. If Scotland ever became independent, it would become an independent member of the EU. In the run-up to the referendum, the Scottish Government and the UK Government debated the accession process. The Scottish Government asserted that "Article 48 [TEU] provides a suitable legal route to facilitate the transition process, by allowing the EU Treaties to be amended through ordinary revision procedure before Scotland becomes independent, to enable it to become a member state at the point of independence".[705] The UK Government, however, opposed the idea stating that

701 Van der Mei, AP, The Outer Limits of the Prohibition of Discrimination on Grounds of Nationality: A Look through the Lens of Union Citizenship, 18 Maastricht Journal of European and Comparative Law, 2011, pp. 62–85, p. 79.

702 Ibid. p. 75.

703 Cf. The Scottish Government, Scotland's Future: Your Guide to an Independent Scotland, Edinburgh: November 2013, pp. 198–199.

704 Ibid. p. 199.

705 Ibid. p. 457.

"[t]he legal basis for becoming a member of the EU is Article 49 [TEU]".[706] It is clear that whatever route an eventual accession process might take, the tuition fees of students from the continuing UK could not be an intra-UK matter anymore.

It is evident that, following independence, students from the continuing UK would be directly discriminated against on grounds of nationality. As the UK government rightly assessed, "it is likely that the existing policy on tuition fees would have to be overturned either to impose tuition fees for Scottish and EU students or to remove the fee system for students from other parts of the UK."[707] In pursuing the policy proposed, "the Scottish Government would face an extremely steep uphill battle to convince the EU institutions that it should be entitled to retain a practice involving systemic direct discrimination against one particular cohort of EU citizens."[708] Hence, it has been suggested that the introduction of "residence conditions and/or [...] quotas" and therefore indirect discrimination might be a possible course of action.[709] The introduction of quotas would, however, certainly not be possible for all degree programmes. So far, the ECJ has held that quotas may be justified on public health grounds. Budgetary concerns have not yet been accepted as a justification. Except for medical and paramedical degree programmes, restrictions would therefore not be in line with the current EU policy.

7.3 Student Grants and Loans: Maintenance Aid and the Mobile Student

The right to maintenance grants or loans for students taking advantage of the cross-border dimension of the higher education landscape is a topic the ECJ has been addressing quite often in the last few years. Still a burning issue, cases concerning student maintenance frequently end up in the national courts and are eventually put before the ECJ. The growth in cross-border higher education and

---

706 UK Government, Scotland Analysis: EU and International Issues, London: January 2014, p. 63.

707 Ibid. p. 73.

708 Nic Shuibhne, N., University Fees and rUK Students: The EU Legal Framework, 2013, Scottish Constitutional Futures Forum, http://www.scottishconstitutionalfutures.org/OpinionandAnalysis/ViewBlogPost/tabid/1767/articleType/ArticleView/articleId/2759/Niamh-Nic-Shuibhne-University-Fees-and-rUK-Students--the-EU-Legal-Framework.aspx.

709 Ibid.

the resulting applications for student maintenance have prompted fears among the Member States that students are engaging in "study grant forum shopping".[710] While at first glance this may sound far-fetched, there might be some validity to these claims. Students have been applying for maintenance aid in Member States where they are not ordinarily resident and sometimes have never been. Member States are worried that the principles of free movement and non-discrimination on grounds of nationality threaten "the ability to secure a fair allocation of the educational resources of the Member State."[711]

Recent ECJ case law regarding student maintenance applications may be divided into three categories:

- students who move to another Member State for the sole purpose of pursuing an education,
- students whose parents are or have been employed in the Member State as migrant workers (i.e. resident workers) or frontier workers (i.e. non-resident workers), and
- students who are nationals of the Member State but have either never lived there or have only lived there for a short period of time. Thus, since they have made use of their right to freedom of movement, it is a situation with a cross-border element. As it is not wholly internal, it falls within the ambit of EU law.

The following sub-chapters shall give an overview on the most important developments.

7.3.1 *Förster* and the Five Year Rule: The Aftermath of *Bidar* or Goodbye to the Genuine Link Requirement for Non-Economically Active Students

Prior to the introduction of Union citizenship, mobile students could not invoke a right for maintenance grants or loans in the host Member State. The only way to have access to welfare benefits was economic activity. Hence, students who did not work themselves and did not have parents with migrant worker status could never qualify. It is indeed one of the great achievements of Union citizenship that

710 Case C-20/12 *Elodie Giersch, Benjamin Marco Stemper, Julien Taminiaux, Xavier Renaud Hodin, Joëlle Hodin v État du Grand-Duché de Luxembourg, intervening parties: Didier Taminiaux*, Judgment of the Court (Fifth Chamber) of 20 June 2013, nyr, para 21.

711 Jørgensen, S., The Right to Cross-Border Education in the European Union, 46 CMLR, 2009, pp. 1567–1590, p. 1567.

pursuant to certain conditions mobile students may be eligible for maintenance aid. A social advantage in accordance with Article 7(2) of Regulation 1612/68, the ECJ had long held that student maintenance aid falls outside the scope of Article 18 TFEU.[712] Thus, only those falling within Regulation 1612/68 had a right to claim such aid. However, since then, Union law has evolved and Union citizenship as well as a legal basis for education policy have been introduced into EU primary law. Since *Bidar*, student maintenance aid – whether in form of grants or loans – is available to students under certain conditions. The ECJ does not differentiate between student grants and state-subsidised student loans. After all, the underlying purpose is the same: "the provision of a state subsidy which is specifically intended to cover the living costs associated with education".[713]

In order to understand *Förster*[714], a case involving a German student in the Netherlands, *Bidar* needs to be looked at more closely. Mr Bidar, a French national, had entered the UK in August 1998 with his mother who underwent medical treatment there. After her untimely death, he stayed in the UK, now living with his grandmother. Mr Bidar completed his secondary education in the UK and enrolled to study economics at University College London, for which he received assistance for tuition fees. Regarding his application for a student loan for his maintenance costs, however, he was told that he was ineligible because he was not settled in the UK.[715] According to the Education (Student Support) Regulations 2001 (the "Student Support Regulations"), financial assistance for students in England and Wales to cover maintenance costs was available in form of loans. Since Bidar had been a full-time student during his time in the UK, he was not eligible for such a loan. Pursuant to the Student Support Regulations, a person was inter alia considered settled in the UK if their residence "has not during any part of that three-year period been wholly or mainly for the purpose of receiving full-time education."[716]

Unfortunately for Bidar, he was not covered by Regulation 1612/68.[717] However, the ECJ considered that

712 Cf. Case C-209/03 *Bidar*, para 38.

713 Cf. Dougan, M., Fees, Grants, Loans and Dole Cheques: Who Covers the Cost of Migrant Education Within the EU?, 1 JCER, 2005, pp. 4–29, p. 14.

714 Case C-158/07 *Jacqueline Förster v Hoofddirectie van de Informatie Beheer Groep* [2008] ECR 8507.

715 Cf. Case C-209/03 *Bidar*, paras 20 and 21.

716 Ibid. paras 12–15.

717 Ibid. para 29.

the situation of a citizen of the Union who is lawfully resident in another Member State falls within the scope of application of the Treaty within the meaning of the first paragraph of Article 12 EC [now Article 18 TFEU] for the purposes of obtaining assistance for students, whether in the form of a subsidised loan or a grant, intended to cover his maintenance costs.[718]

The Court further accepted that EU law had evolved, referring to Article 24(1) of Directive 2004/38 (which was to be implemented until 30 April 2006 and repealed, with effect from said date, Directive 93/96 on the right of residence for students and Directive 90/364 on the right of residence), which states that "[s]ubject to such specific provisions as are expressly provided for in the Treaty and secondary law, all Union citizens residing […] in the territory of the host Member State shall enjoy equal treatment with the nationals of that Member State within the scope of the Treaty." It further referred to Article 24(2) of Directive 2004/38, which stipulates that

the host Member State shall not be obliged to confer entitlement to social assistance […] prior to acquisition of the right of permanent residence, to grant maintenance aid for studies, including vocational training, consisting in student grants or student loans to persons other than workers, self-employed persons, persons who retain such status and members of their families.

Thus, the judges concluded that the grant of student maintenance aid falls within the scope of the Treaty as Community legislature had obviously already taken the view that it does.[719]

When *Bidar* was decided, Directive 93/96 still applied. However, Bidar was not a student in the mobile student kind of sense. Rather, he had already lived in the UK while going through secondary education. Whereas the seventh recital in the preamble to Directive 93/36 set out that "assistance granted to students, does not fall within the scope of the [EEC] Treaty within the meaning of Article 7 [now Article 18 TFEU] thereof" and Article 3 of Directive 93/96 explicitly excluded "any entitlement to the payment of maintenance grants by the host Member State on the part of students benefiting from the right of residence", the ECJ held that

Article 3 of Directive 93/96 does not preclude a national of a Member State who, by virtue of Article 18 EC [now Article 21 TFEU] and Directive 90/364, is lawfully resident in the territory of another Member State where he intends to start or pursue higher education

718 Ibid. para 42.
719 Ibid. para 43.

from relying during that residence on the fundamental principle of equal treatment enshrined in the first paragraph of Article 12 EC [now Article 18 TFEU].[720]

During his secondary education, Bidar had been lawfully resident, meaning that no one had complained that he did not have sufficient resources or that he did not have sickness insurance. Thus, he had been lawfully resident under Article 21 TFEU and Directive 90/364 on the right of residence, granting rights to persons of independent means.[721] The legality of his residence was entirely based on EU law, as he did not have a UK residence permit, which, under UK law, is not obligatory for EU citizens. Hence, it appears that the onus is on the Member State "to show that the individual does not have sufficient resources of sickness insurance [...] rather than on the migrant citizen to show that he has sufficient resources/ medical insurance to entitle him to stay."[722]

The UK Government argued that it was legitimate to ensure that the taxes paid by the students or their parents were sufficient for the justification of subsidised loans and that it was "legitimate to require a genuine link between the student claiming assistance to cover his maintenance costs and the employment market of the host Member State." However, while the ECJ accepted that it was legitimate "to ensure that the grant of assistance to cover the maintenance costs of students from other Member States does not become an unreasonable burden which could have consequences for the overall level of assistance" and therefore grant maintenance aid only to those who had shown "a certain degree of integration" into the host Member State's society, it held that it was not permissible to "require the students concerned to establish a link with its employment market." The Court concluded that a mandatory residence period, such as the three years of ordinary residence required by the Student Support Regulations, was a means of proving "a certain degree of integration" into the host Member State. Due to the Student Support Regulations precluding any student of obtaining a settled status even though lawfully resident, having received a substantial part of their secondary education in the host Member State and therefore having established a genuine link with its society, they were therefore not compatible with Article 18 TFEU.[723]

720 Ibid. para 46.

721 Ibid. para 36.

722 Barnard, C., Case C-209/03, *R (on the application of Danny Bidar) v. London Borough of Ealing, Secretary of State for Education and Skills*, judgment of the Court (Grand Chamber) 15 March 2005, not yet reported, 42 CMLR, 2005, pp. 1465–1489, p. 1472.

723 Cf. Case C-209/03 *Bidar*, paras 55–63.

Bidar was not a judgment that opened floodgates to "grant-tourism" and as a UK Government press officer commented, the number of students who would benefit from the Court's ruling was in fact "very limited".[724] Students coming to the UK in order to start a degree course do not qualify. As Barnard clarifies, the same goes for those who, prior to attending university, have completed their A-levels, a two-year course, in the UK. Hence, the only ones who could qualify as ordinarily resident are those who have already completed their GCSE (General Certificate of Secondary Education) course in the UK. This means that only students who have received a substantial amount of their secondary education in the UK are able to claim maintenance aid for their studies.[725] Following *Bidar*, the Student Support Regulations were altered. Beginning with the academic year 2004/05, EU nationals or the children of such nationals who were "ordinarily resident in England and Wales on the first day of the first academic year of the course" and who have "been ordinarily resident throughout the three-year period preceding the first day of the first academic year of the course in the United Kingdom and Islands", were eligible for maintenance grants and loans.[726]

According to Article 24(2) of the Citizens' Rights Directive, Member States do not have to grant students maintenance aid prior to their acquisition of the right of permanent residence. Pursuant to Article 16(1) of the Citizens' Rights Directive, such right is acquired after "a continuous period of five years in the host Member State". Recital 29 of the preamble to Directive 2004/38 provides that "[t]his Directive should not affect more favourable national provisions." Article 37 of the Citizens' Rights Directive on more favourable national provisions states: "The provisions of this Directive shall not affect any laws, regulations or administrative provisions laid down by a Member State which would be more favourable to the persons covered by this Directive." However, the Citizens' Rights Directive does not contain a non-regression clause forbidding the reduction of the current level of protection. This is why it has been argued that Member States might as well lower their standards to reduce costs.[727]

It appears that the UK has become more cautious in the meantime, preventing "grant-tourism" of students who completed their secondary education in the UK with education being the main purpose of their stay. Para 2 of Part 2 of Schedule

---

724 ECJ establishes EU-wide right for students to loans and grants, EurActiv, 16 March 2005 (last updated 29.1.2010), http://www.euractiv.com/education/ecj-establishes-eu-wide-right-st-news-213557.

725 Cf. Barnard, Case C-209/03, pp. 1474 et seq.

726 SI 2005/1341 The Education (Student Support) (Amendment) Regulations 2005.

727 Cf. Barnard, Case C-209/03, pp. 1482 et seq.

1 of the Student Support Regulations is concerned with students who have not acquired the right of permanent residence when starting their course. They must not have been ordinarily resident during the relevant three-year period preceding the academic year "wholly or mainly for the purpose of receiving full-time education."[728] Exceptions apply if the student is in the UK for the main purpose of being with their parent or spouse/civil partner or if the main purpose of the stay is to remain with relatives "rather than mainly for the purpose of attending school."[729] Para 3 of Part 2 of Schedule 1 of the Student Support Regulations clarifies that students who have acquired the right of permanent residence and who have been ordinarily resident in the UK throughout the relevant three-year period preceding the academic year "wholly or mainly for the purpose of receiving full-time education", qualify if they were ordinarily resident in the EEA or Switzerland immediately before said period of ordinary residence.[730]

On 9 May 2005, following the judgment in *Bidar*, the Informatie Beheer Groep (the "IB-Groep"), the administrative body in charge of the enforcement of Dutch legislation relating to the financing of studies, adopted a Policy rule on the adaptation of applications for maintenance aid for studies ("study finance") for students from the EU, EEA and Switzerland entering into force with retroactive effect from 15 March 2005. Pursuant to it, Union citizens are eligible for study finance in the Netherlands if they have been lawfully resident there for a continuous period of at least five years prior to the application (cf. Articles 24(2) and 16(1) of Directive 2004/38). According to Article 2(2)(1) of the Law on the financing of studies (Wet studiefinanciering 2000, the "WSF 2000"), study finance may be granted to

> (a) students who possess Netherlands nationality,
> (b) students who do not possess Netherlands nationality but are resident in the Netherlands and are treated as Netherlands nationals in respect of the financing of studies by virtue of a treaty or a decision of an organisation of public international law[.]

In 2003, another paragraph was added stipulating that "the requirement that a student be resident in the Netherlands shall not apply to a student on whom that requirement may not be imposed because of a Treaty or a decision of an organisation of public international law."[731]

728 SI 2011/1986 The Education (Student Support) Regulations 2011.

729 2014/15 HE Student Finance Assessing Eligibility Guidance, recital 44, http://www.practitioners.slc.co.uk/media/692622/sfe_assessing_eligibility_guidance_14-15.pdf.

730 SI 2011/1986 The Education (Student Support) Regulations 2011.

731 Case C-158/07 *Förster*, paras 9 and 10.

Ms Förster, a German national, settled in the Netherlands in 2000 to pursue studies as a primary school teacher and subsequently enrolled for a bachelor's degree programme in educational theory at the Hogeschool van Amsterdam. In addition to her studies, Förster took up various jobs. She further received a maintenance grant by the IB-Groep from September 2000 onwards, which she was granted in relation to her status as a migrant worker (cf. Article 7(2) of Regulation No 1612/68). However, she was not gainfully employed from July 2003 to December 2003. Therefore, the IB-Groep ruled by decision of 3 March 2005 that Ms Förster had not retained her migrant worker status and was to repay the maintenance grant for the respective period. Ms Förster challenged the decision before the Rechtbank Alkmaar (Alkmaar District Court). However, it confirmed the previous decision that Ms Förster could not be regarded as a migrant worker for the second half of 2003 and held that she could not rely on *Bidar* because she had not been integrated into Dutch society prior to her degree in educational theory.

Ms Förster appealed the judgment before the Centrale Raad van Beroep (Higher Social Security Court), claiming that she had been "sufficiently integrated" into Dutch society and that she should be regarded as a migrant worker for the respective period.[732] The Centrale Raad van Beroep referred the matter to the ECJ for a preliminary ruling asking whether Article 7 of Regulation 1251/70 on the right of workers to remain in the territory of a Member State after having been employed in that State applied to a student who had moved to the Netherlands for the main purpose of pursuing higher education, had initially been employed on a limited scale but had ceased to work in the meantime. However, the Court negated that this was the case because Förster had neither ceased to work due to retirement or become permanently incapacitated nor had she become employed in another Member State and retained her residence in the Netherlands.[733]

AG Mazák in his opinion also elaborated on whether Förster would be able to profit from former case law holding that Union citizens who had been employed in a Member State "must be regarded as having retained [their] status as a worker provided that there is a link or, as the Court also referred to it, 'continuity' between the previous occupational activity and the studies undertaken." Continuity could indeed be seen as a given as Förster had, before ceasing to work, completed a paid work placement in relation to her studies. AG Mazák argued that the fact that a Union citizen had come to the host Member

732 Ibid. paras 15–23.
733 Ibid. paras 25–33.

State with the principal intention of studying and "was pursuing studies while working as an employed person, does not as such preclude that person [...] from relying on the [said case law]". According to him, the decisive element was whether the work pursued had not been "purely marginal and ancillary" and there was no evidence of abuse.[734] However, the ECJ did not even consider the retention of the worker status. This is without doubt most unsatisfactory and ought to have been discussed.

Moreover, the Centrale Raad van Beroep had enquired whether Directive 93/96 precluded students from invoking Article 12 TEC (now Article 18 TFEU) when applying for maintenance aid. The ECJ held that a Union citizen who had moved to another Member State in order

> to start or pursue education can benefit from a right of residence on the basis of Article 18 EC [now Article 21 TFEU] and Directive 93/96 when he or she fulfils the conditions set out in Article 1 of that directive as regards having sufficient resources and sickness insurance and being enrolled in a recognised educational establishment for the principal purpose of following a vocational training course.[735]

Citing *Bidar*, it held that a Union citizen "who is not economically active may rely on the first paragraph of Article 12 EC [now Article 18 TFEU] where he or she has been lawfully resident in the host Member State for a certain time" with regard to student maintenance aid.[736] The Court further reiterated that although Member States need to, "in the organisation and application of their social assistance systems, show a certain degree of financial solidarity with nationals of other Member States", student maintenace aid should not constitute an unreasonable burden interfering with the overall level of assistance.[737] Students may therefore be required to demonstrate a certain degree of integration into the society of the host Member State. Referring to Directive 2004/38 (although not applicable in the present case), which entails a durational requirement, the Court held that a condition of five years' uninterrupted residence was both appropriate and proportionate for the purpose of guaranteeing that the student was integrated into the society of the host Member State. It is up to the Member States

734 Opinion of Advocate General Mazák, delivered on 10 July 2008, Case C-158/07 *Förster*, paras 76–90.

735 Case C-158/07 *Förster*, para 40.

736 Ibid. para 39.

737 Ibid. para 48.

to lower the threshold: they may grant maintenance aid to students who do not fulfil the residence requirement set by the Citizens' Rights Directive.[738]

The Policy rule in question, which had laid down the residence requirement, had been adopted on 9 May 2005 and entered into force with retroactive effect from 15 March 2005.[739] Introduced to "cover the transitional period between the judgment in *Bidar* and the transposition of Directive 2004/38",[740] it was unclear whether the retroactive application of such a residence requirement was lawful. However, the Court decided that since the respective Policy rule gave greater rights to students, the principle of legal certainty did not preclude the retroactive application of a residence requirement "which makes the right of students from other Member States to a maintenance grant subject to the completion of periods of residence which occurred prior to the introduction of that requirement."[741] However, it was therefore also clear that the concept of the genuine link as we know it had been abolished.

The concept of the genuine or real link has been used to determine whether a Union citizen is sufficiently integrated into the society of the host Member State. In *Förster*, the Court relied solely on the residence requirement and did not take into account any other factors (which, without doubt would have been there considering that Förster had been studying and working in the Netherlands for quite some time). Hence, the "five years of uninterrupted residence" rule is no more than "a mere reflection of the genuine link requirement", making a complex assessment unnecessary.[742] The processing of applications for student maintenance aid has become a lot easier for Member States, if their national law coincides with the outer limits set by the Union legislature. By all accounts, this new legal situation also means that most mobile students will never be able to claim maintenance aid in the host Member State as they will have graduated by the time they qualify for permanent residency.[743] It is hardly surprising that

738 Ibid. paras 49–60.

739 Ibid. para 62.

740 Ibid. para 68.

741 Ibid. para 71.

742 Oršolić Dalessio, T., The Social Dimension of EU Citizenship – A Castle in the Air or Construction Gone Wrong?, 14 German Law Journal, 2013, pp. 869–888, p. 881.

743 Also cf. Golynker, O., Case C-158/07, *Jacqueline Förster v. Hoofddirectie van de Informatie Beheer Groep*, Judgment of the Court (Grand Chamber) of 18 November 2008, not yet reported, CMLR, Vol. 46, 2009, pp. 2021–2039, p. 2026.

Förster has been called a "politically wise" ruling.[744] However, it will also discourage Member States from setting lower thresholds. If a Member State decides not to implement any other measures except for the minimum requirement set by Article 24(2) of Directive 2004/38, i.e. the "five years of uninterrupted residence" rule, administrative burdens can be greatly reduced.

In the future, the concept of the genuine link will therefore essentially be reduced to "the assessment of proportionality of national requirements that provide for a shorter than the maximum possible period of residence".[745] However, so far, criteria have been relatively vague. Thus, it has been argued that the concept of the genuine link needs to be clarified.[746] It has often encompassed the length of residency in the host Member State. However, the ECJ has made it clear that other factors need to be taken into account as well. A genuine link between the applicant and the host Member State may be established through close ties of personal nature such as family relations,[747] past employment,[748] or language skills[749].[750] Union citizens who qualify for permanent residency according to Article 16(1) of Directive 2004/38 have "a secure (though not totally unqualified) right to residency, together with full rights to equal treatment – including access to maintenance grants and student loans."[751]

7.3.2 The Portability of Student Grants and Loans for the Economically Active Aka the Children of Cross-Border Workers: *Commission v Netherlands* and *Giersch*

Recently, the ECJ was concerned with the question of the portability of maintenance aid for children of migrant and frontier or cross-border workers. The Member States at issue were the Netherlands and Luxembourg, two countries with an extensive history of cross-border labour mobility. Besides a considerable

---

744 Van der Mei, AP, Union Citizenship and the Legality of Durational Residence Requirements for Entitlement to Student Financial Aid, 16 Maastricht Journal of European and Comparative Law, 2009, pp. 477–496, p. 485.

745 Golynker, 2009, p. 2026.

746 Cf. Oršolić Dalessio, 2013, p. 883.

747 Cf. Case C-367/11 *Déborah Prete v Office national de l'emploi, Judgment of the Court* (Fourth Chamber) of 25 October 2012, nyr, para 50.

748 Cf. Case C-503/09 *Lucy Stewart v Secretary of State for Work and Pensions* [2011] ECR 6497, para 100.

749 Cf. Joined Cases C-523/11 and C-585/11 *Prinz and Seeberger*, para 38.

750 Cf. Hoogenboom, 2013, pp. 28–29.

751 Dougan, 2005, p. 16.

number of frontier workers from its neighbouring countries Belgium, France and Germany, the Grand Duchy also has a growing inflow of migrant workers. On 1 January 2012, more than 44% of the total population were foreign nationals.[752] Likewise, the Netherlands experience a high inflow of frontier workers from its neighbouring countries Belgium and Germany. German nationals make up for the largest Union citizen immigrant group in the Netherlands, with 377,000 German nationals residing there at the beginning of 2012.[753]

In *Commission v Netherlands*[754] the Law on the financing of studies (Wet studiefinanciering 2000, the "WSF 2000") was an issue yet again. However, this time it concerned the discrimination of children of migrant and frontier workers regarding portable funding, which led the Commission to bring infringement proceedings before the ECJ. With regard to funding for higher education pursued outside the Netherlands, the Netherlands had established the so-called "three out of six years rule". According to Article 2(14)(2) of the WSF 2000, eligibility for portable funding was conditional on the student having resided lawfully in the Netherlands for at least three out of the six years prior to the enrolment at the HEI abroad. This requirement applies irrespective of nationality. The Commission argued that such a provision was indirectly discriminatory, violating Article 45 TFEU on the freedom of movement for workers and Article 7(2) of Regulation 1612/68 which stipulates that nationals of a Member State who are working in another Member State "shall enjoy the same social and tax advantages as national workers." It further held that such a residence requirement was even more discriminatory towards frontier workers as they "by definition, reside in a Member State other than the Member State of employment" and thus would not be able to satisfy the contested rule.[755]

The Netherlands contended that the aim of Article 2(14) of the WSF 2000 was to boost studying abroad. Thus, it claimed that residency in the Netherlands was a prerequisite to encourage mobility. In the alternative, it argued that it was in fact Article 12 of Regulation 1612/68 which applied in the present case. According to it, children of migrant workers shall be admitted to the host Member State's "general educational, apprenticeship and vocational training

752 Cf. OECD, Luxembourg, in: International Migration Outlook 2013, OECD Publishing, 2013, p. 274.
753 Cf. OECD, Netherlands, in: International Migration Outlook 2013, OECD Publishing, 2013, p. 278.
754 Case C-542/09 *European Commission v Kingdom of the Netherlands*, Judgment of the Court of Justice (Second Chamber) of 14 June 2012, nyr.
755 Cf. Case C-542/09 *Commission v Netherlands*, paras 15–18.

courses under the same conditions as the nationals of that State, if such children are residing in its territory." Among other things, the Netherlands cited "unacceptable financial consequences" should the "three out of six years" rule be abolished, fearing that students would abuse the WSF 2000, seeking short-time employment in the Netherlands in order to obtain funding.[756]

However, neither AG Sharpston nor the Court accepted the argument that Article 7(2) of Regulation 1612/68 could not be invoked. Referring to the fourth recital of the preamble to Regulation 1612/68 which provides that the right to free movement extends to frontier workers (and to service providers, as a matter of fact), AG Sharpston stated that workers must neither reside in the host Member State nor enjoy the social advantages there in order to be able to invoke Article 7(2) of Regulation 1612/68. She added that the dependants of a migrant worker "are the indirect beneficiaries of the equal treatment obligation under Article 7(2) because discrimination against them with respect to a social advantage also discriminates against the migrant worker who then has to support the family member" and referred to *Meeusen*, a case which had involved the daughter of a Belgian frontier worker in the Netherlands studying in Antwerp, repeating that maintenance aid was not dependent on a residence requirement.[757] The Court agreed with Sharpston, reiterating settled case law pursuant to which student maintenance aid constitutes a social advantage within the meaning of Article 7(2) of Regulation 1612/68, which children of workers are entitled to if "the worker continues to support the child".[758] They may themselves rely on the respective provision "if, under national law, such funding is granted directly to the student."[759] The scope ratione personae of Article 12 of Regulation 1612/68, the Court explained, was entirely different: it grants a right to education to children of current or former migrant workers regardless of dependency. However, the child must have resided in the host Member State with its parents or a parent while at least one parent resided their as a migrant worker.[760]

756 Ibid. paras 23, 24, 26 and 27.

757 Opinion of AG Sharpston, delivered on 16 February 2012, Case C-542/09 *Commission v Netherlands*, nyr, paras 32 and 33; also cf. Case C-337/97 *C.P.M. Meeusen gegen Hoofddirectie van de Informatie Beheer Groep* [1999] ECR 3289, para 25.

758 Case C-542/09 *Commission v Netherlands*, paras 34 and 35; also cf. Case C-3/90 *M. J. E. Bernini v Minister van Onderwijs en Wetenschappen* [1992] ECR 1071, paras 25 and 29 and Case C-337/97 *Meeusen*, para 19.

759 Cf. Case C-542/09 *Commission v Netherlands*, para 48.

760 Ibid. paras 49 and 50.

With regard to the budgetary considerations, the Court recognised that although they "may underlie a Member State's choice of social policy and influence the nature or scope of the social protection measures which it wishes to adopt, they do not in themselves constitute an aim pursued by that policy and cannot therefore justify discrimination against migrant workers". It thus ruled that differential treatment between migrant workers and national workers was not permissible as this "would imply that the application and the scope of a rule of EU law as fundamental as non-discrimination on grounds of nationality might vary in time and place according to the state of the public finances". It held that students from other Member States who applied for maintenance aid in the host Member State and were considered non-economically active (cf. *Bidar*[761], *Förster*[762]) did not fall under this ruling. They were neither economically active themselves nor children of migrant workers, hence the requirement of "a certain degree of integration into the society" was justifiable in order to avoid that such assistance would become an unreasonable burden for the Member State.[763] In a nutshell, the Court held that a residence requirement such as the one laid down in Article 2(14)(2) of the WSF 2000 "to prove the required degree of integration is [...] inappropriate when the persons concerned are migrant workers or frontier workers." Integration, it further stated, arises from the fact that the migrant worker through taxes "contributes to the financing of the social policies of that State and should profit from them under the same conditions as national workers."[764]

As to "the" argument of the Netherlands that the objective of the relevant provision of the WSF 2000 was to increase student mobility, the Court accepted that this "constitutes an overriding reason relating to the public interest capable of justifying a restriction on the principle of non-discrimination on grounds of nationality." The Netherlands had argued that their scheme of maintenance aid for students studying abroad ran counter the idea that non-resident students studying in the Member State in which they are normally resident would be able to claim portable funding. It further emphasised that the provision in question was supposed to help enrich the Dutch society and employment market as the Netherlands expect the students profiting from the scheme to return after graduation. In order to lawfully restrict one of the fundamental freedoms guaranteed by EU law, a measure needs to be both appropriate and proportionate. Whereas

761 Case C-209/03 *Bidar.*

762 Case C-158/07 *Förster.*

763 Ibid. paras 57–61.

764 Ibid. paras 63 and 66.

the Court accepted that a residence requirement was appropriate, it negated the proportionality of the "three out of six years" rule due to exclusivity. It held that the specific periods of residence required prioritised "an element which is not necessarily the sole element representative of the actual degree of attachment", another possible element obviously being the employment of the parents. Consequently, the Court ruled that the Netherlands had failed to fulfil its obligations under Article 45 TFEU and Article 7(2) of Regulation 1612/68.[765]

Not long after the judgment in *Commission v Netherlands*, a similar case was brought before the ECJ. Luxembourg faced applications for student maintenance aid by children of frontier workers. Ms Giersch, Ms Hodin and Mr Taminiaux were Belgian residents who wanted to start their studies in Belgium. Mr Stemper was resident in Germany and wanted to pursue his studies in the UK. However, they only represented the tip of the iceberg, since, according to the Luxembourg tribunal administratif (Administrative Court), there were some 600 similar actions pending. In the Grand Duchy student maintenance aid is granted in form of grants and loans, which are portable. Studying abroad is not unusual for Luxembourg residents. Indeed, it was a must until recently as it was only in 2003 that the University of Luxembourg was founded. Many students study in the Grand Duchy's neighbouring countries Belgium, France and Germany as well as in Austria. Due to historical reasons – dating back to Empress Maria Theresia who was also Duchess of Luxembourg – the Universities of Innsbruck and Vienna are still "Landesuniversitäten" (state universities) of Luxembourg.[766]

In Luxembourg financial aid for students was covered by the Law of 22 June 2000 on State financial aid for higher education,[767] which was subsequently amended by the Law of 4 April 2005 and the Law of 26 July 2010 (the "amended Law of 22 June 2000").[768] Due to the ECJ ruling in *Giersch*, the amended Law of 22 June 2000 was repealed and replaced by the Law of 24 July 2014.[769] The new law entered into force on 1 August 2014 (cf. Article 13 of the Law of 24 July 2014).

According to Article 2 of the amended Law of 22 June 2000, students qualify for maintenance aid if they are either Luxembourg nationals or a family member of a Luxembourg national and are domiciled in Luxembourg or if they are

765 Ibid. paras 70–89.

766 Cf. Bethscheider, W., Hochschulwesen in Luxemburg, GR-Atlas, http://gr-atlas.uni.lu/index.php/de/articles/ge62/ho497/lu502.

767 *Mémorial* A 2000, p. 1106.

768 *Mémorial* A 2005, p. 786 and *Mémorial* A 2010, p. 2040.

769 *Mémorial* A 2014, p. 2188.

a national of another Member State of the EU or the EEA or Switzerland, reside in Luxembourg and are either employed, self-employed, retain that status or are a family member of a person who qualifies for one of those categories or have acquired the right of permanent residence. There is no difference in residence requirements for Luxembourg nationals and nationals of other Member States, which one could have reason to doubt due to the use of the concepts of "domicile" and "residence". In order to prove eligible for student aid, each student, regardless of nationality, has to provide a certificate of residence.[770] The financial aid is quite substantial. According to Article 3 of the amended Law of 22 June 2000, the maximum amount a student can receive is EUR 17,700 for each academic year. Every student is entitled to a basic amount (EUR 13,000), which may be topped up according to the student's financial and social situation and the tuition fees to be borne by the student.

The applicants in the main proceedings, sons and daughters of frontier workers who, by definition, are non-resident workers, did not reside in the Grand Duchy. They were therefore refused financial aid for their studies, although their parents had been working in the Grand Duchy for between 23 to 32 years.[771] As has been made clear in *Commission v Netherlands*, an economic link, even if it stems from the dependent student's parent, may not be disregarded. However, before the tribunal administratif the Luxembourg Government tried to contest the applicability of Article 7(2) of Regulation 1612/68 by stating that those entitled to financial aid were autonomous students not dependent on their parents. The tribunal administratif rejected this, stating that such aid constituted a social advantage within the meaning of Article 7(2) of Regulation 1612/68. The Luxembourg Government further added that it sought to increase the proportion of Luxembourg residents with a higher education degree. Granting financial aid to students who were not even resident in the Grand Duchy would seriously threaten the accomplishment of this goal, given that it would become an unreasonable burden on public finances.

The tribunal administratif therefore put the question before the ECJ

> whether Article 7(2) of Regulation No 1612/68 must be interpreted as precluding legislation of a Member State, such as that at issue in the main proceedings, which makes the

770 Article 3 of the Règlement grand-ducal du 12 novembre 2010 modifiant le règlement grand-ducal du 5 octobre 2000 concernant l'aide financière de l'Etat pour études supérieures, *Mémorial* A 2010, p. 3430.

771 Cf. Case C-20/12 *Giersch*, para 81.

> grant of financial aid for higher education studies conditional on residence by the student and which differentiates between persons residing in the Member State concerned and those who, not being resident in that Member State, are children of frontier workers carrying out an activity in that Member State, with the aim of bringing about an increase in the proportion of residents who hold a higher education degree while avoiding an excessive financial burden which the grant of such aid to every student would entail.[772]

The Court held that the measure at issue constitutes indirect discrimination on grounds of nationality as residence requirements "operate mainly to the detriment of nationals of others [sic] Member States".[773] Referring to *Bressol*[774] and *Commission v Netherlands*[775], it reiterated that indirect discrimination is prohibited unless objectively justified.[776] In this regard, the Luxembourg Government relied on social and budgetary considerations. It stated that the proportion of Luxembourg residents with a higher education degree was currently at 28% and that an increase was desirable in order to transition to a knowledge-based economy. The Luxembourg Government therefore claimed that it was necessary to achieve a figure of 66% of Luxembourg residents with a higher education degree, however, did not indicate when it planned to reach that goal.[777] It asserted that only Luxembourg residents had formed an attachment with the State's society "of such a kind as to justify the assumption that, having benefited from the possibility offered by the system of aid concerned in order to finance their studies – undertaken as the case may be abroad – they will return to Luxembourg in order to apply their knowledge for the benefit of that country's economic development." Furthermore, the Luxembourg Government insisted that granting financial aid to children of frontier workers not resident in Luxembourg would constitute an unreasonable burden on the State's budget and would put the financial aid system into question.[778]

Regarding the budgetary considerations, the Court rebutted the argument citing *Commission v Netherlands*[779].[780] It did accept the argument surrounding the

772 Case C-20/12 *Giersch*, para 33.
773 Ibid. para 44.
774 Cf. Case C-73/08 *Bressol and Chaverot*, paras 47 and 48.
775 Cf. Case C-542/09 *Commission v Netherlands*, para 55.
776 Cf. Case C-20/12 *Giersch*, para 46.
777 Interestingly, at national level, the Luxembourg Government had put the figure at 40%, the EU 2020 goal. Cf. Case C-20/12 *Giersch*, para 20.
778 Cf. Case C-20/12 *Giersch*, paras 47–50.
779 Cf. Case C-542/09 *Commission v Netherlands*, paras 57 and 58.
780 Cf. Case C-20/12 *Giersch*, paras 51 and 52.

social considerations, stating that promoting higher education was a legitimate objective pointing out that it was in the public interest and acknowledged at the EU level (EU 2020, ET 2020).[781] The Court reiterated that the payment of taxes by virtue of employment creates a link with the society of the host Member State, which is in itself in principle sufficient. However, it also held that distinguishing between migrant and frontier workers may be justifiable as frontier workers are not always as integrated into the society of the host Member State as a migrant worker. It also admitted that resident students might be more likely to return to Luxembourg upon graduation than non-resident students and become integrated into the local labour market. The Court therefore deemed the condition of residence appropriate "for attaining the objective of promoting higher education and of significantly increasing the proportion of Luxembourg residents who hold a higher education degree."[782] However, with regard to proportionality, the Court held that the residence requirement was too exclusive in nature, referring once again to *Commission v Netherlands*[783]. It remarked that

> [a] sufficient attachment of the student in question with the Grand Duchy such as to make it possible to conclude that that probability exists may also be derived from the fact that that student resides alone or with his parents in a Member State which borders upon the Grand Duchy of Luxembourg and that, for a significant period of time, his parents have worked in Luxembourg and live near to that Member State.[784]

The Court also grasped the opportunity to advise the Luxembourg Government of other, more lenient means. It suggested that student loans, the outstanding balance or the non-reimbursement thereof could be made conditional on the student working and residing in the Grand Duchy upon graduation. Moreover, it added that financial aid from the Member State in which the student resides should be taken into account in order to avoid the risk of duplication. Last but not least, it noted that "study grant forum shopping" could be avoided by ensuring that the frontier worker, i.e. the parent of the student, had worked in Luxembourg "for a certain minimum period of time". With regard to the last suggestion, the Court referred to the minimum requirement set by Article 24(2) of Directive 2004/38, according to which a host Member State was not required to grant maintenance

781 Ibid. paras 53–56.
782 Ibid. paras 63–68.
783 Cf. Case C-542/09 *Commission v Netherlands*, para 86.
784 Case C-20/12 *Giersch*, paras 76–78.

aid to students if they had not already acquired a right of permanent residence according to Article 16(1) of Directive 2004/38.[785]

Giersch warrants an explanation. From the outset, it seems a case not even worthy of a preliminary ruling. There are, in fact, no new questions to answer, or so one could have thought. The judgments in *Commission v Netherlands* and *Giersch* could not be more different. The reference to the five-year rule of Directive 2004/38 represents a departure from settled case law. In *Commission v Netherlands* no distinction was made between migrant and frontier workers. Moreover, the ECJ was committed to recital 4 of the preamble to Regulation 1612/68, treating migrant and frontier workers the same. Article 7(2) of Regulation 1612/68 could be invoked regardless of residence. As O'Leary notes, the concept of the genuine or real link, initially created for non-economically active Union citizens "seeking access to social benefits on the basis of a combination of Articles 18, 20 and 21 TFEU and, when necessary or relevant, Regulation 1612/68", is being transposed to the economically active Union citizens.[786] The "game changer" in this regard seems to have been the ECJ's decisions in *Hartmann*[787] and *Geven*[788], in which the Member State of employment refused the payment of child-raising allowances.[789] While it is certainly legitimate to require a frontier worker to contribute substantially to the national labour market and not just engage in minor employment, it is worrisome that special emphasis is now placed on residency. It is understandable that Member States want to prevent abuse of social benefits. Nevertheless, considering that many frontier workers spend their life working in another Member State accusing their children of "study grant forum shopping" might go too far.

When implementing the decision in *Giersch*, Luxembourg took up the misguided reference to the Citizens' Rights Directive. Pursuant to the Law of 19 July 2013 amending the Law of 22 June 2000, children of frontier workers qualify for study maintenance aid if their parents have been employed in the Grand Duchy for an uninterrupted period of at least five years and work at least half of the normal working hours.[790] In the first trimester of 2014, about 161,500 frontier workers were employed in Luxembourg, whereby approximately half of them had

785 Ibid. paras 79 and 80.

786 O'Leary, 2011, p. 534.

787 Case C-212/05 *Gertraud Hartmann v Freistaat Bayern* [2007] ECR 6303.

788 Case C-213/05 *Wendy Geven v Land Nordrhein-Westfalen* ECR [2007] 6347.

789 Cf. O'Leary, S., The Curious Case of Frontier Workers and Study Finance: *Giersch*, 51 CMLR, 2014, pp. 601–622, p. 609.

790 *Mémorial* A 2013, p. 2724.

French nationality and a quarter each came from Belgium and Germany. With 205,000 residents in employment, the number of non-resident workers amounts to 44% of the actual workforce of Luxembourg.[791] If non-resident, the dependent child of a frontier worker may face refusal of student maintenance aid if the parent, although employed in the Grand Duchy for years, has changed jobs or retired.

After having implemented the ECJ's decision in less than a month after it was issued, the Luxembourg Government revised its financial aid law. With the Law of 24 July 2014, a new system was introduced.[792] In accordance with the jurisprudence of the ECJ, dependent children of frontier workers may apply for student grants and loans if their parents have worked in Luxembourg for at least five out of the last seven years (cf. Article 3(5)(b) of the Law of 24 July 2014). Article 8(a) of the Law of 24 July 2014 entails an anti-cumulation rule to avoid overlapping of national benefits. According to Article 8, para 3 of said Law, the student maintenance aid and every other aid (e.g. child allowance) available to students in their State of residence is taken into account when determining the amount of student maintenance aid to be paid by Luxembourg. Hence, non-resident students need to provide confirmation of having applied for student maintenance aid in their State of residence in order to have proof of the exact amount they are entitled to. This amount is then deducted from the Luxembourg student maintenance aid.[793]

It is obvious that EU law is about to be transformed. Whereas economic activity used to be the "master key", opening up the redistributive schemes of the Member States, frontier workers will now face harsher conditions. However, the idea of economic reciprocity is misleading. Whereas migrant workers pay income tax in the host Member State, this is not necessarily the case for frontier workers.[794] There are no rules for taxation at the EU level, meaning that double-taxation agreements are bilateral, existing solely between individual Member States. The income of frontier workers may be taxed in the State of residence or the State of

791 Cf. Emploi salarié intérieur par lieu de résidence et nationalité 1995–2014, Le portail des statistiques – Grand-Duché de Luxembourg, http://www.statistiques.public.lu/stat/TableViewer/tableViewHTML.aspx?ReportId=7252&IF_Language=fra&MainTheme=2&FldrName=3&RFPath=92.

792 *Mémorial* A 2014, p. 2188.

793 Cf. http://www.guichet.public.lu/citoyens/fr/enseignement-formation/etudes-superieures/aides-logement/aide-financiere.

794 Cf. De Witte, F., Who Funds the Mobile Student? Shedding Some Light on the Normative Assumptions Underlying EU Free Movement Law: Commission v. Netherlands, 50 CMLR, 2013, pp. 203–216, p. 207.

employment or both.[795] However, if income tax is levied in the State of employment, excluding frontier workers from welfare benefits is illogical. Until double taxation has been dealt with at the EU level and streamlining has taken place, the ECJ ought to take into account where income taxes are paid and not propose inappropriate thresholds for frontier workers who are contributing to the budget of the respective Member State by virtue of tax. If frontier workers pay income tax in the State of employment, there is no reason why they should be treated differently to migrant workers. The situation would be different if their children received student maintenance aid from their State of residence. However, this can, as the ECJ has rightly stated, be dealt with by introducing anti-cumulation rules. Moreover, there is the possibility of frontier workers falling "between two stools" if they are considered neither sufficiently integrated in their State of residence (i.e. because of not yet having acquired permanent residence) nor in their State of employment (i.e. because they have not worked there for a sufficient amount of time).[796]

7.3.3 The Portability of Student Grants and Loans for the Non-Economically Active: The Genuine Link and "Own" Nationals

The "own" nationals of a Member State receive maintenance aid for studies if they fulfil the eligibility criteria. However, what happens if these nationals want to exercise their right to move freely to another Member State and seek to export their study grants or loans? The German Federal Law on assistance for education and training (Bundesgesetz über individuelle Förderung der Ausbildung – Bundesausbildungsförderungsgesetz, the "BAföG") as amended on 6 December 2011, by the twenty-fourth law amending the Federal Law on assistance for education and training,[797] provides for the portability of education or training grants. Pursuant to Section 17(2) of the BAföG, half of the student grant for higher education is given as a non-repayable grant, the other half as a loan, which must be reimbursed up to but not exceeding an amount of EUR 10,000. According to Section 5(2)(3) of the BAföG, students who have established permanent residence in Germany shall receive a portable education or training grant if they commence or continue their education and training in educational establishments

795 http://ec.europa.eu/taxation_customs/taxation/personal_tax/crossborder_workers/index_en.htm.

796 Hoogenboom, 2013, pp. 40 et seq.

797 BGBl. I, p. 2569.

in a Member State of the EU or in Switzerland. In a recent decision the German Bundesverwaltungsgericht (the Federal Administrative Court, the "BVerwG") held that Section 5(2)(3) of the BAföG is exhaustive, meaning that student grants may only be exported to the Member States of the EU and to Switzerland. It is not portable to the EFTA States that are parties to the EEA, i.e. Iceland, Liechtenstein or Norway.[798]

Section 5(1) of the BAföG defines "permanent residence" as the primary centre of interest of the person concerned. Permanent residency does not require the intention to stay there permanently. A person who resides at a place solely for education and training purposes has not established permanent residence there. According to Section 16(1) of the BAföG, which deals with the duration of grants for education or training abroad, a grant within the meaning of Section 5(2)(1) or (5) of the BAföG shall be paid for a maximum period of one year. Section 16(3) of the BAföG stipulates that in cases referred to in Section 5(2)(3) of the BAföG the grant shall be paid for more than one year only if the student has permanently resided in Germany for a minimum of three years when the student commenced residence abroad after 31 December 2007.

Section 6 of the BAföG provides that German nationals within the meaning of the Grundgesetz (Basic Law), who have their permanent residence in a foreign State in which they attend an education or training establishment or from which they attend an education or training establishment in a neighbouring State, may receive an education or training grant only if justified by specific circumstances. According to the administrative provisions relating to the BAföG (Allgemeine Verwaltungsvorschrift zum Bundesausbildungsförderungsgesetz, the "BAföGVwV"), such circumstances may inter alia relate to the student's personal capacity (e.g. illness or disability of the student), the student's personal life or close family (e.g. illness or disability of the student's parents or family members who require the student's care), reasons relating to the student's studies (e.g. the student frequents a German education and training establishment elsewhere equivalent to the relevant German education and training establishments) or financial reasons (e.g. pursuing education and training in Germany would constitute hardship).

798 Cf. Urteil des 5. Senats vom 10. Januar 2013 – BVerwG 5 C 19.11.

In joined cases *Prinz and Seeberger*[799] and in cases *Meneses*[800] and *Elrick*[801] the ECJ had to deal with German nationals who fell short of the residence requirement of three years and were therefore denied the export of grants to other Member States. Except for Meneses, the applicants in the main proceedings had all been born in Germany but had subsequently left the country by virtue of their parents' employment. However, the cases differ with regard to the applicants' previous exercise of the right to free movement. Whereas Mr Seeberger and Ms Elrick had exercised their right to free movement according to EU law when living in Spain and the UK prior to transferring their permanent residence to Germany, Ms Prinz and Mr Meneses did not do so as they were living in third countries such as Tunisia and Turkey (except for a three year stint in Spain in the case of Mr Meneses). However, in both cases it was the permanent residence in a third country that interfered with the three-year rule of a long enough permanent residence in Germany. As AG Sharpston noted, this does not affect the questions referred to the Court: the applicants are exercising their right to free movement in order to study in another Member State, where they resided before is not part of the analysis.[802]

Ms Prinz was born in Germany and lived in Tunisia for ten years, whereby she resided in Germany from September 1993 until April 1994. Upon her definitive return to Germany in January 2007, she pursued her secondary education in Frankfurt and obtained her upper secondary diploma, the German Abitur, in June 2009. In September 2009, she began her studies in the Netherlands. She was awarded a student grant for the academic year 2009/2010, however, her grant application for the following academic year was rejected on the grounds that she had failed to fulfil the residence requirement laid down by Section 16(3) of the BAföG because she had not continously resided in Germany for three years and was therefore not eligible to claim such a grant for a period of more than one year.

Mr Seeberger was born in Germany and attended primary and secondary school there until 1994. From 1994 until December 2005 he lived in Spain. In October 2009, he had himself entered into the Munich population register. Nevertheless, he maintained that he had already taken up permanent residence in

799 Joined Cases C-523/11 and C-585/11 *Prinz and Seeberger*.

800 Case C-220/12 *Andreas Ingemar Thiele Meneses v Region Hannover*, Judgment of the Court of Justice (Third Chamber) of 24 October 2013, nyr.

801 Case C-275/12 *Elrick*.

802 Cf. Opinion of Advocate General Sharpston, delivered on 21 February 2013, Joined Cases C-523/11 and C-585/11 *Laurence Prinz v Region Hannover and Philipp Seeberger v Studentenwerk Heidelberg*, Judgment of the Court of Justice (Third Chamber) of 18 July 2013, nyr, para 30.

Germany in January of 2006. In September 2009, he commenced his studies in Spain. His application for a study grant was rejected on the grounds that he did not qualify for a grant under Section 16(3) of the BAföG because he had not complied with the set out residence requirement, being resident in Spain.

Neither Ms Prinz nor Mr Seeberger applied for student maintenance aid in either the Netherlands or Spain or at least there is no indication that they did.[803] With regard to Ms Prinz this would not have been possible anyway as she did neither fulfil the five-year rule which applies to non-economically active students in the Netherlands nor is there any indication that she qualified as a migrant worker.

The Verwaltungsgericht Hannover and the Verwaltungsgericht Karlsruhe (German administrative courts), at which Ms Prinz and Mr Seeberger had brought actions, both decided to halt proceedings and refer the matter to the ECJ. The ECJ was essentially asked whether EU law precludes national legislation, which does not allow for education or training grants on the grounds alone that students exercising their right to freedom of movement and residence under Articles 20 and 21 TFEU had not already had permanent residence in their Member State of origin for at least three years.

The Court noted that Ms Prinz and Mr Seeberger were both German nationals who enjoyed Union citizen status under Article 20(1) TFEU and consequently, were able to exercise the rights conferred on Union citizens and invoke them if such exercise be denied, including against their Member State of origin.[804] Pursuant to Article 165(1) TFEU, the organisation of the education system falls into the competence of the Member States. However, such competence needs to "be exercised in compliance with European Union law and, in particular, in compliance with the Treaty provisions on the freedom to move and reside within the territory of the Member States, as conferred by Article 21(1) TFEU".[805] National legislation, which is to the detriment of certain nationals of that Member State because they took advantage of the opportunities available to them under EU law, restricts the right to move and reside freely within the territory of the Member States and at the same time contradicts Article 6(e) TFEU and the second indent

803 Ibid. para 35.

804 Joined Cases C-523/11 and C-585/11 *Prinz and Seeberger*, para 23.

805 Ibid. para 26. Also cf. Joined Cases C-11/06 and C-12/06 *Rhiannon Morgan v Bezirksregierung Köln and Iris Bucher v Landrat des Kreises Düren* [2007] ECR 9161, para 24 and the case-law cited.

of Article 165(2) TFEU, which aim to encourage student mobility.[806] Citing Morgan and Bucher, the Court reiterated that

> where a Member State provides for a system of education or training grants which enables students to receive such grants if they pursue studies in another Member State, it must ensure that the detailed rules for the award of those grants do not create an unjustified restriction of the right to move and reside within the territory of the Member States laid down in Article 21 TFEU[.][807]

The Court held that the residence requirement laid down in Section 16(3) of the BAföG "even though it applies without distinction to German nationals and other citizens of the European Union, constitutes a restriction on the right to freedom of movement and residence enjoyed by all citizens of the Union pursuant to Article 21 TFEU" and is "likely to dissuade nationals [...] from exercising their right to freedom of movement and residence in another Member State, given the impact that exercising that freedom is likely to have on the right to the education or training grant."[808]

The German Government argued that a requirement of a minimum level of integration such as the three-year rule laid down in Section 16(3) of the BAföG was justified because it "preserves the national scheme for education grants for studies abroad by protecting the State paying the grant from an unreasonable financial burden."[809] It presented data from the Statistisches Bundesamt (federal statistical office) and submitted that without a residence requirement approximately one million Germans living abroad with half a million of them in the neighbouring Member States (numbers from 2008) as well as certain non-nationals would qualify for portable funding for their entire studies.[810] However, as AG Sharpston so poignantly pointed out, it was doubtful that all German nationals residing in other Member States "from babes in arms to old-age pensioners" would want to pursue studies and rely on the German BAföG.[811] She further emphasised that

> [a]s EU law currently stands, it is unreasonable to require a Member State to assume financial responsibility for a student who has no connection to it. The opposite proposition

806 Joined Cases C-523/11 and C-585/11 *Prinz and Seeberger*, paras 27 and 29.

807 Ibid. para 30. Also cf. Joined Cases C-11/06 and C-12/06 *Morgan and Bucher*, para 28.

808 Joined Cases C-523/11 and C-585/11 *Prinz and Seeberger*, paras 31 and 32.

809 Ibid. para 34.

810 Opinion of Advocate General Sharpston, Joined Cases C-523/11 and C-585/11 *Prinz and Seeberger*, para 61.

811 Ibid. para 62.

would imply that the Member States have agreed on full financial solidarity for funding students and that there is full 'mobility' of that social advantage, which is clearly not the case.[812]

Furthermore, the three-year rule is not necessarily appropriate to determine the integration into German society. Whereas a German national who has lived elsewhere for 17 years and returns to Germany three years prior to exporting the study grant qualifies under the three-year rule, this is not the case with a German national who has lived in Germany for 17 years and leaves three years prior to starting to study in another Member State. AG Sharpston also pointed out that the three-year rule allowed a Bulgarian national to move to Germany three years prior to commencing studies in Poland or his Member State of origin and be entitled to a study grant out of the German public budget. From her point of view, the three-year rule was therefore not flexible enough.[813] The Court thus held that "a sole condition of residence [...] risks [...] excluding from funding students who, despite not having resided for an uninterrupted period of three years in Germany immediately prior to studying abroad, are nevertheless sufficiently connected to German society." Finding the three-year rule to be too exclusive, the Court noted that other factors needed to be taken into account such as whether the applicant had been educated in his Member State of origin for a significant period of time or was attached to the Member State in any other way such as by "his family, employment, language skills or the existence of other social and economic factors."[814]

Mr Meneses, a German national born in Brazil, has his permanent residence in Turkey, where his parents live. He attended German schools in Turkey (from 2001 to 2004 and from 2007 to 2009) and Spain (from 2004 to 2007) and in June 2009 obtained his upper secondary diploma, the German Abitur. From June 2009 to April 2010, he resided in South America. In the summer semester 2010, he began to study law at the University of Würzburg, Germany. During the winter semester 2010/11, he changed to the University of Maastricht, Netherlands. His application for an education and training grant was rejected on the ground that according to Section 6 of the BAföG, which allows German nationals who have their permanent residence abroad to derogate from the three-year rule of

812 Ibid. para 70.
813 Ibid. paras 94–96.
814 Cf. Joined Cases C-523/11 and C-585/11 *Prinz and Seeberger*, para 38.

Section 5(2)(3) of the BAföG, such grants may be awarded only under specific circumstances.[815]

The Verwaltungsgericht Hannover (a German administrative court), where Mr Meneses had brought an action, essentially asked the Court whether the right of free movement and residence conferred on Union citizens by Articles 20 and 21 TFEU precludes national legislation, which makes the award of education and training grants for studies for nationals of the same Member State with a permanent residence abroad conditional on the education establishment being either in the State of permanent residence or in a neighbouring State thereof and on specific circumstances which justify such a grant. However, the Court found that the derogations to the three-year rule as provided for by Section 6 of the BAföG and the supplementary provisions of the BAföGVwV do "not depend at all on the existence of factors connecting the applicant for the grant and German society."

Ms Elrick was born in Germany. Her permanent residence is at her parents' home in Germany. From 1998 onwards, she mainly resided in the UK, where she completed her secondary school education. In September 2008, she commenced a one-year course leading to a diploma in travel. According to Section 2(1)(2) of the BAföG, education and training grants are awarded for attendance of vocational schools ("Berufsfachschulen") which do not require prior completion of a course of vocational education or training provided that the course is of at least two years' duration and leads to a vocational qualification. Moreover, students need to meet certain criteria such as that they do not live at their parents' home and there is no educational establishment near their parents' home offering an equivalent course (cf. Section 2(1a)(1) of the BAföG). Section 5(4)(3) of the BAföG stipulates that Section 5(2)(3) of the BAföG only applies to studies at an educational establishment equivalent to vocational school classes ("Berufsfachschulklassen") within the meaning of Section 2(1)(2) of the BAföG. Because Ms Elrick attended a one-year course instead of a course of at least two years' duration as specified in Section 2(1)(2) of the BAföG, her application for an education and training grant was rejected.

According to the Verwaltungsgericht Hannover (a German administrative court), where Ms Elrick had brought an action, she would have been eligible for an education and training grant had she undertaken such a (two-year) course in Germany. Travelling to and from an adequate educational establishment to her parents' home would have taken her over two hours a day. She would therefore

815 Cf. Case C-220/12 *Meneses*, paras 8–12.

have had to find accommodation elsewhere. Hence, Ms Elrick would have met the conditions in Section 2(1a)(1) of the BAföG and, in principle, been eligible for an education and training grant in Germany.[816]

The ECJ was essentially asked whether the relevant German national law was compatible with Articles 20 and 21 TFEU. The German Government contended that the purpose of the BAföG was "to carry out a qualitative selection of the types of education or training courses subsidised".[817] However, the Court noted that legislation that

> makes the award of an education or training grant for a course undertaken abroad subject to the condition that the course in question be equivalent to a course provided by a vocational school ('Berufsfachschulklasse') leading to a vocational qualification following a course of study of two years, constitutes a restriction within the meaning of Article 21 TFEU, since a grant would be awarded to an applicant in the same personal situation as Ms Elrick to undertake in Germany a course equivalent to that which she pursued in another Member State.[818]

The German Government further contended that it was its intention to make education and training grants only available for courses that offer graduates attractive career prospects in that they have "the highest chance of success in the labour market." Students attending courses leading to weak qualifications, such as the one at issue, which according to the German Government is only suitable for general vocational guidance and "can only slightly improve the student's chances in the labour market",[819] are therefore not eligible for such a grant.

Germany has not yet implemented the Court's decisions in *Prinz and Seeberger*, *Meneses* and *Elrick* into national law. This will happen when the BAföG is next amended through the twenty-fifth law amending the Federal Law on assistance for education and training. In the meantime, the Federal Ministry of Education and Research has ordered the regional authorities by decree (24 July 2013 and 20 November 2013) to implement the aforementioned rulings.[820] On 20 August 2014, the German Government adopted a draft law on the twenty-fifth law

816 Cf. Case C-275/12 *Elrick*, paras 12–14.
817 Ibid. para 27.
818 Ibid. para 28.
819 Ibid. para 31.
820 Cf. Deutscher Bundestag – 17. Wahlperiode, Drucksache 17/14577, Schriftliche Fragen mit den in der Woche vom 12. August 2013 eingegangenen Antworten der Bundesregierung, 16.08.2013, pp. 90–91; Deutscher Bundestag – 18. Wahlperiode, Drucksache 18/115, Schriftliche Fragen mit den in der Woche vom 25. November 2013 eingegangenen Antworten der Bundesregierung, 29.11.2013, pp. 57–58.

amending the Federal Law on assistance for education and training.[821] According to Article 1(1)(a)(bb) of the draft law on the twenty-fifth law amending the Federal Law on assistance for education and training, a new third sentence shall be introduced into Section 5(2) of the BAföG. Implementing the decisions in *Prinz and Seeberger* and *Meneses*, it lays down that students that fall within the scope of Section 8(1)(1)–(5) of the BAföG must not have established permanent residence in Germany if they are able to prove a sufficient level of integration with other factors.[822] The decisions in *Prinz and Seeberger* and *Meneses* are only applicable to German nationals. The new provision in Section 5(2) of the BAföG will go beyond the rulings of the ECJ. By referring not only to Section 8(1)(1) of the BAföG but also to Section 8(1)(2)–(5) of the BAföG, it observes the principle of non-discrimination on grounds of nationality by including Union citizens who have the right to permanent residence in Germany, spouses or partners and children of Union citizens entitled to freedom of movement and Union citizens whose previous employment in Germany is related to the vocational training in question. Under the same conditions, this also applies to EEA citizens and to spouses or partners and children of EEA citizens. Third-country nationals who have a permanent residence permit or an EU long-term residence permit are also covered.

As the draft law on the twenty-fifth law amending the Federal Law on assistance for education and training explains, the current version of the BAföG does not differentiate between those entitled to freedom of movement and those who are not.[823] Furthermore, Section 5(4)(3)–(4) of the BAföG shall be changed to implement the decision in *Elrick*. Students studying at vocational schools and trade or technical schools ("Berufsfachschulen" and "Fachschulen") in other Member States of the EU shall receive education and training grants for courses that lead to a vocational qualification even if they are not of two years' duration (cf. Article 1(1)(b)(cc) of the draft law on the twenty-fifth law amending the Federal Law on assistance for education and training).

821 Entwurf eines Fünfundzwanzigsten Gesetzes zur Änderung des Bundesausbild ungsförderungsgesetzes, http://www.bmbf.de/pubRD/Regierungsentwurf_25._BAfoeGAendG.pdf.

822 "Satz 1 ist auf die in § 8 Absatz 1 Nummer 1 bis 5 bezeichneten Auszubildenden auch dann anzuwenden, wenn sie ihren ständigen Wohnsitz nicht im Inland haben, aber nach den besonderen Umständen des Einzelfalls ihre hinreichende Verbundenheit zum Inland anderweitig nachweisen."

823 Entwurf eines Fünfundzwanzigsten Gesetzes zur Änderung des Bundesausbildung sförderungsgesetzes, p. 38.

8. Regionalism in the European Union: Taking Education to a Whole New Level

While national governments are formidable participants in EU policy making, control has slipped away from them. [...] the locus of political control has changed.[824]

8.1 EU Cohesion Policy and Education and Training

In a time of multi-level governance, policy areas have to be approached from various levels. Depending on whether a Member State is organised as a federal, regionalised or unitary state, the local and regional levels may also be competent in regard to the content and organisation of education and vocational training (cf. Articles 165(1) and 166(1) TFEU). Thus, it is vital to encourage and foster cross-border, transnational and interregional cooperation in education and training. With a total of 273 regions (NUTS 2 according to the Nomenclature of Territorial Units for Statistics), there is quite a potential for cooperation at the regional level. With the Lisbon Treaty, territorial cohesion was added to the Union's objectives. Article 3(3) TEU explicitly stipulates that the Union "shall promote economic, social and territorial cohesion". Furthermore, "territorial cohesion" has been inserted into Title XVIII ("Economic, Social and Territorial Cohesion"), which provides the foundations for cohesion policy. Article 174, para 1 TFEU reads "[i]n order to promote its overall harmonious development, the Union shall develop and pursue its actions leading to the strengthening of its economic, social and territorial cohesion." According to Article 174, para 3 TFEU, "particular attention shall be paid to [...] cross-border [...] regions." There have been tendencies to limit cohesion policy to the poorer regions of the EU. These are, however, not compatible with EU primary law as it stands.[825]

Alongside economic and social cohesion, territorial cohesion is becoming increasingly important. The EU's cohesion policy supports cross-border

824 Hooghe, L, and G. Marks, Multi-Level Governance and European Integration, Rowman & Littlefield: Lanham, 2001, p. 2.

825 Kramer, E., European Parliament, DG for Internal Policies (Policy Department B: Structural and Cohesion Policies), Impact on and Practical Implications of the Lisbon Treaty for Cohesion Policy, 2010, p. 7, http://www.europarl.europa.eu/webnp/webdav/site/myjahiasite/users/emartinezdealosmoner/public/Impact%20on%20and%20practical%20implications%20of%20the%20Lisbon%20Treaty%20for%20Cohesion%20Policy.pdf.

(transfrontier), transnational and interregional cooperation. More than ever before, the Treaties respect the systems of government of the Member States. Since the Treaty of Lisbon, the subsidiarity provision explicitly refers to the regional and local level, thus accepting their autonomy. Article 5(3) TEU reads

> [u]nder the principle of subsidiarity, in areas which do not fall within its exclusive competence, the Union shall act only if and in so far as the objectives of the proposed action cannot be sufficiently achieved by the Member States, either at *central level* or at *regional and local level*, but can rather, by reason of the scale or effects of the proposed action, be better achieved at Union level.

The Union consists of three federal states (Austria, Belgium and Germany) as well as several regionalised states, some of which have only introduced regional or so-called "meso" or intermediate levels in recent years.[826] Hence, the recognition of regional and local authorities and their competence at the EU level is important. Article 4(2) TEU stipulates that "[t]he Union shall respect the equality of Member States before the Treaties as well as their national identities, inherent in their fundamental structures, political and constitutional, inclusive of *regional and local self-government*."

Given the importance of subsidiarity in the field of education, i.e. Member States are solely responsible "for the content of teaching and the organisation of education systems and their cultural and linguistic diversity" (Article 165(1) TFEU) and for the content and organisation of vocational training (Article 166(1) TFEU) as well as the fact that competence and policy-making responsibility is usually shared with the sub-national level in federal and regionalised states,[827] the acknowledgement of all actors of multi-level governance (i.e. EU, Member State and sub-national level) in the subsidiarity provision is crucial. In the past, the regions perceived the process of European integration as a potential threat to their powers. The German *Länder* successfully insisted upon a constitutional amendment because they were not involved in the decision-making process at the EU level with regard to German education policy.[828] The Lisbon Treaty's emphasis on

---

826 Cf. European University Institute, Study on the Division of Powers between the European Union, the Member States, and Regional and Local Authorities, European University Institute: Florence, 2008, pp. 24 et seq.

827 Cf. Committee of the Regions, Regional and Local Powers in Europe: Education and Youth, Culture, Public Health, Transeuropean Networks and Regional and Structural Policy, CoR Studies E-4/2002, Office for Official Publications of the European Communities: Luxembourg, 2002, p. 82.

828 Schade, A., A Research Topic in Education Law and Policy: The Development of Regionalism and Federalism in Europe and their Impact on Educational Policy and

the local and regional level gives rise to hope that the regions will be able to act as a link between the EU (and the Member States) and the civil society and thus bring EU educational policy closer to the citizens.

Cohesion policy and structural funds serve as a central implementing tool of ET 2020. The ESF and the ERDF are keys to promoting education and training. In the 2007–2013 programming period alone, about 10% of the total cohesion envelope, that is EUR 32 billion (ESF: EUR 25 billion, ERDF: 7 billion), were directly spent on education and training.[829] The ESF is the main financial instrument to invest in education and training. Its mission includes inter alia to "encourage a high level of education and training for all and support the transition between education and employment for young people" (Article 2(1) of Regulation 1304/2013[830], the "ESF Regulation"). The ESF supports "Member States in pursuing the priorities and headline targets of the Union strategy for smart, sustainable and inclusive growth (the "Europe 2020 strategy") and by allowing Member States to address their specific challenges with regard to achieving the Europe 2020 strategy objectives". The ESF thus takes into account "the relevant Integrated Guidelines and relevant country-specific recommendations adopted in accordance with Article 121(2) and Article 148(4) TFEU and, where appropriate, at national level, the national reform programmes as well as other relevant national strategies and reports" (Article 2(2) ESF Regulation). Article 3(1)(c) of the ESF Regulation defines four investment priorities, which focus on education and training directly:

(i) Reducing and preventing early school-leaving and promoting equal access to good quality early-childhood, primary and secondary education including formal, non-formal and informal learning pathways for reintegrating into education and training;
(ii) Improving the quality and efficiency of, and access to, tertiary and equivalent education with a view to increasing participation and attainment levels, especially for disadvantaged groups;

Administration, 4 European Journal for Education Law and Policy, 2000, pp. 35–39, p. 36.

829 European Commission, Channelling Cohesion Policy Funds Towards Education and Training: What to Expect from the New Regulatory Framework?, DGVT Meeting in Ireland, 21–22 May 2013, Agenda Item II, Document 2, http://www.education.ie/en/press-events/conferences/ireland-s-presidency-of-the-eu/conference-21-22-may-2013/channelling-cohesion-policy-funds-towards-education-and-training.pdf.

830 Regulation (EU) No 1304/2013 of the European Parliament and of the Council of 17 December 2013 on the European Social Fund and repealing Council Regulation (EC) No 1081/2006, OJ L 347, 20.12.2013, pp. 470–486.

(iii) Enhancing equal access to lifelong learning for all age groups in formal, non-formal and informal settings, upgrading the knowledge, skills and competences of the workforce, and promoting flexible learning pathways including through career guidance and validation of acquired competences;
(iv) Improving the labour market relevance of education and training systems, facilitating the transition from education to work, and strengthening vocational education and training systems and their quality, including through mechanisms for skills anticipation, adaptation of curricula and the establishment and development of work-based learning systems, including dual learning systems and apprenticeship schemes[.]

The ERDF, on the other hand, supports "investment in [...] educational infrastructure" (Article 3(1)(d) of Regulation 1301/2013[831], the "ERDF Regulation"). The investment priorities of the ERDF are in line with the investment priorities set out by the ESF (Article 5(10) of the ERDF Regulation). The ERDF also co-finances INTERREG EUROPE (2014–2020), the new generation of INTERREG programmes, which fosters cross-border, transnational and regional cooperation.[832]

8.2 Cross-Border Cooperation in Europe

The importance of cross-border cooperation became part of the European integration process soon after the signing of the founding Treaties. Initially, however, cooperation did not take place within the EU framework. Instead, the early development of cross-border cooperation was subject to informal initiatives at the local and regional level. In 1958, the EUREGIO (Gronau/Enschede), a Dutch-German cross-border region comprising 129 cities, municipalities and districts (25 Dutch and 104 German ones), was founded.[833] Cross-border regions are defined as territorial units, which include "contiguous sub-national units from two or more nation states".[834] They are especially challenging within public governance because of their "atypical, non-nested territorial set-up": made up of "municipalities, districts and other subnational jurisdictions – belong[ing] to

831 Regulation (EU) No 1301/2013 of the European Parliament and of the Council of 17 December 2013 on the European Regional Development Fund and on specific provisions concerning the Investment for growth and jobs goal and repealing Regulation (EC) No 1080/2006, OJ L 347, 20.12.2013, pp. 289–302.

832 http://www.interreg4c.eu/fileadmin/User_Upload/PDFs/INTERREG_EUROPE_-_final.pdf.

833 http://www.euregio.eu.

834 Perkmann, M., Construction of New Territorial Scales: A Framework and Case Study of the EUREGIO Cross-border Region, 41 Regional Studies, 2007, pp. 253–266, p. 254.

different nation states, they do not operate in a conventional context of public administration defined by legal competences and decision-making mechanisms rooted in public law."[835]

In 1980, the CoE opened the *European Outline Convention on Transfrontier Co-operation between Territorial Communities or Authorities*, also called Madrid Convention, for signature in order to encourage and facilitate cross-border co-operation between regional and local communities or authorities (it has currently been ratified by 38 of the 47 Member States of the CoE).[836] The convention, which includes model and outline agreements, statutes and contracts, came into force in 1981. However, as the Standing Conference of Local and Regional Authorities of Europe (CLRAE) pointed out, "the major obstacle to the effective application of the convention is that the acts accomplished in this way by local and regional authorities have no legal value within their respective States".[837] The Madrid Convention has been supplemented by three Additional Protocols. The first one, the Additional Protocol signed in 1995, addressed the issue by stating that "territorial communities or authorities may set up a transfrontier co-operation body, which may or may not have legal personality."[838] In the event that the cooperation body has legal personality, it "shall be as defined in the law of the Contracting Party in which its headquarters are located."[839]

There are different types of cross-border regions. One can generally distinguish between micro cross-border regions (e.g. Euregio, also European Region or Euroregion), which operate on a high cooperation intensity and "usually have a council, a presidency, subject-matter oriented working groups and a common secretariat", and macro cross-border regions (e.g. the Working Community of the Alpine Regions (ARGE ALP) founded in 1972, the Alps-Adriatic Working Community founded in 1978, or the Working Community of the Western Alps

835 Ibid. p. 259.

836 European Outline Convention on Transfrontier Co-operation between Territorial Communities or Authorities (1980) CETS No. 106, (in force since 22 December 1981).

837 Explanatory Report to the Additional Protocol to the European Outline Convention on Transfrontier Co-operation between Territorial Communities or Authorities (1995) CETS No. 159, para 3.

838 Article 3 of the Additional Protocol to the European Outline Convention on Transfrontier Co-operation between Territorial Communities or Authorities (1995) CETS No. 159.

839 Ibid. Article 4(1).

(COTRAO) founded in 1982), where the intensity of cooperation is considerably lower.[840] Whereas Euroregions have flourished in recent years, the development of Working Communities has come to a standstill. This can be well illustrated on the basis of the situation in Austria: small-scale or micro cross-border regions were non-existent before the accession to the EU. However, since the first were established in 1994 (EUREGIO Bayerischer Wald-Böhmerwald-Sumava, EUREGIO Inn-Salzach), "many of the Working Communities have largely stagnated in terms of political importance and budgets".[841] Nevertheless, since 2009, macro cross-border cooperation is on the rise again in form of so-called macro-regional strategies. These are integrated frameworks that "address common challenges faced by a defined geographical area relating to Member States and third countries located in the same geographical area which thereby benefit from strengthened cooperation contributing to achievement of economic, social and territorial cohesion."[842] The EU Strategy for the Alpine Region (EUSALP), which is currently under development, would essentially constitute an advancement of the ARGE ALP.[843] However, this would not mean the end of the ARGE ALP. On the contrary, as an existing institution, it would be integrated into the macro-region.

In 2006 and 2009, respectively, the EU presented two new frameworks for cross-border cooperation. Under the Austrian Council presidency in the first half of 2006, the first instrument for cross-border, transnational and interregional cooperation with a legal personality, the European Grouping of Territorial Cooperation (EGTC), was agreed on. Based on Article 159, para 3 TEC (now Article 175, para 3 TFEU), which allows "for specific actions to be decided upon outside the [Structural] Funds [...] in order to achieve the objective of social and economic cohesion envisaged by the Treaty",[844] Regulation 1082/2006[845], the

840 Perkmann, M., Cross-Border Regions in Europe: Significance and Drivers of Regional Cross-border Co-operation, 10 European Urban and Regional Studies, 2003, pp. 153–171, pp. 158–160.

841 Ibid. p. 166.

842 http://ec.europa.eu/regional_policy/cooperate/macro_region_strategy/index_en.cfm.

843 EU gibt grünes Licht für "Makroregion Alpen", EurActiv, 20 December 2013 (last updated 7 March 2014), http://www.euractiv.de/regionalpolitik/artikel/eu-gibt-gruenes-licht-fuer-makroregion-alpen-008382.

844 Recital 1 to the Preamble of Regulation 1082/2006.

845 Regulation (EC) No 1082/2006 of the European Parliament and of the Council of 5 July 2006 on a European grouping of territorial cooperation (EGTC), OJ L 210, 31.7.2006, pp. 19–24.

"EGTC Regulation", was adopted on 5 July 2006 and entered into force on 1 August 2006 (cf. Article 18, para 1 EGTC Regulation). Except for Article 16 of the EGTC Regulation, which stipulates that "Member States shall make such provisions as are appropriate to ensure the effective application of this Regulation", it became applicable on 1 August 2007 (cf. Article 18, para 2 EGTC Regulation). At the end of 2013, the EGTC Regulation was amended. Regulation 1302/2013[846] was adopted on 17 December 2013 and entered into force on 21 December 2013. It became applicable on 22 June 2014 (cf. Article 3 of Regulation 1302/2013).

According to Article 3(1) of the EGTC Regulation as amended, an EGTC may be made up of the following entities:

(a) Member States or authorities at national level;
(b) regional authorities;
(c) local authorities;
(d) public undertakings or bodies governed by public law;
(e) undertakings entrusted with operations of services of general economic interest in compliance with applicable Union and national law;
(f) national, regional or local authorities, or bodies or public undertakings, equivalent to those referred to under point (d), from third countries, subject to the conditions laid down in Article 3a.

According to Article 2(1)(b) of Directive 2004/17,[847] a "public undertaking" is defined as "any undertaking over which the contracting authorities may exercise directly or indirectly a dominant influence by virtue of their ownership of it, their financial participation therein, or the rules which govern it". A dominant influence is presumed if the authorities concerned

- hold the majority of the undertaking's subscribed capital, or
- control the majority of the votes attaching to shares issued by the undertaking, or
- can appoint more than half of the undertaking's administrative, management or supervisory body.

---

846 Regulation (EU) No 1302/2013 of the European Parliament and of the Council of 17 December 2013 amending Regulation (EC) No 1082/2006 on a European grouping of territorial cooperation (EGTC) as regards the clarification, simplification and improvement of the establishment and functioning of such groupings, OJ L 347, 20.12.2013, pp. 303–319.

847 Directive 2004/17/EC of the European Parliament and of the Council of 31 March 2004 coordinating the procurement procedures of entities operating in the water, energy, transport and postal services sectors, OJ L 134, 30.4.2004, pp. 1–113.

Pursuant to Article 1(9) of Directive 2004/18[848], a "body governed by public law" is a body which is

(a) established for the specific purpose of meeting needs in the general interest, not having an industrial or commercial character;
(b) having legal personality; and
(c) financed, for the most part, by the State, regional or local authorities, or other bodies governed by public law; or subject to management supervision by those bodies; or having an administrative, managerial or supervisory board, more than half of whose members are appointed by the State, regional or local authorities, or by other bodies governed by public law.

According to Article 3(2) of the EGTC Regulation as amended, the members of an EGTC must be "located on the territory of at least two Member States". Exceptions may apply for neighbouring third countries or overseas countries or territories (OCTs) (cf. Article 3(a)(2) and (5) of the EGTC Regulation as amended).

The tasks of EGTCs inter alia include Structural Funds management, strategic cooperation as well as "if appropriate, acting as a vehicle for the operational implementation of a cooperation project."[849] Pursuant to Article 7(3), subpara 1 of the EGTC Regulation as amended, an EGTC may carry out its tasks "with or without financial support from the Union." Hence, as the second recital of the preamble to Regulation 1302/2013 sets out, "[t]he establishment of an EGTC [...] is not automatically linked with any legal or financial advantages". However, the establishment of an EGTC without EU funding will most likely only be an option for authorities.

As set out in the eighth recital of the preamble to Regulation 1302/2013 amending the EGTC Regulation,

> it should be possible to use EGTCs in the future to jointly manage public services with a particular focus on services of general economic interest or on infrastructure. Other private or public law actors should also be able, therefore, to become members of an EGTC. Consequently, "public undertakings" as defined in Directive 2004/17/EC of the European Parliament and of the Council, and undertakings entrusted with the operation of services of general economic interest, in fields such as education and training [...] should be covered as well.

848 Directive 2004/18/EC of the European Parliament and of the Council of 31 March 2004 on the coordination of procedures for the award of public works contracts, public supply contracts and public service contracts, OJ L 134, 30.4.2004, pp. 114–240.

849 Committee of the Regions, The European Grouping of Territorial Cooperation – EGTC, January 2007, CdR 117/2007 (Study), p. 7.

This opens up a whole new perspective. Whereas the fields of activity of various EGTCs (among them several Euregios) include education and training,[850] the amendment of the EGTC Regulation is bound to be a breakthrough in the field as educational establishments have the possibility of forming EGTCs themselves. However, it would most certainly be useful for them to interact with already existing EGTCs made up of national, regional or local authorities as they would be able to pass on their experience and (legal) expertise. The fifth recital of the preamble to Regulation 1302/2013 reads that EGTCs, which pursuant to Article 1(4) of the EGTC Regulation "have in each Member State the most extensive legal capacity accorded to legal persons under that Member State's national law", may conclude "agreements with other EGTCs [...] for the purposes of carrying out joint cooperation projects". Hence, such joint cooperation projects could be carried out in the field of education and training. Existing EGTCs could therefore take EGTCs made up of schools or HEIs under their wings and play a coordinating role.

In October 2009, the European Council adopted the first macro-regional strategy, the EU Strategy for the Baltic Sea Region (EUSBSR), involving Sweden, Finland, Estonia, Latvia, Lithuania, Poland, Germany and Denmark.[851] Almost two years later, in June 2011, it endorsed the EU Strategy for the Danube Region (EUSDR), which involves nine EU members (Germany, Austria, Hungary, the Czech Republic, the Slovak Republic, Slovenia, Bulgaria, Romania and Croatia) as well as five third countries (Serbia, Bosnia and Herzegovina, Montenegro, Ukraine and Moldova).[852] The EUSBSR and the EUSDR have acted as a blueprint for further macro-regional strategies. In June 2014, the Commission launched the EU Strategy for the Adriatic and Ionian Region (EUSAIR), which covers four EU members (Croatia, Greece, Italy, and Slovenia) and four third countries (Albania, Bosnia and Herzegovina, Montenegro and Serbia).[853] Moreover, the European Council has already invited "the Commission, in cooperation with Member States, to elaborate an EU Strategy for the Alpine Region by

850 Cf. Committee of the Regions, EGTC Monitoring Report 2013: Towards the New Cohesion Policy, European Union: 2014.

851 European Council Conclusions, Brussels, 29–30 October 2009, point 35.

852 European Council Conclusions, Brussels, 23–24 June 2011, p. 13.

853 Communication from the Commission to the European Parliament, the Council, the European Economic and Social Committee and the Committee of the Regions concerning the European Union Strategy for the Adriatic and Ionian Region, COM(2014) 357 final, Brussels, 17.6.2014.

June 2015."[854] The EUSALP covers five EU members (Austria, France, Germany, Italy and Slovenia) and two third countries (Liechtenstein and Switzerland).

Macro-regions have been defined as "catchment areas bound by common history and collective memory, geography, climate and culture".[855] They constitute "an area including territory from a number of different countries or regions [including third countries or regions thereof] associated with one or more common features or challenges."[856] A "tool of European integration and increased territorial cohesion", macro-regional strategies "can be understood as a focussed and prioritised use of existing European, national, regional and even local policies [...] that span national borders".[857] They are built on the principle of the "3 NOs": no new EU funding, no new legislation and no new institutions. Instead, macro-regional strategies shall "provide an integrated framework that allows the European Union and Member States to identify needs and match them to the available resources through co-ordination of appropriate policies."[858] The Commission is heavily involved, taking on responsibility for the "co-ordination, monitoring, reporting, facilitation of the implementation and follow-up."[859] In order to be effective, macro-regional strategies need to rely on multi-level governance. Hence, sub-national and national levels as well as the civil society are involved in a bottom-up process, allowing them to "plan together and align funding."[860] The relevant actors have to identify synergies between existing policies and initiatives as they do not receive any additional EU funding.

---

854 Cf. European Council Conclusions, Brussels, 19–20 December 2013, point 50.

855 European Parliament, Opinion of the Committee on Culture and Education for the Committee on Regional Development on the evolution of EU macro-regional strategies: present practice and future prospects, especially in the Mediterranean (2011/2179(INI)), 2.3.2012.

856 http://ec.europa.eu/regional_policy/cooperate/baltic/pdf/macroregional_strategies_2009.pdf.

857 Dubois, A., Hedin, S., Schmitt, P. and J. Sterling, EU Macro-regions and Macro-regional Strategies – A Scoping Study, Nordregio Electronic Working Paper No 4, 2009, pp. 10 and 31.

858 Communication from the Commission to the European Parliament, the Council, the European Economic and Social Committee and the Committee of the Regions concerning the European Union Strategy for the Baltic Sea Region, COM(2009) 248 final, 10.6.2009, p. 7.

859 Ibid. p. 10.

860 Report from the Commission to the European Parliament, the Council, the European Economic and Social Committee and the Committee of the Regions concerning the added value of macro-regional strategies, COM(2013) 468 final, 27.6.2013, p. 4.

Whereas EGTCs tend to work on a micro-regional level, exceptions being the EGTC Sécretariat du Sommet de la Grande Région, which involves the Grand Duchy of Luxembourg and the Walloon Region, for example, macro-regional strategies are dominated by states, although they may by restricted to regions. This is the case with Germany, which has been the only country involved in two macro-regional strategies so far. Hamburg, Schleswig-Holstein and Mecklenburg-Western Pomerania participate in the EUSBSR while Baden-Württemberg and Bavaria participate in the EUSDR.[861] Moreover, Germany will also be involved in the EUSALP, the latest macro-regional strategy of the EU. However, the concepts of the EGTC and the macro-regional strategy may be more closely associated with each other in the future. The fifth recital to the preamble of Regulation 1302/2013 reads that EGTCs may conclude agreements in order to allow for the "more efficient operation of macro-regional strategies." Recital 19 to the preamble of Regulation 1302/2013 sets out that the purpose of EGTCs "should be extended to cover the facilitation and promotion of territorial cooperation in general, including strategic planning and the management of regional and local concerns in line with Cohesion Policy and other Union policies, thus contributing [...] to the implementation of macro-regional strategies." Hence, in theory, a macro-region could be organised as an EGTC.

8.3 Macro-regional Strategies and the Implementation of EU Education Policy

Both the EUSBSR and the EUSDR have incorporated education and training into their fields of activity. Macro-regions do not receive any additional EU funding. This is why the Council and the Commission have drawn attention to funding sources which may not have been used due to "a lack of information, of technical knowledge or of resources in order to comply with the manifold challenges of the application processes."[862] Therefore, macro-regions "should fully utilise the ESIF, the pre-accession and neighbourhood instruments in non-EU countries, but also all other available sources of EU and national funding."[863]

---

861 Schymik, C., Modellversuch Makroregion: Die EU-Strategien für den Ostsee- und den Donauraum, SWP-Studie, 2011, p. 8.

862 EUSDR Report June 2012, Priority Area 09: To Invest in People and Skills, p. 10.

863 EUSDR Report June 2013, Priority Area 09: To Invest in People and Skills: Education and Training, Labour Market, Marginalised Groups, p. 8.

One of the three objectives (previously four pillars[864]) of the EUSBSR is to "increase prosperity". The EUSBSR focusses on 17 priority areas. With the Priority Area "Education – Developing innovative education and youth", the EUSBSR intends to contribute towards achieving the EU 2020/ET 2020 goals. Actions include:

(1) The development of "new methods for training entrepreneurship and innovation":

The Baltic Training Programme, which inter alia supports the internationalisation of vocational education and training, serves as a flagship project;

(2) "To meet the challenge of demographic changes and to combat youth unemployment":

The dual system, which is already in place in the Baltic Sea Region (BSR) members Denmark, Germany and Finland, serves as a blueprint to other BSR members;

(3) "Making lifelong learning and mobility a reality within the BSR":

This includes providing information on mobility (funding, insurance, etc.) and "support in matchmaking with partners abroad". The BSR mobility database and a Baltic summer job programme are listed as potential flagship initiatives;

(4) "Enhance cooperation – on a voluntary basis – between the regional universities of the BSR":

This includes inter alia the coordination of research areas or mobility exchange of students as well as professors and researchers. The Baltic University Programme, which is the largest network of universities in the BSR, serves as a flagship project;

(5) "Closer integration and cooperation of youth policy structures using the 'Structured dialogue' as an influential instrument for involving young people in decision-making":

This includes inter alia the dissemination of knowledge through exchange with local, regional or national level politicians;

(6) "Closer integration and cooperation of youth policy structures, focusing on the local level":

---

864 Cf. http://balticsea-region.eu/about.

This includes inter alia the creation of municipal cooperation structures for the promotion of exchange of professionals and youth in the BSR;

(7) Social inclusion:
"[F]ostering social dialogue and cooperation on social development in the BSR" shall combat early school leaving.[865]

One of the four pillars of the EUSDR is "building prosperity". The EUSDR focusses on 11 priority areas. With Priority Area "To Invest in People and Skills", the EUSDR intends to contribute towards achieving the EU 2020/ET 2020 goals. Actions include

(1) "To enhance performance of education systems through closer cooperation of education institutions, systems and policies";
(2) "To foster cooperation between key stakeholders of labour market, education and research policies in order to develop learning regions and environments":

This includes inter alia a project on know-how transfer for the ESF administration;

(3) "To support creativity and entrepreneurship":

Action 3 focusses on "transversal key competences, entrepreneurship education and the promotion of innovative learning environments and creative partnerships between education, culture, civil society and the economy";

(4) "To support lifelong learning and expanding learning mobility" (departing from the Action Plan[866], action 4 now incorporates the original actions 4 and 5);
(5) "To promote equity, social cohesion and active citizenship through education and training" (action 5 new);
(6) "To improve cross-sector policy coordination to address demographic and migration challenges";

865 Commission Staff Working Document, Action Plan accompanying the Communication from the Commission to the European Parliament, the Council, the European Economic and Social Committee and the Committee of the Regions: European Union Strategy for the Baltic Sea Region, SEC(2009) 712/2 (revised February 2013), pp. 78–82.

866 Commission Staff Working Document, Action Plan accompanying the Communication from the Commission to the European Parliament, the Council, the European Economic and Social Committee and the Committee of the Regions: European Union Strategy for the Danube Region, SEC(2010) 1489 final, 8 December 2010, p. 72.

(7) "To fight poverty and social exclusion of marginalised communities in the Danube Region, especially the Roma communities" (departing from the Action Plan[867], action 7 now incorporates the original actions 7 and 8);
(8) "To promote gender equality on the labour market, especially in payment" (action 8 new).[868]

The EUSAIR, which was launched in 2014, also emphasises the value of education and training. Contrary to the EUSBSR and the EUSDR where education and training feature as priority areas, the approach of the EUSAIR is different: education and training serve as a cross-cutting issue. Under Pillar 1 "Blue Growth", the topic "Fisheries and aquaculture" includes the action "Developing skills". It focusses on the promotion and the strengthening of "networks of academies and training institutes to develop specific educational and (joint) training programs for fishermen and aquaculture farmers on innovative fishing and aquaculture techniques and safety at work."[869] Under Pillar 2 "Connecting the Region", the topic "Maritime transport" includes the action "Improving and harmonising traffic monitoring and management". It lists capacity building activities such as "training, education programmes, standardization and interoperability" in order to "improv[e] the application of international legal requirements" as possible projects.[870] Moreover, the topic "Intermodal connections to the hinterland", which includes the action "Developing the Western Balkans comprehensive network", lists capacity building and the development of communication activities such as "training, education programmes, seminars" that aim "at improving the application of international legal requirements in the field of environmental impact assessment of transport and energy infrastructures" as possible projects. Under Pillar 3 "Environmental Quality", the topic "marine environment" includes the action "Address diffuse sources". It focusses on education and training activities for farmers in order to increase awareness for environmentally friendly farming.[871]

---

867 Ibid. p. 73.

868 EUSDR Report June 2013, pp. 11–15.

869 Commission Staff Working Document, Action Plan accompanying the Document Communication from the Commission to the European Parliament, the Council, the European Economic and Social Committee and the Committee of the Regions concerning the European Union Strategy for the Adriatic and Ionian Region, SWD(2014) 190 final, 17.6.2014, pp. 15–16.

870 Ibid. p. 28.

871 Ibid. p. 45.

The planned EUSALP does not include education and training. Nevertheless, Pillar 1 "Fostering sustainable growth and promoting innovation in the Alps: from theory to practice, from research centres to enterprises" focusses on the development of research capacity, which undeniably includes providing for qualified personnel.[872]

8.4 The EGTC European Region Tyrol-South Tyrol-Trentino: Education and Training at the Crossroads

The construction of Euroregions varies: they may be created artificially or share historical, economic or social roots.[873] The EGTC European Region Tyrol–South Tyrol–Trentino, which is made up of the Province of Tyrol, the Autonomous Province of Bolzano/Bozen and the Autonomous Province of Trento, falls into the latter category. Until 1918, Tyrol, i.e. North Tyrol (Nordtirol) and East Tyrol (Osttirol), South Tyrol (Südtirol) and Trentino were part of the County of Tyrol. In the aftermath of WWI (cf. the 1919 Treaty of St. Germain), the Austro-Hungarian Empire was dismantled and South Tyrol and Trentino ceded to Italy. An example of Europe's "scars of history", the Austrian-Italian border is "the result of geography being repeatedly pillaged by history, or the environment by politics, or culture by economic interests and national prestige [...] drawn for historical reasons which have, for the most part, ceased to be reasons".[874]

The members of the EGTC European Region Tyrol–South Tyrol–Trentino are regions with legislative power. According to Article 2 of the Austrian Federal Constitutional Law (Bundes-Verfassungsgesetz, the "BV-G"), Austria is a federal State composed of nine autonomous federal provinces[875] (*Bundesländer* or *Länder* in German). The provinces are vested with legislative and administrative competence unless the constitution states otherwise (cf. Article 15(1) B-VG). The areas in which the federal State has legislative and administrative competence are listed in Article 10 B-VG. Article 11 B-VG lists the areas in which legislation is the responsibility of the federal State whereas administration is the responsibility of

---

872 DG REGIO, An EU Strategy for the Alpine Region (EUSALP) Core Document, 3.7.2014, http://ec.europa.eu/eusurvey/files/d6f334e8-64a9-422b-b7b8-36b336f25e89.

873 Cf. Schoen, N., The State's Power in the Euroregion Tyrol-South Tyrol/Alto Adige-Trentino, in: J. de Janny et al. (eds.), Walking the Tightrope: Europe between Europeanisation and Globalisation, Euroculture: Groningen, pp. 45–64, p. 49.

874 De Rougemont in Committee of the Regions, The European Grouping of Territorial Cooperation – EGTC, January 2007, CdR 117/2007 (Study), p. 17.

875 This term is used interchangeably with the term "federal states".

the provinces. Article 12 B-VG lists the areas in which the federal State provides the legislative framework and the provinces are responsible for the implementation of legislation and administration. Italy is a regionalised State, which is made up of 20 regions (regioni). Each of these regions has a statute that defines their competences (Article 123 of the Italian Constitution). According to Article 116, para 1 of the Italian Constitution, five regions are autonomous regions with special status (regioni autonome a statuto speciale). Compared to the fifteen regions with ordinary status, the autonomous regions are vested with "some genuine and exclusive legislative competencies."[876] Moreover, the statutes of the autonomous regions are adopted by constitutional law (cf. Article 116, para 1 of the Italian Constitution). The region Trentino-South Tyrol is composed of the Autonomous Provinces of Trento and Bolzano/Bozen (cf. Article 116, para 2 of the Italian Constitution). The 1972 special statute for the region Trentino-South Tyrol lays down the legislative and administrative competences of the Autonomous Provinces of Trento and Bolzano/Bozen.[877]

Since 1991, the regional parliaments of Tyrol, South Tyrol and Trentino (the regional parliament of Vorarlberg initially took part, but retreated to observer status) have been meeting for joint sessions ("Dreier-Landtag"). However, initiating cross-border cooperation proved complicated. Italy has made declarations with respect to the Madrid Convention, one of it being that Article 3(2) of said Convention should come into effect. Hence, an inter-state agreement is necessary for cross-border cooperation. Moreover, in regard to Article 2(2) of the Madrid Convention, "Italian territorial authorities empowered to conclude the agreements and arrangements covered by this Convention must, unless they are directly adjacent to a foreign State, be situated within 25 km of the border."[878] In 1993, Austria and Italy concluded a framework agreement on cross-border

876 Committee of the Regions, Regional and Local Powers in Europe: Employment, Social Policy, Environment, Transport and Vocational Training, CoR Studies E-1/2002, Office for Official Publications of the European Communities: Luxembourg, 2001, p. 40.

877 Dekret des Präsidenten der Republik vom 31. August 1972, Nr. 670, in: Autonome Provinz Bozen-Südtirol, Das neue Autonomiestatut, 14th ed., Südtiroler Landesregierung: Bozen, 2009.

878 List of Declarations made with respect to the European Outline Convention on Transfrontier Co-operation between Territorial Communities or Authorities (1980) CETS No. 106.

cooperation of local and regional authorities, which entered into force in 1995.[879] According to Articles 1 and 2 of said framework agreement, the contracting states commit themselves to fostering cross-border cooperation by supporting initiatives of the region Trentino-South Tyrol, the Autonomous Provinces of Trento and Bolzano/Bozen as well as the municipalities and associations of provincial and local authorities that are, even if only partially, situated within 25 km of the Austrian border and the Austrian provinces, municipalities and local authorities.

Whereas the Austrian-Italian cross-border cooperation was facilitated through the efforts to move towards an ever-closer Union, the increase of European cross-border cooperation, the ratification of the Madrid Convention and Austria's accession to the EU,[880] the attempt to institute a European Region Tyrol-South Tyrol-Trentino "*qua* public body project", i.e. "as a formal authority recognised by public law in both countries", had to be abandoned.[881] In fact, the opening of a common office of the European Region Tyrol-South Tyrol-Trentino in Brussels in 1995 was heavily criticized by the Italian State and was even the subject of an action before the Italian Constitutional Court.[882] In May 1998, a resolution concerning the cross-border cooperation within the framework of a Euroregion was adopted at a joint session of the regional parliaments.[883] In October 2009, a resolution concerning the establishment of the EGTC European Region Tyrol-South Tyrol-Trentino was adopted at a joint session of the regional parliaments.[884]

---

879 Rahmenabkommen zwischen der Republik Österreich und der Italienischen Republik über die Grenzüberschreitende Zusammenarbeit von Gebietskörperschaften, BGBl. Nr. 421/1995.

880 Cf. Zeller, K., Die rechtlichen Grundlagen für eine verstärkte Zusammenarbeit in der Europaregion Tirol, in: Laimer, S. (ed.), EUREGIO – quo vadis?, Athesia/NWV: Bozen/Graz/Wien, 2006, pp. 65–74, p. 65.

881 Perkmann, M., Cross-border Co-operation as Policy Entrepreneurship: Explaining the Variable Success of European Cross-border Regions, CSGR Working Paper No. 166/05, 2005, p. 21.

882 Romeo, C., Tirol Südtirol Trentino: Ein historischer Überblick, EVTZ Europaregion Tirol Südtirol Trentino: Bozen, 2012, p. 129.

883 Beschluss betreffend die Vereinbarung über die grenzüberschreitende Zusammenarbeit im Rahmen einer Europaregion zwischen der Autonomen Provinz Bozen-Südtirol, der Autonomen Provinz Trient und dem Land Tirol, Gemeinsame Sitzung der Landtage von Südtirol, Tirol, Trentino und Vorarlberger Landtag im Beobachterstatus, Meran, 19 May 1998.

884 Beschluss Nr. 1 betreffend Projekt zur Einrichtung eines Europäischen Verbundes für territoriale Zusammenarbeit (EVTZ) mit der Bezeichnung "Euregio Südtirol/Alto Adige, Tirol und Trentino", Gemeinsame Sitzung der Landtage von Südtirol, Tirol,

Following the resolution, the regional authorities of Tyrol, South Tyrol and Trentino opened a common office of the EGTC European Region Tyrol-South Tyrol-Trentino in Bolzano/Bozen.[885] In June 2011, the Convention on the EGTC European Region Tyrol-South Tyrol-Trentino was signed.[886] It was the first EGTC in Austria, the second in Italy and the 21st in the EU.[887]

8.4.1 Education in Context: Actions and Activities

In Austria, the federal State has competence for legislation on and administration of education and training unless the Federal Constitutional Law provides otherwise (cf. Article 14(1) B-VG). The responsibility for legislation on and administration of pre-school education rests with the provinces (cf. Article 14(4)(b) B-VG). With regard to compulsory schooling (primary school, lower secondary school (Hauptschule, Neue Mittelschule) and pre-vocational school), the federal State provides the legislative framework whereas the provinces are responsible for the implementation of legislation and administration. It is up to them to provide for the framework organisation, i.e. structure, organisational forms, establishment, maintenance, dissolution, school districts, class size and class time (cf. Article 14(3)(b) B-VG). The provinces are responsible for the legislation on and the administration of compulsory school teachers (except for the "Bundeslehrer" (grammar school teachers) at the Neue Mittelschulen; these are teachers with a university degree that usually teach at the Bundesgymnasien (grammar schools)) (cf. Article 14(4)(a) B-VG). The provinces have no competence as far as grammar schools (Bundesgymnasien), which provide education for the lower and the upper secondary level, are concerned. With regard to vocational schools for agriculture and forestry, the federal State provides the legislative framework whereas the provinces are responsible for the implementation of legislation and administration (cf. Article 14a(4)(a) B-VG). Support for youth activities (i.e. out-of-school

Trentino und Vorarlberger Landtag im Beobachterstatus, Mezzocorona, 29 October 2009.

885 Europaregion Tirol-Südtirol-Trentino, Gemeinsame Erklärung anlässlich der Arbeitssitzung der Regierungen von Tirol, Südtirol und Trentino, Innsbruck, 15 October 2009.

886 Übereinkunft über die Errichtung des Europäischen Verbundes für Territoriale Zusammenarbeit "Europaregion Tirol-Südtirol-Trentino" zwischen dem Land Tirol, der Autonomen Provinz Bozen-Südtirol und der autonomen Provinz Trient, 11 June 2011.

887 Cf. http://www.europaregion.info/de/evtz-europaregion.asp.

youth work) falls under the responsibility of the provinces.[888] Moreover, the provinces have legislative and administrative competence in sports.

In Italy, the State has exclusive competence (competenza esclusiva statale) with regard to legislation on general education standards (cf. Article 117, para 2, litera n of the Italian Constitution). Except for vocational training, the State has concurrent legislative competence (competenza concorrente) in education, subject to the autonomy of the educational institutions (cf. Article 117, para 3 of the Italian Constitution). According to Article 8(26)–(29) of the 1972 special statute for the region Trentino-South Tyrol, the Autonomous Provinces of Trento and Bolzano/Bozen have legislative competence for pre-schools, school welfare with regard to the educational sectors in which they have legislative competence, school buildings and vocational training. Article 9(2) of the 1972 special statute for the region Trentino-South Tyrol provides that the Autonomous Provinces of Trento and Bolzano/Bozen have concurrent legislative competence for primary schools and lower and upper secondary schools. The autonomy is particularly pronounced with regard to education in the Autonomous Province of Bolzano/Bozen. The population of South Tyrol contains a large portion of German speakers. Moreover, there is a Ladin minority. Hence, Article 19, paras 1 and 2 of the 1972 special statute for the region Trentino-South Tyrol provides for education in German and Ladin. Whereas education in German is available from pre-school to upper secondary school, education in Ladin is only available at pre-school and primary school. In Italy, the regions are responsible for developing and implementing youth policy programmes.[889] Furthermore, the Autonomous Provinces of Trento and Bolzano/Bozen have concurrent legislative competence for sport (cf. Article 9(11) of the 1972 special statute for the region Trentino-South Tyrol). As far as the Autonomous Provinces of Trento and Bolzano/Bozen have legislative competence, they also have administrative competence (cf. Article 16(1) of the 1972 special statute for the region Trentino-South Tyrol).

All of the members of the EGTC European Region Tyrol-South Tyrol-Trentino are vested with (a certain amount of) competence in the education sector. Hence, cooperation in this area is one of the objectives of the EGTC European Region Tyrol-South Tyrol-Trentino. Article 5(2)(b)(i) of the Convention and the Statute

888 Cf. Bundesministerium für Wirtschaft, Familie und Jugend, Jugendpolitik in Österreich: Ein kurzer Überblick, Bundesministerium für Wirtschaft, Familie und Jugend: Wien, 2009, p. 6.

889 http://extranet.cor.europa.eu/divisionpowers/countries/MembersLP/Italy/Policy-Areas-Obligatory/Pages/Youth-and-Sport.aspx.

of the EGTC European Region Tyrol-South Tyrol-Trentino stipulates that the EGTC promotes territorial development in education. Article 7(1)(a) of the Convention and the Statute of the EGTC provides that projects in education shall entail encouraging contacts between pupils, the expansion of language instruction and cooperation in the field of teacher training. Interestingly, education is always listed first among the areas of cooperation. Whereas one could argue that this is due to the German term for education being "Bildung" (Italian: "formazione"), this is most certainly not the case. On the contrary, cooperation in education is a priority for the EGTC European Region Tyrol-South Tyrol-Trentino. It goes much further than the Alpine Convention, an international territorial treaty between the Alpine states Austria, France, Germany, Italy, Liechtenstein, Monaco, Slovenia and Switzerland and the EU, and the aforementioned ARGE ALP.[890]

Cross-border cooperation in education is and has always been at the heart of the members of the EGTC European Region Tyrol-South Tyrol-Trentino. At their joint sessions, the state governments have often emphasised the importance of multilingualism. After all, three languages, German, Italian and Ladin, are spoken within the region Trentino-South Tyrol.[891] The regional parliaments have therefore requested that the respective regional governments consider whether it would be possible to introduce German/Italian as a compulsory subject at school.[892] Moreover, they suggested that SLA could be fostered with the help of

890 Cf. Schroeder, W. and N. Ehlotzky, Zustand und Perspektiven grenzüberschreitender Kooperation im Alpenraum, in: P. Hilpold, C. Perathoner and W. Steinmair (eds.), Rechtsvergleichung an der Sprachgrenze, Peter Lang: Frankfurt am Main, 2011, pp. 67–114, pp. 100 et seq.

891 South Tyrol has a population of 505,067. 62.3% (314,604) are German-speaking, 23.4% (118,120) are Italian-speaking and 4.1% (20,548) are Ladin-speaking (numbers from 2011). Cf. Autonome Provinz Bozen-Südtirol, Demografisches Handbuch für Südtirol, Landesinstitut für Statistik: Bozen, 2014, p. 118. The Trentino has a population of 526,510. 3.5% (18,550) of the population are Ladin-speaking. 0.3% (1,660) of the population speak Mocheno ("Fersentalerisch") and 0.2% (1,072) of the population speak Cimbrian ("Zimbrisch"), Germanic languages related to Bavarian (numbers from 2011). Cf. http://www.statistica.provincia.tn.it/binary/pat_statistica_new/popolazione/15CensGenPopolazione.1340956277.pdf.

892 Beschluss Nr. 17 betreffend Förderung der Kenntnisse der deutschen und italienischen Sprache sowie des Ladinischen und anderer Minderheitensprachen, Gemeinsame Sitzung der Landtage von Südtirol, Tirol und dem Trentino sowie Vorarlberger Landtag im Beobachterstatus, Meran, 30 March 2011.

content and language integrated learning (CLIL).[893] However, the introduction of CLIL is controversial since Article 19(1) of the 1972 special statute for the region Trentino-South Tyrol provides that the medium of instruction in pre-schools, primary and secondary schools in the Autonomous Province of Bolzano/Bozen must be the native language of the students. In 2013, the South Tyrolean regional government nonetheless adopted a resolution allowing for CLIL pilot projects in a restricted form (e.g. CLIL in a maximum of two subjects).[894] Contrary to South Tyrol, CLIL has already been established at various schools in Trentino. Whereby the choices in regard to the medium of instruction, i.e. German and English, appear broadly balanced at primary level (139 English/120 German CLIL projects), English predominates at lower secondary (86 English/42 German/8 English and German CLIL projects) and upper secondary level (97 English/43 German CLIL projects) (numbers taken from the academic year 2011/12).[895]

In 2005, the Province of Tyrol and the Autonomous Province of Trento concluded a memorandum of agreement.[896] They stressed the importance of multilingualism, stating that the fostering thereof ensures the appreciation of the cultural and social heritage. The Province of Tyrol and the Autonomous Province of Trento agreed to set up bilingual education (German-Italian/Italian-German) at two primary schools in Innsbruck and Trento, respectively (point 1). From the academic year 2005/06 onwards, teachers provide bilingual education for one class of each year, i.e. year one to four in Innsbruck and year one to five in Trento (starting with year one) at the respective primary schools (point 3). For this purpose, Tyrol and Trentino provide the necessary teaching staff (point 5). In 2010, the Province of Tyrol and the Autonomous Province of Trento signed a supplementary agreement.[897] With the academic year 2010/11, the regions provide for

893 Beschluss Nr. 20 betreffend Zielsetzung Zweisprachigkeit 2020, Gemeinsame Sitzung der Landtage von Südtirol, Tirol und dem Trentino sowie Vorarlberger Landtag im Beobachterstatus, Meran, 30 March 2011, point 3.

894 Beschluss Nr. 1034, Sprachprojekte und Sachfachunterricht mit der CLIL-Methodik an den deutschsprachigen Grund-, Mittel- und Oberschulen, Südtiroler Landesregierung, 8 July 2013.

895 Provincia autonoma di Trento Dipartimento Istruzione, Analisi Quantitativa Esperienze di Insegnamento in Modalita' CLIL (Content and Language Integrated Learning), pp. 15, 23 and 28, https://www.vivoscuola.it/c/document_library/get_file?uuid=8d280ec3-ba54-4f8f-9e0b-7323fd2bc58d&groupId=10137.

896 Vereinbarungsprotokoll zwischen dem Land Tirol und der autonomen Provinz Trient, Innsbruck, 20 April 2005.

897 Zusatzvereinbarung gemäß Punkt 3) letzter Absatz des Vereinbarungsprotokolls zwischen dem Land Tirol und der autonomen Provinz Trient, unterzeichnet in

four members of staff each (point 5). The supplementary agreement does not differentiate between primary and lower secondary schools anymore (in the 2005 memorandum of agreement, secondary schools were mentioned, however, it was not clear, whether bilingual education would be established at secondary school level). The oversight role belongs to the respective school authorities (point 11). This agreement shall apply until 2015, after which the application is automatically extended unless the Province of Tyrol or the Autonomous Province of Trento explicitly request otherwise (point 14). The Province of Tyrol and the Autonomous Province of Trento further signed a memorandum on the exchange of teaching staff.[898] The duration of the exchange shall be one week, whereby a teacher from Tyrol teaches at a school in Trentino and vice versa. This exchange takes place at primary and lower secondary school level.

In 2014, the Province of Tyrol and the Autonomous Province of Trento concluded another memorandum of understanding, which entered into force on 1 September 2014.[899] Whereas the cooperation in the school sector focussed on primary and lower secondary schools, it has now been extended to upper secondary schools. Under the arrangements for cooperation of the EGTC European Region Tyrol-South Tyrol-Trentino, a focus shall be put on individual exchange programmes for students and teachers. Furthermore, exchange programmes at class level and joint school projects and initiatives shall be introduced (point 1). Target groups are upper secondary schools (point 2). Host families of exchange students in Tyrol or Trentino, respectively, will receive financial support.[900]

It is apparent that Tyrol and Trentino are pushing for cooperation in the school sector, whereas South Tyrol maintains a low profile. Of course, Tyrol and Trentino (which has a bigger population of Italian speakers compared to South Tyrol) benefit the most in regard to teacher and student exchange. However, in a recent survey (June-August 2013), the South Tyroleans ranked education third

---

Innsbruck am 20. April 2005, und Änderungen des Protokolls, San Michele all'Adige, 22 May 2010.

898 Memorandum zwischen dem Land Tirol und der autonomen Provinz Trient zum Projekt Austausch von Lehrkräften, San Michele all'Adige, 22 May 2010.

899 Grundsatzvereinbarung zur Intensivierung und besonderen Förderung von Austauschprogrammen für Schüler/innen und Lehrer/innen sowie von Schulkooperationen und schulübergreifenden Projekten zwischen Schulen aus der autonomen Provinz Trient und dem Bundesland Tirol, Völs am Schlern, 5 July 2014.

900 Cf. Tirol und Trentino fördern Austausch von Schülern, Der Standard, 7 July 2014, http://derstandard.at/2000002786422/Tirol-und-Trentino-foerdern-Austausch-von-Schuelern.

(11.7% of the people questioned) when asked about the fields (11 in total) in which they wished for closer cooperation. For comparison, a wish for closer cooperation in education was only expressed by 7.3% of the people questioned in Trentino (ranked sixth) and 2.9% of the people questioned in Tyrol (ranked eighth). In the overall result (all the people questioned in the three regions), education ranked fifth (7.3% of the people questioned).[901] Evidently, there is support from the population for closer cooperation in the school sector.

With the EGTC European Region Tyrol-South Tyrol-Trentino as an intermediary, first contacts have been made between three primary schools in Tyrol, South Tyrol and Trentino. The aim is to establish a partnership for the exchange of experiences between students, teachers and families in the European Region.[902] Undoubtedly, South Tyrolean schools will gradually enhance cooperation with its neighbouring regions.

The University of Innsbruck functions as "Landesuniversität" (state university) for South Tyrol. In 1997, the University of Bolzano/Bozen was founded. However, the University of Innsbruck has not become any less important for the Autonomous Province of Bolzano/Bozen. In the fall semester 2012/13, 4,071 South Tyroleans studied in Innsbruck.[903] This is not without reason. With the academic year 1973/74, the University of Innsbruck in collaboration with the University of Padova started to offer courses in Italian law.[904] In the beginning, there was no legal basis for an Italian law programme. Hence, students were allowed to undertake a so-called "studium irregulare" choosing courses in Italian law.[905] This did not change until Austria and Italy signed a bilateral agreement on university cooperation in 1982.[906] Article 1 of said agreement allows

---

901 Traweger, C. and G. Pallaver, Kommunikation, Kooperation, Integration in der Europaregion Tirol-Südtirol-Trentino: Die Meinung der Bevölkerung, STUDIA: Innsbruck, 2014, pp. 73–76.

902 Zwischenbericht über den Stand der Umsetzung der Beschlüsse, die von den Landtagen von Südtirol, Tirol, Trentino und dem Vorarlberger Landtag im Beobachterstatus am 30. März 2011 in Meran verabschiedet wurden, March 2012, pp. 43–44.

903 Cf. Statistik Austria, Bildung in Zahlen: Tabellenband, Verlag Österreich: Wien, 2014, p. 321.

904 Cf. Klecatsky, HR and I. Winkler, Das Studium des italienischen Rechts an der Universität Innsbruck als Beitrag zur transnationalen Sicherung der Südtiroler Autonomie, in: W. Fiedler und G. Ress (eds.), Verfassungsrecht und Völkerrecht: Gedächtnisschrift für Wilhelm Karl Geck, Heymanns: Köln, 1989, pp. 451–466, p. 457.

905 Cf. http://www.uibk.ac.at/italienisches-recht/ueber_uns/ueber_uns.html.de.

906 Abkommen zwischen der Republik Österreich und der Italienischen Republik über die Zusammenarbeit der Universitäten, BGBl. Nr. 423/1983.

for inter-university agreements. Article 2(1) of said agreement provides for the introduction of "integrated" programmes ("integrierte Studienprogramme") at one or both of the universities that are parties to an inter-university agreement. Such an agreement must, in particular, include jointly developed curricula as well as provide that courses are held at one or both universities by lecturers from the contracting state parties (cf. Article 3(2) of said agreement). While the bilateral agreement entered into force in 1983, it was not until 1986 that an integrated diploma programme in Italian law was established at the University of Innsbruck.[907] In most of the courses Italian features as the medium of instruction. However, some are taught in German.[908] Graduates receive the academic title "Magister/a iuris", which equals the Italian "Laurea in giurisprudenza".[909] With the academic year 2012/13, a PhD double degree programme in Italian law was introduced. Students receive a PhD from the University of Innsbruck and a "Dottorato di ricerca in materie giuridiche" from the University of Padova.[910] Considering that the exchange of notes between Austria and Italy does not include the recognition of doctoral degrees (in Italy, research doctorates were only introduced in 1980[911]),[912] the PhD double degree programme in Italian law is an opportunity to receive academic recognition in both countries. The integrated diploma programme in Italian law and the PhD double degree in Italian law represent the most extensive collaboration between the universities of Innsbruck and Padova as they concern all stages of tertiary education.

---

907 Vereinbarung zwischen der Universität Innsbruck und der Universität Padua über die gemeinsame Durchführung eines Studienprogrammes "Integriertes Diplomstudium der Rechtswissenschaften", BGBl. Nr. 3/1986, amended through BGBl. Nr. 189/1987 and BGBl. III Nr. 262/2001.

908 Cf. http://www.uibk.ac.at/italienisches-recht/studium/studium.html.de.

909 Cf. 45. Notenwechsel zwischen der Regierung der Republik Österreich und der Regierung der Italienischen Republik über die gegenseitige Anerkennung akademischer Grade und Titel samt Anlage, BGBl. III Nr. 45/2001.

910 Anlage zum Mitteilungsblatt der Leopold-Franzens-Universität Innsbruck vom 14. Mai 2012, 26. Stück, Nr. 273.

911 Cf. Siller, S., Rechtliche Grundlagen der Bildungskooperation unter besonderer Berücksichtigung der Zusammenarbeit im universitären Bereich, in: P. Hilpold, C. Perathoner and W. Steinmair (eds.), Rechtsvergleichung an der Sprachgrenze, Peter Lang: Frankfurt am Main, 2011, pp. 481–513, p. 495.

912 Cf. Fraenkel-Haeberle, C., Die Anerkennung akademischer und beruflicher Titel zwischen Italien und Österreich, in: P. Hilpold, C. Perathoner and W. Steinmair (eds.), Rechtsvergleichung an der Sprachgrenze, Peter Lang: Frankfurt am Main, 2011, pp. 515–535, p. 523.

In 2002, the Universities of Bolzano/Bozen, Innsbruck and Trento signed a joint memorandum of understanding concerning the "Bolzano, Innsbruck, Trento Joint School for Information Technology" (BIT School).[913] Today, the BIT School, a PhD School, is thriving. The first phase was completed from 2009–2011. The BIT School is currently in its second phase, which lasts from 2012–2014.[914] In 2013, the Universities of Bolzano/Bozen, Innsbruck and Trento signed a framework agreement.[915] As set out in recitals (a) and (b) of the preamble to the framework agreement, the universities intend to foster the establishment of joint courses, develop collaborative projects and establish research networks. Pursuant to Article 1 of the framework agreement, the universities aspire to develop a permanent cooperation. This shall encourage mobility of students and lecturers. Professors and researchers shall be able to be associated with more than one HEI. Hence, they would be appointed to one university, while also carrying out teaching and research at one of the other universities concerned (cf. Article 3 of the framework agreement). Students shall be able to attend courses or modules that are subject to the curriculum at one of the partner universities. Moreover, lecturers shall organise study trips in coordination with each other (cf. Article 5 of the framework agreement). The universities plan to increase their cooperation within the Erasmus programme as well as to expand mobility projects within bilateral or multilateral frameworks. Furthermore, the mobility of students shall be facilitated by full academic recognition of periods of study at one of the partner universities (cf. Article 7 of the framework agreement).

Whereas youth policy is usually treated as a separate policy in the Member States,[916] the EGTC European Region Tyrol-South Tyrol-Trentino and its members

---

913 http://www.europaregion.info/de/marksteine-der-europaregion.asp; for the joint Memorandum of Understanding cf. http://www.google.at/url?sa=t&rct=j&q=&esrc=s&source=web&cd=1&ved=0CCAQFjAA&url=http%3A%2F%2Fwww.uibk.ac.at%2Fipoint%2Fnews%2Funi_und_die_welt%2F20020315%2Fbit-mou%2Fmou-final_en.doc&ei=i5jmU6DwGMSMOO-YgIgL&usg=AFQjCNEi7Lkgfq-1x8NUstRx-r6b1ZdgvA&bvm=bv.72676100,d.ZWU.

914 Überblick: Laufende gemeinsame Initiativen und Projektvorhaben der Universitäten von Bozen, Innsbruck und Trient, http://www.uibk.ac.at/public-relations/presse/archiv/2013/429/dokumente/dok_20130816121352_97018ebde1.pdf, pp. 3–4.

915 Rahmenabkommen zwischen der Freien Universität Bozen und der Leopold-Franzens-Universität Innsbruck und der Università degli Studi di Trento, Alpbach, 18 August 2013.

916 Committee of the Regions, Regional and Local Powers in Europe: Education and Youth, Culture, Public Health, Transeuropean Networks and Regional and Structural Policy, 2002, p. 81.

pursue an integrated approach, involving education, training, youth and sport. Besides the agreements between the Province of Tyrol and the Autonomous Province of Trento in the school sector or the regional universities in the higher education sector, the EGTC organises youth festivals and summer camps which feature language learning activities (German-Italian/Italian-German), with the latest addition being a joint sports camp.[917] The EGTC therefore embodies all the objectives set out in the Erasmus+ programme (cf. Regulation (EU) No. 1288/2013). With the Erasmus+ programme a special focus has been set on partnerships in regard to interregional and cross-border cooperation in the fields of education, training, youth and sport. According to Article 2(18) of the Erasmus+ programme, "partnership"

> means an agreement between a group of institutions and/or organisations in different Programme countries to carry out joint European activities in the fields of education, training, youth and sport or establishing a formal or informal network in a relevant field such as joint learning projects for pupils and their teachers in the form of class exchanges and individual long-term mobility, intensive programmes in higher education and cooperation between regional and local authorities to foster inter-regional, including cross-border, cooperation; it may be extended to institutions and/or organisations from partner countries with a view to strengthening the quality of the partnership[.]

Thus, the EGTC European Region Tyrol-South Tyrol-Trentino could either coordinate and implement actions and projects itself or serve as a platform for institutions and/or organisations, which seek to develop such partnerships. Applications for Erasmus+ grants could therefore include either strategic or collaborative partnerships.

8.4.2 The Erasmus+ Programme: An Option for the EGTC European Region Tyrol-South Tyrol-Trentino?

With regard to Erasmus+ grants for education, training and youth, Articles 8(1)(1) and 14(1)(a) of the Erasmus+ Regulation provide that strategic partnerships including institutions and/or organisations involved in education, training and youth may receive funding for transnational "cooperation for innovation and the exchange of good practices" (key action 2). They may aim "to develop initiatives addressing one or more fields of education[,] training and youth and promote innovation, exchange of experience and know-how between different types

917 Cf. http://www.europaregion.info/de/projekte-jugend.asp.

of organisations involved in education, training and youth or in other relevant fields."[918] Strategic partnerships may include

- activities that strengthen the cooperation between organisations with a view to establishing **exchanges** [sic] **of practices**;
- activities that promote the development, testing and/or implementation of **innovative practices** in the field of education, training and youth;
- activities that facilitate the **recognition and validation of knowledge, skills and competences** acquired through formal, non-formal and informal learning;. [sic]
- activities of **cooperation between regional authorities** to promote the development of education, training and youth systems and their integration in actions of local and regional development;
- transnational initiatives fostering entrepreneurial mind-sets and skills, to encourage **active citizenship and entrepreneurship (including social entrepreneurship)**.[919]

Strategic Partnerships can "also organise **training, teaching or learning activities** of individuals, in so far as they bring added value to the achievement of the project's objectives."[920]

Strategic partnerships involve at least three institutions and/or organisations from three different programme countries. Institutions and/or organisations from partner countries may take part if they bring "an essential added value to the project" but may not act as applicants.[921] On condition that a strategic partnership exclusively involves schools, promotes cooperation between local or regional school authorities or is situated in the youth field, it does not need to involve partners from more than two programme countries. If such a strategic partnership involves local or regional school authorities, it must include at least a school and a local organisation which is "active in another fields [sic] of education, training and youth or in the labour market" from each programme country. Regarding schools-only partnerships or partnerships in the youth field, two partners, one from each programme country, will suffice.[922] Hence, key action 2 would be ideal for the EGTC European Region Tyrol-South Tyrol-Trentino as no other programme or partner countries would be necessary. Eligible activities for strategic partnerships (this excludes learner activities and staff/youth worker long-term activities from and to partner countries) that foresee "training, teaching or learning activities" include:

918 European Commission, Erasmus+: Programme Guide, 2014, p. 15.
919 Ibid. p. 96.
920 Ibid.
921 Ibid.
922 Ibid. p. 97.

- Blended mobility combining short-term physical mobility (less than 2 months) with virtual mobility;
- Short-term exchanges of groups of pupils (5 days to 2 months);
- Intensive Study Programmes (5 days to 2 months);
- Long-term study mobility of pupils (2 to 12 months);
- Long-term teaching or training assignments (2 to 12 months);
- Long-term mobility of youth workers (2 to 12 months);
- Short-term joint staff training events (5 days to 2 months).[923]

Hence, Erasmus+ grants could, for example, be used for the teacher exchange between the Province of Tyrol and the Autonomous Province of Trento. Moreover, the newly introduced individual exchange programmes for students and teachers and the exchange programmes at class level would qualify. Furthermore, the activities that the EGTC European Region Tyrol-South Tyrol-Trentino organises, such as summer camps that include language courses, could be financed through the Erasmus+ programme. The maximum grant awarded for a strategic partnership amounts to EUR 150,000 per year.[924] Considering that the EGTC's overall budget for 2013 amounted to EUR 520,000 (the members contribute EUR 150,000 each) and specific project funding (Interreg, Autonomous Region),[925] an Erasmus+ grant would certainly be most useful.

With regard to Erasmus+ grants for sport, Article 17(1)(a) of the Erasmus+ Regulation provides that collaborative partnerships may receive funding for transnational activities which "focus in particular on grassroots sport". Public bodies, which are responsible for sport, and non-profit organisations may take part in collaborative partnerships that "should involve an appropriate and diverse range of partners in order to benefit from different experiences, profiles and expertise and to produce relevant and high quality project results."[926] Activities may include

- networking among key stakeholders;
- identification and sharing of good practices;
- development and implementation of training and educational modules;
- activities to increase the competences of multipliers in the field of sport and to develop monitoring and
- benchmarking of indicators, notably as regards the promotion of ethical behaviours and codes of conduct among sportspeople;

923 Ibid. p. 98.

924 Ibid. p. 103.

925 Cf. Committee of the Regions, EGTC Monitoring Report 2013, 2014, p. 67.

926 European Commission, Erasmus+: Programme Guide, 2014, p. 185.

- awareness-raising activities on the value of sport and physical activity in relation to the personal, social and professional development of individuals;
- activities to improve the evidence-base of sport to tackle societal and economic challenges (collection of data, surveys, consultations, etc.);
- activities to promote innovative synergies between the field of sport and the fields of health, education, training and youth;
- conferences, seminars, meetings, events and awareness-raising actions underpinning the aforementioned activities.[927]

Collaborative partnerships target cooperation within programme countries and must involve at least five public bodies or non-profit organisations from five different programme countries.[928] Institutions and/or organisations from partner countries may take part if they bring "an essential added value to the project" but may not act as applicants.[929] The maximum grant awarded amounts to EUR 500,000 and at maximum 80% of the total eligible costs.[930] Whereas a collaborative partnership might not be as interesting to the EGTC European Region Tyrol-South Tyrol-Trentino as a strategic partnership because it involves so many partners, nearby programme countries such as Germany (e.g. Bavaria) and Liechtenstein or France, which like Austria and Italy will be involved in the EUSALP, would be an option. Moreover, if Switzerland (e.g. the Canton of Graubünden which borders Tyrol, South Tyrol and Liechtenstein and would thus be ideal for a collaboration) reverts to being a programme country (due to the partner country status, the participation of Swiss institutions and/or organisations depends on whether they add essential value to the project), finding project partners in the immediate vicinity of the EGTC European Region Tyrol-South Tyrol-Trentino should be manageable considering that Bavaria and the aforementioned regions form a contiguous area.

927 Ibid.
928 Ibid. p. 186.
929 Ibid. p. 185.
930 Ibid. p. 189.

9. Outlook and Concluding Remarks

Rooted in functional spillover, education has developed into a fully-fledged EU policy within its own right. It has been propelled from the margins of European integration to its very centre. Under the aegis of the EU, the national and sub-national levels actively cooperate in education and training. Increasing cross-border cooperation is a focal point of the Erasmus+ programme. Partnerships may be set up in the fields of education, vocational training, youth and sport. The Erasmus+ programme further supports cooperation between education and training and the world of work. For the first time ever, a student loan guarantee enables students to undertake a Master's degree abroad. Studying and training abroad boosts the employability of graduates. With international experience, they are half as likely to be trapped in long-term unemployment as their stay-at-home counterparts. In fact, there is a significant difference in the unemployment rate between those who studied or trained abroad and those who did not. Five years after earning their degree, the unemployment rate of graduates who studied or trained abroad is 23% lower.[931] The Erasmus+ programme is instrumental for increasing the employment rate of recent graduates, which is one of the targets of ET 2020. Apart from the Member States, Erasmus+ programme countries include the EEA EFTA States, Turkey and the former Yugoslav Republic of Macedonia. Student and staff exchanges are further possible between numerous partner countries, making Erasmus+ the most international exchange programme.

Through the introduction of the horizontal social clause (cf. Article 9 TFEU), the Lisbon Treaty has made the promotion of education and training the top priority. The interplay between education and training and the other policies of the EU is more visible than ever. This has been demonstrated with respect to cohesion policy, where the investment priorities of the ESF and the ERDF include education and training. Most importantly, the Lisbon Treaty has added a new dimension to cohesion policy: territorial cohesion (cf. Article 174, para 1 TFEU). The Lisbon Treaty has further extended youth policy, aiming to make democratic participation more tangible to young people. In addition, it has introduced a legal basis for sport, allowing the Union to officially operate a sport policy. Further amendments include the alignment of Article 166(4) TFEU on

931 Erasmus Impact Study confirms EU student exchange scheme boosts employability and job mobility, Press Release, 22 September 2014 (IP/14/1025).

vocational training with Article 165(4) TFEU on education, youth and sport. For the first time ever, Council recommendations may thus be adopted under either of these two provisions. Furthermore, the protection of fundamental rights has been strengthened through the CFREU's incorporation into primary law. Article 14 CFREU, which includes the right to education, the right to access to vocational and continuing training, the parental right to decide on the religious, philosophical and/or pedagogical direction of the child's education and the freedom to found educational establishments, is therefore binding. Moreover, the Union has been vested with explicit treaty-making power for the external dimension (cf. Article 216(1) TFEU).

Education and training have significantly changed the European legal landscape. The primary carer of a dependent person who qualifies for a right of residence under the Citizens' Rights Directive derives a right of residence. The EU has turned into a political entity that is more integrated than the US, where state universities have quotas for out-of-state students and charge them considerably higher tuition fees than in-state students.[932] This is unimaginable in the EU, where public universities may not directly discriminate against Union citizens. However, the freedom of movement of persons, which after all is the linchpin of Union citizenship, has also generated alarming headlines. Times have been troublesome for Member States with an open admission policy. Students who do not qualify for admission in Germany or France are flooding HEIs in Austria and Belgium. In order to take control of the situation, Austria and Belgium have introduced quotas for medical and paramedical studies. However, they have not yet obtained the Commission's blessings. The decision of the Commission is crucial and the further development of EU education law will largely depend on it. Infringement proceedings against Austria and Belgium have been suspended until December 2016. They have until then to show that the restrictive measures are necessary and proportional and therefore in accordance with EU law.

The concept of Union citizenship and the principle of non-discrimination on grounds of nationality are without doubt the greatest achievement of EU law. However, there is no question that there are adverse effects and the impact on Member States with an open admission policy is likely to be immense. The education systems are the responsibility of the Member States. The smaller the Member State, the lower the level of tax revenues. Provided that they wish to maintain an open admission policy, they must be prepared to accept each and

932 Cf. Jacobs, 2007, p. 595.

every applicant from all over the EU.[933] Member States are basically forced to implement selective and competitive admission criteria or to stop heavily subsidising higher education. Minimum grades, entrance examinations and/or high tuition fees may be the only way to ensure that the studying conditions will allow for a high quality tertiary education system. Intra-EU mobility is at the heart of the European idea. However, educating masses of students who leave upon graduation comes at a high cost. It is therefore up to the Member States to arrange for better employment and working conditions for recent graduates. Moreover, a debate at the EU level on financial compensation between the Member States in like manner to the Nordic Council would be a first step.

Student maintenance aid is a burning issue. It is not surprising that the rationale of the free movement of persons has changed from "the idea that labour will move to where it is needed and/or where it or the individual free mover can flourish" to that it "is a good thing, what is important is that the student returns to the Member State which has financed the studies in question and that he or she settles in that Member State and contributes to the development of its economy rather than the economic development of the internal market as a whole."[934] The ECJ has just delivered several rulings on student grants and loans, clarifying the right to student maintenance aid. Student grants and loans for children of cross-border workers are portable. Durational residency requirements for the portability of student maintenance aid for "own" nationals are too general and exclusive in nature to determine the sufficient integration into the society of a Member State. Other factors need to be taken into account as well as the right to freedom of movement and residence (cf. Articles 20 and 21 TFEU) would be infringed otherwise. The ECJ has not yet ruled on the portability of student grants and loans of Union citizens with a right to permanent residence. However, when implementing the rulings of the ECJ, Germany will already provide for Union citizens with a right to permanent residence. The latest rulings of the ECJ are important, as non-economically active students residing in a host Member State do not have a right to student maintenance aid unless they have a permanent right of residence. These rulings also raise the question of double financing. In order to avoid cumulation of student maintenance aid, the implementation of anti-cumulation rules will be useful.

933 Opinion of Advocate General Sharpston, Case C-73/08 *Bressol and Chaverot*, para 106.
934 O'Leary, 2014, p. 614.

Cohesion policy is trending. Bridging borders and sectors is en vogue. This is a good thing, especially for EU education policy. Cross-border, transnational and interregional cooperation helps to identify common education and training needs. A bottom-up process is essential to tackle problems on the sub-national and national level. Eventually, good practice examples may even be interesting for the Union as a whole. As has been shown, education and training is a focal point of the EUSBSR and the EUSDR. It is also featured in the newly launched EUSAIR. The EGTC European Region Tyrol-South Tyrol-Trentino is a prime example of how EU education policy can be implemented at the regional level. A hub for cross-border and interregional cooperation, the EGTC European Region Tyrol-South Tyrol-Trentino fosters collaboration in the fields of education, vocational training, youth and sport which are covered by the Erasmus+ programme. Under key action 2, funding is available for strategic partnerships in the fields of education, vocational training and youth. Subject to certain conditions, strategic partnerships do not require partner institutions and/or organisations from more than two programme countries. Collaborative partnerships in the field of sport include large-scale projects in the sense that the partner institutions and/or organisations need to come from at least five different countries. However, they could still be of interest for the EGTC European Region Tyrol-South Tyrol-Trentino. Considering that the Province of Tyrol, the Autonomous Province of Bolzano/Bozen and the Autonomous Province of Trento are members of the ARGE ALP, partner institutions and/or organisations from the Alpine states could be found via said network.

In conclusion, EU education policy has proven to be effective on the national and sub-national level. Territorial cooperation between neighbouring regions (or countries) is resulting in common projects in education and training. Robert Schuman once rightly pointed out, "Europe will not be made all at once, or according to a single plan. It will be built through concrete achievements which first create a de facto solidarity."[935] This holds true for education and training. As we consciously move forward in the European integration process, the role of the regions is becoming increasingly prevalent. In federal and regionalised states, education is one of the bastions of sub-national competence. Whether the regions contribute to macro-regional strategies or cooperate on the micro-regional level, the future development of EU education policy will likely be more of a bottom-up than a top-down process. The ECJ has been the main driving

935 The Schuman Declaration, 9 May 1950, http://europa.eu/about-eu/basic-information/symbols/europe-day/schuman-declaration/index_en.htm.

force for a long time and its jurisdiction has yielded substantial benefits for those in education and training. Although there may always be some issues that will have to be left to the courts, it is clear that the foundations of EU education law have been laid. With its extensive jurisdiction on student maintenance aid, the ECJ has put an answer to an urgent question for those currently in education. Twenty-eight Member States with their own priorities, policies and education systems are not easily brought in line. The EU 2020 Strategy and ET 2020 establish a common basis. Interaction among the vertical dimension (EU, national and sub-national level) as well as the horizontal dimension (e.g. social partners, non-governmental organisations) is crucial for policy dialogue. Hence, it is safe to say that the future of EU education policy lies in the added value of multi-level governance.

References

Books and Articles

Alston, P. and J. Weiler, An 'Ever Closer Union' in Need of a Human Rights Policy: The European Union and Human Rights, in: P. Alston, M. Bustelo and J. Heenan (eds.), The EU and Human Rights, OUP: Oxford, 1999, pp. 3–66

Amann, CU, Bilingual Education: A Token for Crosscultural Pragmatics?, Diploma Thesis, University of Innsbruck, 2011

Anderson, D. and C. Murphy, The Charter of Fundamental Rights: History and Prospects in Post-Lisbon Europe, EUI LAW Working Papers, 2011

Bache, I., The Europeanization of Higher Education: Markets, Politics or Learning?, 44 JCMS, 2006, pp. 231–248

Barnard, C., Education and Vocational Training, in: D. Phillips (ed.), Aspects of Education and the European Union, Oxford Studies in Comparative Education, 5(2) (Triangle: Wallingford (OX)), 1995, pp. 13–28

Barnard, C., Of Students and Babies, 64 Cambridge Law Journal, 2005, pp. 560–563

Barnard, C., Case C-209/03, *R (on the application of Danny Bidar) v. London Borough of Ealing, Secretary of State for Education and Skills*, judgment of the Court (Grand Chamber) 15 March 2005, not yet reported, 42 CMLR, 2005, pp. 1465–1489

Barrett, G., Family Matters: European Community Law and Third-Country Family Members, 40 CMLR, 2003, pp. 369–421

Becker, GS, Human Capital: A Theoretical and Empirical Analysis with Special Reference to Education, 3rd ed., Chicago UP: Chicago, 1993

Becker, P. and R. Primova, Die Europäische Union und die Bildungspolitik, Diskussionspapier Forschungsgruppe EU-Integration, SWP: Berlin, April 2009

Bergan, S., The Recognition of Qualifications: Legal Basis and Practical Implementation, 2 Journal of the EHEA, 2012, pp. 73–92

Bernard, N., A "New Governance" Approach to Economic, Social and Cultural Rights in the EU, in: T. Hervey and J. Kenner (eds.), Economic and Social Rights under the EU Charter of Fundamental Rights, Hart Publishing: Oxford, 2003, pp. 247–268

Bernsdorff, N., Charta Artikel 14 Recht auf Bildung, in: Meyer, J. (ed.), Charta der Grundrechte der Europäischen Union, 3rd ed., 2010

Blanke, HJ, Art. 165/166 AEUV, in: E. Grabitz, M. Hilf and M. Nettesheim (eds.), Das Recht der Europäischen Union, CH Beck: München, 44. Ergänzungslieferung, May 2011

Blanke, HJ, Article 4, in: HJ Blanke and S. Mangiameli (eds.), The Treaty on European Union (TEU): A Commentary, Springer: Heidelberg, 2013, pp. 185–253

Blitz, BK, From Monnet to Delors: Educational Co-operation in the European Union, 12 Contemporary European History, 2003, pp. 197–212

Bode, S., Europarechtliche Gleichbehandlungsansprüche Studierender und ihre Auswirkungen in den Mitgliedstaaten: Zur Reichweite des Diskriminierungsverbots im Hochschulbereich unter besonderer Berücksichtigung der Unionsbürgerschaft, Nomos: Baden-Baden, 2005

Böhlmark, A. and M. Lindahl, Independent Schools and Long-run Educational Outcomes – Evidence from Sweden's Large Scale Voucher Reform, CESifo Working Paper No. 3866, 2012

Bruun, N., Lörcher, K. and I. Schömann, Introduction, in: N. Bruun, K. Lörcher and I. Schömann (eds.), The Lisbon Treaty and Social Europe, Hart Publishing: Oxford, 2012

Budischowsky, J., Art. 162 AEUV, in: Mayer, H., Kommentar zu EUV und AEUV unter Berücksichtigung der österreichischen Judikatur und Literatur, Manz: Wien, 2010, pp. 3–7

Budischowsky, J., Art. 165, 166 AEUV, in: Mayer, H., Kommentar zu EUV und AEUV unter Berücksichtigung der österreichischen Judikatur und Literatur, Manz: Wien, 2010, pp. 10–31

Carlier, JY, Case C-200/02, *Man Lavette Chen and Kunqian Catherine Zhu v Secretary of State for the Home Department*, Judgment of the Court of Justice (Full Court) of 19 October 2004, 42 CMLR, 2005, pp. 1121–1131

Chalmers, D., Davies, G. and G. Monti, European Union Law: Cases and Materials, 2nd ed., Cambridge UP: Cambridge, 2010

Conway, G., Conflicts of Competence Norms in EU Law and the Legal Reasoning of the ECJ, 11 German Law Journal, 2010, pp. 966–1005

Corbett, A., Ideas, Institutions and Policy Entrepreneurs: Towards a New History of Higher Education in the European Community, 38 European Journal for Education, 2003, pp. 315–330

Corbett, A., Education and the Lisbon Strategy, in: P. Copeland and D. Papadimitriou (eds.), The EU's Lisbon Strategy: Evaluating Success, Understanding Failure, Palgrave: Basingstoke, 2012, pp. 149–167

Corrias, L., The Passivity of Law: Competence and Constitution in the European Court of Justice, Springer: Heidelberg, 2011

Cort, P., The EC Discourse on Vocational Training: How a 'Common Vocational Training Policy' Turned into a Lifelong Learning Strategy, 2 Vocations and Learning, 2009, pp. 87–107

Craig, P. and G. de Búrca, EU Law: Text, Cases and Materials, 5th ed., OUP: Oxford, 2011

Craig, P., Integration, Democracy and Legitimacy, in: P. Craig and G. de Búrca (eds.), The Evolution of EU Law, 2nd ed., OUP: Oxford, 2011, pp. 13–40

Dehmel, A., Making a European Area of Lifelong Learning a Reality? Some Critical Reflections on the European Union's Lifelong Learning Policies, 42 Comparative Education, 2006, pp. 49–62

De Búrca, G., The Evolution of EU Human Rights Law, in: P. Craig and G. de Búrca (eds.), The Evolution of EU Law, 2nd ed., OUP: Oxford, 2011, pp. 465–497

De Waele, H., The Role of the European Court of Justice in the Integration Process: A Contemporary and Normative Assessment, 6 HanseLR, 2010, pp. 3–26

De Witte, B., Introduction, in: B. de Witte (ed.), European Community Law of Education, Nomos: Baden-Baden, pp. 9–18

De Witte, F., Who Funds the Mobile Student? Shedding Some Light on the Normative Assumptions Underlying EU Free Movement Law: Commission v. Netherlands, 50 CMLR, 2013, pp. 203–216

Dougan, M., Fees, Grants, Loans and Dole Cheques: Who Covers the Cost of Migrant Education Within the EU?, 1 JCER, 2005, pp. 4–29

Dubois, A., Hedin, S., Schmitt, P. and J. Sterling, EU Macro-regions and Macro-regional Strategies – A Scoping Study, Nordregio Electronic Working Paper No 4, 2009

Editorial, Editorial Comments: Two-speed European Citizenship? Can the Lisbon Treaty Help Close the Gap?, 45 CMLR, 2008, pp. 1–11

Edward, D. and R. Lane, Edward and Lane on European Union Law, Edward Elgar: Cheltenham, 2013

Ertl, H., The European Union and Education and Training: An Overview of Policies and Initiatives, in: D. Phillips and H. Ertl (eds.), Implementing European Union Education and Training Policy: A Comparative Study of Issues in Four Member States, Kluwer Academic: Dordrecht, 2003, pp. 13–39

European University Institute, Study on the Division of Powers between the European Union, the Member States, and Regional and Local Authorities, European University Institute: Florence, 2008

Field, J., The European Union and the Learning Society: Congested Sovereignty in an Age of Globalisation, in: F. Coffield (ed.), A National Strategy for Lifelong Learning, Newcastle University: Newcastle upon Tyne, 1997, pp. 95–111

Field, J., European Dimensions: Education, Training and the European Union, Higher Education Policy Series 39, Jessica Kingsley: London, 1998

Flynn, J., Gravier: Suite du Feuilleton, in: B. de Witte (ed.), European Community Law of Education, Nomos: Baden-Baden, 1989, pp. 95–112

Foster, N., EU Law: Directions, 3rd ed, OUP: Oxford, 2012

Fraenkel-Haeberle, C., Die Anerkennung akademischer und beruflicher Titel zwischen Italien und Österreich, in: P. Hilpold, C. Perathoner and W. Steinmair (eds.), Rechtsvergleichung an der Sprachgrenze, Peter Lang: Frankfurt am Main, 2011, pp. 515–535

Frenz, W., Kommunikationsgrundrechte, in: W. Frenz, Handbuch Europarecht, Band 4: Europäische Grundrechte, Springer: Berlin, 2009, pp. 531–730

Frenz, W., Bildung, Jugend, Sport, in: W. Frenz, Handbuch Europarecht, Band 6: Institutionen und Politiken, Springer: Berlin, 2011, pp. 1139–1163

Frenz, W., Europäische Bildungspolitik, 64 DÖV, 2011, pp. 249–259

Funk, BC, Verfassungsrechtliche Dimensionen des österreichischen Hochschulrechts, in: W. Berka, C. Brünner and W. Hauser (eds.), Handbuch des österreichischen Hochschulrechts (2nd ed.), NWV: Wien, 2012, pp. 31–50

Garben, S., Case C-73/08, *Nicolas Bressol and Others, Céline Chaverot and Others v. Gouvernement de la Communauté française*, Judgment of the Court (Grand Chamber) of 13 April 2010, nyr, 47 CMLR, 2010, pp. 1493–1510

Garben, S., EU Higher Education Law: The Bologna Process and Harmonization by Stealth, Kluwer: Alphen aan den Rijn, 2011

Gérard, M., Financing Bologna, the Internationally Mobile Students in European Higher Education, CESifo Working Paper No 2391, 2008

Gérard, M., Financing Bologna Students' Mobility, Taxation Paper No 26, Office for Official Publications of the European Communities: Luxembourg, 2010

Gérard, M., Who Is to Pay for Mobile Students?, in: A. Curaj et al. (eds.), European Higher Education at the Crossroads: Between the Bologna Process and National Reforms, Springer: Dordrecht, 2012, pp. 727–748

Gérard, M. and S. Uebelmesser, Globalization and Access to Higher Education – Policy Implications, CESifo DICE Report 2013/2, pp. 3–10

Gori, G., Towards an EU Right to Education, Kluwer Law International: The Hague, 2001

Gori, G., Article 14, in: S. Peers, T. Hervey and J. Kenner, The EU Charter of Fundamental Rights: A Commentary, Hart Publishing: Oxford, 2014, pp. 401–422

Golynker, O., Case C-158/07, *Jacqueline Förster v. Hoofddirectie van de Informatie Beheer Groep*, Judgment of the Court (Grand Chamber) of 18 November 2008, not yet reported, CMLR, Vol. 46, 2009, pp. 2021–2039

Gornitzka, A., Bologna in Context: A Horizontal Perspective on the Dynamics of Governance Sites for a Europe of Knowledge, 45 European Journal of Education, 2010, pp. 535–548

Gornitzka, A., The Open Method of Coordination as Practice – A Watershed in European Education Policy?, ARENA Working Paper No. 16, December 2006, pp. 14–15;

Grosjean, E., Forty Years of Cultural Cooperation at the Council of Europe, 1954–94, 31 European Education, 1999, pp. 11–37

Guild, E., Peers, S. and J. Tomkin, The EU Citizenship Directive: A Commentary, OUP: Oxford, 2014

Hablitzel, H., Subsidiaritätsprinzip und Bildungskompetenzen im Vertrag über die Europäische Union, Pustet: Regensburg, 1994

Hablitzel, H., Harmonisierungsverbot und Subsidiaritätsprinzip im europäischen Bildungsrecht, 55 DÖV, 2002, pp. 407–414

Hake, BJ, Lifelong Learning Policies in the European Union: Developments and Issues, 29 Compare: A Journal of Comparative and International Education, 1999, pp. 53–69

Halász, G., European Coordination of National Education Policies from the Perspective of the New Member Countries, in: R. Standaert (ed.), Becoming the Best: Educational Ambitions for Europe, CIDREE: Enschede, 2003, pp. 89–118

Halász, G., European Union: The Strive for Smart, Sustainable and Inclusive Growth, in: Y. Wang (ed.), Education Policy Trends in G20 Members, Springer: Heidelberg, 2013, pp. 267–286

Harris, N., Equal Rights in Education in the UK (England), 4 IJELP, 2008, pp. 4–15

Hilpold, P., Bildung in Europa – Unter besonderer Berücksichtigung der EU-Bildungsprogramme, Nomos: Baden-Baden, 1995

Hilpold, P., Unionsbürgerschaft und Sprachenrechte in der EU, 122 JBl, 2000, pp. 93–101

Hilpold, P., Hochschulzugang und Unionsbürgerschaft: Das Urteil EuGH vom 7.7.2005 in der Rechtssache C-147/03, Kommission gegen Österreich, EuZW, 2005, pp. 647–652

Hilpold, P., Unionsbürgerschaft und Bildungsrechte oder: Der EuGH-Richter als "Künstler", in: GH Roth and P. Hilpold (eds.), Der EuGH und die Souveränität der Mitgliedsstaaten: eine kritische Analyse richterlicher Rechtssschöpfung auf ausgewählten Rechtsgebieten, Linde/Stämpfi/Boorberg: Wien/Bern/Stuttgart, 2008, pp. 11–53

Hilpold, P., Unterhaltsstipendien für Unionsbürger – Die Rechtssache "Förster" und die Grenzen mitgliedstaatlicher Solidarität, EuZW, 2009, pp. 40–43

Hilpold, P. Nichtdiskriminierung und Unionsbürgerschaft, in: M. Niedobitek (ed.), Europarecht – Politiken der Union, Walter de Gruyter: Berlin, 2014, pp. 1–96

Hodgson, D., International Protection of the Right to Education, Max Planck Encyclopedia of Public International Law, Max Planck Institute for Comparative Public Law and International Law: Heidelberg and OUP, 2013

Hoogenboom, A., Mobility of Students and the Financial Sustainability of Higher Education Systems in the EU: A Union of Harmony or Irreconcilable Differences?, 9 CYEL, 2013, pp. 15–59

Hooghe, L, and G. Marks, Multi-Level Governance and European Integration, Rowman & Littlefield: Lanham, 2001

Hüfner, K., The Human Rights Approach to Education in International Organisations, 46 European Journal of Education, 2011, pp. 117–126

Jacobs, FG, Citizenship of the European Union – A Legal Analysis, 13 European Law Journal, 2007, pp. 591–610

Jones, HC, Testimony, in: L. Pépin, The History of European Cooperation in Education and Training: Europe in the Making – An Example, Office for Official Publications of the European Communities: Luxembourg, 2006, pp. 39–42

Jørgensen, S., The Right to Cross-Border Education in the European Union, 46 CMLR, 2009, pp. 1567–1590

Kirsch, M. and Y. Beernaert, Short Cycle Higher Education in Europe: Level 5: The Missing Link, EURASHE: Brussels, 2011

Kaczorowska, A., European Union Law, Routledge: Abingdon, 2013

Kasparovsky, H., The Impact of EU Law on Austrian Higher Education Curricula, 4 ICL Journal, 2010, pp. 582–589

Käsper, K., Free Movement of Students in the EU, in: T. Kerikmäe (ed.), Protecting Human Rights in the EU: Controversies and Challenges of the Charter of Fundamental Rights, Springer: Heidelberg, 2014, pp. 145–159

Klecatsky, HR and I. Winkler, Das Studium des italienischen Rechts an der Universität Innsbruck als Beitrag zur transnationalen Sicherung der Südtiroler Autonomie, in: W. Fiedler und G. Ress (eds.), Verfassungsrecht und Völkerrecht: Gedächtnisschrift für Wilhelm Karl Geck, Heymanns: Köln, 1989, pp. 451–466

Kotzur, M., Die Bildungskompetenzen der Europäischen Union nach Art. 165, 166 AEUV, in: K. Odendahl (ed.), Europäische (Bildungs-)Union?, BWV: Berlin/NWV: Wien, 2011, pp. 107–130

Kollonay-Lehoczky, C., Lörcher, K. and I. Schömann, The Lisbon Treaty and the Charter of Fundamental Rights of the European Union, in: N. Bruun, K. Lörcher, and I. Schömann (eds.), The Lisbon Treaty and Social Europe, Hart Publishing: Oxford, 2012, pp. 61–105

Kunoy, B., A Union of National Citizens: The Origins of the Court's Lack of Avant-Gardisme in the Chen Case, 43 CMLR, pp. 179–190

Lange, B. and N. Alexiadou, New Forms of European Union Governance in the Education Sector? A Preliminary Analysis of the Open Method of Coordination, 6 EERJ, 2007, pp. 321–335

Leal-Arcas, R., The European Union's New Common Commercial Policy after the Treaty of Lisbon, in: M. Trybus and L. Rubini (eds.), The Treaty of Lisbon and the Future of European Law and Policy, Edward Elgar: Cheltenham, 2012, pp. 262–284

Lenaerts, K., ERASMUS: Legal Basis and Implementation, in: B. de Witte (ed.), European Community Law of Education, Nomos: Baden-Baden, 1989, pp. 113–125

Lenaerts, K., The Principle of Subsidiarity and the Environment in the European Union: Keeping the Balance of Federalism, 17 Fordham International Law Journal, 1993, pp. 846–895

Lenaerts, K., Education in European Community Law after "Maastricht", 31 CMLR, 1994, pp. 7–41

Lenaerts, K., 'Civis Europaeus Sum': From the Cross-border Link to the Status of Citizen of the Union, 3 Online Journal on free movement of workers within the European Union, 2011, pp. 6–18

Lenaerts, K., Exploring the Limits of the EU Charter of Fundamental Rights, 8 ECLR, 2012, pp. 375–403

Lenaerts, K., Die EU-Grundrechtecharta: Anwendbarkeit und Auslegung, EuR, 2012, pp. 3–17

Mächtle, CI, Bildungsspezifische Implikationen des allgemeinen Diskriminierungsverbots und der Freizügigkeit, Peter Lang: Frankfurt am Main, 2010

Margedant, U., Bildungspolitik, in: J. Bergmann (ed.), Handlexikon der Europäischen Union, 4th ed., Nomos: Baden-Baden, 2012, pp. 148–152

Marks, G., Structural Policy and Multilevel Governance in the EC, in: AW Cafruny and GG Rosenthal (eds.), The State of the European Community Volume 2: The Maastricht Debates and Beyond, Lynne Rienner: Boulder, 1993, pp. 391–410

Martens, K. and KD Wolf, Boomerangs and Trojan Horses: The Unintended Consequences of Internationalising Education Policy Through the EU and the OECD, in: A. Amaral et al. (eds.), European Integration and the

Governance of Higher Education and Research, Springer: Dordrecht, 2009, pp. 81–107

Mentick, D. and F. Goudappel, The Education Provision in the Charter of Fundamental Rights of the European Union: A Bleak Perspective, 4 European Journal for Education Law and Policy, 2000, pp. 145–148

Miles, G. et al., Foundations for the LPC 2013–2014, OUP: Oxford, 2013

Niedobitek, M., Artikel 165 AEUV, in: R. Streinz (ed.), EUV/AEUV: Vertrag über die Europäische Union und Vertrag über die Arbeitsweise der Europäischen Union, 2nd ed., CH Beck: München, 2012

Niedobitek, M., Artikel 166 AEUV, in: R. Streinz (ed.), EUV/AEUV: Vertrag über die Europäische Union und Vertrag über die Arbeitsweise der Europäischen Union, 2nd ed., CH Beck: München, 2012

Nino, M., The Protection and Promotion of Sport in the European Union Following the Treaty of Lisbon and the Bernard Ruling, in: G. Ziccardi Capaldo (ed.), 1 The Global Community Yearbook of International Law and Jurisprudence 2010, OUP: New York, 2012, pp. 179–194

Norberg, S. et al., The European Economic Area: EEA Law: A Commentary on the EEA Agreement, Fritzes (Kluwer): Stockholm, 1993

Nóvoa, A. and W. de Jong-Lambert, Educating Europe: An Analysis of EU Educational Policies, in: D. Phillips and H. Ertl (eds.), Implementing European Union Education and Training Policy: A Comparative Study of Issues in Four Member States, Kluwer Academic: Dordrecht, 2003, pp. 41–72

O'Brien, C., Case C-310/08 *London Borough of Harrow v. Nimco Hassan Ibrahim and Secretary of State for the Home Department*, Judgment of the Court (Grand Chamber) of 23 February 2010, nyr., Case C-480/08 *Maria Teixeira v. London Borough of Lambeth and Secretary of State for the Home Department*, Judgment of the Court (Grand Chamber) of 23 February 2010, nyr., 48 CMLR, 2011, pp. 203–225

Obwexer, W., Der Beitritt der EU zur EMRK: Rechtsgrundlagen, Rechtsfragen und Rechsfolgen, EuR, 2012, pp. 115–148

Odendahl, K., Bildung, Kultur, Forschung und technologische Entwicklung, in: M. Niedobitek (ed.), Europarecht – Politiken der Union, De Gruyter: Berlin, 2014, pp. 1005–1064

O'Leary, S., Free Movement of Persons and Services, in: P. Craig and G. de Búrca (eds.), The Evolution of EU Law, 2nd ed., OUP: Oxford, 2011, pp. 499–545

O'Leary, S., The Curious Case of Frontier Workers and Study Finance: *Giersch*, 51 CMLR, 2014, pp. 601–622

Oršolić Dalessio, T., The Social Dimension of EU Citizenship – A Castle in the Air or Construction Gone Wrong?, 14 German Law Journal, 2013, pp. 869–888

Ott, A. and R. Wessel, The EU's External Relations Regime: Multilevel Complexity in an Expanding Union, in: S. Blockmans and A. Lazowski (eds.), The European Union and Its Neighbours: A Legal Appraisal of the EU's Policies of Stabilisation, Partnership and Integration, T.M.C. Asser Press: The Hague, 2006, pp. 19–60

Papadopoulos, GS, Education 1960–1990: The OECD Perspective, OECD: Paris, 1994

Papadopoulos, GS, The OECD Approach to Education in Retrospect: 1960–1990, 46 European Journal of Education, 2011, pp. 85–86

Papatsiba, V., Making Higher Education More European through Student Mobility? Revisiting EU Initiatives in the Context of the Bologna Process, 42 Comparative Education, 2006, pp. 93–111

Pépin, L., The History of European Cooperation in Education and Training: Europe in the Making - An Example, Office for Official Publications of the European Communities: Luxembourg, 2006

Pépin, L., The History of EU Cooperation in the Field of Education and Training: How Lifelong Learning Became a Strategic Objective, 42 European Journal of Education, 2007, pp. 121–132

Pépin, L., Education in the Lisbon Strategy: Assessment and Prospects, 46 European Journal of Education, 2011, pp. 25–35

Perkmann, M., Cross-Border Regions in Europe: Significance and Drivers of Regional Cross-border Co-operation, 10 European Urban and Regional Studies, 2003, pp. 153–171

Perkmann, M., Cross-border Co-operation as Policy Entrepreneurship: Explaining the Variable Success of European Cross-border Regions, CSGR Working Paper No. 166/05, 2005

Perkmann, M., Construction of New Territorial Scales: A Framework and Case Study of the EUREGIO Cross-border Region, 41 Regional Studies, 2007, pp. 253–266

Pollack, MA, The End of Creeping Competence? EU-Policy Making Since Maastricht, 38 JCMS, 2000, pp. 519–538

Radtke, F., Die Erziehungswissenschaft der OECD - Aussichten auf die neue Performanz-Kultur, 14 Erziehungswissenschaft, 2003, pp. 109–136

Ramirez, P., Article 10, in: HJ Blanke and S. Mangiameli (eds.), The Treaty on European Union (TEU): A Commentary, Springer: Heidelberg, 2013, pp. 417–447

Rechberger-Bechter, C., Europäische Gemeinschaft in der Bildungspolitik: Zuständigkeiten und Handlungsmöglichkeiten, Nomos: Wien, 2008

Romeo, C., Tirol Südtirol Trentino: Ein historischer Überblick, EVTZ Europaregion Tirol Südtirol Trentino: Bozen, 2012

Ruffert, M., Artikel 165 AEUV, in: C. Calliess and M. Ruffert, EUV/AEUV, 4th ed., CH Beck: München, 2011

Ruffert, M., Artikel 166 AEUV, in: C. Calliess and M. Ruffert, EUV/AEUV, 4th ed., CH Beck: München, 2011

Ryba, R., Educational Changes in Europe, in: D. Phillips (ed.), Aspects of Education and the European Union, Oxford Studies in Comparative Education, 5(2) (Triangle: Wallingford (OX)), 1995, pp. 63–75

Schade, A., A Research Topic in Education Law and Policy: The Development of Regionalism and Federalism in Europe and their Impact on Educational Policy and Administration, 4 European Journal for Education Law and Policy, 2000, pp. 35–39

Scharpf, FW, The Asymmetry of European Integration or Why the EU Cannot Be a "Social Market Economy", 8 Socio-Economic Review, 2010, pp. 211–250

Schoen, N., The State's Power in the Euroregion Tyrol-South Tyrol/Alto Adige-Trentino, in: J. de Janny et al. (eds.), Walking the Tightrope: Europe between Europeanisation and Globalisation, Euroculture: Groningen, pp. 45–64

Schroeder, W. and N. Ehlotzky, Zustand und Perspektiven grenzüberschreitender Kooperation im Alpenraum, in: P. Hilpold, C. Perathoner and W. Steinmair (eds.), Rechtsvergleichung an der Sprachgrenze, Peter Lang: Frankfurt am Main, 2011, pp. 67–114

Schymik, C., Modellversuch Makroregion: Die EU-Strategien für den Ostsee- und den Donauraum, SWP-Studie, 2011

Senden, L., Soft Law in European Union Community Law, Hart Publishing: Oxford, 2004

Shaw, J., Hunt, J. and C. Wallace, Economic and Social Law of the European Union, Palgrave Macmillan: Basingstoke, 2007

Shaw, J., Citizenship: Contrasting Dynamics at the Interface of Integration and Constitutionalism, in: P. Craig and G. de Búrca (eds.), The Evolution of EU Law, 2nd ed., OUP: Oxford, 2011, pp. 575–609

Siekmann, R., Introduction to International and European Sports Law: Capita Selecta, T.M.C. Asser Press: The Hague, 2012

Siller, S., Rechtliche Grundlagen der Bildungskooperation unter besonderer Berücksichtigung der Zusammenarbeit im universitären Bereich, in: P. Hilpold, C. Perathoner and W. Steinmair (eds.), Rechtsvergleichung an der Sprachgrenze, Peter Lang: Frankfurt am Main, 2011, pp. 481–513

Smismans, S., How to Be Fundamental with Soft Procedures? The Open Method of Coordination and Fundamental Social Rights, in: G. de Búrca and B. de Witte (eds.), Social Rights in Europe, OUP: Oxford, 2005, pp. 217–238

Snyder, F., The Effectiveness of European Community Law: Institutions, Processes, Tools and Techniques, 56 The Modern Law Review, 1993, pp. 19–54

Stalford, H., Transferability of Qualifications and EU Migrant Children, in: J. Shaw (ed.), Social Law and Policy in an Evolving European Union, Hart Publishing: Oxford, 2000, pp. 243–258

Streinz, T., Fraternal Twins: The European Union and the Council of Europe, in: H. de Waele and JJ Kuipers (eds.), The European Union's Emerging International Identity: Views from the Global Arena, Brill: Leiden, 2013, pp. 101–129

Tauch, C., EU Higher Education Issues and Priorities for 2010–2020, 1 Journal of the European Higher Education Area, 2011, pp. 65–90

Teichler, U., Changes of ERASMUS under the Umbrella of SOCRATES, 5 Journal of Studies in International Education, 2001, pp. 201–227

Tomaševski, K., Human Rights Obligations: Making Education Available, Accessible, Acceptable and Adaptable, Right to Education Primers No. 3, Novum Grafiska: Gothenburg, 2001

Towara, C. Das Rechts auf Bildung gemäß Art. 14 der Charta der Grundrechte der EU, in: Odendahl, K. (ed.), Europäische (Bildungs-)Union?, 2011, NWV: Wien/BWV: Berlin, pp. 75–106

Tryfonidou, A., Redefining the Outer Boundaries of EU Law: The Zambrano, McCarthy and Dereci Trilogy, 18 European Public Law, 2012, pp. 493–526

Traweger, C. and G. Pallaver, Kommunikation, Kooperation, Integration in der Europaregion Tirol-Südtirol-Trentino: Die Meinung der Bevölkerung, STUDIA: Innsbruck, 2014

Trubek, DM and LG Trubek, Hard and Soft Law in Europe, 11 European Law Journal, 2005, pp. 343–364

Van Craeyenest, F., La nature juridique des résolutions sur la coopération en matière d'éducation, in: B. de Witte (ed.), European Community Law of Education, Nomos: Baden-Baden, 1989, pp. 127–133

Van der Mei, AP, Union Citizenship and the 'De-Nationalisation' of the Territorial Welfare State: Comments on Case C-456/02 *Trojani* and Case C-209/03 *Bidar*, 7 European Journal of Migration and Law, 2005, pp. 203–211

Van der Mei, AP, Union Citizenship and the Legality of Durational Residence Requirements for Entitlement to Student Financial Aid, 16 Maastricht Journal of European and Comparative Law, 2009, pp. 477–496

Van der Mei, AP, Free Movement of Students and the Protection of National Educational Interests: Reflections on Bressol and Chaverot, 13 European Journal of Migration and Law, 2011, pp. 123–134

Van der Mei, AP, The Outer Limits of the Prohibition of Discrimination on Grounds of Nationality: A Look through the Lens of Union Citizenship, 18 Maastricht Journal of European and Comparative Law, 2011, pp. 62–85

Vedder, C., Artikel 165 AEUV, in: C. Vedder and W. Heintschel von Heinegg (eds.), Europäisches Unionsrecht, Nomos: Baden-Baden, 2012, pp. 699–703

Vedder, C., Artikel 166 AEUV, in: C. Vedder and W. Heintschel von Heinegg (eds.), Europäisches Unionsrecht, Nomos: Baden-Baden, 2012, pp. 703–705

Vergès, J., La voie intergovernmentale: Le "Livre Bleu" Français, in: B. de Witte (ed.), European Community Law of Education, Nomos: Baden-Baden, 1989, pp. 135–144

Vielle, P., How the Horizontal Social Clause Can be Made to Work: The Lessons of Gender Mainstreaming, in: N. Bruun, K. Lörcher and I. Schömann (eds.), The Lisbon Treaty and Social Europe, Hart Publishing: Oxford, 2012, pp. 105–121

Wagner, V., Article 14 – Right to Education, in: EU Network of Independent Experts on Fundamental Rights, Commentary of the Charter of Fundamental Rights of the European Union, 2006, pp. 141–148

Walkenhorst, H. The Changing Role of EU Education Policy – a Critical Assessment, Paper for the EUSA Ninth Biennial International Conference, March 31–April 2, 2005

Walkenhorst, H., Explaining Change in EU Education Policy, 15 Journal of European Public Policy, 2008, pp. 567–587

Wallace, C. and J. Shaw, Education, Multiculturalism and the Charter of Fundamental Rights of the European Union, in: T. Hervey and J. Kenner (eds.), Economic and Social Rights under the EU Charter of Fundamental Rights – A Legal Perspective, Hart Publishing: Oxford, 2003, pp. 223–246

Ward, P., Family Law in Ireland, Alphen aan den Rijn: Kluwer Law International, 2010

Warleigh-Lack, A. and R. Drachenberg, Policy Making in the European Union, in: M. Cini and N. Perez-Solorzano Borragan (eds.), European Union Politics, 4th ed., 2013, OUP: Oxford, pp. 199–212

Weatherill, S., The Limits of Legislative Harmonization Ten Years After *Tobacco Advertising*: How the Court's Case Law has Become a "Drafting Guide", 12 German Law Journal, 2011, pp. 827–864

Weiler, J. and S. Fries, A Human Rights Policy for the European Community and Union: The Question of Competences, in: P. Alston, M. Bustelo and J. Heenan (eds.), The EU and Human Rights, OUP: Oxford, 1999, pp. 147–165

Weiß, W., Artikel 207 AEUV, in: E. Grabitz, M. Hilf, and M. Nettesheim (eds.), Das Recht der Europäischen Union, CH Beck: München, 49. Ergänzungslieferung, 2012

Winkler, R., The Right to Education according to Article 14 of the Charter of Fundamental Rights, 1 IJELP, 2005, pp. 60–65

Woolcock, S. The Treaty of Lisbon and the European Union as an Actor in International Trade, ECIPE Working Paper No. 1, 2010

Zeller, K., Die rechtlichen Grundlagen für eine verstärkte Zusammenarbeit in der Europaregion Tirol, in: S. Laimer (ed.), EUREGIO – quo vadis?, Athesia/NWV: Bozen/Graz/Wien, 2006

Zilioli, C., The Recognition of Diplomas and Its Impact on Educational Policies, in: B. de Witte (ed.), European Community Law of Education, Nomos: Baden-Baden, 1989, pp. 51–70

Web Sources

By Author

Barnard, C., Competence Review: The Internal Market, https://www.gov.uk/government/uploads/system/uploads/attachment_data/file/226863/bis-13-1064-competence-review-internal-market.pdf

Bethscheider, W., Hochschulwesen in Luxemburg, GR-Atlas, http://gr-atlas.uni.lu/index.php/de/articles/ge62/ho497/lu502

Garner, BA, Garner's Dictionary of Legal Usage, http://www.oxforddictionaries.com

Grossman, A., Birthright Citizenship as Nationality of Convenience, Proceedings, Council of Europe, Compendium of Texts on the 3rd European Conference on "The Nationality and the Child", Strasbourg: 11–12 October 2004, published 17 April 2008, pp. 109–121, http://uniset.ca/naty/CJ-S-NAT_2008_2_en.pdf

Guild, E., The Court of Justice of the European Union and Citizens of the Union: A Revolution Underway? The Zambrano Judgment of 8 March 2011, http://eudo-citizenship.eu/search-results/453-the-court-of-justice-of-the-european-union-and-citizens-of-the-union-a-revolution-underway-the-zambrano-judgment-of-8-march-2011

Kramer, E., European Parliament, DG for Internal Policies (Policy Department B: Structural and Cohesion Policies), Impact on and Practical Implications of the Lisbon Treaty for Cohesion Policy, 2010, http://www.europarl.europa.eu/webnp/webdav/site/myjahiasite/users/emartinezdealosmoner/public/Impact%20on%20and%20practical%20implications%20of%20the%20Lisbon%20Treaty%20for%20Cohesion%20Policy.pdf

Nic Shuibhne, N., University Fees and rUK Students: The EU Legal Framework, 2013, Scottish Constitutional Futures Forum, http://www.scottishconstitutionalfutures.org/OpinionandAnalysis/ViewBlogPost/tabid/1767/articleType/

ArticleView/articleId/2759/Niamh-Nic-Shuibhne-University-Fees-and-rUK-Students--the-EU-Legal-Framework.aspx

Parrish, R. et al., The Lisbon Treaty and EU Sports Policy: Study, European Parliament: Brussels, 2010, http://www.europarl.europa.eu/meetdocs/2009_2014/documents/cult/dv/esstudyeusportspolicy/esstudyeusportspolicyen.pdf

Schoukens, P., From Soft Monitoring to Enforceable Action: A Quest for New Legal Approaches in the EU Fight Against Social Exclusion, Policy Paper by Euroforum KU Leuven, April 2013, https://www.kuleuven.be/euroforum/viewpic.php?LAN=E&TABLE=DOCS&ID=858

Shafiq, M. and J. Myers, Educational Vouchers and Social Cohesion: A Statistical Analysis of Student Civic Attitudes in Sweden, 1999–2009, American Journal of Education, forthcoming, http://www.ncspe.org/publications_files/OP218.pdf

Weston, BH, Human Rights, Encyclopædia Britannica Online, last updated 20.3.2014, http://www.britannica.com/EBchecked/topic/275840/human-rights

Newspaper Articles

Sweden admits Lisbon Agenda "failure", EurActiv, 3 June 2009, http://www.euractiv.com/priorities/sweden-admits-lisbon-agenda-fail-news-221962

ECJ establishes EU-wide right for students to loans and grants, EurActiv, 16 March 2005 (last updated 29.1.2010), http://www.euractiv.com/education/ecj-establishes-eu-wide-right-st-news-213557

EU gibt grünes Licht für "Makroregion Alpen", EurActiv, 20 December 2013 (last updated 7 March 2014), http://www.euractiv.de/regionalpolitik/artikel/eu-gibt-gruenes-licht-fuer-makroregion-alpen-008382

Frank, M. and T. Schultz, Dr. Austria, Süddeutsche Zeitung, 17 May 2010, http://www.sueddeutsche.de/karriere/deutsche-studenten-in-oesterreich-dr-austria-1.45835-2

Myklebust, JP, New Nordic agreement on compensation for students, University World News, Issue No. 246, 31 October 2012, http://www.universityworldnews.com/article.php?story=20121031163939447

Tirol und Trentino fördern Austausch von Schülern, Der Standard, 7 July 2014, http://derstandard.at/2000002786422/Tirol-und-Trentino-foerdern-Austausch-von-Schuelern

Miscellaneous Web Sources in Order of Appearance

Final Report of the European Convention Working Group V "Complementary Competencies", CONV 375/1/02, 4 November 2002, http://european-convention.europa.eu/pdf/reg/en/02/cv00/cv00375-re01.en02.pdf

http://conventions.coe.int/Treaty/Commun/ChercheSig.asp?NT=018&CM=&DF=&CL=ENG

Rapporteur Group on Education, Culture, Sport and Youth, New structures for European Cultural Co-operation, GR-C(2001)38 revised 22 October 2001, https://wcd.coe.int/ViewDoc.jsp?id=232495

http://www.cvce.eu/recherche/unit-content/-/unit/en/72d9869d-ff72-493e-a0e3-bedb3e671faa/841836b7-7c9e-4fc4-b0f2-b452f31c6078

Inventory of the OEEC, Historical Archives of the European Communities, EUI, http://archives.eui.eu/en/fonds/173448?item=OEEC

http://www.eesc.europa.eu/?i=portal.en.about-the-committee

Final Communiqué of the Hague Summit, English Source: Membership of the European Communities: Implications for Ireland, Laid by the Government Before Each House of the Oireachtas, The Stationery Office: Dublin, April 1970, pp. 109–112, http://www.cvce.eu/obj/final_communique_of_the_hague_summit_2_december_1969-en-33078789-8030-49c8-b4e0-15d053834507.html

www.ec.europa.eu/esf

http://cor.europa.eu/en/activities/commissions/educ/Pages/role.aspx#

http://europa.eu/legislation_summaries/glossary/green_paper_en.htm

http://europa.eu/legislation_summaries/glossary/white_paper_en.htm

Berlin Declaration, German Presidency of the Council of the European Union, 2007, http://en.wikisource.org/wiki/Berlin_Declaration

European Commission, DG EAC, Education and Training within Europe, DGVT Meeting in Ireland, 21–22 May 2013, Agenda Item II, Document 1, https://www.education.ie/en/Press-Events/Conferences/Ireland-s-Presidency-of-the-EU/Conference-21-22-May-2013/Education-and-Training-within-Europe-2020-Strategy.pdf

http://ec.europa.eu/europe2020/making-it-happen/index_en.htm

http://epp.eurostat.ec.europa.eu/statistics_explained/index.php/Glossary:Early_leaver_from_education_and_training.

http://ec.europa.eu/europe2020/pdf/themes/28_tertiary_education.pdf

https://europass.cedefop.europa.eu

https://www.youthpass.eu

http://europa.eu/legislation_summaries/institutional_affairs/treaties/lisbon_treaty/ai0020_en.htm

http://ecctis.co.uk/naric

http://www.bverfg.de/entscheidungen/es20090630_2bve000208en.html

http://ec.europa.eu/education/policy/international-cooperation/index_en.htm

Information Note on the Participation of Switzerland in Erasmus+, http://ec.europa.eu/programmes/erasmus-plus/news/2014/20140209_en.htm

The former Yugoslav Republic of Macedonia joins Erasmus+, http://ec.europa.eu/programmes/erasmus-plus/news/2014/20140610-erasmus_en.htm

Turkey latest country to join Erasmus+, http://ec.europa.eu/programmes/erasmus-plus/news/2014/20140620_en.htm

http://eacea.ec.europa.eu

http://eacea.ec.europa.eu/bilateral_cooperation/eu_canada/index_en.php

http://eacea.ec.europa.eu/bilateral_cooperation/eu_us/index_en.php

http://www.ua.ac.be/main.aspx?c=.ELA&n=63187

Fifth Negotiation Meeting Between the CDDH AD HOC Negotiation Group and the European Commission on the Accession of the European Union to the European Convention on Human Rights, Final Report to the CDDH, 47+1(2013)008rev2, Strasbourg, 10 June 2013, http://www.coe.int/t/dghl/standardsetting/hrpolicy/accession/Meeting_reports/47_1(2013)008rev2_EN.pdf

Accession by the European Union to the European Convention on Human Rights: Answers to Frequently Asked Questions, 30 April 2013, http://www.coe.int/t/dghl/standardsetting/hrpolicy/accession/Accession_documents/EU_accession-QA_updated_2013_E.pdf

http://www.parliament.uk/about/how/sovereignty

Council of Europe, European Committee of Social Rights: Conclusions 2012, France, http://www.coe.int/t/dghl/monitoring/socialcharter/conclusions/State/France2012_en.pdf

Council of Europe, The Right to Education under the European Social Charter: Information Document prepared by the Secretariat of the ESC, 17 November 2006, https://www.coe.int/t/dghl/monitoring/socialcharter/Theme%20factsheets/FactsheetEducation_en.pdf

European Commission, Eurydice – Facts and Figures: Compulsory Education in Europe 2013/14: http://eacea.ec.europa.eu/education/eurydice/documents/facts_and_figures/compulsory_education_EN.pdf

2014/15 HE Student Finance Assessing Eligibility Guidance, http://www.practitioners.slc.co.uk/media/692622/sfe_assessing_eligibility_guidance_14-15.pdf

Emploi salarié intérieur par lieu de résidence et nationalité 1995–2014, Le portail des statistiques – Grand-Duché de Luxembourg, http://www.statistiques.public.lu/stat/TableViewer/tableViewHTML.aspx?ReportId=7252&IF_Language=fra&MainTheme=2&FldrName=3&RFPath=92.

http://www.guichet.public.lu/citoyens/fr/enseignement-formation/etudes-superieures/aides-logement/aide-financiere

http://ec.europa.eu/taxation_customs/taxation/personal_tax/crossborder_workers/index_en.htm

Entwurf eines Fünfundzwanzigsten Gesetzes zur Änderung des Bundesausbildungsförderungsgesetzes, http://www.bmbf.de/pubRD/Regierungsentwurf_25._BAfoeGAendG.pdf

European Commission, Channelling Cohesion Policy Funds Towards Education and Training: What to Expect from the New Regulatory Framework?, DGVT Meeting in Ireland, 21–22 May 2013, Agenda Item II, Document 2, http://www.education.ie/en/press-events/conferences/ireland-s-presidency-of-the-eu/conference-21-22-may-2013/channelling-cohesion-policy-funds-towards-education-and-training.pdf

http://www.interreg4c.eu/fileadmin/User_Upload/PDFs/INTERREG_EUROPE_-_final.pdf

http://www.euregio.eu

http://ec.europa.eu/regional_policy/cooperate/macro_region_strategy/index_en.cfm

http://ec.europa.eu/regional_policy/cooperate/baltic/pdf/macroregional_strategies_2009.pdf

http://balticsea-region.eu/about

DG REGIO, An EU Strategy for the Alpine Region (EUSALP) Core Document, 3.7.2014, http://ec.europa.eu/eusurvey/files/d6f334e8-64a9-422b-b7b8-36b336f25e89

http://www.europaregion.info/de/evtz-europaregion.asp

http://extranet.cor.europa.eu/divisionpowers/countries/MembersLP/Italy/Policy-Areas-Obligatory/Pages/Youth-and-Sport.aspx

http://www.statistica.provincia.tn.it/binary/pat_statistica_new/popolazione/15CensGenPopolazione.1340956277.pdf

Provincia autonoma di Trento Dipartimento Istruzione, Analisi Quantitativa Esperienze di Insegnamento in Modalita' CLIL (Content and Language Integrated Learning), https://www.vivoscuola.it/c/document_library/get_file?uuid=8d280ec3-ba54-4f8f-9e0b-7323fd2bc58d&groupId=10137

http://www.uibk.ac.at/italienisches-recht/ueber_uns/ueber_uns.html.de

http://www.uibk.ac.at/italienisches-recht/studium/studium.html.de

http://www.europaregion.info/de/marksteine-der-europaregion.asp

Joint Memorandum of Understanding, http://www.google.at/url?sa=t&rct=j&q=&esrc=s&source=web&cd=1&ved=0CCAQFjAA&url=http%3A%2F%2Fwww.uibk.ac.at%2Fipoint%2Fnews%2Funi_und_die_welt%2F20020315%2Fbit-mou%2Fmou-final_en.doc&ei=i5jmU6DwGMSMOO-

YgIgL&usg=AFQjCNEi7Lkgfq-1x8NUstRx-r6b1ZdgvA&bvm=bv.72676100,d.ZWU

Überblick: Laufende gemeinsame Initiativen und Projektvorhaben der Universitäten von Bozen, Innsbruck und Trient, http://www.uibk.ac.at/public-relations/presse/archiv/2013/429/dokumente/dok_20130816121352_97018ebde1.pdf

http://www.europaregion.info/de/projekte-jugend.asp

The Schuman Declaration, 9 May 1950, http://europa.eu/about-eu/basic-information/symbols/europe-day/schuman-declaration/index_en.htm

Case Law

ECJ Case Law

Case C-11/70 *Internationale Handelsgesellschaft mbH v Einfuhr und Vorratsstelle für Getreide und Futtermittel* [1970] ECR 1125

Case C-9/74 *Casagrande v Landeshauptstadt München* [1974] ECR 773

Case C-293/83 *Françoise Gravier v City of Liège* [1985] ECR 593

Case C-45/86 *Commission v Council* [1987] ECR 1493

Case C-309/85 *Bruno Barra v Belgian State and City of Liège* [1988] ECR 355

Case C-24/86 *Vincent Blaizot v University of Liège and Others* [1988] ECR 379

Case 42/87 *Commission of the European Communities v Kingdom of Belgium* [1988] ECR 5445

Case C-197/86 *Steven Malcolm Brown v The Secretary of State for Scotland* [1988] ECR 3205

Case C-263/86 *Belgian State v René Humbel and Marie-Thérèse Humbel née Edel* [1988] ECR 5365

Case 242/87 *Commission of the European Communities v Council of the European Communities* [1989] ECR 1425

Case C-322/88 *Grimaldi v Fonds des maladies professionelles* [1989] ECR 4407

Case C-308/89 *Carmina di Leo v Land Berlin* [1990] ECR 4185

Case C-260/89 *ERT v DEP* [1991] ECR 2925

Case C-300/89 *Commission v Council* [1991] ECR 2867

Case C-3/90 *M. J. E. Bernini v Minister van Onderwijs en Wetenschappen* [1992] ECR 1071

Case C-155/91 *Commission v Council* [1993] ECR 939

Case C-7/94 *Landesamt für Ausbildungsförderung Nordrhein-Westfalen v Lubor Gaal* [1995] ECR 1031

Case C-473/93 *Commission of the European Communities v Grand Duchy of Luxemburg* [1996] ECR 3207

Case C-85/96 *María Martínez Sala v Freistaat Bayern* [1998] ECR 2691

Case C-39/86 *Sylvie Lair v Universität Hannover* [1998] ECR 3161

Case C-274/96 *Criminal proceedings against Horst Otto Bickel and Ulrich Franz* [1998] ECR 7637

Case C-337/97 *C.P.M. Meeusen gegen Hoofddirectie van de Informatie Beheer Groep* [1999] ECR 3289

Case C-376/98 *Germany v European Parliament and Council* [2000] ECR 8419

Case C-184/99 *Rudy Grzelczyk v Centre public d'aide sociale d'Ottignies-Louvain-la-Neuve* [2001] ECR 6193

Case C-224/98 *Marie-Nathalie D'Hoop v Office national de l'emploi* [2002] ECR 6191

Case C-413/99 *Baumbast and R v Secretary of State for the Home Department* [2002] ECR 7091

Case C-476/98 *Commission v Germany* [2002] ECR 9855

Case C-65/03 *Commission of the European Communities v Kingdom of Belgium* [2004] ECR 6427

Case C-200/02 *Kunqian Catherine Zhu and Man Lavette Chen v Secretary of State for the Home Department* [2004] ECR 9925

Case C-209/03 *The Queen, on the application of Dany Bidar v London Borough of Ealing and Secretary of State for Education and Skills* [2005] ECR 2119

Case C-147/03 *Commission of the European Communities v Republic of Austria* [2005] ECR 5969

Case C-540/03 *European Parliament v Council* [2006] ECR 5769

Case C-212/05 *Gertraud Hartmann v Freistaat Bayern* [2007] ECR 6303

Case C-213/05 *Wendy Geven v Land Nordrhein-Westfalen* [2007] ECR 6347

Joined Cases C-11/06 and C-12/06 *Rhiannon Morgan v Bezirksregierung Köln and Iris Bucher v Landrat des Kreises Düren* [2007] ECR 9161

Case C-158/07 *Jacqueline Förster v Hoofddirectie van de Informatie Beheer Groep* [2008] ECR 8507

Case C-310/08 *London Borough of Harrow v Nimco Hassan Ibrahim and Secretary of State for the Home Department* [2010] ECR 1065

Case C-480/08 *Maria Teixeira v London Borough of Lambeth and Secretary of State for the Home Department* [2010] ECR 1107

Case C-73/08 *Nicolas Bressol and Others and Céline Chaverot and Others v Gouvernement de la Communauté française* [2010] ECR 2735

Case C-34/09 *Gerardo Ruiz Zambrano v Office national de l'emploi (ONEm)* [2011] ECR 1177

Case C-434/09 *Shirley McCarthy v Secretary of State for the Home Department* [2011] ECR 3375

Case C-503/09 *Lucy Stewart v Secretary of State for Work and Pensions* [2011] ECR 6497

Case C-256/11 *Murat Dereci and Others v Bundesministerium für Inneres* [2011] ECR 11315

Case C-542/09 *European Commission v Kingdom of the Netherlands*, Judgment of the Court of Justice (Second Chamber) of 14 June 2012, nyr

Case C-367/11 *Déborah Prete v Office national de l'emploi*, Judgment of the Court (Fourth Chamber) of 25 October 2012, nyr

Case C-20/12 *Elodie Giersch, Benjamin Marco Stemper, Julien Taminiaux, Xavier Renaud Hodin, Joëlle Hodin v État du Grand-Duché de Luxembourg, intervening parties: Didier Taminiaux*, Judgment of the Court (Fifth Chamber) of 20 June 2013, nyr

Joined Cases C-523/11 and C-585/11 *Laurence Prinz v Region Hannover and Philipp Seeberger v Studentenwerk Heidelberg*, Judgment of the Court of Justice (Third Chamber) of 18 July 2013, nyr

Case C-220/12 *Andreas Ingemar Thiele Meneses v Region Hannover*, Judgment of the Court of Justice (Third Chamber) of 24 October 2013, nyr

Case C-275/12 *Samantha Elrick v Bezirksregierung Köln*, Judgment of the Court of Justice (Third Chamber) of 24 October 2013, nyr

ECJ Advocate General Opinions

Opinion of Advocate General Warner, delivered on 11 June 1974, Case C-9/74 *Casagrande v Landeshauptstadt München* [1974] ECR 773

Opinion of Advocate General Léger, delivered on 10 December 1996, Case C-233/94 *Germany v European Parliament and Council* [1997] ECR 2405

Opinion of Advocate General Fennelly, delivered on 15 June 2000, Case C-376/98 *Germany v European Parliament and Council* [2000] ECR 8419

Opinion of Advocate General Jacobs, delivered on 20 January 2005, Case C-147/03 *Commission of the European Communities v Republic of Austria* [2005] ECR 5969

Opinion of Advocate General Ruiz-Jarabo Colomer, delivered on 20 March 2007, Joined Cases C-11/06 and C-12/06 *Rhiannon Morgan v Bezirksregierung Köln and Iris Bucher v Landrat des Kreises Düren* [2007] ECR 9161

Opinion of Advocate General Mazák, delivered on 10 July 2008, Case C-158/07 *Jacqueline Förster v Hoofddirectie van de Informatie Beheer Groep* [2008] ECR 8507

Opinion of Advocate General Sharpston, delivered on 25 June 2009, Case C-73/08 *Nicolas Bressol and Others and Céline Chaverot and Others v Gouvernement de la Communauté française* [2010] ECR 2735

Opinion of Advocate General Trstenjak, delivered on 22 September 2011, Case C-411/10 *N. S. v Secretary of State for the Home Department* [2011] ECR 13905

Opinion of Advocate General Sharpston, delivered on 16 February 2012, Case C-542/09 *European Commission v Kingdom of the Netherlands*, nyr

Opinion of Advocate General Sharpston, delivered on 21 February 2013, Joined Cases C-523/11 and C-585/11 *Laurence Prinz v Region Hannover and Philipp Seeberger v Studentenwerk Heidelberg*, Judgment of the Court of Justice (Third Chamber) of 18 July 2013, nyr

ECJ Opinions

Opinion 1/76 [1977] ECR 741

Opinion 2/94 *Accession by the Community to the European Convention for the Protection of Human Rights and Fundamental Freedoms* [1996] ECR 1763

ECtHR Case Law

Case "Relating to Certain Aspects of the Laws on the Use of Languages in Education in Belgium" v Belgium (Merits) [1968] 1 EHRR 252

Kjeldsen, Busk Madsen and Pedersen v Denmark [1976] 1 EHRR 711

Member State Case Law

Belgium

Arrêt de la Cour constitutionnelle No. 89/2011 du 31 mai 2011, numéros du rôle: 4034 et 4093

Germany

Lisbon Judgment, BVerfG, 2 BvE 2/08 vom 30.6.2009

Verwaltungsgericht Gelsenkirchen, Beschlüsse vom 28.9.2011, Aktenzeichen 6 L 941/11; 6 L 929/11; 6 L 940/11 und 6 L 942/11

Oberverwaltungsgericht Nordrhein-Westfalen, Beschlüsse vom 6.10.2011, Aktenzeichen 13 B 1214/11, 13 B 1215/11, 13 B 1216/11, 13 B 1217/11 and 13 B 1218/11

Oberverwaltungsgericht Nordrhein-Westfalen, Beschlüsse vom 8.11.2011, Aktenzeichen 13 B 1209/11, 13 B 1210/11, 13 B 1211/11, 13 B 1212/11, 13 B 1213/11 and 13 B 1224/11

Urteil des 5. Senats vom 10. Januar 2013 – BVerwG 5 C 19.11

EU Documents

Legislation

Agreement on the European Economic Area, OJ L 1, 3.1.1994, pp. 3–522; and EFTA States' official gazettes

Commission Decision 2008/785/EC of 9 October 2008 amending Commission Decision 2005/56/EC setting up the Education, Audiovisual and Culture Executive Agency for the management of Community action in the fields of education, audiovisual and culture in application of Council Regulation (EC) No 58/2003, OJ L 269, 10.10.2008, pp. 11–13

Council Decision 63/266/EEC of 2 April 1963 Laying Down General Principles for Implementing a Common Vocational Training Policy, English Special Edition: Series I Volume 1963–1964, pp. 25–2

Council Decision 87/327/EEC of 15 June 1987 Adopting the European Community Action Scheme for the Mobility of University Students, OJ L 166, 25.6.1987, pp. 20–24

Council Decision 1999/311/EC of 29 April 1999 adopting the third phase of the trans-European cooperation scheme for higher education (Tempus III) (2000–2006), OJ L 120, 8.5.1999, pp. 30–36

Council Decision 2006/910/EC of 4 December 2006 concerning the conclusion of the Agreement between the European Community and the United States of America renewing the cooperation programme in higher education and vocational education and training: Agreement between the European Community and the United States of America renewing a programme of cooperation in higher education and vocational education and training, OJ L 346, 9.12.2006, p. 33–40

Council Decision 2006/964/EC of 18 December 2006 on the conclusion of the Agreement between the European Community and the Government of Canada establishing a framework for cooperation in higher education, training and youth: Agreement between the European Community and the Government of Canada establishing a framework for cooperation in higher education, training and youth, OJ L 397, 30.12.2006, pp. 14–21

Council Directive 2000/43/EC of 29 June 2000 implementing the principle of equal treatment between persons irrespective of racial or ethnic origin, OJ L 180, 19.7.2000, pp. 22–26

Council Directive 73/148/EEC of 21 May 1973 on the abolition of restrictions on movement and residence within the Community for nationals of Member States with regard to establishment and the provision of services, OJ L 172, pp. 14–16

Council Directive 90/364/EEC of 28 June 1990 on the right of residence, OJ L 180, 13.7.1990, pp. 26–27

Decision No 1720/2006/EC of the European Parliament and of the Council of 15 November 2006 Establishing an Action Programme in the Field of Lifelong Learning, OJ L 327, 24.11.2006, pp. 45–68

Decision of the EEA Joint Committee amending Protocol 31 to the EEA Agreement, on cooperation in specific fields outside the four freedoms No 140/2012 of 13 July 2012, OJ L 309, 8.11.2012, pp. 23–24

Decision No 110/2014 (OJ L [to be published] and EEA Supplement No [to be published]), e.i.f. 17.5.2014

Directive 2004/17/EC of the European Parliament and of the Council of 31 March 2004 coordinating the procurement procedures of entities operating in the water, energy, transport and postal services sectors, OJ L 134, 30.4.2004, pp. 1–113

Directive 2004/18/EC of the European Parliament and of the Council of 31 March 2004 on the coordination of procedures for the award of public works contracts, public supply contracts and public service contracts, OJ L 134, 30.4.2004, pp. 114–240

Directive 2005/36/EC of the European Parliament and of the Council of 7 September 2005 on the recognition of professional qualifications, OJ L 255, 30.9.2005, pp. 22–142

Regulation (EC) No 1082/2006 of the European Parliament and of the Council of 5 July 2006 on a European grouping of territorial cooperation (EGTC), OJ L 210, 31.7.2006, pp. 19–24

Regulation (EU) No 1288/2013 of the European Parliament and of the Council of 11 December 2013 establishing 'Erasmus+': the Union programme for education, training, youth and sport and repealing Decisions No 1719/2006/EC, No 1720/2006/EC and No 1298/2008/EC Text with EEA relevance, OJ L 347, 20.12.2013, pp. 50–73

Regulation (EU) No 1301/2013 of the European Parliament and of the Council of 17 December 2013 on the European Regional Development Fund and on specific provisions concerning the Investment for growth and jobs goal and repealing Regulation (EC) No 1080/2006, OJ L 347, 20.12.2013, pp. 289–302

Regulation (EU) No 1302/2013 of the European Parliament and of the Council of 17 December 2013 amending Regulation (EC) No 1082/2006 on a European grouping of territorial cooperation (EGTC) as regards the clarification, simplification and improvement of the establishment and functioning of such groupings, OJ L 347, 20.12.2013, pp. 303–319

Regulation (EU) No 1304/2013 of the European Parliament and of the Council of 17 December 2013 on the European Social Fund and repealing Council Regulation (EC) No 1081/2006, OJ L 347, 20.12.2013, pp. 470–486

Other Documents

Amended proposal for a Directive of the European Parliament and of the Council on the right of citizens of the Union and their family members to move and reside freely within the territory of the Member States, COM(2003) 199 final

Call for proposals – EACEA/37/10, EU-Canada Programme for Co-operation in Higher Education, Training and Youth Transatlantic Exchange Partnerships – Transatlantic Degree Partnerships, OJ C 323, 30.11.2010, pp. 20–22

Call for proposals – EACEA/36/10, EU-US Cooperation in Higher Education and Vocational Training, Atlantis: Actions for Transatlantic Links and Academic Networks in Training and Integrated Studies Call for proposals 2011, OJ C 2, 5.1.2011, pp. 2–4

Cancellation of the EU-US Atlantis Call for Proposals EACEA/36/10, OJ C 142, 13.5.2011, p. 29

Charter of Fundamental Rights of the European Union, OJ C 303, 14 December 2007, pp. 1–16

Cologne European Council, Presidency Conclusions, 3 and 4 June 1999

Commission's Action Plan for skills and mobility, Communication from the Commission to the Council, the European Parliament, the Economic and Social Committee and the Committee of the Regions, COM(2002) 72 final, 13.2.2002

Commission Staff Working Document, Action Plan accompanying the Communication from the Commission to the European Parliament, the Council, the European Economic and Social Committee and the Committee of the Regions: European Union Strategy for the Baltic Sea Region, SEC(2009) 712/2 (revised February 2013)

Commission Staff Working Document, Action Plan accompanying the Communication from the Commission to the European Parliament, the Council, the European Economic and Social Committee and the Committee of the Regions: European Union Strategy for the Danube Region, SEC(2010) 1489 final, 8 December 2010

Commission Staff Working Document, Action Plan accompanying the Document Communication from the Commission to the European Parliament, the Council, the European Economic and Social Committee and the Committee of the Regions concerning the European Union Strategy for the Adriatic and Ionian Region, SWD(2014) 190 final, 17.6.2014

Commission Working Document Consultation on the Future "EU 2020" Strategy, Brussels, 24.11.2009, COM(2009) 647 final

Communication on the principle of subsidiarity, adopted by the Commission on 27 October 1992, for transmission to the Council and Parliament, Bulletin of the European Communities, No. 10, 1992, pp. 116–126

Communication from the Commission to the Council, Education in the European Community, COM(74) 253 final/2, 17 March 1974, Bulletin of the European Communities, Supplement 3/74

Communication from the Commission to the European Parliament, the Council, the European Economic and Social Committee and the Committee of the Regions of 3 July 2008 – Improving Competences for the 21st Century: An Agenda for European Cooperation on Schools, COM(2008) 425 final

Communication from the Commission to the European Parliament, the Council, the European Economic and Social Committee and the Committee of the Regions concerning the European Union Strategy for the Baltic Sea Region, COM(2009) 248 final, 10.6.2009

Communication from the Commission, Europe 2020: A Strategy for Smart, Sustainable and Inclusive Growth, COM(2010) 2020 final, 3.3.2010

Communication from the Commission to the European Parliament, the Council, the European Economic and Social Committee and the Committee of the Regions: Developing the European Dimension in Sport, COM(2011) 12 final, 18.1.2011

Communication from the Commission to the European Parliament, the Council, the European Economic and Social Committee and the Committee of the Regions: European higher education in the world, COM(2013) 499 final, Brussels, 11.7.2013

Communication from the Commission to the European Parliament, the Council, the European Economic and Social Committee and the Committee of the Regions, Taking Stock of the Europe 2020 Strategy for Smart, Sustainable and Inclusive Growth, Brussels, 19.3.2014, COM(2014) 130 final/2

Communication from the Commission to the European Parliament, the Council, the European Economic and Social Committee and the Committee of the Regions concerning the European Union Strategy for the Adriatic and Ionian Region, COM(2014) 357 final, Brussels, 17.6.2014

Corrigendum to call for proposals – EACEA/36/10 – EU-US Cooperation in Higher Education and Vocational Training – Atlantis: Actions for Transatlantic Links and Academic Networks in Training and Integrated Studies – Call for proposals 2011, OJ C 108, 7.4.2011, p. 26

Council Conclusions of 12 May 2009 on a Strategic Framework for European Cooperation in Education and Training (ET 2020), OJ C 119, 28.5.2009, pp. 2–10

Declaration by Germany, Austria and Belgium on Subsidiarity, OJ C 340, 10.11.1997, p. 143

Detailed work programme on the follow-up of the objectives of education and training systems in Europe, OJ C 142, 14.6.2002, pp. 1–22

European Commission, Erasmus+ Programme Guide: Valid as of 1 January 2014, Version 3, 9.4.2014

European Commission White Paper – A New Impetus for European Youth, COM(2001) 681 final, 21.11.2001

European Council Conclusions, Brussels, 29–30 October 2009

European Council Conclusions, Brussels, 17 June 2010

European Council Conclusions, Brussels, 23–24 June 2011

European Council Conclusions, Brussels, 19–20 December 2013

European Parliament, Committee on Legal Affairs, Rapporteur: MM Ortega, Working Document on Institutional and Legal Implications of the Use of "Soft Law" Instruments, 14.2.2007, PE 384.581v02-00 (DT\653346EN.doc)

European Parliament, Opinion of the Committee on Culture and Education for the Committee on Regional Development on the evolution of EU macro-regional strategies: present practice and future prospects, especially in the Mediterranean (2011/2179(INI)), 2.3.2012

EP-Resolution on Education and Training in the Run-up to 1993, OJ C 150, 15.6.1992, pp. 366–370

European Parliament Resolution of 4 September 2007 on institutional and legal implications of the use of 'soft law' instruments (2007/2028(INI)), OJ C 187E, 24.7.2008, pp. 75–79

European Parliament Resolution of 20 February 2008 on the Treaty of Lisbon (2007/2286(INI)), OJ C 184 E, 6.8.2009, pp. 25–30

Explanations relating to the Charter of Fundamental Rights, OJ C 303, 14 December 2007, pp. 17–35

General Guidelines for Drawing up a Community Action Programme on Vocational Training, OJ C 81, 12.8.1971, pp. 5–11 (Unofficial Translation, accessed via EUR-Lex)

Green Paper on the European Dimension of Education, COM(93) 457 final, 29 September 1993

Janne, H., For a Community Policy on Education, Bulletin of the European Communities, Supplement 10/73

Joint Declaration by the European Parliament, the Council and the Commission, OJ C 103, 27.4.1977

2012 Joint Report of the Council and the Commission on the implementation of the Strategic Framework for European Cooperation in Education and Training (ET 2020): Education and Training in a Smart, Sustainable and Inclusive Europe, OJ C 70, 8.3.2012, pp. 9–18

Lisbon European Council 23 and 24 March 2000, Presidency Conclusions

Meetings of the Heads of State or Government (Summit), Paris, 19–21 October 1972, Bulletin of the European Communities, No. 10, 1972, pp. 15–24

Presidency Conclusions of the Nice European Council Meeting, 7, 8 and 9 December 2000

Presidency Conclusions of the Brussels European Council Meeting, 11 and 12 December 2008

Proposal for a Council Decision adopting the European Community Action Scheme for the Mobility of University Students, COM(85) 756 final, OJ C 73, 2.4.1986, pp. 4–7

Proposal for a Council Decision on the position to be adopted, on behalf of the European Union, in the EEA Joint Committee concerning an amendment to Protocol 31 to the EEA Agreement, on cooperation in specific fields outside the four freedoms, 11.3.2014, COM(2014) 142 final

Recommendation of the European Parliament and of the Council of 23 April 2008 on the establishment of the European Qualifications Framework for lifelong learning, OJ C 111, 6.5.2008, pp. 1–7

Recommendation of the European Parliament and of the Council of 18 June 2009 on the Establishment of a European Credit System for Vocational Education and Training (ECVET), OJ C 155, 8.7.2009, pp. 11–18

Report from the Commission to the European Parliament, the Council, the European Economic and Social Committee and the Committee of the Regions concerning the added value of macro-regional strategies, COM(2013) 468 final, 27.6.2013

Resolution of the Ministers for Education meeting within the Council of 16 November 1971 on Cooperation in the Field of Education, European Educational Policy Statements, 3rd ed., Office for Official Publications of the European Communities: Luxembourg, 1988, p. 11

Resolution of the Ministers of Education, Meeting within the Council, of 6 June 1974 on Cooperation in the Field of Education, OJ C 98, 20.8.1974, p. 2

Resolution of the Council and of the Ministers of Education meeting within the Council of 9 February 1976 Comprising an Action Programme in the Field of Education, OJ C 38, 19.2.1976, pp. 1–5

Resolution of the Council and the Ministers of Education meeting within the Council on the European dimension in education of 24 May 1988, OJ C 177, 6.7.1988, pp. 5–7

Resolution of the Council and of the representatives of the Governments of the Member States, meeting within the Council of 27 June 2002 regarding the framework of European cooperation in the youth field, OJ C 168, 13.7.2002, pp. 2–5

White Paper Growth, Competitiveness, Employment: The Challenges and Ways Forward into the 21st Century COM(93) 700 final, Bulletin of the European Communities, Supplement 6/93

White Paper on Education and Training – Teaching and Learning – Towards the Learning Society, COM(95) 590 final

White Paper on Sport, COM(2007) 391 final

Press Releases

1976–2006: Thirty Years of European Cooperation in Education, Press Release, 23 February 2006 (IP/06/12)

Free movement of students: the Commission sends letters of formal notice to Austria and Belgium, Press Release, 24 January 2007 (IP/07/06)

Access to higher education: the Commission suspends its infringement cases against Austria and Belgium, Press Release, 28 November 2007 (IP/07/1788)

Lisbon Treaty Turns Committee of the Regions into Subsidiarity Watchdog, Press Release, 4 December 2009 (COR/09/113)

Austria and Belgium given more time to justify quotas, Press Release, 18 December 2012 (IP/12/1388)

Erasmus Impact Study confirms EU student exchange scheme boosts employability and job mobility, Press Release, 22 September 2014 (IP/14/1025)

Publications

European Commission, Affirming Fundamental Rights in the European Union: Time to Act, Report of the Expert Group on Fundamental Rights, Office for Official Publications of the European Communities: Luxembourg, 1999

European Commission, The European Higher Education Area in 2012: Bologna Process Implementation Report, Education, Audiovisual and Culture Executive Agency: Brussels, 2012

European Commission, Education and Training Monitor 2012, Publications Office of the European Union: Luxembourg, 2012

European Commission, Education and Training Monitor 2013, Publications Office of the European Union: Luxembourg, 2013

European Commission, EU Guidelines on Dual Careers of Athletes, Publications Office of the European Union: Luxembourg, 2013

Committee of the Regions, Regional and Local Powers in Europe: Employment, Social Policy, Environment, Transport and Vocational Training, CoR Studies E-1/2002, Office for Official Publications of the European Communities: Luxembourg, 2001

Committee of the Regions, Regional and Local Powers in Europe: Education and Youth, Culture, Public Health, Transeuropean Networks and Regional and Structural Policy, CoR Studies E-4/2002, Office for Official Publications of the European Communities: Luxembourg, 2002

Committee of the Regions, The European Grouping of Territorial Cooperation – EGTC, January 2007, CdR 117/2007 (Study)

Committee of the Regions, Key Dates in the History of the Committee of the Regions: 1994–2009, Publications Office of the European Union: Luxembourg, 2009

Committee of the Regions, EGTC Monitoring Report 2013: Towards the New Cohesion Policy, European Union: 2014

Report from the High Level Group chaired by Wim Kok, Facing the Challenge: The Lisbon Strategy for Growth and Employment, Office for Official Publications of the European Communities: Luxembourg, 2004

International Documents

Legislation

Additional Protocol to the European Outline Convention on Transfrontier Co-operation between Territorial Communities or Authorities (1995) CETS No. 159

Convention of the OEEC

Convention on the Recognition of Qualifications concerning Higher Education in the European Region (1997) CETS No. 165

European Agreement on Continued Payment of Scholarships to Students Studying Abroad (1969) CETS No. 69

European Convention on the Equivalence of Diplomas leading to Admission to Universities (1953) CETS No. 15

European Convention on the Equivalence of Periods of University Study (1956) CETS No. 21

European Convention on the Academic Recognition of University Qualifications (1959) CETS No. 32

European Convention on the General Equivalence of Periods of University Study (1990) CETS No. 138

European Cultural Convention CETS (1954) CETS No. 18

European Outline Convention on Transfrontier Co-operation between Territorial Communities or Authorities (1980) CETS No. 106

Modified Brussels Treaty

Statute of the Council of Europe (1949) CETS No. 1

Other Documents

Committee on Economic, Social and Cultural Rights, General Comment 11 on the plans of action for primary education (Twentieth session, 1999), UN Doc. E/C.12/1999/4 (1999)

Committee on Economic, Social and Cultural Rights, General Comment 13 on the right to education (Twenty-first session, 1999), UN Doc. E/C.12/1999/10 (1999)

Explanatory Report to the Additional Protocol to the European Outline Convention on Transfrontier Co-operation between Territorial Communities or Authorities (1995) CETS No. 159

Explanatory Report to the revised European Social Charter (1996) CETS No. 163

Explanatory Report to Protocol No. 14 to the Convention for the Protection of Human Rights and Fundamental Freedoms, amending the control system of the Convention (2004) CETS No. 194

List of Declarations made with respect to the European Outline Convention on Transfrontier Co-operation between Territorial Communities or Authorities (1980) CETS No. 106

Recommendation No. R (92) 13 Rev of the Committee of Ministers to Member States on the Revised European Sports Charter, adopted by the Committee of Ministers on 24 September 1992 at the 480th meeting of the Ministers' Deputies and revised at their 752nd meeting on 16 May 2001

Resolution (76) 3 of the Committee of Ministers of the Council of Europe on committee structures, terms of reference and working methods, 18 February 1976

Publications

European Social Charter (revised), European Committee of Social Rights, Conclusions 2008 – Volume 1 (Albania, Andorra, Armenia, Azerbaijan, Belgium,

Bulgaria, Cyprus, Estonia, Finland, France, Georgia, Ireland, Italy), Council of Europe Publishing: Strasbourg, 2008

OECD, How Is International Student Mobility Shaping Up?, Education Indicators in Focus, No. 14, OECD Publishing, 2013

OECD, Luxembourg, in: International Migration Outlook 2013, OECD Publishing, 2013

OECD, Netherlands, in: International Migration Outlook 2013, OECD Publishing, 2013

National Documents

Bilateral Agreements

Abkommen zwischen der Republik Österreich und der Italienischen Republik über die Zusammenarbeit der Universitäten, BGBl. Nr. 423/1983

Kulturabkommen zwischen der Republik Österreich und dem Großherzogtum Luxemburg, BGBl. Nr. 372/1972, in der Fassung des Zusatzprotokolls, BGBl. Nr. 588/1986

Rahmenabkommen zwischen der Republik Österreich und der Italienischen Republik über die Grenzüberschreitende Zusammenarbeit von Gebietskörperschaften, BGBl. Nr. 421/1995

Österreich – Liechtenstein: Abkommen über Gleichwertigkeiten im Bereich der Reifezeugnisse und des Hochschulwesens, BGBl. III Nr. 176/1997

Exchange of Notes

45. Notenwechsel zwischen der Regierung der Republik Österreich und der Regierung der Italienischen Republik über die gegenseitige Anerkennung akademischer Grade und Titel samt Anlage, BGBl. III Nr. 45/2001

Legislation

Austria

Articles 17, 17a and 18 of the Austrian Basic Law (Staatsgrundgesetz)

Bundesgesetz vom 15. Juli 1966 über die Studien an den wissenschaftlichen Hochschulen (Allgemeines Hochschul-Studiengesetz – AHStG), BGBl. Nr. 177/1966

Bundesgesetz über die Studien an den Universitäten (Universitäts-Studiengesetz – UniStG), BGBl. I Nr. 48/1997

Bundesgesetz über die Organisation der Universitäten und ihre Studien (Universitätsgesetz 2002 – UG), BGBl. I Nr. 120/2002, consolidated version

Verordnung des Bundesministers für Wissenschaft und Verkehr über die Festlegung von Personengruppen bei der Zulassung zu ordentlichen Studien (Personengruppenverordnung), BGBl. II Nr. 211/1997

Verordnung des Bundesministers für Wissenschaft und Forschung über die Festlegung von Personengruppen bei der Zulassung zu ordentlichen Studien (Personengruppenverordnung 2014 – PersGV 2014), BGBl. II Nr. 340/2013

Bulgaria

Articles 23 and 53 of the Bulgarian Constitution

Belgium

Arrêté royal déterminant les conditions et la procédure d'octroi de l'équivalence des diplômes et certificats d'études étrangers, 20 July 1971, published in Moniteur belge, 5 Ausgust 1971, p. 9254

Arrêté du Gouvernement de la Communauté française établissant l'équivalence entre certains titres étrangers de fin d'études secondaires et le certificat homologué d'enseignement secondaire supérieur, 17 May 1999, published in Moniteur belge, 25 September 1999, p. 36182

Article 24 of the Belgian Constitution

Décret régulant le nombre d'étudiants dans certains cursus de premier cycle de l'enseignement supérieur, 16.6.2006, published in Moniteur Belge 6.7.2006, p. 34055

Croatia

Articles 63, 64, 66, 67, 68 and 69 of the Croatian Constitution

Cyprus

Article 20 of the Cypriot Constitution

Czech Republic

Articles 16, 26 and 33 of the Charter of Fundamental Rights and Freedoms

Denmark

Section 76 of the Danish Constitution (Danmarks Riges Grundlov)

Estonia

Article 37 of the Estonian Constitution

Finland

Section 16 of the Finnish Constitution

France

Arrêté du 28 octobre 2009 relatif à la première année commune aux études de santé, JORF, No. 266, 17.11.2009, p. 19838

Section 13 of the Preamble to the French Constitution

Germany

Articles 6 and 7 of the German Basic Law (Grundgesetz)

Greece

Article 16 of the Greek Constitution

Hungary

Article XI of the Fundamental Law

Ireland

Articles 2, 9(2)(1) and 42 of the Irish Constitution (Bunreacht na hÉireann)

Italy

Articles 30, 33, 34, 116, 117 and 123 of the Italian Constitution

Beschluss Nr. 1034, Sprachprojekte und Sachfachunterricht mit der CLIL-Methodik an den deutschsprachigen Grund-, Mittel- und Oberschulen, Südtiroler Landesregierung, 8 July 2013

Dekret des Präsidenten der Republik vom 31. August 1972, Nr. 670, in: Autonome Provinz Bozen-Südtirol, Das neue Autonomiestatut, 14th ed., Südtiroler Landesregierung: Bozen, 2009

Latvia

Article 112 of the Latvian Constitution

Lithuania

Articles 40, 41 and 42 of the Lithuanian Constitution

Luxembourg

Article 23 of the Luxembourg Constitution

Règlement grand-ducal du 12 novembre 2010 modifiant le règlement grand-ducal du 5 octobre 2000 concernant l'aide financière de l'Etat pour études supérieures, Mémorial A 2010, p. 3430

Malta

Articles 2, 10, 11, 12 and 17 of the Maltese Constitution

Netherlands
Article 23 of the Dutch Constitution

Poland
Article 70 of the Polish Constitution

Portugal
Articles 43, 73, 74, 75, 76 and 77 of the Portuguese Constitution

Romania
Article 32 of the Romanian Constitution

Slovakia
Article 42 of the Slovakian Constitution

Slovenia
Articles 54, 57 and 58 of the Slovenian Constitution

Spain
Article 27 of the Spanish Constitution

Sweden
Section 2 of Chapter 1 and Section 18 of Chapter 2 of the Instrument of Government (Regeringsformen)

UK
SI 2005/1341 The Education (Student Support) (Amendment) Regulations 2005

SI 2011/1986 The Education (Student Support) Regulations 2011

The Education (Fees) (Scotland) Regulations 2011

Other Documents

Germany

Deutscher Bundestag – 4. Wahlperiode, Drucksache IV/567, Allgemeine Grundsätze zur Durchführung einer gemeinsamen Politik der Berufsausbildung (Vorschlag der Kommission an den Rat vom 5. Oktober 1961)

Deutscher Bundestag – 17. Wahlperiode, Drucksache 17/14577, Schriftliche Fragen mit den in der Woche vom 12. August 2013 eingegangenen Antworten der Bundesregierung, 16.08.2013

Deutscher Bundestag – 18. Wahlperiode, Drucksache 18/115, Schriftliche Fragen mit den in der Woche vom 25. November 2013 eingegangenen Antworten der Bundesregierung, 29.11.2013

Publications

Austria

Bundesministerium für Wirtschaft, Familie und Jugend, Jugendpolitik in Österreich: Ein kurzer Überblick, Bundesministerium für Wirtschaft, Familie und Jugend: Wien, 2009

Statistik Austria, Bildung in Zahlen: Tabellenband, Verlag Österreich: Wien, 2014

Italy

Autonome Provinz Bozen-Südtirol, Demografisches Handbuch für Südtirol, Landesinstitut für Statistik: Bozen, 2014

UK

House of Lords, European Union Committee, The Treaty of Lisbon: An Impact Assessment, Volume I: Report, The Stationery Office Limited: London, 2008

House of Lords, European Union Committee, The Treaty of Lisbon: An Impact Assessment, Vol. II: Evidence, The Stationery Office Limited: London, 2008

The Scottish Government, Scotland's Future: Your Guide to an Independent Scotland, Edinburgh: November 2013

UK Government, Scotland Analysis: EU and International Issues, London: January 2014

Documents Relating to the Macro-regional Strategies

EUSDR Report June 2012, Priority Area 09: To Invest in People and Skills

EUSDR Report June 2013, Priority Area 09: To Invest in People and Skills: Education and Training, Labour Market, Marginalised Groups

Documents Relating to the EGTC European Region Tyrol-South Tyrol-Trentino

Vereinbarung zwischen der Universität Innsbruck und der Universität Padua über die gemeinsame Durchführung eines Studienprogrammes „Integriertes Diplomstudium der Rechtswissenschaften", BGBl. Nr. 3/1986, amended through BGBl. Nr. 189/1987 and BGBl. III Nr. 262/2001

Beschluss betreffend die Vereinbarung über die grenzüberschreitende Zusammenarbeit im Rahmen einer Europaregion zwischen der Autonomen Provinz Bozen- Südtirol, der Autonomen Provinz Trient und dem Land Tirol, Gemeinsame Sitzung der Landtage von Südtirol, Tirol, Trentino und Vorarlberger Landtag im Beobachterstatus, Meran, 19 May 1998

Vereinbarungsprotokoll zwischen dem Land Tirol und der autonomen Provinz Trient, Innsbruck, 20 April 2005

Europaregion Tirol-Südtirol-Trentino, Gemeinsame Erklärung anlässlich der Arbeitssitzung der Regierungen von Tirol, Südtirol und Trentino, Innsbruck, 15 October 2009

Beschluss Nr. 1 betreffend Projekt zur Einrichtung eines Europäischen Verbundes für territoriale Zusammenarbeit (EVTZ) mit der Bezeichnung „Euregio Südtirol/Alto Adige, Tirol und Trentino", Gemeinsame Sitzung der Landtage von Südtirol, Tirol, Trentino und Vorarlberger Landtag im Beobachterstatus, Mezzocorona, 29 October 2009

Zusatzvereinbarung gemäß Punkt 3) letzter Absatz des Vereinbarungsprotokolls zwischen dem Land Tirol und der autonomen Provinz Trient, unterzeichnet in Innsbruck am 20. April 2005, und Änderungen des Protokolls, San Michele all'Adige, 22 May 2010

Memorandum zwischen dem Land Tirol und der autonomen Provinz Trient zum Projekt Austausch von Lehrkräften, San Michele all'Adige, 22 May 2010

Beschluss Nr. 17 betreffend Förderung der Kenntnisse der deutschen und italienischen Sprache sowie des Ladinischen und anderer Minderheitensprachen, Gemeinsame Sitzung der Landtage von Südtirol, Tirol und dem Trentino sowie Vorarlberger Landtag im Beobachterstatus, Meran, 30 March 2011

Beschluss Nr. 20 betreffend Zielsetzung Zweisprachigkeit 2020, Gemeinsame Sitzung der Landtage von Südtirol, Tirol und dem Trentino sowie Vorarlberger Landtag im Beobachterstatus, Meran, 30 March 2011

Übereinkunft über die Errichtung des Europäischen Verbundes für Territoriale Zusammenarbeit „Europaregion Tirol-Südtirol-Trentino" zwischen dem Land Tirol, der Autonomen Provinz Bozen-Südtirol und der autonomen Provinz Trient, 11 June 2011

Zwischenbericht über den Stand der Umsetzung der Beschlüsse, die von den Landtagen von Südtirol, Tirol, Trentino und dem Vorarlberger Landtag im Beobachterstatus am 30. März 2011 in Meran verabschiedet wurden, March 2012

Anlage zum Mitteilungsblatt der Leopold-Franzens-Universität Innsbruck vom 14. Mai 2012, 26. Stück, Nr. 273

Rahmenabkommen zwischen der Freien Universität Bozen und der Leopold-Franzens-Universität Innsbruck und der Università degli Studi di Trento, Alpbach, 18 August 2013

Grundsatzvereinbarung zur Intensivierung und besonderen Förderung von Austauschprogrammen für Schüler/innen und Lehrer/innen sowie von Schulkooperationen und schulübergreifenden Projekten zwischen Schulen aus der autonomen Provinz Trient und dem Bundesland Tirol, Völs am Schlern, 5 July 2014

Miscellaneous

Written evidence from Erna Hjaltested, Senior Legal Officer, EEA Co-ordination Division, EFTA, 14 January 2013, in: House of Commons, Foreign Affairs Committee, The Future of the European Union: UK Government Policy, First Report of Session 2013–14, Vol. II

Written evidence from Tore Grønningsæter, Senior Information and Communication Officer, EFTA, 26 March 2014 (file with author)

Völkerrecht, Europarecht und Internationales Wirtschaftsrecht

Herausgegeben von Peter Hilpold und August Reinisch

Band 1 Florian Razesberger: The International Criminal Court. The Principle of Complementarity. 2006.

Band 2 Christian Wimpissinger: Steuerliche Verlustverrechnung nach EG-Recht. 2006.

Band 3 Christina Knahr: Participation of Non-State Actors in the Dispute Settlement System of the WTO: Benefit or Burden? 2007.

Band 4 Daniela Kröll: Toward Multilateral Competition Law? After Cancún: Reevaluating the Case for Additional International Competition Rules Under Special Consideration of the WTO Agreement. 2007.

Band 5 Georg Nolte / Peter Hilpold (Hrsg.): Auslandsinvestitionen – Entwicklung großer Kodifikationen – Fragmentierung des Völkerrechts – Status des Kosovo. Beiträge zum 31. Österreichischen Völkerrechtstag 2006 in München. 2008.

Band 6 Irmgard Marboe: Die Berechnung von Entschädigung und Schadenersatz in der internationalen Rechtsprechung. 2009.

Band 7 Peter Neumann: United Nations Procurement Regime. Description and Evaluation of the Legal Framework in the Light of International Standards and of Findings of an Inquiry into Procurement for the Iraq Oil-for-Food Programme. 2008.

Band 8 Kirsten Schmalenbach / Wolfgang Benedek (Hrsg.): Von Terrorismusbekämpfung bis Klimaschutz. Beiträge zum 32. Österreichischen Völkerrechtstag 2007 in Altaussee. 2008.

Band 9 Stephan Wittich / August Reinisch / Andrea Gattini (Hrsg.): Kosovo – Staatsschulden – Notstand – EU-Reformvertrag – Humanitätsrecht. Beiträge zum 33. Österreichischen Völkerrechtstag 2008 in Conegliano. 2009.

Band 10 Peter Hilpold (Hrsg.): Das Selbstbestimmungsrecht der Völker. Vom umstrittenen Prinzip zum vieldeutigen Recht? 2009.

Band 11 Peter Hilpold / Christoph Perathoner (Hrsg.): Immigration und Integration. Völkerrechtliche und europarechtliche Antworten auf eine zentrale Herausforderung der Zeit. 2010.

Band 12 Claudia Alfons: Recognition and Enforcement of Annulled Foreign Arbitral Awards. An Analysis of the Legal Framework and its Interpretation in Case Law and Literature. 2010.

Band 13 Peter Hilpold / Walter Steinmair / Christoph Perathoner (Hrsg.): Rechtsvergleichung an der Sprachgrenze. 2011.

Band 14 Werner Schroeder / Jelka Mayr-Singer (Hrsg.): Völkerstrafrecht, Rechtsschutz und Rule of Law. Das Individuum als Herausforderung für das Völkerrecht. Beiträge zum 34. Österreichischen Völkerrechtstag 2009 in Tramin/Südtirol. 2011.

Band 15 Werner Petritz: Vor dem Aus? Der Vertrag über die Nichtweiterverbreitung von Kernwaffen. Funktion und Relevanz anhand zweier Beispiele. 2012.

Band 16 Kirsten Schmalenbach (Hrsg.): Aktuelle Herausforderungen des Völkerrechts. Beiträge zum 36. Österreichischen Völkerrechtstag 2011. Unter Mitarbeit von Lando Kirchmair. 2012.

Band 17 Ruth Steger: Staatenimmunität und Kriegsverbrechen. Das IGH-Urteil im Verfahren Deutschland gegen Italien vom 03.02.2012. 2013.

Band 18 Christoph Vedder (Hrsg.): Völkerrecht 2012. Richterliche Praxis und politische Realität. Beiträge zum 37. Österreichischen Völkerrechtstag 2012. Unter Mitarbeit von Manuel Indlekofer. 2013.

Band 19 Wolfgang Benedek / Hans-Peter Folz / Hubert Isak / Matthias C. Kettemann / Renate Kicker (Hrsg.): Bestand und Wandel des Völkerrechts. Beiträge zum 38. Österreichischen Völkerrechtstag 2013 in Stadtschlaining. 2014.

Band 20 Andrea Bockley / Ursula Kriebaum / August Reinisch (Hrsg.): Nichtstaatliche Akteure und Interventionsverbot. Beiträge zum 39. Österreichischen Völkerrechtstag 2014 in Klosterneuburg. 2015.

Band 21 Caroline U. Amann: The EU Education Policy in the Post-Lisbon Era. A Comprehensive Approach. 2015.

www.peterlang.com

www.ingramcontent.com/pod-product-compliance
Ingram Content Group UK Ltd.
Pitfield, Milton Keynes, MK11 3LW, UK
UKHW021843100926
8556IPUK00019B/1014

9 783631 666159